Please remember that this is a library book,
and that it belongs only temporarily to each
person who uses it. Be considerate. Do
not write in this, or any, library book.

Taking SIDES

Clashing Views on Controversial Issues in Drugs and Society

Fourth Edition

Taking
SIDES

Clashing Views on
Controversial Issues in
Drugs and Society

Fourth Edition

Edited, Selected, and with Introductions by

Raymond Goldberg
State University of New York College at Cortland

Dushkin/McGraw-Hill
A Division of The McGraw-Hill Companies

To Norma, Tara, and Greta

Photo Acknowledgments

Cover image: © 2000 by PhotoDisc, Inc.

Cover Art Acknowledgment

Charles Vitelli

Library of Congress Cataloging-in-Publication Data

Main entry under title:
    Taking sides: clashing views on controversial issues in drugs and society/edited, selected, and with introductions by Raymond Goldberg.—4th ed.
    Includes bibliographical references and index.
    1. Drug abuse—Social aspects. I. Goldberg, Raymond, *comp.*

362.29

0-07-303193-3   ISSN: 1094-7566

 Printed on Recycled Paper

PREFACE

One of the hallmarks of a democratic society is the freedom of its citizens to disagree. This is no more evident than on the topic of drugs. The purpose of this fourth edition of *Taking Sides: Clashing Views on Controversial Issues in Drugs and Society* is to introduce drug-related issues that (1) are pertinent to the reader and (2) have no clear resolution. In the area of drug abuse, there is much difference of opinion regarding drug prevention, causation, and treatment. For example, should drug abuse be prevented by increasing enforcement of drug laws or by making young people more aware of the potential dangers of drugs? Is drug abuse caused by heredity, personality characteristics, or environment? Is drug abuse a medical, legal, or social problem? Are individuals who inject drugs best served by the provision of clean needles or improved treatment? Are self-help groups the most effective treatment for drug abusers?

There are many implications to how the preceding questions are answered. If addiction to drugs is viewed as hereditary rather than as the result of flaws in one's character or personality, then a biological rather than a psychosocial approach to treatment may be pursued. If the consensus is that the prevention of drug abuse can be achieved by eliminating the availability of drugs, then more money and effort will be allocated for interdiction and law enforcement than education. If drug abuse is viewed as a legal problem, then prosecution and incarceration will be the goal. If drug abuse is identified as a medical problem, then abusers will be given treatment. However, if drug abuse is deemed a social problem, then energy will be directed at underlying social factors, such as poverty, unemployment, health care, and education. Not all of the issues have clear answers. One may favor increasing penalties for drug violations *and* improving treatment services. And it is possible to view drug abuse as a medical *and* social *and* legal problem.

The issues debated in this volume deal with both legal and illegal drugs. Although society seems most interested in illegal drugs, it is quite pertinent to address issues related to legal drugs because they cause more deaths and disabilities. No one is untouched by drugs, and everybody is affected by drug use and abuse. Billions of tax dollars are channeled into the war on drugs. Thousands of people are treated for drug abuse, often at public expense. The drug trade spawns crime and violence. Medical treatment for illnesses and injuries resulting from drug use and abuse creates additional burdens to an already extended health care system. Babies born to mothers who used drugs while pregnant are entering schools, and teachers are expected to meet the educational needs of these children. Ritalin is prescribed to tens of thousands of students to deal with their lack of attention in the classroom. Drunk drivers represent a serious threat to our health and safety while raising the cost of

Make it more difficult when *Society more reason to* *abortion* *or more reason* *see if they can listen to the eye*

everyone's auto insurance. The issues debated here are not on whether or not drug abuse is a problem but what should be done to rectify this problem.

Many of these issues have an immediate impact on the reader. For example, Issue 3, *Should Congress Impose a Lower Blood Alcohol Concentration Limit for Drunk Driving?* will affect the amount of alcohol that people consume before driving. Issue 8, *Should Tobacco Products Be More Closely Regulated?* is relevant to smokers and nonsmokers because restrictions on smoking are discussed. Issue 13, *Is Prozac Overprescribed?* is important because millions of people have been diagnosed with clinical depression. And the question *Should Marijuana Be Legalized for Medicinal Purposes?* (Issue 9) may become relevant for many readers or their loved ones someday.

Plan of the book   In this fourth edition of *Taking Sides: Clashing Views on Controversial Issues in Drugs and Society,* there are 38 selections dealing with 19 issues. Each issue is preceded by an *introduction* and followed by a *postscript.* The purpose of the introduction is to provide some background information and to set the stage for the debate as it is argued in the "yes" and "no" selections. The postscript summarizes the debate and challenges some of the ideas brought out in the two selections, which can enable the reader to see the issue in other ways. Included in the postscripts are additional suggested readings on the issue. Also, Internet site addresses (URLs) have been provided at the beginning of each part, which should prove useful as starting points for further research. The issues, introductions, and postscripts are designed to stimulate readers to think about and achieve an informed view of some of the critical issues facing society today. At the back of the book is a list of all the *contributors to this volume,* which gives information on the physicians, professors, and policymakers whose views are debated here.

Taking Sides: Clashing Views on Controversial Issues in Drugs and Society is a tool to encourage critical thinking. In reading an issue and forming your own opinion you should not feel confined to adopt one or the other of the positions presented. Some readers may see important points on both sides of an issue and may construct for themselves a new and creative approach. Such an approach might incorporate the best of both sides, or it might provide an entirely new vantage point for understanding.

Changes to this edition   This fourth edition represents a significant revision. Four of the 19 issues are completely new: *Should Congress Impose a Lower Blood Alcohol Concentration Limit for Drunk Driving?* (Issue 3); *Should Young People Be Taught How to Use Marijuana?* (Issue 6); *Does Drug Abuse Treatment Work?* (Issue 18); and *Are Antidrug Media Campaigns Effective?* (Issue 19). For eight of the issues retained from the previous edition, one or both selections were replaced to reflect more current points of view: Issue 1 on the legalization of drugs; Issue 7 on harm reduction as a drug control policy goal; Issue 8 on the regulation of tobacco products; Issue 9 on legalizing marijuana for medicinal purposes; Issue 11 on nicotine; Issue 14 on tobacco advertising;

Issue 15 on abstinence for alcoholics; and Issue 16 on the effectiveness of Drug Abuse Resistance Education (DARE). In addition, for Issue 4, *Should Needle Exchange Programs Be Supported?* one selection has been replaced and the issue question has been modified to provide a new focus. In all, there are 17 new selections.

A word to the instructor To facilitate the use of *Taking Sides,* an *Instructor's Manual With Test Questions* (multiple-choice and essay) and a general guidebook called *Using Taking Sides in the Classroom,* which discusses methods and techniques for implementing the pro-con approach into any classroom setting, can be obtained through the publisher. An online version of *Using Taking Sides in the Classroom* and a correspondence service for Taking Sides adopters can be found at http://www.dushkin.com/usingts/. For students, we offer a field guide to analyzing argumentative essays called *Analyzing Controversy: An Introductory Guide,* with exercises and techniques to help them to decipher genuine controversies.

Taking Sides: Clashing Views on Controversial Issues in Drugs and Society is only one title in the Taking Sides series. If you are interested in seeing the table of contents for any of the other titles, please visit the Taking Sides Web site at http://www.dushkin.com/takingsides/.

Acknowledgments A number of people have been most helpful in putting together this fourth edition. I would like to thank those professors who adopted the third edition of this book and took the time to make suggestions for this subsequent edition:

Donald Brodeur
Sacred Heart University

Mark Kaelin
Montclair State University

Owen Cater
California State University,
  Sacramento

I am also grateful to my students and colleagues, who did not hesitate to share their perceptions and to let me know what they liked and disliked about the third edition. Without the editorial staff at Dushkin/McGraw-Hill, this book would not exist. The insightful and professional contributions of Ted Knight, list manager for the Taking Sides program, were most valuable. His thoughtful perceptions and encouragement were most appreciated. In no small way can my family be thanked. I am grateful for their patience and support.

Raymond Goldberg
State University of New York College at Cortland

CONTENTS IN BRIEF

CONTENTS

Ethan A. Nadelmann, director of the Lindesmith Center, maintains that the war on drugs has been futile and counterproductive. He feels that drug abstinence cannot be achieved through legal mandates and that a pragmatic approach is needed. University of Delaware professor James A. Inciardi and his associate Christine A. Saum contend that the war on drugs is not a failure and that legalizing drugs would worsen drug-related problems.

Barry McCaffrey, director of the Office of National Drug Control Policy, argues that the importation of drugs must be stopped to reduce drug use and abuse. He maintains that a coordinated international effort is needed to combat the increased production of heroin, cocaine, and marijuana. Mathea Falco, president of Drug Strategies, a nonprofit policy institute, asserts that the emphasis should not be on curtailing the availability of drugs but on factors that contribute to Americans' use of drugs. She contends that blaming other countries for drug-related problems in the United States is one way for politicians to deflect criticism from themselves.

U.S. senator Paul D. Wellstone and his colleagues argue that the federal government should support a law establishing .08 as the national blood alcohol concentration (BAC) level for drunk driving. Prompted by the thousands of deaths caused annually by people driving under alcohol's influence, they contend that there are fewer fatal automobile crashes in states with a .08 BAC standard. U.S. senator Trent Lott and his colleagues maintain that establishing BAC standards should be left to individual states, not to the federal government. They argue that their opponents' desire to mandate a national standard for BAC is another example of the federal government overstepping its boundaries.

In their review of various studies, professor of epidemiology and medicine David Vlahov and Benjamin Junge, evaluation director for the Baltimore Needle Exchange Program, found that needle exchange programs successfully reduced the transmission of the virus that causes AIDS. In addition, many people who participated in needle exchange programs reduced their drug use and sought drug abuse treatment. The Office of National Drug Control Policy, an executive agency that determines policies and objectives for the U.S. drug control program, sees needle exchange programs as an admission of defeat and a retreat from the ongoing battle against drug use, and it argues that compassion and treatment are needed, not needles.

Paul A. Logli, an Illinois prosecuting attorney, argues that it is the government's duty to enforce every child's right to begin life with a healthy, drug-free mind and body. Logli maintains that pregnant women who use drugs should be prosecuted because they may harm the life of their unborn children. Writer Sue Mahan asserts that the prosecution of pregnant drug users is unfair because poor women are more likely to be the targets of such prosecution. Mahan argues that instead of treating these women as criminals, both society and these women would be better served by the provision of adequate prenatal care and treatment.

Marsha Rosenbaum, director of the Lindesmith Center in San Francisco, California, supports teaching young people how to use marijuana responsibly in order to reduce the potential problems of marijuana use. She argues that telling young people that they should not use marijuana and relating horror stories connected to its use have not reduced marijuana use. Writers Wayne Hall and Nadia Solowij maintain that marijuana causes numerous medical, psychological, perceptual-motor, and academic problems and that its use should be discouraged.

Robert J. MacCoun, an associate professor in the Graduate School of Public Policy at the University of California, Berkeley, supports efforts to minimize problems associated with drugs. He states that a harm reduction approach will not resolve all drug problems, but he feels that reducing those problems is a desirable goal. Clinical professor of psychiatry Robert L. DuPont and clinical assistant professor Eric A. Voth argue that there is insufficient evidence that a policy of harm reduction is beneficial and that the notion of harm reduction is just another way for some people to rationalize legalizing drugs.

Writer Edward L. Koven asserts that current restrictions on tobacco products are minimal compared to restrictions on other products. He also contends that the negative effects of smoking tobacco, especially secondhand smoke, justify more restrictive regulations, such as banning tobacco use in public places. John Hood, vice president of the John Locke Foundation in Raleigh, North Carolina, argues that the tobacco industry is already heavily regulated, that smokers should have the freedom to choose to smoke, and that the Food and Drug Administration is attempting to intrude too much into the lives of individuals.

Professor of psychiatry Lester Grinspoon and law lecturer James B. Bakalar argue that anecdotal evidence indicates that marijuana has medical benefits for patients suffering from chemotherapy nausea, AIDS, glaucoma, chronic pain, epilepsy, and migraine headaches. They assert that the federal government is prohibiting its use without justification. Robert L. DuPont, a clinical professor of psychiatry, contends that the medicinal value of marijuana is questionable and inconclusive. He maintains that the many people who support marijuana use for medical purposes are ultimately looking for a way to establish marijuana use for nonmedical purposes.

Psychologist Stanton Peele, an expert on alcoholism and addiction, asserts that physicians should recommend that their patients drink alcohol in moderate amounts. He maintains that numerous studies demonstrate the benefits of moderate alcohol use in reducing the risk of coronary heart disease, the leading cause of death in the United States. Albert B. Lowenfels, a professor at New York Medical College, contends that recommending moderate alcohol consumption is not prudent, especially since many people come from families with histories of alcohol abuse. He argues that it is inappropriate to extol the merits of moderate alcohol use to people who have abstained throughout their lives.

Janet Brigham, a research psychologist at SRI International in Menlo Park, California, maintains that nicotine is a powerfully addictive drug and that overcoming addiction to tobacco is as difficult as overcoming addiction to alcohol, heroin, or cocaine. She also argues that calling nicotine dependence a "habit" minimizes its addictiveness. Assistant professor of psychology Richard J. DeGrandpre contends that cigarette addiction is due to social, cultural, and economic factors and not because of physical dependence on nicotine. DeGrandpre asserts that nicotine replacement to help people stop smoking is not especially effective and that it is not just the nicotine that smokers desire when they light up a cigarette.

Harvard Medical School professor Richard Bromfield contends that physicians are often too eager to prescribe Ritalin for children with attention deficit/hyperactivity disorder (ADHD). Bromfield is concerned that Ritalin's long-term effects have not been adequately researched and that its overuse may be masking other childhood disorders. George Washington Medical School professor Jerry Wiener maintains that Ritalin has been proven to be safe and effective. Wiener argues that attention deficit/hyperactivity disorder is underdiagnosed in many instances and that children who could benefit from the use of Ritalin often do not receive it.

Writer Mark Nichols states that many physicians prescribe Prozac too read-ily and that Prozac is used too often for ordinary problems of daily living such as discontent and irritability. He contends, moreover, that its long-term effects are not known and that some people experience negative psycholog-ical reactions while on Prozac. Health and psychology writer Nancy Wartik maintains that Prozac is helpful for treating chronic depression, especially among women, and that Prozac's purported dangers are overexaggerated. She asserts that if there were less adverse publicity surrounding Prozac, more people could benefit from its use.

Richard W. Pollay, a professor of business, argues for greater regulation of the tobacco industry because it has a history of presenting misleading and in-accurate information. He also maintains that cigarette advertising influences the perceptions, attitudes, and smoking behavior of young people. Journalist Jacob Sullum disputes the contention that cigarette advertising influences young people to start smoking. He maintains that there is no proof that a ban on advertising would have any impact on smoking rates.

Professor of health Thomas Byrd maintains that Alcoholics Anonymous (AA) provides more effective treatment for alcoholics than psychiatrists, members of the clergy, or hospital treatment centers. Byrd contends that AA is the most powerful and scientific program, in contrast to all other therapies. Psychol-ogist Stanton Peele questions the effectiveness of AA and supports instead alcohol treatment programs that are tailored to meet the different needs of alcoholics. Peele argues that for some alcoholics, the concept of a lifetime of abstinence may be counterproductive and that many alcoholics are capable of controlling their drinking behavior.

Researcher Michele Alicia Harmon reports that Drug Abuse Resistance Education (DARE) had a positive impact on fifth-grade students in terms of attitudes against substance abuse, assertiveness, positive peer association, association with drug-using peers, alcohol use within the previous year, and prosocial norms. Drug researchers Richard R. Clayton et al. maintain that despite DARE's popularity, it does not produce less drug use among its participants. They argue that the money that is spent by the federal government to fund DARE could be used for more effective drug prevention programs.

Sociology professor Ellis Cashmore argues that the notion that anabolic steroid use violates the rules of fair play is illogical because competition has never been predicated on fair play. Joannie M. Schrof, an associate editor of *U.S. News and World Report*, asserts that athletes who take anabolic steroids are not fully aware of the drugs' potential adverse effects.

Psychology professor John B. Murray contends that drug abuse treatment, especially methadone maintenance, has been shown to reduce illegal opiate use, curtail criminal activity, and lower rates of HIV infection. Assistant professor of psychology Robert Apsler questions the effectiveness of drug abuse treatment and whether or not drug addicts would go for treatment if services were expanded.

Barry McCaffrey, director of the Office of National Drug Control Policy (ONDCP), argues that the attitudes and behaviors of young people regarding drug use are affected by antidrug media campaigns. He therefore supports the federal government's spending millions of dollars for antidrug public service announcements. David R. Buchanan, an assistant professor of community health studies, and professor of health education Lawrence Wallack argue that antidrug media campaigns are not only ineffective but may result in a backlash. They maintain that many drug-prevention messages are inaccurate, and they question the value of the scare tactics that are part of most antidrug announcements.

INTRODUCTION

Drugs: Divergent Views

Raymond Goldberg

AN OVERVIEW OF THE PROBLEM

No one is immune to the effects of drugs. Very few topics generate as much debate and concern as drugs. Drugs and issues related to drugs are evident in every aspect of life. There is much dismay that drug use and abuse cause many of the problems that plague society. Individuals, families, and communities are adversely affected by drug abuse, and many people wonder if morality will continue to decay because of drugs. The news media are replete with horrendous stories about people under the influence of drugs committing crimes against others, senseless drug-related deaths, men and women who compromise themselves for drugs, and women who deliver babies that are addicted or impaired by drugs.

From conception until death, almost everyone is touched by drug use. In some cases, stimulants such as Ritalin are prescribed for children so that they can learn or behave better in school. Some students take stimulants so that they can stay up late to write a term paper or lose a few pounds. Many teenagers take drugs because they want to be accepted by their friends who use drugs or to deal with daily stress. For many people, young and old, the elixir for relaxation may be sipped, swallowed, smoked, or sniffed. Some people who live in poverty-stricken conditions anesthetize themselves with drugs as a way to escape from their environment. On the other hand, some individuals who seem to have everything immerse themselves in drugs, possibly out of boredom. To cope with the ailments that come with getting older, the elderly often rely on drugs. Many people use drugs to confront their pains, problems, frustrations, and disappointments. Others take drugs simply because they like the effects or out of curiosity.

BACKGROUND ON DRUGS

Despite one's feelings about drug use, drugs are an integral part of society. The popularity of various drugs rises and falls with the times. For example, according to annual surveys of 8th-, 10th-, and 12th-grade students in the United States, the use of LSD and marijuana have increased throughout the 1990s despite a decline in use throughout the 1980s (Johnston, O'Malley, and Bachman, 1998). Especially alarming is the fact that the largest increase has occurred among 8th-grade students.

Understanding the history and role of drugs in society is critical to our ability to address drug-related problems. Drugs are believed to have been used throughout human history. Alcohol played a significant role in the early history of the United States. According to Lee (1963), for example, the Pilgrims landed at Plymouth Rock because they ran out of beer. Marijuana use dates back nearly 5,000 years, when the Chinese Emperor Shen Nung prescribed it for medical ailments like malaria, gout, rheumatism, and gas pains. Hallucinogens have existed since the beginning of humankind. About 150 of the estimated 500,000 different plant species have been used for hallucinogenic purposes (Schultes and Hofmann, 1979).

Opium, from which narcotics are derived, was alluded to often by the ancient Greeks and Romans; opium is referred to in Homer's *Odyssey* (circa 1000 B.C.). In the Arab world opium and hashish were widely used (primarily because alcohol was forbidden). The Arabs were introduced to opium through their trading in India and China. Arab physician Avicenna (A.D. 1000) wrote an extremely complete medical textbook in which he describes the benefits of opium. Ironically, Avicenna died from an overdose of opium and wine. Eventually, opium played a central role in a war between China and the British government.

Caffeine is believed to be the most commonly consumed drug throughout the world. More than 9 out of every 10 Americans consume caffeine. Coffee dates back to A.D. 900, when, to stay awake during lengthy religious vigils, Muslims in Arabia drank coffee. However, coffee was later condemned because the Koran, the holy book of Islam, described coffee as an intoxicant (Brecher, 1972). Drinking coffee became a popular activity in Europe, although it was banned for a short time. In the mid-1600s, coffeehouses were prime locations for men to converse, relax, and do business. Medical benefits were associated with coffee, although England's King Charles II and English physicians tried to prohibit its use.

One function of coffeehouses was as places of learning. For a one-cent cup of coffee, one could listen to well-known literary and political leaders (Meyer, 1954). Lloyd's of London, the famous insurance company, started around 1700 from Edward Lloyd's coffeehouse. However, not everyone was pleased with these "penny universities," as they were called. In 1674, in response to the countless hours men spent at the coffeehouses, a group of women published a pamphlet titled *The Women's Petition Against Coffee*, which criticized coffee use. Despite the protestations against coffee, its use proliferated. Today, more than 325 years later, coffeehouses are still flourishing as centers for relaxation and conversation.

Coca leaves, from which cocaine is derived, have been chewed since before recorded history. Drawings found on South American pottery illustrate that coca chewing was practiced before the rise of the Incan Empire. The coca plant was held in high regard: considered a present from the gods, it was used in religious rituals and burial ceremonies. When the Spaniards arrived in South America, they tried to regulate coca chewing by the natives but were unsuccessful. Cocaine was later included in the popular soft drink Coca-Cola. Another stimulant, amphetamine, was developed in the 1920s and was originally used to treat narcolepsy. It was later prescribed for treating asthma and for weight loss. Today the stimulant Ritalin is given to more than 1 million school-age children annually to address attention deficit disorders. This raises the question of whether or not Ritalin is being overprescribed (Issue 12).

Minor tranquilizers, also called "antianxiety drugs," were first marketed in the early 1950s. The sales of these drugs were astronomical. Drugs to reduce anxiety were in high demand. Another group of antianxiety drugs are benzodiazepines. Two well-known benzodiazepines are Librium and Valium; the latter ranks as the most widely prescribed drug in the history of American medicine. Xanax, which has replaced Valium as the tranquilizer of choice, is one of the five most precribed drugs in the United States today. Minor tranquilizers are noteworthy because they are legally prescribed to alter one's consciousness. Mind-altering drugs existed prior to minor tranquilizers, but they were not prescribed for that purpose.

COMBATING DRUG PROBLEMS

The debates in *Taking Sides: Clashing Views on Controversial Issues in Drugs and Society* confront many important drug-related issues. For example, what is the most effective way to reduce drug abuse? Should laws preventing drug use and abuse be more strongly enforced, or should drug laws be less punitive? How can the needs of individuals be met while serving the greater good of society? Should drug abuse be seen as a public health problem or a legal problem? Are drugs an American problem or an international problem? The debate regarding whether or not the drug problem should be fought nationally or internationally is addressed in Issue 2. One could argue that America would benefit most by focusing its attention on stopping the proliferation of drugs in other countries.

One of the oldest debates concerns whether or not drug use should be legal. Issue 1 deals with this question. In recent years this debate has become more intense because well-known individuals such as political analyst William F. Buckley, Jr., and economist Milton Friedman have come out in support of legalization. For many people the issue is not whether drug use is good or bad but whether or not people should be punished for taking drugs. One question that is basic to this debate is whether drug legalization causes more or less damage than drug criminalization. A related issue, Issue 7, discusses whether or not the United States should adopt a drug policy that focuses on harm reduction. A pertinent issue concerns needle exchange programs, in which clean needles are provided to individuals who inject themselves with drugs (Issue 4). There are obvious inherent dangers to injecting drugs; yet does the provision of sterile needles help these people? Should people be given equipment that is used for an illegal act? What has been the effect of needle exchange programs in cities where they have been instituted?

In a related matter, should potentially harmful drugs be restricted even if they may be of medical benefit? Some people are concerned that drugs used for medical reasons may be illegally diverted. Yet most people agree that patients should have access to the best medicine available. In referenda in numerous states, voters have approved the medical use of marijuana. Is the federal government consistent in allowing potentially harmful drugs to be used for medical purposes? For example, narcotics are often prescribed for pain relief. Is there a chance that patients who are given narcotics will become addicted? Issue 9 debates whether or not marijuana has a legitimate medical use. Issue 6 also focuses on marijuana, specifically on the fact that many young people use it illegally. Should they be informed of its potential harm, or should they be discouraged from using it at all?

Many of the issues discussed in this book deal with drug prevention. As with most controversial issues, there is a lack of consensus on how to prevent drug-related problems. For example, Issue 5 debates whether or not prosecuting women who use drugs during pregnancy will affect drug use by other women who become pregnant. Will pregnant women avoid prenatal care because they fear prosecution? Will newborns be better served if pregnant women who use drugs are charged with child abuse? Are these laws discriminatory, since most cases that are prosecuted involve poor women?

Some contend that drug laws discriminate not only according to social class but also according to age and ethnicity. Many drug laws in the United States were initiated because of their association with different ethnic groups: Opium smoking was made illegal after it was associated with Chinese immigrants (Musto, 1991); cocaine became illegal after it was linked with blacks; and marijuana was outlawed after it was linked with Hispanics.

Drug-related issues are not limited to illegal drugs. Tobacco and alcohol are two pervasive legal drugs that generate much debate. For example, should there be stricter regulations on tobacco products (Issue 8)? The answer to this questions may depend on whether or not nicotine is viewed as an addictive drug (Issue 11). With regard to alcohol, Issue 10 looks at whether or not physicians should promote moderate alcohol use. A factor in this debate is whether or not alcoholism is hereditary, which may determine whether alcoholics should totally abstain from alcohol or whether they can learn to drink moderately (Issue 15). Other issues relating to legal drugs deal with whether or not the legal blood alcohol concentration limit for driving while intoxicated should be lowered (Issue 3) and whether or not the antidepressant drug Prozac is overprescribed (Issue 13).

GATEWAY DRUGS

An inhalant is a type of drug that is popular with many young people. Like tobacco and alcohol, inhalants are considered "gateway" drugs, which are drugs that are often used as a prelude to other, usually illegal, drugs. Inhalants are composed of numerous products, ranging from paints and solvents to glues, aerosol sprays, petroleum products, cleaning supplies, and nitrous oxide (laughing gas). Inhalant abuse in the United States is a relatively new phenomenon. It seems that until the media starting reporting on the dangers of inhalant abuse, its use was not particularly common (Brecher, 1972). This raises a question regarding the impact of the media on drug use. Issue 19 examines the effect of public service announcements on teen drug use.

Advertisements are an integral part of the media, and their influence can be seen in the growing popularity of cigarette smoking among adolescents. In the 1880s cigarette smoking escalated in the United States. One of the most important factors contributing to cigarettes' popularity at that time was the development of the cigarette-rolling machine (previously, cigarettes could be rolled at a rate of only four per minute). Also, cigarette smoking, which was considered an activity reserved for men, began to be seen as an option for women. As cigarettes began to be marketed toward women, cigarette smoking became more widespread. Issue 14 deals with whether or not the Food and Drug Administration should prohibit tobacco advertising. As one can see from this introduction, numerous factors affect drug use. One argument is that if young people were better educated about the hazards of drugs and were taught how to understand the role of the media, then limits on advertising would not be necessary.

DRUG PREVENTION AND TREATMENT

Some people maintain that educating young people about drugs is one way to prevent drug use and abuse. Studies show that by delaying the onset of drug use, the likelihood of drug abuse is reduced. In the past, however, drug education had little impact on drug-taking behavior (Goldberg, 1997). Some programs have actually resulted in increased drug use because they stimulated curiosity. Does this suggest that drug education is detrimental or that more effective programs need to be developed? One nationwide program that deals with drug use is Drug Abuse Resistance Education (DARE). Issue 16 examines whether or not DARE effectively reduces the incidence of drug use and abuse.

Another way to reduce drug abuse that has been heavily promoted is drug abuse treatment. However, is drug abuse treatment effective? Does it prevent recurring drug abuse, reduce criminal activity and violence, and halt the spread of drug-related disease? Issue 18 examines whether or not drug abuse treatment affects these outcomes. A study by Glass (1995) showed that methadone maintenance, a treatment for heroin addiction, may have some benefits. But do those benefits outweigh the costs of the treatment? If society feels that treatment is a better alternative to incarceration, it is imperative to know if treatment works.

DISTINGUISHING BETWEEN DRUG USE, MISUSE, AND ABUSE

Although the terms *drug, drug misuse,* and *drug abuse* are commonly used, they have different meanings to different people. Defining these terms may seem simple at first, but many factors affect how they are defined. Should a definition for a drug be based on its behavioral effects, its effects on society, its pharmacological properties, or its chemical composition? One simple, concise definition of a drug is "any substance that produces an effect on the mind, body, or both." One could also define a drug by how it is used. For example, if watching television or listening to music are forms of escape from daily problems, then they may be considered drugs.

Legal drugs cause far more death and disability than illegal drugs, but society appears to be most concerned with the use of illegal drugs. The potential harms of legal drugs tend to be minimized. By viewing drugs as illicit substances only, people can fail to recognize that commonly used substances such as caffeine, tobacco, alcohol, and over-the-counter preparations are drugs. If these substances are not perceived as drugs, then people might not acknowledge that they can be misused or abused.

Definitions for misuse and abuse are not affected by a drug's legal status. Drug misuse refers to the inappropriate or unintentional use of drugs. Someone who smokes marijuana to improve his or her study skills is misusing marijuana because the drug impairs short-term memory. Drug abuse alludes to physical, emotional, financial, intellectual, or social consequences arising from chronic drug use. Under this definition, can a person abuse food, aspirin, soft drinks, or chocolate? Also, should a person be free to make potentially unhealthy choices?

THE COST OF THE WAR ON DRUGS

The U.S. government spends billions of dollars each year to curb the rise in drug use. A major portion of that money goes toward law enforcement. Vast sums of money are used by the military to intercept drug shipments, while foreign governments are given money to help them with their own wars on drugs. A smaller portion of the funds is used for treating and preventing drug abuse. One strategy to eliminate drug use is drug testing. Currently, men and women in the military, athletes, industry employees, and others are subject to random drug testing.

The expense of drug abuse to industries is staggering: Experts estimate that almost 20 percent of workers in the United States use dangerous drugs while at work; and the cost of drug abuse to employers is approximately $120 billion each year (Brookler, 1992). Compared to nonaddicted employees, drug-dependent employees are absent from their jobs more often, and drug users are less likely to maintain stable job histories than nonusers (Kandel, Murphy, and Kraus, 1985). In its report *America's Habit: Drug Abuse, Drug Trafficking and Organized Crime*, the President's Commission on Organized Crime supported testing all federal workers for drugs. It further recommended that federal contracts be withheld from private employers who do not implement drug-testing procedures (Brinkley, 1986).

A prerequisite to being hired by many companies is passing a drug test. Drug testing may be having a positive effect. From 1987 to 1994 the number of workers testing positive declined 57 percent (Center for Substance Abuse Prevention, 1995). Many companies have reported a decrease in accidents and injuries after the initiation of drug testing (Angarola, 1991). However, most Americans consider drug testing degrading and dehumanizing (Walsh and Trumble, 1991). An important question is, What is the purpose of drug testing? Drug testing raises three other important questions: (1) Does drug testing prevent drug use? (2) Is the point of drug testing to help employees with drug problems or to get rid of employees who use drugs? and (3) How can the civil rights of employees be balanced against the rights of companies?

Athletes are periodically screened for use of anabolic steroids and other drugs to enhance performance. Issue 17 discusses this practice and raises the question of whether or not it is anybody's business but the individual athlete's if he or she uses steroids or other drugs. This issue also raises questions regarding the ability of athletic governing bodies to determine which athletes are using drugs.

How serious is the drug problem? Is it real, or is there simply an unreasonable hysteria regarding drugs? In the United States there has been a growing intolerance toward drug use during the last 20 years (Musto, 1991). Drugs are a problem for many people. Drugs can affect one's physical, social, intellectual, and emotional health. Ironically, some people take drugs *because* they produce these effects. Individuals who take drugs receive some kind of reward from the drug; the reward may come from being associated with others who use drugs or from the feelings derived from the drug. If these rewards were not present, people would likely cease using drugs.

The disadvantages of drugs are numerous: they interfere with career aspirations and individual maturation. They have also been associated with violent behavior; addiction; discord among siblings, children, parents, spouses, and friends; work-related problems; financial troubles; problems in school; legal predicaments; accidents; injuries; and death. Yet are drugs the cause or the symptom of the problems that people have? Perhaps drugs are one aspect of a larger scenario in which society is experiencing much change and in which drug use is merely another thread in the social fabric.

REFERENCES

R. T. Angarola, "Substance-Abuse Testing in the Workplace: Legal Issues and Corporate Responses," in R. H. Coombs and L. J. West, eds., *Drug Testing: Issues and Options* (Oxford University Press, 1991).

E. M. Brecher, *Licit and Illicit Drugs* (Little, Brown, 1972).

J. Brinkley, "Drug Use Held Mostly Stable or Better," *The New York Times* (October 10, 1986).

R. Brookler, "Industry Standards in Workplace Drug Testing," *Personnel Journal* (April 1992), pp. 128–132.

Drug-Free for a New Century, Center for Substance Abuse Prevention, Substance Abuse and Mental Health Services Administration (1995).

R. M. Glass, "Methadone Maintenance: New Research on a Controversial Treatment," *Journal of the American Medical Association* (vol. 269, no. 15, 1995), pp. 1995–1996.

R. Goldberg, *Drugs Across the Spectrum* (Morton Publishing, 1997).

L. D. Johnston, P. O. O'Malley, and J. G. Bachman, *Monitoring the Future* (National Institute on Drug Abuse, 1998).

D. B. Kandel, D. Murphy, and D. Kraus, "Cocaine Use in Young Adulthood: Patterns of Use and Psychosocial Correlates," in N. J. Kozel and E. H. Adams, eds., *Cocaine Use in America: Epidemiologic and Clinical Perspectives* (National Institute on Drug Abuse, 1985).

H. Lee, *How Dry We Were: Prohibition Revisited* (Prentice Hall, 1963).

H. Meyer, *Old English Coffee Houses* (Rodale Press, 1954).

D. F. Musto, "Opium, Cocaine and Marijuana in American History," *Scientific American* (July 1991), pp. 40–47.

R. E. Schultes and A. Hofmann, *Plants of the Gods: Origins of Hallucinogenic Use* (McGraw-Hill, 1979).

J. M. Walsh and J. G. Trumble, "The Politics of Drug Testing," in R. H. Coombs and L. J. West, eds., *Drug Testing: Issues and Options* (Oxford University Press, 1991).

On the Internet . . .

National Institute on Drug Abuse (NIDA)
The National Institute on Drug Abuse is an agency of the federal government that publishes reports on topics ranging from drug use trends to the effects of various drugs. In addition, NIDA conducts workshops dealing with drug prevention.
http://www.nida.nih.gov/nidatoc.html

The UCLA Drug Abuse Research Center (DARC)
The UCLA Drug Abuse Research Center investigates psychosocial and epidemiological issues pertaining to drug use and abuse. The DARC also conducts evaluations of interventions regarding drug dependence.
http://www.medsch.ucla.edu/som/npi/DARC/default.htm

The American Council for Drug Education (ACDE)
The American Council for Drug Education is a nonprofit organization that gathers, analyzes, monitors, and disseminates information pertaining to substance abuse as well as develops programs to reduce substance abuse.
http://www.acde.org

The Office of National Drug Control Policy (ONDCP)
The Office of National Drug Control Policy develops and coordinates the policies, goals, and objectives of the United States' drug control program for reducing the use of illicit drugs. *http://www.whitehousedrugpolicy.gov*

The Lindesmith Center
With locations in New York City and San Francisco, California, the Lindesmith Center examines many policy issues as they relate to drug abuse and harm reduction, as well as advocates different approaches to resolving drug problems. The center maintains a resource library and conducts frequent seminars. *http://www.lindesmith.org*

PART 1

Drugs and Public Policy

Drug abuse causes a myriad of problems for society: The psychological and physical effects of drug abuse can be devastating; many drugs are addictive; drugs wreak havoc on families; disability and death result from drug overdoses; and drugs are frequently implicated in crimes, especially violent crimes. Identifying drug-related problems is not difficult. What is unclear is the best course of action to take when dealing with these problems.

Three scenarios exist for dealing with drugs: policies can be made more restrictive, they can be made less restrictive, or they can remain the same. The position one takes depends on whether drug use and abuse are seen as legal, social, or medical problems. Perhaps the issue is not whether drugs are good or bad but how to minimize the harm of drugs. The debates in this section explore these issues.

■ Should Drugs Be Legalized?

■ Should the United States Put More Emphasis on Stopping the Importation of Drugs?

■ Should Congress Impose a Lower Blood Alcohol Concentration Limit for Drunk Driving?

■ Should Needle Exchange Programs Be Supported?

■ Should Pregnant Drug Users Be Prosecuted?

■ Should Young People Be Taught How to Use Marijuana?

■ Is Harm Reduction a Desirable National Drug Control Policy Goal?

■ Should Tobacco Products Be More Closely Regulated?

ISSUE 1

Should Drugs Be Legalized?

YES: Ethan A. Nadelmann, from "Commonsense Drug Policy," *Foreign Affairs* (January/February 1998)

NO: James A. Inciardi and Christine A. Saum, from "Legalization Madness," *The Public Interest* (Spring 1996)

ISSUE SUMMARY

YES: Ethan A. Nadelmann, director of the Lindesmith Center, maintains that the war on drugs has been futile and counterproductive. He feels that drug abstinence cannot be achieved through legal mandates and that a pragmatic approach is needed.

NO: University of Delaware professor James A. Inciardi and his associate Christine A. Saum contend that the war on drugs is not a failure and that legalizing drugs would worsen drug-related problems.

In 1999 the federal government allocated $19 billion to control drug use and to enforce laws that are designed to protect society from the perils created by drug use. Some people believe that the government's war on drugs could be more effective but that governmental agencies and communities are not fighting hard enough to stop drug use. They also hold that laws to halt drug use are too few and too lenient. Others contend that the war against drugs is unnecessary; that, in fact, society has already lost the war on drugs. These individuals feel that the best way to remedy drug problems is to end the fight altogether by ending the criminalization of drug use.

There are conflicting views among both liberals and conservatives on whether or not legislation has had the intended result of curtailing the problems of drug use. Many argue that legislation and the criminalization of drugs has been counterproductive in controlling drug problems. Some suggest that the criminalization of drugs have actually contributed to and worsened the social ills associated with drugs. Proponents of drug legalization maintain that the war on drugs, not drugs themselves, is damaging to American society. They do not advocate drug use; they argue only that laws against drugs exacerbate problems related to drugs.

Proponents of drug legalization argue that the strict enforcement of drug laws damages American society because it drives people to violence and crime. These people overburden the court system, thus rendering it ineffective. Moreover, proponents contend that the criminalization of drugs fuels organized crime, allows children to be pulled into the drug business, and makes illegal drugs themselves more dangerous because they are manufactured without government standards or regulations. Hence, drugs may be adulterated or of unidentified potency. Legalization advocates also argue that legalization would take the profits out of drug sales, thereby decreasing the value of and demand for drugs. In addition, the costs resulting from law enforcement are far greater to society than the benefits of criminalization.

Some legalization advocates argue that the federal government's prohibition stance on drugs is an immoral and impossible objective. To achieve a "drug-free society" is self-defeating and a misnomer because drugs have always been a part of human culture. Furthermore, prohibition efforts indicate a disregard for the private freedom of individuals because they assume that individuals are incapable of making their own choices. Drug proponents assert that their personal sovereignty should be respected over any government agenda, including the war on drugs.

People who favor legalizing drugs feel that legalization would give the government more control over the purity and potency of drugs and that the international drug trade would be regulated more effectively. Legalization, they argue, would take the emphasis off of law enforcement policies and allow more effort to be put toward education, prevention, and treatment. Decriminalization advocates assert that most of the negative implications of drug prohibition would disappear.

Opponents of this view maintain that legalization is not the solution to drug problems and that it is a very dangerous idea. Legalization, they assert, will drastically increase drug use because if drugs are more accessible, more people will turn to drugs. This upsurge in drug use will come at an incredibly high price: American society will be overrun with drug-related accidents, loss in worker productivity, and hospital emergency rooms filled with drug-related emergencies. Drug treatment efforts would be futile because users would have no legal incentive to stop taking drugs. Also, users may prefer drugs rather than rehabilitation, and education programs may be ineffective in dissuading children from using drugs. Advocates of drug legalization maintain that drug abuse is a "victimless crime" in which the only person being hurt is the drug user. Legalization opponents argue that this notion is ludicrous and dangerous because drug use has dire repercussions for all of society. Drugs can destroy the minds and bodies of many people. Also, regulations to control drug use have a legitimate social aim to protect society and its citizens from the harm of drugs. Legalization opponents maintain that criminalization is not immoral or a violation of personal freedom to individuals. Rather, criminalization allows a standard of control to be established in order to preserve human character and society as a whole.

In the following selections, Ethan A. Nadelmann explains why he feels drugs should be legalized, while James A. Inciardi and Christine A. Saum describe the detrimental effects that they believe would occur as a result of drug legalization.

YES

Ethan A. Nadelmann

COMMONSENSE DRUG POLICY

In 1988 Congress passed a resolution proclaiming its goal of "a drug-free America by 1995." U.S. drug policy has failed persistently over the decades because it has preferred such rhetoric to reality, and moralism to pragmatism. Politicians confess their youthful indiscretions, then call for tougher drug laws. Drug control officials make assertions with no basis in fact or science. Police officers, generals, politicians, and guardians of public morals qualify as drug czars—but not, to date, a single doctor or public health figure. Independent commissions are appointed to evaluate drug policies, only to see their recommendations ignored as politically risky. And drug policies are designed, implemented, and enforced with virtually no input from the millions of Americans they affect most: drug users. Drug abuse is a serious problem, both for individual citizens and society at large, but the "war on drugs" has made matters worse, not better.

Drug warriors often point to the 1980s as a time in which the drug war really worked. Illicit drug use by teenagers peaked around 1980, then fell more than 50 percent over the next 12 years. During the 1996 presidential campaign, Republican challenger Bob Dole made much of the recent rise in teenagers' use of illicit drugs, contrasting it with the sharp drop during the Reagan and Bush administrations. President [Bill] Clinton's response was tepid, in part because he accepted the notion that teen drug use is the principal measure of drug policy's success or failure; at best, he could point out that the level was still barely half what it had been in 1980.

In 1980, however, no one had ever heard of the cheap, smokable form of cocaine called crack, or drug-related HIV infection or AIDS. By the 1990s, both had reached epidemic proportions in American cities, largely driven by prohibitionist economics and morals indifferent to the human consequences of the drug war. In 1980, the federal budget for drug control was about $1 billion, and state and local budgets were perhaps two or three times that. By 1997, the federal drug control budget had ballooned to $16 billion, two-thirds of it for law enforcement agencies, and state and local funding to at least that. On any day in 1980, approximately 50,000 people were behind bars for violating a drug law. By 1997, the number had increased eightfold, to

From Ethan A. Nadelmann, "Commonsense Drug Policy," *Foreign Affairs*, vol. 77, no. 1 (January/February 1998). Copyright © 1998 by The Council on Foreign Relations, Inc. Reprinted by permission of *Foreign Affairs*.

about 400,000. These are the results of a drug policy overreliant on criminal justice "solutions," ideologically wedded to abstinence-only treatment, and insulated from cost-benefit analysis.

Imagine instead a policy that starts by acknowledging that drugs are here to stay, and that we have no choice but to learn how to live with them so that they cause the least possible harm. Imagine a policy that focuses on reducing not illicit drug use per se but the crime and misery caused by both drug abuse and prohibitionist policies. And imagine a drug policy based not on the fear, prejudice, and ignorance that drive America's current approach but rather on common sense, science, public health concerns, and human rights. Such a policy is possible in the United States, especially if Americans are willing to learn from the experiences of other countries where such policies are emerging. . . .

REEFER SANITY

Cannabis, in the form of marijuana and hashish, is by far the most popular illicit drug in the United States. More than a quarter of Americans admit to having tried it. Marijuana's popularity peaked in 1980, dropped steadily until the early 1990s, and is now on the rise again. Although it is not entirely safe, especially when consumed by children, smoked heavily, or used when driving, it is clearly among the least dangerous psychoactive drugs in common use. In 1988 the administrative law judge for the Drug Enforcement Administration, Francis Young, reviewed the evidence and concluded that "marihuana, in its natural form, is one of the safest therapeutically active substances known to man."

As with needle exchange and methadone treatment, American politicians have ignored or spurned the findings of government commissions and scientific organizations concerning marijuana policy. In 1972 the National Commission on Marihuana and Drug Abuse—created by President Nixon and chaired by a former Republican governor, Raymond Shafer—recommended that possession of up to one ounce of marijuana be decriminalized. Nixon rejected the recommendation. In 1982 a panel appointed by the National Academy of Sciences reached the same conclusion as the Shafer Commission.

Between 1973 and 1978, with attitudes changing, 11 states approved decriminalization statutes that reclassified marijuana possession as a misdemeanor, petty offense, or civil violation punishable by no more than a $100 fine. Consumption trends in those states and in states that retained stricter sanctions were indistinguishable. A 1988 scholarly evaluation of the Moscone Act, California's 1976 decriminalization law, estimated that the state had saved half a billion dollars in arrest costs since the law's passage. Nonetheless, public opinion began to shift in 1978. No other states decriminalized marijuana, and some eventually recriminalized it.

Between 1973 and 1989, annual arrests on marijuana charges by state and local police ranged between 360,000 and 460,000. The annual total fell to 283,700 in 1991, but has since more than doubled. In 1996, 641,642 people were arrested for marijuana, 85 percent of them for possession, not sale, of the drug. Prompted by concern over rising marijuana use among adolescents and fears of being labeled soft on drugs, the Clinton administration launched its own anti-marijuana campaign in 1995. But the administration's claims to have identified new risks of marijuana consumption—including a purported link between marijuana and violent behavior—have not withstood scrutiny.[1] Neither Congress nor the White House seems likely to put the issue of marijuana policy before a truly independent advisory commission, given the consistency with which such commissions have reached politically unacceptable conclusions.

In contrast, governments in Europe and Australia, notably in the Netherlands, have reconsidered their cannabis policies. In 1976 the Baan Commission in the Netherlands recommended, and the Dutch government adopted, a policy of separating the "soft" and "hard" drug markets. Criminal penalties for and police efforts against heroin trafficking were increased, while those against cannabis were relaxed. Marijuana and hashish can now be bought in hundreds of "coffeeshops" throughout the country. Advertising, open displays, and sales to minors are prohibited. Police quickly close coffeeshops caught selling hard drugs. Almost no one is arrested or even fined for cannabis possession, and the government collects taxes on the gray market sales.

In the Netherlands today, cannabis consumption for most age groups is similar to that in the United States. Young Dutch teenagers, however, are less likely to sample marijuana than their American peers; from 1992 to 1994, only 7.2 percent of Dutch youths between the ages of 12 and 15 reported having tried marijuana, compared to 13.5 percent of Americans in that age bracket. Far fewer Dutch youths, moreover, experiment

with cocaine, buttressing officials' claims of success in separating the markets for hard and soft drugs. Most Dutch parents regard the "reefer madness" anti-marijuana campaigns of the United States as silly.

Dutch coffeeshops have not been problem free. Many citizens have complained about the proliferation of coffeeshops, as well as nuisances created by foreign youth flocking to party in Dutch border cities. Organized crime involvement in the growing domestic cannabis industry is of increasing concern. The Dutch government's efforts to address the problem by more openly and systematically regulating supplies to coffeeshops, along with some of its other drug policy initiatives, have run up against pressure from abroad, notably from Paris, Stockholm, Bonn, and Washington. In late 1995 French President Jacques Chirac began publicly berating The Hague for its drug policies, even threatening to suspend implementation of the Schengen Agreement allowing the free movement of people across borders of European Union (EU) countries. Some of Chirac's political allies called the Netherlands a narco-state. Dutch officials responded with evidence of the relative success of their policies, while pointing out that most cannabis seized in France originates in Morocco (which Chirac has refrained from criticizing because of his government's close relations with King Hassan). The Hague, however, did announce reductions in the number of coffeeshops and the amount of cannabis customers can buy there. But it still sanctions the coffeeshops, and a few municipalities actually operate them.

Notwithstanding the attacks, in the 1990s the trend toward decriminalization of cannabis has accelerated in Europe. Across much of Western Europe, possession and even minor sales of the drug are effectively decriminalized. Spain decriminalized private use of cannabis in 1983. In Germany, the Federal Constitutional Court effectively sanctioned a cautious liberalization of cannabis policy in a widely publicized 1994 decision. German states vary considerably in their attitude; some, like Bavaria, persist in a highly punitive policy, but most now favor the Dutch approach. So far the Kohl administration has refused to approve state proposals to legalize and regulate cannabis sales, but it appears aware of the rising support in the country for Dutch and Swiss approaches to local drug problems.

In June 1996 Luxembourg's parliament voted to decriminalize cannabis and push for standardization of drug laws in the Benelux countries. The Belgian government is now considering a more modest decriminalization of cannabis combined with tougher measures against organized crime and heroin traffickers. In Australia, cannabis has been decriminalized in South Australia, the Australian Capital Territory (Canberra), and the Northern Territory, and other states are considering the step. Even in France, Chirac's outburst followed recommendations of cannabis decriminalization by three distinguished national commissions. Chirac must now contend with a new prime minister, Lionel Jospin, who declared himself in favor of decriminalization before his Socialist Party won the 1997 parliamentary elections. Public opinion is clearly shifting. A recent poll found that 51 percent of Canadians favor decriminalizing marijuana.

WILL IT WORK?

Both at home and abroad, the U.S. government has attempted to block resolutions supporting harm reduction, suppress scientific studies that reached politically inconvenient conclusions, and silence critics of official drug policy. In May 1994 the State Department forced the last-minute cancellation of a World Bank conference on drug trafficking to which critics of U.S. drug policy had been invited. That December the U.S. delegation to an international meeting of the U.N. Drug Control Program refused to sign any statement incorporating the phrase "harm reduction." In early 1995 the State Department successfully pressured the World Health Organization to scuttle the release of a report it had commissioned from a panel that included many of the world's leading experts on cocaine because it included the scientifically incontrovertible observations that traditional use of coca leaf in the Andes causes little harm to users and that most consumers of cocaine use the drug in moderation with few detrimental effects. Hundreds of congressional hearings have addressed multitudinous aspects of the drug problem, but few have inquired into the European harm-reduction policies described above. When former Secretary of State George Shultz, then–Surgeon General M. Joycelyn Elders, and Baltimore Mayor Kurt Schmoke pointed to the failure of current policies and called for new approaches, they were mocked, fired, and ignored, respectively—and thereafter mischaracterized as advocating the outright legalization of drugs.

In Europe, in contrast, informed, public debate about drug policy is increasingly common in government, even at the EU level. In June 1995 the European Parliament issued a report acknowledging that "there will always be a demand for drugs in our societies... the policies followed so far have not been able to prevent the illegal drug trade from flourishing." The EU called for serious consideration of the Frankfurt Resolution, a statement of harm-reduction principles supported by a transnational coalition of 31 cities and regions. In October 1996 Emma Bonino, the European commissioner for consumer policy, advocated decriminalizing soft drugs and initiating a broad prescription program for hard drugs. Greece's minister for European affairs, George Papandreou, seconded her. Last February the monarch of Liechtenstein, Prince Hans Adam, spoke out in favor of controlled drug legalization. Even Raymond Kendall, secretary general of Interpol, was quoted in the August 20, 1994, *Guardian* as saying, "The prosecution of thousands of otherwise law-abiding citizens every year is both hypocritical and an affront to individual, civil and human rights ... Drug use should no longer be a criminal offense. I am totally against legalization, but in favor of decriminalization for the user."

One can, of course, exaggerate the differences between attitudes in the United States and those in Europe and Australia. Many European leaders still echo Chirac's U.S.–style antidrug pronouncements. Most capital cities endorse the Stockholm Resolution, a statement backing punitive prohibitionist policies that was drafted in response to the Frankfurt Resolution. And the Dutch have had to struggle against French and other efforts to standardize more punitive drug laws and policies within the EU.

Conversely, support for harm-reduction approaches is growing in the United States, notably and vocally among public health professionals but also, more discreetly, among urban politicians and police officials. Some of the world's most innovative needle exchange and other harm-reduction programs can be found in America. The 1996 victories at the polls for California's Proposition 215, which legalizes the medicinal use of marijuana, and Arizona's Proposition 200, which allows doctors to prescribe any drug they deem appropriate and mandates treatment rather than jail for those arrested for possession, suggest that Americans are more receptive to drug policy reform than politicians acknowledge.

But Europe and Australia are generally ahead of the United States in their willingness to discuss openly and experiment pragmatically with alternative policies that might reduce the harm to both addicts and society. Public health officials in many European cities work closely with police, politicians, private physicians, and others to coordinate efforts. Community policing treats drug dealers and users as elements of the community that need not be expelled but can be made less troublesome. Such efforts, including crackdowns on open drug scenes in Zurich, Bern, and Frankfurt, are devised and implemented in tandem with initiatives to address health and housing problems. In the United States, in contrast, politicians presented with new approaches do not ask, "Will they work?" but only, "Are they tough enough?" Many legislators are reluctant to support drug treatment programs that are not punitive, coercive, and prison-based, and many criminal justice officials still view prison as a quick and easy solution for drug problems.

The lessons from Europe and Australia are compelling. Drug control policies should focus on reducing drug-related crime, disease, and death, not the number of casual drug users. Stopping the spread of HIV by and among drug users by making sterile syringes and methadone readily available must be the first priority. American politicians need to explore, not ignore or automatically condemn, promising policy options such as cannabis decriminalization, heroin prescription, and the integration of harm-reduction principles into community policing strategies. Central governments must back, or at least not hinder, the efforts of municipal officials and citizens to devise pragmatic approaches to local drug problems. Like citizens in Europe, the American public has supported such innovations when they are adequately explained and allowed to prove themselves. As the evidence comes in, what works is increasingly apparent. All that remains is mustering the political courage.

NOTES

1. Lynn Zimmer and John P. Morgan, *Marijuana Myths, Marijuana Facts: A Review of the Scientific Evidence*, New York: Lindesmith Center, 1997.

NO

James A. Inciardi and Christine A. Saum

LEGALIZATION MADNESS

Frustrated by the government's apparent inability to reduce the supply of illegal drugs on the streets of America, and disquieted by media accounts of innocents victimized by drug-related violence, some policy makers are convinced that the "war on drugs" has failed. In an attempt to find a better solution to the "drug crisis" or, at the very least, to try an alternative strategy, they have proposed legalizing drugs.

They argue that, if marijuana, cocaine, heroin, and other drugs were legalized, several positive things would probably occur: (1) drug prices would fall; (2) users would obtain their drugs at low, government-regulated prices, and they would no longer be forced to resort to crime in order to support their habits; (3) levels of drug-related crime, and particularly violent crime, would significantly decline, resulting in less crowded courts, jails, and prisons (this would allow law-enforcement personnel to focus their energies on the "real criminals" in society); and (4) drug production, distribution, and sale would no longer be controlled by organized crime, and thus such criminal syndicates as the Colombian cocaine "cartels," the Jamaican "posses," and the various "mafias" around the country and the world would be decapitalized, and the violence associated with drug distribution rivalries would be eliminated.

By contrast, the anti-legalization camp argues that violent crime would not necessarily decline in a legalized drug market. In fact, there are three reasons why it might actually increase. First, removing the criminal sanctions against the possession and distribution of illegal drugs would make them more available and attractive and, hence, would create large numbers of new users. Second, an increase in use would lead to a greater number of dysfunctional addicts who could not support themselves, their habits, or their lifestyles through legitimate means. Hence crime would be their only alternative. Third, more users would mean more of the violence associated with the ingestion of drugs.

These divergent points of view tend to persist because the relationships between drugs and crime are quite complex and because the possible outcomes of a legalized drug market are based primarily on speculation. However, it is

From James A. Inciardi and Christine A. Saum, "Legalization Madness," *The Public Interest*, no. 123 (Spring 1996). Copyright © 1996 by National Affairs, Inc. Reprinted by permission of the author and *The Public Interest*.

possible, from a careful review of the existing empirical literature on drugs and violence, to make some educated inferences.

CONSIDERING "LEGALIZATION"

Yet much depends upon what we mean by "legalizing drugs." Would all currently illicit drugs be legalized or would the experiment be limited to just certain ones? True legalization would be akin to selling such drugs as heroin and cocaine on the open market, much like alcohol and tobacco, with a few age-related restrictions. In contrast, there are "medicalization" and "decriminalization" alternatives. Medicalization approaches are of many types, but, in essence, they would allow users to obtain prescriptions for some, or all, currently illegal substances. Decriminalization removes the criminal penalties associated with the possession of small amounts of illegal drugs for personal use, while leaving intact the sanctions for trafficking, distribution, and sale.

But what about crack-cocaine? A quick review of the literature reveals that the legalizers, the decriminalizers, and the medicalizers avoid talking about this particular form of cocaine. Perhaps they do not want to legalize crack out of fear of the drug itself, or of public outrage. Arnold S. Trebach, a professor of law at American University and president of the Drug Policy Foundation, is one of the very few who argues for the full legalization of all drugs, including crack. He explains, however, that most are reluctant to discuss the legalization of crack-cocaine because, "it is a very dangerous drug. . . . I know that for many people the very thought of making crack legal destroys any inclination they might have had for even thinking about drug-law reform."

There is a related concern associated with the legalization of cocaine. Because crack is easily manufactured from powder cocaine (just add water and baking soda and cook on a stove or in a microwave), many drug-policy reformers hold that no form of cocaine should be legalized. But this weakens the argument that legalization will reduce drug-related violence; for much of this violence would appear to be in the cocaine- and crack-distribution markets.

To better understand the complex relationship between drugs and violence, we will discuss the data in the context of three models developed by Paul J. Goldstein of the University of Illinois at Chicago. They are the "psychopharmacological," "economically compulsive," and "systemic" explanations of violence. The first model holds, correctly in our view, that some individuals may become excitable, irrational, and even violent due to the ingestion of specific drugs. In contrast, taking a more economic approach to the behavior of drug users, the second holds that some drug users engage in violent crime mainly for the sake of supporting their drug use. The third model maintains that drug-related violent crime is simply the result of the drug market under a regime of illegality.

PSYCHOPHARMACOLOGICAL VIOLENCE

The case for legalization rests in part upon the faulty assumption that drugs themselves do not cause violence; rather, so goes the argument, violence is the result of depriving drug addicts of drugs or of the "criminal" trafficking in drugs. But, as researcher Barry Spunt points out,

"Users of drugs do get violent when they get high."

Research has documented that chronic users of amphetamines, methamphetamine, and cocaine in particular tend to exhibit hostile and aggressive behaviors. Psychopharmacological violence can also be a product of what is known as "cocaine psychosis." As dose and duration of cocaine use increase, the development of cocaine-related psychopathology is not uncommon. Cocaine psychosis is generally preceded by a transitional period characterized by increased suspiciousness, compulsive behavior, fault finding, and eventually paranoia. When the psychotic state is reached, individuals may experience visual, as well as auditory, hallucinations, with persecutory voices commonly heard. Many believe that they are being followed by police or that family, friends, and others are plotting against them.

Moreover, everyday events are sometimes misinterpreted by cocaine users in ways that support delusional beliefs. When coupled with the irritability and hyperactivity that cocaine tends to generate in almost all of its users, the cocaine-induced paranoia may lead to violent behavior as a means of "self-defense" against imagined persecutors. The violence associated with cocaine psychosis is a common feature in many crack houses across the United States. Violence may also result from the irritability associated with drug-withdrawal syndromes. In addition, some users ingest drugs before committing crimes to both loosen inhibitions and bolster their resolve to break the law.

Acts of violence may result from either periodic or chronic use of a drug. For example, in a study of drug use and psychopathy among Baltimore City jail inmates, researchers at the University of Baltimore reported that cocaine use was related to irritability, resentment, hostility, and assault. They concluded that these indicators of aggression may be a function of drug effects rather than of a predisposition to these behaviors. Similarly, Barry Spunt and his colleagues at National Development and Research Institutes (NDRI) in New York City found that of 269 convicted murderers incarcerated in New York State prisons, 45 percent were high at the time of the offense. Three in 10 believed that the homicide was related to their drug use, challenging conventional beliefs that violence only infrequently occurs as a result of drug consumption.

Even marijuana, which pro-legalizers consider harmless, may have a connection with violence and crime. Spunt and his colleagues attempted to determine the role of marijuana in the crimes of the homicide offenders they interviewed in the New York State prisons. One-third of those who had ever used marijuana had smoked the drug in the 24-hour period prior to the homicide. Moreover, 31 percent of those who considered themselves to be "high" at the time of committing murder felt that the homicide and marijuana were related. William Blount of the University of South Florida interviewed abused women in prisons and shelters for battered women located throughout Florida. He and his colleagues found that 24 percent of those who killed their abusers were marijuana users while only 8 percent of those who did not kill their abusers smoked marijuana.

AND ALCOHOL ABUSE

A point that needs emphasizing is that alcohol, because it is legal, accessible, and inexpensive, is linked to violence to a far greater extent than any illegal drug. For example, in the study just cited, it was found that an impressive 64 percent of those women who eventually killed their abusers were alcohol users (44 percent of those who did not kill their abusers were alcohol users). Indeed, the extent to which alcohol is responsible for violent crimes in comparison with other drugs is apparent from the statistics. For example, Carolyn Block and her colleagues at the Criminal Justice Information Authority in Chicago found that, between 1982 and 1989, the use of alcohol by offenders or victims in local homicides ranged from 18 percent to 32 percent.

Alcohol has, in fact, been consistently linked to homicide. Spunt and his colleagues interviewed 268 homicide offenders incarcerated in New York State correctional facilities to determine the role of alcohol in their crimes: Thirty-one percent of the respondents reported being drunk at the time of the crime and 19 percent believed that the homicide was related to their drinking. More generally, Douglass Murdoch of Quebec's McGill University found that in some 9,000 criminal cases drawn from a multinational sample, 62 percent of violent offenders were drinking shortly before, or at the time of, the offense.

It appears that alcohol reduces the inhibitory control of threat, making it more likely that a person will exhibit violent behaviors normally suppressed by fear. In turn, this reduction of inhibition heightens the probability that intoxicated persons will perpetrate, or become victims of, aggressive behavior.

When analyzing the psychopharmacological model of drugs and violence, most of the discussions focus on the offender and the role of drugs in causing or facilitating crime. But what about the victims? Are the victims of drug- and alcohol-related homicides simply casualties of someone else's substance abuse? In addressing these questions, the data demonstrates that victims are likely to be drug users as well. For example, in an analysis of the 4,298 homicides that occurred in New York City during 1990 and 1991, Kenneth Tardiff of Cornell University Medical College found that the victims of these offenses were 10 to 50 times more likely to be cocaine users than were members of the general population. Of the white female victims, 60 percent in the 25- to 34-year age group had cocaine in their systems; for black females, the figure was 72 percent. Tardiff speculated that the classic symptoms of cocaine use—irritability, paranoia, aggressiveness—may have instigated the violence. In another study of cocaine users in New York City, female high-volume users were found to be victims of violence far more frequently than low-volume and nonusers of cocaine. Studies in numerous other cities and countries have yielded the same general findings —that a great many of the victims of homicide and other forms of violence are drinkers and drug users themselves.

ECONOMICALLY COMPULSIVE VIOLENCE

Supporters of the economically compulsive model of violence argue that in a legalized market, the prices of "expensive drugs" would decline to more affordable levels, and, hence, predatory crimes would become unnecessary. This argument is based on several specious assumptions. First, it assumes that there is empirical support for what has been referred to as the "enslavement theory of addiction." Second, it assumes that people addicted to drugs commit crimes only for the purpose of supporting their habits. Third, it assumes that, in a legalized market, users could obtain as much of the drugs as they wanted whenever they wanted. Finally, it assumes that, if drugs are inexpensive, they will be affordable, and thus crime would be unnecessary.

With respect to the first premise, there has been for the better part of this century a concerted belief among many in the drug-policy field that addicts commit crimes because they are "enslaved" to drugs, and further that, because of the high price of heroin, cocaine, and other illicit chemicals on the black market, users are forced to commit crimes in order to support their drug habits. However, there is no solid empirical evidence to support this contention. From the 1920s through the end of the 1960s, hundreds of studies of the relationship between crime and addiction were conducted. Invariably, when one analysis would support the posture of "enslavement theory," the next would affirm the view that addicts were criminals first and that their drug use was but one more manifestation of their deviant lifestyles. In retrospect, the difficulty lay in the ways that many of the studies had been conducted: Biases and deficiencies in research designs and sampling had rendered their findings of little value.

Studies since the mid 1970s of active drug users on the streets of New York, Miami, Baltimore, and elsewhere have demonstrated that the "enslavement theory" has little basis in reality. All of these studies of the criminal careers of drug users have convincingly documented that, while drug use tends to intensify and perpetuate criminal behavior,

it usually does not initiate criminal careers. In fact, the evidence suggests that among the majority of street drug users who are involved in crime, their criminal careers are well established prior to the onset of either narcotics or cocaine use. As such, it would appear that the "inference of causality"—that the high price of drugs on the black market itself causes crime—is simply false.

Looking at the second premise, a variety of studies show that addicts commit crimes for reasons other than supporting their drug habit. They do so also for daily living expenses. For example, researchers at the Center for Drug and Alcohol Studies at the University of Delaware who studied crack users on the streets of Miami found that, of the active addicts interviewed, 85 percent of the male and 70 percent of the female interviewees paid for portions of their living expenses through street crime. In fact, one-half of the men and one-fourth of the women paid for 90 percent or more of their living expenses through crime. And, not surprisingly, 96 percent of the men and 99 percent of the women had not held a legal job in the 90-day period before being interviewed for the study.

With respect to the third premise, that in a legalized market users could obtain as much of the drugs as they wanted whenever they wanted, only speculation is possible. More than likely, however, there would be some sort of regulation, and hence black markets for drugs would persist for those whose addictions were beyond the medicalized or legalized allotments. In a decriminalized market, levels of drug-related violence would likely either remain unchanged or increase (if drug use increased).

As for the last premise, that cheap drugs preclude the need to commit crimes to obtain them, the evidence emphatically suggests that this is not the case. Consider crack-cocaine: Although crack "rocks" are available on the illegal market for as little as two dollars in some locales, users are still involved in crime-driven endeavors to support their addictions. For example, researchers Norman S. Miller and Mark S. Gold surveyed 200 consecutive callers to the 1-800-COCAINE hotline who considered themselves to have a problem with crack. They found that, despite the low cost of crack, 63 percent of daily users and 40 percent of non-daily users spent more than $200 per week on the drug. Similarly, interviews conducted by NDRI researchers in New York City with almost 400 drug users contacted in the streets, jails, and treatment programs revealed that almost one-half of them spent over $1,000 a month on crack. The study also documented that crack users—despite the low cost of their drug of choice—spent more money on drugs than did users of heroin, powder cocaine, marijuana, and alcohol.

SYSTEMIC VIOLENCE

It is the supposed systemic violence associated with trafficking in cocaine and crack in America's inner cities that has recently received the attention of drug-policy critics interested in legalizing drugs. Certainly it might appear that, if heroin and cocaine were legal substances, systemic drug-related violence would decline. However, there are two very important questions in this regard: First, is drug-related violence more often psychopharmacological or systemic? Second, is the great bulk of systemic violence related to the distribution of crack? If most of the drug-related violence is psychopharmacological in nature, and if sys-

temic violence is typically related to crack—the drug generally excluded from consideration when legalization is recommended—then legalizing drugs would probably *not* reduce violent crime.

Regarding the first question, several recent studies conducted in New York City tend to contradict, or at least not support, the notion that legalizing drugs would reduce violent systemic-related crime. For example, Paul J. Goldstein's ethnographic studies of male and female drug users during the late 1980s found that cocaine-related violence was more often psychopharmacological than systemic. Similarly, Kenneth Tardiff's study of 4,298 New York City homicides found that 31 percent of the victims had used cocaine in the 24-hour period prior to their deaths. One of the conclusions of the study was that the homicides were not necessarily related to drug dealing. In all likelihood, as victims of homicide, the cocaine users may have provoked violence through their irritability, paranoid thinking, and verbal or physical aggression—all of which are among the psychopharmacological effects of cocaine.

Regarding the second question, the illegal drug most associated with systemic violence is crack-cocaine. Of all illicit drugs, crack is the one now responsible for the most homicides. In a study done in New York City in 1988 by Goldstein and his colleagues, crack was found to be connected with 32 percent of all homicides and 60 percent of all drug-related homicides. Furthermore, although there is evidence that crack sellers are more violent than other drug sellers, this violence is not confined to the drug-selling context—violence potententials appear to precede involvement in selling.

Thus, though crack has been blamed for increasing violence in the marketplace, this violence actually stems from the psychopharmacological consequences of crack use. Ansley Hamid, a professor of anthropology at the John Jay College of Criminal Justice in New York, reasons that increases in crack-related violence are due to the deterioration of informal and formal social controls throughout communities that have been destabilized by economic processes and political decisions. If this is the case, does anyone really believe that we can improve these complex social problems through the simple act of legalizing drugs?

DON'T JUST SAY NO

The issue of whether or not legalization would create a multitude of new users also needs to be addressed. It has been shown that many people do not use drugs simply because drugs are illegal. As Mark A.R. Kleiman, author of *Against Excess: Drug Policy for Results*, recently put it: "Illegality by itself tends to suppress consumption, independent of its effect on price, both because some consumers are reluctant to disobey the law and because illegal products are harder to find and less reliable as to quality and labeling than legal ones."

Although there is no way of accurately estimating how many new users there would be if drugs were legalized, there would probably be many. To begin with, there is the historical example of Prohibition. During Prohibition, there was a decrease of 20 percent to 50 percent in the number of alcoholics. These estimates were calculated based on a decline in cirrhosis and other alcohol-related deaths; after Prohibition ended, both of these indicators increased.

Currently, relatively few people are steady users of drugs. The University of Michigan's *Monitoring the Future* study reported in 1995 that only two-tenths of 1 percent of high-school seniors are daily users of either hallucinogens, cocaine, heroin, sedatives, or inhalants. It is the addicts who overwhelmingly consume the bulk of the drug supply—80 percent of all alcohol and almost 100 percent of all heroin. In other words, there are significantly large numbers of non-users who have yet to even try drugs, let alone use them regularly. Of those who begin to use drugs "recreationally," researchers estimate that approximately 10 percent go on to serious, heavy, chronic, compulsive use. Herbert Kleber, the former deputy director of the Office of National Drug Control Policy, recently estimated that cocaine legalization might multiply the number of addicts from the current 2 million to between 18 and 50 million (which are the estimated numbers of problem drinkers and nicotine addicts).

This suggests that drug prohibition seems to be having some very positive effects and that legalizing drugs would not necessarily have a depressant effect on violent crime. With legalization, violent crime would likely escalate; or perhaps some types of systemic violence would decline at the expense of greatly increasing the overall rate of violent crime. Moreover, legalizing drugs would likely increase physical illnesses and compound any existing psychiatric problems among users and their family members. And finally, legalizing drugs would not eliminate the effects of unemployment, inadequate housing, deficient job skills, economic worries, and physical abuse that typically contribute to the use of drugs.

POSTSCRIPT

Should Drugs Be Legalized?

Nadelmann asserts that utilizing the criminal justice system to eradicate drug problems simply does not work. He argues that international control efforts, interdiction, and domestic law enforcement are ineffective and that many problems associated with drug use are the consequences of drug regulation policies. He maintains that decriminalization is a feasible and desirable means of dealing with the drug crisis.

Inciardi and Saum charge that the advantages of maintaining illegality far outweigh any conceivable benefits of decriminalization. They profess that if drug laws were relaxed, the result would be more drug users and, thus, more drug addicts and more criminal activity. Also, there is the possibility that more drug-related social problems would occur. Inciardi and Saum conclude that society cannot afford to soften its position on legalization.

Legalization proponents argue that drug laws have not worked and that the drug battle has been lost. They believe that drug-related problems would disappear if legalization were implemented. Citing the legal drugs alcohol and tobacco as examples, legalization opponents argue that decriminalizing drugs would not decrease profits from the sale of drugs (the profits from cigarettes and alcohol are incredibly high). Moreover, opponents argue, legalizing a drug does not make its problems disappear (alcohol and tobacco have extremely high addiction rates as well as a myriad of other problems associated with their use).

Many European countries have a system of legalized drugs, and most have far fewer addiction rates and lower incidences of drug-related violence and crime than the United States. However, would the outcomes of decriminalization in the United States be the same as in Europe? Legalization in the United States could still be a tremendous risk because its drug problems could escalate and recriminalizing drugs would be difficult. This was the case with Prohibition in the 1920s, which, in changing the status of alcohol from legal to illegal, produced numerous crime- and alcohol-related problems.

Many good articles debate the pros and cons of drug legalization. These include "Strange Bedfellows: Ideology, Politics, and Drug Legalization," by Erich Goode, *Society* (May/June 1998); "Drug Legalization: Time for a Real Debate," by Paul Stares, *The Brookings Review* (Spring 1996); "Legalization of Narcotics: Myths and Reality," by Joseph Califano, *USA Today* (March 1997); and "Drug Policy: Should the Law Take a Back Seat?" by Virginia Berridge, *The Lancet* (February 3, 1996). Also, the February 12, 1996, issue of *The National Review* features a number of prominent individuals discussing whether or not the war on drugs has been lost.

ISSUE 2

Should the United States Put More Emphasis on Stopping the Importation of Drugs?

YES: Barry McCaffrey, from *The National Drug Control Strategy, 1997* (1997)

NO: Mathea Falco, from "U.S. Drug Policy: Addicted to Failure," *Foreign Policy* (Spring 1996)

ISSUE SUMMARY

YES: Barry McCaffrey, director of the Office of National Drug Control Policy, argues that the importation of drugs must be stopped to reduce drug use and abuse. If the supply of drugs being trafficked across American borders is reduced, then there will be fewer drug-related problems. He maintains that a coordinated international effort is needed to combat the increased production of heroin, cocaine, and marijuana.

NO: Mathea Falco, president of Drug Strategies, a nonprofit policy institute, asserts that the emphasis should not be on curtailing the availability of drugs but on factors that contribute to Americans' use of drugs. She contends that blaming other countries for drug-related problems in the United States is one way for politicians to deflect criticism from themselves. Moreover, she argues, people involved in the drug trade in other countries have little incentive to end their involvement.

Since the beginning of the 1990s, overall drug use in the United States has increased. Up to now, interdiction has not proven to be successful in slowing the flow of drugs into the United States. Drugs continue to cross U.S. borders at record levels. This point may signal a need for stepped-up international efforts to stop the production and trafficking of drugs. Conversely, it may illustrate the inadequacy of the current strategy. Should the position of the U.S. government be to improve and strengthen current measures or to try an entirely new approach?

Some people contend that rather than attempting to limit illegal drugs from coming into the United States, more effort should be directed at reducing the demand for drugs and improving treatment for drug abusers. Foreign countries would not produce and transport drugs like heroin and cocaine into the United States if there were no market for them. Drug policies, some people maintain, should be aimed at the social and economic conditions underlying domestic drug problems, not at interfering with foreign governments.

Many U.S. government officials believe that other countries should assist in stopping the flow of drugs across their borders. Diminishing the supply of drugs by intercepting them before they reach the user is another way to eliminate or curtail drug use. Critical elements in the lucrative drug trade are multinational crime syndicates. One premise is that if the drug production, transportation, distribution, and processing functions as well as the money laundering operations of these criminal organizations can be interrupted and eventually crippled, then the drug problem would abate.

In South American countries such as Peru, Colombia, and Bolivia, where coca—from which cocaine is processed—is cultivated, economic aid has been made available to help the governments of these countries fight the cocaine kingpins. An alleged problem is that a number of government officials in these countries are corrupt or fearful of the cocaine cartel leaders. One proposed solution is to go directly to the farmers and offer them money to plant crops other than coca. This tactic, however, failed in the mid-1970s, when the U.S. government gave money to farmers in Turkey to stop growing opium poppy crops. After one year the program was discontinued due to the enormous expense, and opium poppy crops were once again planted.

Drug problems are not limited to the Americas. Since the breakup of the Soviet Union, for example, there has been a tremendous increase in opium production in many of the former republics. These republics are in dire need of money, and one source of income is opium production. Moreover, there is lax enforcement by police officials in these republics.

There are many reasons why people are dissatisfied with the current state of the war on drugs. For example, in the war on drugs, the *casual* user is generally the primary focus of drug use deterrence. This is viewed by many people as a form of discrimination because the vast majority of drug users and sellers who are arrested and prosecuted are poor, members of minorities, homeless, unemployed, and/or disenfranchised. Also, international drug dealers who are arrested are usually not the drug bosses but lower-level people working for them. Finally, some argue that the war on drugs should be redirected away from interdiction and enforcement because they feel that the worst drug problems in society today are caused by legal drugs, primarily alcohol and tobacco.

The following selections address the issue of whether or not the war on drugs should be fought on an international level. Barry McCaffrey takes the view that international cooperation is absolutely necessary if we are to stem the flow of drugs and maintain world order. Mathea Falco argues that an international approach to dealing with drugs avoids the real issues that lead to drug abuse.

YES

Barry McCaffrey

THE NATIONAL DRUG CONTROL STRATEGY, 1997

INITIATIVES TO SHIELD OUR FRONTIERS

America's place in the world—its status as global leader, economic giant, and bastion of democracy—ensures that extraordinary numbers of people will come to our shores, air terminals, and borders on various modes of transport. According to the U.S. Customs Service, each year sixty million people enter our country on more than 675,000 commercial and private flights. Another six million come by sea and 370 million by land. In addition, 116 million vehicles cross the land borders with Canada and Mexico. More than 90,000 merchant and passenger ships dock at our ports, carrying more than nine million shipping containers and four hundred million tons of cargo, while another 157,000 smaller vessels visit our many coastal towns. Amid voluminous trade, drug traffickers seek to hide illegal substances that destroy our citizens and ruin neighborhoods. Through concerted effort, we can limit illegal drugs entering our country from abroad while maintaining open, free-flowing commerce, tourism, and international exchange that help make our nation great.

Preventing Drug Trafficking Across the Southwest Border

If a single geographic region were to be identified as a microcosm of America's drug problem, it would be the U.S.–Mexican border. Cocaine, heroin, methamphetamine, and marijuana all cross into the United States here, hidden among the eighty-four million cars, 232 million people, and 2.8 million trucks that the Customs Service estimates cross the thirty-eight ports of entry spanning nearly two thousand miles. American and Mexican ranchers often are harmed by violent bands of drug runners openly crossing their property. Border areas suffer from disproportionate levels of crime and violence due to the abundance of illegal drugs. The general population is terrified by increasingly sophisticated organizations that ply their vicious trade across what is otherwise a historic setting that marks the conflux of two great nations and their cultures.

From Barry McCaffrey, Office of National Drug Control Policy, *National Drug Control Strategy, 1997* (February 1997). Washington, DC: Government Printing Office, 1997. Notes omitted.

The current situation must be changed. Significant reinforcements have been committed to the substantial resources already focused on the southwest border. Approximately a thousand Border Patrol agents and 150 Immigration and Naturalization inspectors, 625 U.S. Customs Service agents and inspectors, fifty Drug Enforcement agents, seventy FBI agents, and additional Deputy U.S. Marshals will be added in fiscal year 1997. Advanced technological equipment, sophisticated sensors, and long-range infrared night-vision devices have been installed near the border. A variety of intelligence agencies have been tracking the flow of illegal drugs, enhancing interdiction operations, and pursuing drug-trafficking organizations. The Southwest Border Initiative, Southwest Border Council, Southwest Border HIDTA [High Intensity Drug Trafficking Area], Joint Task Force-Six, OCDETF, and the Attorney General's Executive Committee and Operation Alliance have stepped up activities, expanding coordination with state and local agencies. Bilateral working groups have been established with Mexico to achieve the rule of law.

However, illegal drugs are still crossing the border. This tough problem is complicated by illegal immigration, corruption, and questions of jurisdiction, policy, and law. To meet these challenges, we are pursuing an overarching framework to complement individual inspection and interdiction operations, focus resources, provide timely and accurate information that can secure evidence for specific cases, and anticipate strategic and tactical activities of drug traffickers. We will also coordinate efforts among many agencies devoted to the issue, harness technologies in an integrative fashion so that one system complements the other, and work more closely with Mexicans for the common good.

Closing the Caribbean "Back Door"

The DEA estimates that the second-most-significant drug trafficking route into the U.S. is through the Caribbean, specifically Puerto Rico and the U.S. Virgin Islands. Puerto Rico is a natural point of entry because of its central location amid major lines of commerce and transportation and the absence of customs inspections for domestic cargo moving between the island and U.S. mainland. The consequences of this trafficking have been devastating for Puerto Rico, the Virgin islands, and many island nations of the Caribbean. Cocaine sold in Puerto Rico is cheaper than anywhere else in the United States. Violent gangs control nearly a thousand drug-distribution points throughout the island and victimize more than three hundred public housing areas. Puerto Rico has the second highest per capita murder rate in the United States.

In response to the threat posed by international drug trafficking in the Caribbean, the United States established the Puerto Rico–U.S. Virgin Islands High Intensity Drug Trafficking Area (HIDTA) in 1994. To combat drug trafficking and money laundering, HIDTA brings together twenty-six agencies and more than six hundred federal, state, and local personnel forming ten task forces and an intelligence coordination center. During FY '96, HIDTA participants arrested 417 individuals, confiscated 14,500 kilograms of cocaine, and seized eight million dollars in assets and currency.

The United States Coast Guard and United States Customs Service have also worked to constrict this illegal drug route into the United States. Their operations feature expanded marine and air enforcement, more cargo examinations, and frequent searches of small vessels. From March 1 through December 31, 1996, the Customs Service's Operation Gateway produced the seizure of 28,507 pounds of cocaine, 3,060 pounds of marijuana, sixty-two pounds of heroin, and $2.2 million and 129 arrests in the Puerto Rico/U.S. Virgin Islands area. In the last three months of 1996, the Coast Guard seized seven vessels, 13,897 pounds of cocaine, forty pounds of heroin, and made nineteen arrests. Interdiction can help stop drugs from entering our country.

We continue to work closely with our Caribbean allies to guard the approaches to Puerto Rico and deny narco-traffickers safe haven anywhere in the region while complying with international law. We currently have bilateral enforcement agreements in place with sixteen countries in or bordering the Caribbean. Negotiations are underway with an additional six countries, and we are working to expand agreements that help protect island nations possessing small law-enforcement establishments from the onslaught of international criminal organizations that violate their sovereignty and corrupt their economies and democratic institutions. Multinational counterdrug operations in the Caribbean provide an additional force multiplier. For example, British, French, and Dutch Naval forces participate in fully coordinated operations helping to block smuggling routes out of South America.

Addressing Other Drug Entry Points

The greater our success at interrupting drug trafficking along any particular border, the more traffickers attempt to introduce illegal drugs elsewhere.

South Florida, for example, continues to be a key site for drugs coming into the U.S. and for money moving out —despite the successful disruption of the air bridge that brought cocaine during the last decade from Colombia to the southeastern United States. Mexican coastal ports are entry points for drugs being smuggled northward across our southwest border, necessitating interdiction operations on key trafficking routes through the eastern Pacific and western Caribbean. New York City remains the primary port of entry for Southeast Asian heroin. Ports in the Pacific Northwest and along the Pacific coast—as well as the border with Canada and any airport that handles international cargo or passengers —are vulnerable to drug trafficking.

Consequently, we must develop a comprehensive, coordinated capability that allows the federal government to focus resources in response to shifting drug-trafficking threats. We must be proactive in efforts to keep drug traffickers from penetrating our sovereign territory. Existing organizations and initiatives— like the three Joint Inter-Agency Task Forces (East, West, South), the Domestic Air Interdiction Coordination Center, Joint Task Force-Six, and Operation Alliance, which address the southwest border problem, as well as HIDTAs and other cooperative interagency efforts— must remain the building blocks for this effort.

INITIATIVES TO REDUCE DRUG AVAILABILITY

Only sustained commitment can reduce the supply of illegal drugs. The basic principles of supply reduction are straightforward. A five-stage grower-to-user chain links the drug producer in a foreign land with the consumer in the United States. The stages are: cultivation, processing, transit, wholesale distribution, and retail sales on the street. The U.S. government's international drug control programs target the first three links in this chain: cultivation, processing, and transit. International drug control programs have demonstrated that they can be particularly effective when they focus on severing the chain at the source. When drug crops or synthetic drug laboratories are eliminated, fewer drugs enter the system. This approach is analogous to removing a tumor before it metastasizes.

Opposing international criminal organizations that traffic in drugs at all stages of their operation and in all their operating environments is essential. The global drug trade has spawned large trafficking organizations with an almost limitless capacity to subvert the economic and political systems of underdeveloped countries. In our own hemisphere, the two countries that have faced the longest struggle against drug traffickers—Colombia and Mexico—have been plagued by widespread drug corruption. Efforts to break these organizations must be supported by public information that depicts the true nature of drug traffickers, endorses the elements countering them, and supports the rule of law.

The success of our international drug control policies depends on the political will and institutional capability of other countries to implement programs that reduce and ultimately eliminate cultivation of illicit drug crops and suppress the production, trafficking, and abuse of illegal drugs. Consequently, we are convinced that our drug control programs must be complemented by efforts to strengthen democratic institutions in key drug producing and transit countries.

Encouraging Other Nations to Confront Drug Production and Trafficking

The Certification Process.   One way to pressure foreign governments to stand up against drug trafficking organizations is through periodic public scrutiny of their counterdrug record. The U.S. government does so through the annual process of certifying the counterdrug performance of narcotics producing and transit countries. Performance is evaluated in terms of cooperation with U.S. efforts, or unilateral efforts to comply with the goals and objectives of the 1988 United Nations Convention Against Illicit Traffic in Narcotics, Drugs, and Psychotropic Substances.

This annual certification process gives the President an international platform for candid, public evaluation of major drug source and transit countries. While denial of certification carries important foreign assistance sanctions as well as a mandatory U.S. vote against multilateral development banks lending money to such countries, the major sanction is public opprobrium at failing the standard. This process has proved increasingly effective. It has fostered the development of realistic performance benchmarks and increased cooperation in important countries.

Bilateral Cooperation with Mexico. The principal mechanism for counterdrug cooperation with Mexico is the High Level Contact Group on Drug Control formed in March 1996. This bilateral group of senior officials meets periodically while subordinate working groups are in continuous contact. The Contact Group on Drug Control operates at the cabinet level and has instituted a number of broad initiatives, including a shared assessment of the drug threat and a bi-national counterdrug strategy. Key elements of that strategy include: measures to strengthen border security, actions to ensure criminals cannot escape justice in one country by flight to another, improved information sharing, reduction of drug use in both countries, anti–money laundering initiatives, cooperation to interrupt drug shipments destined for both Mexico and the U.S., and concentration of law enforcement efforts on trafficking organizations that operate in both countries.

Progress, while not uniform across the board, has been significant. The criminal drug organizations that operate in both our countries are ruthless, violent, flexible, and defiant of national sovereignty. The corrupting power of thirty billion dollars of illegal drug money is an enormous threat to the democratic institutions of both Mexico and the United States. Notable successes include: the Mexican government's passage of important anti-crime legislation, U.S. training for anti-drug units of Mexican police and Armed Forces as well as in money laundering investigations for investigators and prosecutors from the Mexican Treasury and Attorney General's office. Mexico continues to implement one of the world's most successful drug crop eradication programs. Drug seizures by Mexican authorities increased significantly in 1996; heroin seizures were up 78 percent and cocaine seizures up 21 percent.

To build on these successes, we must continue working with our counterparts to insulate law enforcement organizations from corruption and build Mexican counterdrug capabilities. A major bilateral concern is the cross-border activity of Mexican trafficking organizations and their ability to hold Mexican author-ities at bay. Finally, we must be cognizant of sovereignty concerns in this complex relationship as we broaden the bilateral counterdrug effort. Drug traffickers have developed complex infrastructures and multiple routes in Mexico over the better part of a decade. These criminal organizations can be pursued, but success will take a long-term commitment on the part of dedicated, honest, and courageous Mexican authorities and sustained, cooperative efforts by the United States.

Making Cocaine Less Available

Cocaine is currently our most dangerous illicit drug. It is responsible for more addiction, health problems, economic dislocation, and social costs than any other illegal substance. It is also more vulnerable to international supply reduction than other foreign-produced drugs. Our national efforts against coca cultivation and the production and trafficking of cocaine are guided by Presidential Decision Directive 14, the Western Hemisphere counterdrug strategy. U.S. anti-cocaine activities fall into the following three categories: reduction of cultivation, interdiction, and actions against trafficking organizations.

Reduction of Cultivation. Nearly all the cocaine consumed in the United States is produced from coca crops grown in Bolivia, Colombia, and Peru. In 1995, enough coca was grown on 214,800 hectares of land in these three countries to produce 780 metric tons of cocaine for the world market. Eighty percent of the cocaine in the United States comes from Peruvian coca crops. A top international drug policy priority is support for the efforts of Bolivia, Colombia, and Peru to reduce coca cultivation. Our forthcoming regional initiative, whose goal is nothing less than complete elimination within the next decade of cultivation of coca destined for illicit cocaine production, will focus on alternative economic development in Peru. These efforts will recognize that drug cultivation in source countries is an important means of employment and income for some of the poorest members of society. To be successful, drug crop reduction programs must include measures to resolve socio-economic factors that promote the cultivation of illegal drug crops.

Interdiction. Since 1993, global seizures averaged 270 metric tons of cocaine, leaving approximately five-hundred tons potentially available for consumption each year. U.S. cocaine seizures by themselves averaged 112 tons a year over the same period.

Within South America, a sustained, U.S.–supported interdiction effort continues to disrupt the air, river, maritime, and land transportation of cocaine base from Bolivia and Peru to Colombia. By the end of 1996, Peru and Colombia seized or destroyed dozens of drug trafficker aircraft, resulting in a two-thirds reduction in the number of detected trafficker flights over the Andean ridge region compared with the number of flights detected before the denial program was launched in early 1995. As coca cultivation subsequently exceeded drug trafficker transportation capabilities, average coca prices in Peru dropped by 50 percent over the same time period. We have demonstrated that interdiction efforts in the source country zone can disrupt trafficking patterns significantly. Our challenges now are to work with host nations to: restrict further the air movement of coca products between and within Bolivia, Peru, Brazil, and Colombia; block drug traf-

fickers from developing alternative river, ground, and maritime routes; and assist South American nations in preventing drug trafficking organizations from violating their sovereign air, land, and sea space.

In the "transit zone" of the Caribbean, Central America, Mexico, and the eastern Pacific waters, U.S. interdiction seeks to prevent traffickers from moving cocaine. An effective transit zone interdiction program requires flexible, in-depth, intelligence-driven defenses. Drug traffickers are adaptable, and they will react to our successes by shifting routes and changing modes of transportation. We must be equally flexible and give the traffickers no quarter as we respond to their moves. This objective will require that we—in concert with our regional allies—maintain a "defense in depth," taking aggressive action in source countries, throughout the transit zone, and at our borders.

International coordination and cooperation are important components of our interdiction effort. U.S. interdiction agencies do not by themselves have sufficient resources to address the trafficking threat. Bilateral or multilateral agreements, sharing intelligence and information, and conducting combined operations with our allies can multiply the effectiveness of the regional interdiction effort. Improving the interdiction capabilities of committed nations will also increase the effectiveness of our transit zone efforts. Finally, technology and intelligence can help us employ limited assets against high pay-off targets.

Actions Against Trafficking Organizations. Even after the arrest of major Cali Mafia leaders, Colombian drug syndicates continue to be the preeminent cocaine producing and trafficking organizations. They purchase the majority of semi-finished cocaine base from Bolivian or Peruvian farmers. Along with Mexican poly-drug traffickers and others, they increasingly move the illicit drug to the United States and elsewhere. The power, wealth, and sophistication of Colombian, Mexican, and other drug syndicates pose enormous threats to governmental and judicial institutions in many Western hemisphere countries.

Our successes against these and other international criminal organizations have been increasing. U.S.–supported Colombian law enforcement efforts have resulted in the arrest or surrender of the top seven leaders of the Cali drug cartel. U.S. support for other nations helped disrupt and dismantle trafficking organizations, including the Jose Castrillon organization based in Colombia and Panama. This crime syndicate was responsible for the maritime shipment of several multi-ton loads of cocaine destined for the United States. While the sentences announced to date by the Colombian government have been inadequate considering the magnitude of the crimes committed, cocaine traffickers are operating in an increasingly hostile environment. Our international cocaine control strategy will continue to include an across-the-spectrum attack on these criminal organizations.

Making Heroin Less Available

Efforts against production and trafficking of heroin are guided by the President's heroin control policy of November 1995 (PDD-44). Potential global heroin production has increased about 60 percent in the past eight years to about 360 metric tons. Heroin is not just an American problem. U.S. demand (estimated between four and thirteen metric tons)

is equivalent to only a fraction of that potential.

The heroin interdiction challenge is enormous. Central governments in the two major source countries, Afghanistan and Burma, have limited powers. U.S. access and influence there is also extremely limited. Trafficking organizations are highly cohesive and difficult to penetrate. They use multiple trafficking routes and methods. Heroin flows through East Asia, the Middle East, the Former Soviet Union, Nigeria, South Africa, and South America, following the paths of least resistance and avoiding law enforcement. Heroin is a low bulk, high value commodity. An individual courier traveling aboard a commercial airliner can use body-carry techniques and ingestion to conceal several million dollars worth of heroin. Larger multi-kilogram amounts have been found hidden in commercial cargo shipments. Consequently, the worldwide seizure of morphine base/heroin in 1995 consisted of only thirty-two metric tons while U.S. seizures were just 1.3 metric tons. The recent increase in heroin production in Colombia underscores the diffuse nature of the international heroin challenge. Just a few years ago, Colombia was an insignificant producer of heroin. Now, its potential heroin production (six tons in 1995) represents a significant portion of the estimated U.S. demand. South American heroin is being sold in the U.S. at higher purity levels and lower prices than South East Asian heroin to garner larger market shares, and is in some areas becoming an important source of heroin.

The United States will work through diplomatic and public channels to promote international awareness of the heroin threat, help strengthen law enforcement efforts in heroin source and transit countries, bring cooperative law enforcement to bear against processing and trafficking, act against illegal financial systems that bankroll heroin trafficking activities, and promote the United Nations International Drug Control Program (UNDCP) and other multilateral and regional engagement in opium poppy and heroin control programs in source countries where U.S. bilateral influence is limited by political and security constraints. America will support continuing programs by Colombia and Mexico to eradicate opium poppy and will move promptly against any other illicit opium poppy cultivation encountered in the Western hemisphere.

Countering the Methamphetamine Threat

Methamphetamine abuse is a significant problem on the West Coast and in the Southwest and Midwest; it is also moving eastward. This drug is problematic because it is easily manufactured, inexpensive, and incredibly addictive. Methamphetamine is the "poor man's cocaine" and has the potential to assume national prominence if its use is not curtailed. Current law enforcement efforts against the production and distribution of methamphetamine are guided by the *Department of Justice National Methamphetamine Strategy* released in April 1996. This document serves as the basis for an expanded response that integrates treatment and prevention initiatives.

The principal foreign source of methamphetamine is Mexico. Mexican trafficking groups use existing cocaine smuggling networks to funnel methamphetamine into the United States. Through the High Level Contact Group on Drug Control, the United States will continue supporting Mexican government efforts to identify and destroy methamphetamine production, storage, or shipment activities and act against criminal organizations engaged in this traffic. The U.S. will also cooperate with other industrialized countries, the U.N. Drug Control Program, and multilateral organizations to limit international commerce in methamphetamine precursors and prevent illicit diversion or trafficking in domestic or foreign methamphetamines.

Domestically, the drug is produced in clandestine laboratories using toxic and highly explosive mixtures of hydriotic acid, phosphene gas, and red phosphorous. These chemicals are either smuggled into the country or illegally diverted from legitimate sources. The Methamphetamine Control Act of 1996 addressed this problem by controlling precursor chemicals and increasing criminal penalties for possession and distribution. Meth labs are mostly short-term, "one-batch" facilities commonly established in rural or sparsely populated areas to preclude detection as a result of the chemicals' odors. Nevertheless, federal and state lab seizures are increasing as a result of law enforcement attention to this emerging drug threat.

Measuring and Reducing Domestic Cannabis Cultivation

Marijuana remains the most-commonly-used illegal drug in the United States. Much of the marijuana smoked in the U.S. is cultivated domestically—commercially, privately, outdoors, and indoors. However, we have no accurate estimate of the extent of domestic marijuana cultivation. Our domestic cannabis crop reduction efforts must be supported by accurate information about drug crop locations and potentials. The Office of

National Drug Control Policy will coordinate the development of a domestic marijuana crop measurement program.

Controlling the Diversion of Drug-essential Chemicals

The production of illegal drugs requires enormous quantities of precursor chemicals. Clearly, drug production can be curtailed if the necessary precursor chemicals can be prevented from being diverted for this purpose. The importance of controlling chemicals has been internationally accepted. Article 12 of the 1988 United Nations Convention Against Illicit Traffic in Narcotic Drugs and Psychotropic Substance establishes the obligation for parties to the treaty to control their chemical commerce to prevent diversion to illicit drug manufacture. The Convention lists twenty-two chemicals as most necessary to drug manufacture and, therefore, subject to control.

International cooperation between enforcement and regulatory agencies is essential to the prevention of diversion of precursor chemicals. Information exchange to verify the legitimacy of proposed transactions in regulated chemicals is the key element to such cooperation. The United States continues to urge adoption of chemical control regimes by governments that do not have them. Our goal is to continue and expand the cooperation until sharing of information on proposed transactions in regulated chemicals is routine. We need to demonstrate that all sources of information must be queried, not only those in the exporting and importing countries, and that information sharing can occur without jeopardizing commercial confidentiality.

NO

Mathea Falco

U.S. DRUG POLICY: ADDICTED TO FAILURE

As Americans struggle to define their national security interests in the post–Cold War world, drug control enjoys strong political support from both parties. When asked to rank "very important" foreign policy goals, 85 per cent of the American public place "stopping the flow of drugs" at the top of the list, according to the 1995 Chicago Council on Foreign Relations national survey. For that reason, international drug-control programs will survive the congressional assault on the foreign affairs budget. Voter opposition to foreign aid does not yet extend to eradication and interdiction programs intended to stem the flow of drugs from abroad. Indeed, U.S.-supported antidrug programs in Latin America now represent almost 20 per cent of total American foreign assistance to the region, compared with only 3 per cent a decade ago.

The popular view that other countries are largely responsible for America's drug problems has deep historic roots. When the first drug laws were adopted early in this century, drugs were associated with immigrant groups and minorities: opium with Chinese laborers in the West; cocaine with blacks; and marijuana with Mexican immigrants in the Southwest. These drugs were seen as foreign threats to America's social fabric, undermining traditional moral values and political stability. Today the perceived link between foreigners and drugs still prompts the U.S. government to use diplomacy, coercion, money, and even military force to try to stop drugs from entering the country.

The supply-side approach is logically compelling. If there were no drugs coming in, the argument goes, then there would be no drug problem. And even if foreign drugs cannot be eliminated entirely, the laws of the marketplace dictate that reducing the supply will drive up the price, which in turn will deter potential users from trying drugs and force addicts to either go "cold turkey" or seek treatment. The critical assumption is that curtailing foreign supplies is the most effective way to cut drug abuse in the United States.

This supply-side approach to drugs has powerful political appeal. Blaming foreigners for America's recurring drug epidemics provides convenient if distant targets for public anger that might otherwise be directed toward elected officials. Getting foreign farmers to stop growing drug crops seems easier than curbing America's appetite for drugs. Moreover, intercepting incoming drugs in the air or on the high seas appears to be the kind of technological challenge Americans are uniquely capable of meeting. If our scientists could land men on the moon, then surely we can shut off the drug traffic.

The supply-side approach to drug control has been thoroughly tested by both Republican and Democratic administrations. President Richard Nixon, faced with rising heroin and marijuana use in the late 1960s, closed a key U.S.-Mexican border crossing to convince Mexico to take action against illegal drug production. He also stepped up diplomatic pressure against Turkey, a major opium source for the notorious "French Connection" heroin traffickers, and provided narcotics-control assistance to Mexico and Turkey. Presidents Gerald Ford and Jimmy Carter continued programs of crop eradication, substitution, and overseas law-enforcement spending tens of millions of dollars during the 1970s.

At the end of the seventies, Turkey was no longer a significant source far illegal heroin, although the government allowed some farmers to grow opium for the international pharmaceutical industry. Due to intensive aerial opium eradication, Mexico's share of the U.S. heroin market declined sharply, from between 70 and 80 per cent in 1975 to 30 per cent in 1979. During the same period, heroin addiction in the United States also declined, in large part because addicts faced with rising heroin prices went into treatment, which was then widely available.

Unfortunately, the success of these supply-reduction programs was limited and brief. Production in other regions quickly expanded to fill American demand: Southeast Asia's Golden Triangle (Burma, Laos, and Thailand) and South Asia's Golden Crescent (Afghanistan, Iran, and Pakistan) became primary heroin sources. By 1983, Mexico had again become a major supplier, as opium cultivation spread to more remote areas only nominally controlled by the government.

President Ronald Reagan gave unprecedented resources to supply-control efforts. Just as he intended to shield the United States from Soviet missiles through the Strategic Defense Initiative, so, too, did Reagan try to seal the borders against the flow of drugs that threatened the nation's security. Funding for interdiction and international supply-control programs jumped from $416 million in 1981 to $1.6 billion in 1987, constituting about one-third of total federal antidrug spending.

President George Bush followed similar policies. In September 1989, in his first televised presidential address, Bush announced that, "we will for the first time make available the appropriate resources of America's Armed forces. We will intensify our efforts against drug smugglers on the high seas, in international airspace, and at our borders."

The Defense Department initially resisted congressional efforts to enlist the military in the drug war. However, when faced with major budget cuts after the collapse of the Soviet Union, the Defense Department embraced a drug-fighting mission, protecting some endangered programs by reclassifying them as drug-related. For example, over-the-horizon radar systems designed to guard against Soviet missiles overflying Canada were redirected southward to watch for drug-smuggling aircraft. By 1991, the Defense

Department had captured the largest share of the $2 billion drug-interdiction budget.

Although President Bill Clinton has generally endorsed his predecessors' emphasis on curtailing drug supplies, voices within the administration and the Congress express increasing skepticism about the effectiveness of America's international drug war. In September 1993, a National Security Council (NSC) interagency review concluded that interdiction had not succeeded in slowing the flow of cocaine, confirming the findings of several previous General Accounting Office (GAO) studies. Although interdiction funding had been cut substantially in the Bush administration's last budget, funding fell further under Clinton, dropping to approximately $1.3 billion by 1995.

The NSC policy review argued that stopping drugs close to their source of production might prove a more effective strategy than traditional interdiction efforts. Funding for overseas narcotics-control programs had declined from an estimated $660 million in 1992 to about $330 million in 1994. Following the NSC recommendation, the administration requested substantial increases in the fiscal 1995 budget for source-country programs, but the Democratic-controlled Congress refused to fund them. Noting that Congress had approved the $2.2 billion five-year Andean Strategy, begun in 1989 under the Bush administration to help Bolivia, Colombia, and Peru reduce illicit drug activities, the House Appropriations Committee's 1995 report on foreign operations concluded that

> there are no signs that actual levels of cocaine reaching U.S. shores has changed. . . . We thus find ourselves continuing to march steadily down a path towards devoting more and more resources to helicopters, vehicles, police and army bases, and weaponry, while not doing enough to fund comprehensive economic solutions. . . . The program has done little in its country programs to ensure sustainability, and thus the Committee has no confidence that the reforms achieved so far will stick.

The new Republican Congress has sharply criticized Clinton's shift away from interdiction, calling this a litmus test of his determination to combat drugs. In July 1995, the House of Representatives voted to eliminate the White House Office of National Drug Control Policy (ONDCP), which develops the administration's annual drug strategy and coordinates federal antidrug efforts. While the Senate subsequently restored ONDCP under threat of presidential veto, its budget was cut by one-third. Critics contended that ONDCP's budget would be better spent on interdiction. According to Senator Richard Shelby (R-Alabama), his appropriations subcommittee "voted to terminate" ONDCP in order to provide "full funding for . . . drug interdiction efforts with the $10 million in savings."

Congressional enthusiasm for interdiction does not extend to source-country programs, which two key House committee chairmen characterized as "tried-and-failed crop eradication and alternative development initiatives" in an open letter to Clinton in 1995. Congress cut $98 million from the Clinton administration's requested $213 million for the State Department's source-country efforts in the fiscal 1996 budget.

SUPPLY-CONTROL SCORECARD

Since 1981, American taxpayers have spent $23 billion on international drug control. Yet drug supplies have increased substantially both at home and abroad. Worldwide opium production has more than doubled in the past decade and now exceeds 3,400 tons per year, the equivalent of 340 tons of heroin. From 1984 to 1994, coca production almost doubled, although the United States provided more than $2 billion in narcotics-control assistance to Bolivia, Colombia, and Peru, the world's largest coca producers. Meanwhile, drug prices in the United States have fallen precipitously. Heroin now sells for less than half its 1981 street price, and heroin purity exceeds 60 per cent in many cities, compared with only 7 per cent in 1981. Cocaine prices have dropped by two-thirds. The administrator of the Drug Enforcement Administration (DEA), Thomas Constantine, testified before the House International Relations Subcommittee on the Western Hemisphere in March 1995 that "drug availability and purity of cocaine and heroin are at an all-time high."

Some congressional critics blame the apparent failure of interdiction on a lack of resources, arguing that budget cuts of one-third since 1992 have hindered federal efforts to intercept foreign drug traffic. Others blame Clinton's strategic shift away from efforts to interrupt drug traffic through the Caribbean, Central America, and Mexico in favor of trying to eliminate the *production* of drugs in Bolivia, Colombia, and Peru. In June 1995, Joseph Kelley, a top analyst for international affairs at the GAO, testified that the U.S. international antidrug effort suffers from weak management and poor coordination.

The underlying problem, however, is not operational. Increased resources and better implementation will not make foreign supply-control efforts more successful in driving up drug prices in the United States. The supply-side strategy is fatally flawed for several reasons, which follow.

The economics of drug cultivation mitigate against sustained reductions in supply. Drug crops can be grown very cheaply almost anywhere in the world, and poor farmers have strong economic incentives to adapt to changing conditions. If one production area is wiped out, lost crops can easily be replaced. In Peru, for example, a fungal infestation of coca crops in the early 1990s pushed cultivation into more remote, previously uncultivated areas of the Huallaga Valley. In the 1970s in Mexico, the government's opium-eradication campaign drove farmers to change their cultivation techniques, growing opium poppies in much smaller patches under large-leafed crops, such as banana trees, which made aerial detection difficult.

The number of countries producing drugs has significantly increased in the past two decades. Although coca is a traditional crop in Bolivia, Colombia, and Peru, it is now being grown in other South American countries, and worldwide poppy cultivation continues to expand. In the Central Asian republics, opium is an important source of revenue, while cocaine traffickers in Colombia are diversifying into heroin from locally grown opium poppies. (Before 1991, Colombia had never grown opium.) Marijuana is essentially a weed grown in every temperate region of the world, including many parts of the United States.

Drug crops are the mainstay of many poor countries, where farmers have few comparable alternatives. In Bolivia, for example, where the per capita gross national product (GNP) is $770 a year, an acre of coca yields about $475 annually, compared with $35–$250 for crops such as bananas and grapefruit—if there are buyers. In Kyrgyzstan, per capita GNP was only $610 in 1994, but a pound of opium brings $400 in local markets or can be bartered for canned goods, cooking oil, and other commodities.

The real but brief success of U.S. efforts to reduce Turkish and Mexican drug production in the 1970s has not been matched. Despite continuing U.S. pressure, source-country governments have been unable or unwilling to undertake sustained drug-eradication campaigns. The reductions in cultivation that do occur are symbolic, since the eradicated crops tend to be more than offset by new plantings. For example, from 1987 to 1993, the Bolivian government devoted $48 million in U.S. aid to pay farmers to eradicate 26,000 hectares of coca. During the same period, Bolivian farmers planted more than 35,000 new hectares of coca. Some observers have concluded that U.S. eradication efforts in Bolivia are little more than a coca support program at U.S. taxpayers' expense.

The only successful example of a large-scale reduction in illicit drug cultivation in recent years occurred in Thailand, where rapid economic growth has produced opportunities more lucrative than opium farming. After decades of supplying the world heroin market, Thailand now imports opium from neighboring Burma to support its own addicts. However, some Thais continue to play a significant role in international drug trafficking and money laundering.

The United States consumes a relatively small portion of worldwide drug production. In 1993, Americans used eight metric tons of heroin, less than 4 per cent of worldwide production, according to the DEA. The U.S. cocaine market absorbs less than one-third of total global production. Domestic marijuana consumption accounts for 817 tons per year: As much as half of that total is grown illegally in the United States.

The great bulk of foreign drug production is consumed in countries other than the United States—often in the regions where the drug crops are grown. Burma, Laos, and Thailand, for example, have almost 500,000 opium and heroin addicts, while India, Iran, and Pakistan account for several million more. According to the World Health Organization, drug abuse is regarded as an emerging "public health and social problem" in Central and East European countries. Cocaine supply appears to be on the rise; heroin addiction is also either increasing or maintaining high levels throughout Europe. In recent years, the abuse of coca paste (known as *basuco*) and cocaine has become a major problem in the South American producer and transit countries. Even if the U.S. demand for drugs declined precipitously, foreign drug suppliers have ready markets in every region of the world and would not stop production.

America's annual drug demand can be supplied from a relatively small growing area and transported in a few airplanes. The illegal drugs Americans consume are grown worldwide and can be cultivated on very little acreage. A poppy field roughly the area of northwest Washington, D.C.—25 square miles—can supply the American heroin market for a year. The annual demand for cocaine can be met from coca fields less than one-quarter the size of Rhode Island, or about 300 square miles.

Effectively reducing the flow of drugs into the United States is exceedingly difficult not only because America's borders are long and porous, but because relatively small amounts of heroin and cocaine are involved. Three DC-3A or five Cessna Caravan turboprop planes could carry the nation's annual heroin supply, while three Boeing 747 cargo planes or 12 trailer trucks could transport the necessary cocaine.

The price structure of the drug market severely limits the potential impact of interdiction and source-country programs. By far, the largest drug-trade profits are made at the level of street sales, not in foreign poppy or coca fields or on the high seas. The total cost of cultivating, refining, and smuggling cocaine to the United States accounts for less than 12 per cent of retail prices here. RAND estimates that the total cost of growing and importing heroin accounts for an even smaller fraction of the retail price. Even if the United States were able to seize half the cocaine coming from South America—or eradicate half the coca crop—the price of cocaine in U.S. cities would increase by less than 5 per cent. Thus, massive interdiction and drug-eradication efforts are far less effective in making drugs more expensive than is enforcement directed at U.S. street markets. Police patrols aimed at increasing the "hassle" factor that drug dealers and drug buyers face exert a much greater impact in discouraging domestic drug abuse and drug crime. These patrols also help deter street violence related to drug dealing.

CONCENTRATE ON DOMESTIC DEMAND

After a century of criticizing other countries for being the source of America's drug problem, it is time to recognize that any lasting solutions lie here at home. In the continuing debate over the supply-side drug strategy, we should remember that the steepest declines in drug use occurred during a period when drug availability was rapidly increasing. In 1982, the National Household Survey showed that 23.3 million Americans used illicit drugs. By 1991, when drug prices hit record lows, only 12.5 million people reported illicit drug use. This dramatic decline reflected public awareness that drugs were harmful as well as growing social disapproval of drug use. Following the death of sports star Len Bias from a cocaine overdose in 1986, cocaine use declined by half, particularly among better-educated Americans inclined to respond to health information.

Unfortunately, these downward trends have now reversed. Marijuana use among eighth graders has doubled since 1992, and illicit drug use among high school seniors is climbing for the first time in a decade. Recent surveys reveal that a majority of both teenagers and adults view drugs as less harmful than they did four years ago. This shift in public attitudes presages further increases in drug problems, particularly among young people for whom the 1980s are ancient history.

Moreover, the drugs of choice in the recent upsurge are primarily domestic, not foreign. Teenagers are using marijuana, LSD, and amphetamines—all of which are produced illegally within the United States. Younger children are turning to common household substances, such as glue, solvents, and aerosols, that are virtually impossible to control. In 1995, one in five eighth graders reported using these inhalants, which produce instant highs and can be lethal.

Experience has shown that reducing demand is the key to sustained progress against drug abuse. A 1994 RAND study, *Controlling Cocaine: Supply Versus Demand Programs,* found that treatment is far more effective than either interdiction or source-country programs in reducing cocaine consumption. Specifically, $34 million invested in treatment reduces annual cocaine use by the same amount as $366 million invested in interdiction or $783 million in source-country programs.

Most Americans do not realize that treatment works—not always, and often not the first time, but eventually. National studies that have followed tens of thousands of addicts through different kinds of programs report that one of the most important factors is the length of time in treatment. One-third of those who stay in treatment longer than three months are drug-free a year after leaving treatment. The success rate jumps to two-thirds when treatment lasts a year or longer. And some programs that provide intensive, highly structured therapy report even better results.

Yet since the early 1980s, treatment has been a low priority nationwide as drug interdiction and enforcement have dominated state and federal spending. In 1995, treatment represented only one-fifth of the more than $13 billion federal drug budget compared with one-quarter 10 years earlier, well before the cocaine epidemic created millions of new addicts. About 40 per cent of the nation's drug addicts cannot get treatment due to inadequate funding for treatment facilities.

Education is the key to protecting our children from drugs, no matter where the offending substances are produced. In the past decade, prevention programs have been developed that significantly reduce new drug use among teenagers. These programs, built on social-learning theory, teach children how to recognize pressures that influence them to smoke, drink, and use drugs and how to resist these pressures through role-playing in the classroom. The impact of these programs is much greater when prevention includes families, media, and the community in a comprehensive effort to discourage drug use. Nonetheless, Congress cut funding for in-school drug education by reducing the Safe and Drug Free Schools Program budget for 1996 from $441 million to $200 million—less than one-sixth the total federal budget for interdiction.

TOWARD A NEW DRUG POLICY

Since America's international drug strategy has not reduced drug problems in this country, should the United States support *any* international efforts to control the illicit drug trade? Yes, to the extent that global cooperation can be effective against the multinational drug networks that undermine the stability of political and financial institutions throughout the world. For example, countries formerly controlled by the Soviet Union in Central Asia and Eastern Europe, as well as Russia itself, are being weakened by the activities of transnational criminal drug syndicates. Many burgeoning entrepreneurs in the newly independent republics have learned that hard drugs are a ready substitute for hard currency in international markets. Opium production in Tajikistan, Turkmenistan, and Uzbekistan has doubled since 1990. Law enforcement in the former Soviet Union is now sporadic at best and is already riven by rampant corruption. In many areas, drug traffickers operate unchallenged.

In this hemisphere, the power of the drug traffickers directly threatens two important democracies, Colombia and Mexico. Although the arrests of the Cali drug lords in August 1995 were an important victory for the Colombian government in its bloody war against the cocaine cartels, Colombia continues to be the world's primary cocaine producer. Evidence that President Ernesto Samper Pizano and some of his Cabinet ministers may have taken cartel money has severely strained Colombia's relations with the United States. Continuing allegations of corruption raise doubts about the government's viability.

The "Colombianization" of Mexico, where drug traffickers penetrated the highest levels of the former Salinas administration and may be involved in high-level assassinations, directly threatens U.S. economic and political interests. Recent revelations that Raul Salinas de Gortari banked at least $84 million in drug money in Switzerland while his brother was president have rocked public confidence in the political system that has governed Mexico for more than 60 years. Although the current president, Ernesto Zedillo, has pledged to clean up drug corruption, he may not have sufficient power to do so. Shortly after Zedillo's most recent pledge, in November 1995, a jet owned by the Cali cartel, loaded with cocaine, landed in Baja California. Witnesses report that the plane was unloaded by uniformed Mexican federal police, who subsequently attempted to conceal the fuselage. The cocaine, estimated to be worth $100 million, has "disappeared."

The failure of American efforts to curtail the flow of drugs into the United States should not cause us to abandon the effort at a time when drug traffic is growing rapidly. The passage of the North American Free Trade Agreement (NAFTA) raised concerns among many in this country that Mexican traffickers would now be able to operate unchecked across the border. Outspoken NAFTA opponents, such as California Democratic senator Dianne Feinstein, have threatened to overturn the treaty largely because of these concerns. Although border controls have very little practical impact on drug availability in America, tough inspections send an important political message that the United States will not tolerate traffickers. The U.S. decision in December 1995 to delay NAFTA's unrestricted-trucking provisions reflects the administration's concern about negative public reaction to removing existing restraints—however weak—on cross-border traffic.

The globalization of national economies broadens the reach of the traffickers, who conduct annual business estimated to be valued at $180 to $300 billion worldwide. In this rapidly evolving scenario, the United States has much to share with other countries in the areas of narcotics intelligence, law enforcement, judicial reform, education, and treatment. For example, DEA intelligence was critically important in facilitating the Colombian government's arrests of the Cali cartel leaders. The FBI, the DEA, and other U.S. enforcement agencies are currently training their Russian counterparts in crime-control techniques, including the surveillance of drug networks.

In addition, the United States can take a leading role in improving international efforts to undermine the money-laundering activities that safeguard the profits of drug traffickers. More than 100 governments have ratified the 1988 United Nations Convention

Against Illicit Traffic in Narcotic Drugs and Psychotropic Substances, a worldwide framework for attacking money laundering and bank secrecy. But a dozen governments representing major financial centers have yet to ratify the convention, and enforcement by participating governments remains inconsistent. While some progress has been made in opening up traditional safe havens for drug money—such as Switzerland and the Bahamas—money laundering is increasing in the rapidly growing East Asian and Pacific financial centers. In his October 1995 speech at the United Nations's 50th anniversary, President Clinton highlighted the need for greater international cooperation against money laundering, threatening economic sanctions against countries that refuse to adopt antilaundering measures.

The computer-aided expansion of world trade and financial services complicates monitoring and enforcement for even the most capable governments. Indeed, according to the State Department, "U.S. financial systems continue to be exploited, at levels probably not approached by any other country." Major banks and investment firms in the United States have been implicated in money laundering, and, in June 1995, three former Justice Department officials were indicted for obstructing justice and assisting the Cali cartel in laundering its prof-its. By pursuing such major corruption cases, the United States can set an example for other countries beset by high-level involvement in drug trafficking. Still, the $375 million combined budget of the U.S. Organized Crime Drug Enforcement Task Forces—an interagency program that investigates and prosecutes high-level drug traffickers—remains less than one-fourth the level of federal spending on interdiction and international supply-control programs.

International narcotics control, if no longer subject to the elusive counts of drugs eradicated or seized, can serve America's larger interests in strengthening democratic institutions and freeing countries from the grip of criminal organizations. The arrests of the Cali cartel may not have made an appreciable difference in cocaine's availability in the United States, but they are an encouraging indication of that government's determination to fight the drug traffickers. Still, it is important to remember that lasting answers to America's drug problem lie here at home, not abroad. Providing drug-prevention programs for every school child will curb domestic drug abuse more than trying to reduce overseas drug crops. In the final analysis, offering treatment to the nation's addicts will do more to reduce drug consumption than additional drug seizures at the source of production, on the high seas, or at the border.

POSTSCRIPT

Should the United States Put More Emphasis on Stopping the Importation of Drugs?

The drug trade spawns violence; people die from using drugs or by dealing with people in the drug trade; families are ruined by the effects of drugs on family members; prisons are filled with tens of thousands of people who were and probably still are involved with illegal drugs; and drugs can devastate aspirations and careers. The adverse consequences of drugs can be seen everywhere in society. How should the government determine the best course of action to follow in remedying the negative effects of drugs?

Two paths that are traditionally followed involve reducing either the supply or the demand for drugs. Four major agencies involved in the fight against drugs in the United States—the Drug Enforcement Administration (DEA), the Federal Bureau of Investigation (FBI), the U.S. Customs Service, and the U.S. Coast Guard—have seized thousands of pounds of marijuana, cocaine, and heroin during the past few years. Drug interdiction appears to be reducing the availability of drugs. But what effect does drug availability have on use?

Annual surveys of 8th-, 10th-, and 12th-grade students indicate that availability is not a major factor in drug use. Throughout the 1980s drug use declined dramatically even though marijuana and cocaine could be obtained easily. According to the surveys, the perceived harm of these drugs, not their availability, is what affects students' drug use. As individuals' perceptions of drugs as harmful increase, usage decreases; as perceptions of harm decrease, usage increases.

Efforts to prevent drug use may prove fruitless if people have a natural desire to alter their consciousness. In his 1989 book *Intoxication: Life in the Pursuit of Artificial Paradise* (E. P. Dutton), Ronald Siegel contends that the urge to alter consciousness is as universal as the craving for food and sex.

Articles that examine international efforts to deal with the issue of drugs include "A Global Empirical Review of Drug Crop Eradication and the United Nations' Crop Substitution and Alternative Development Strategies," by Graham Farrell, *Journal of Drug Issues* (vol. 2, 1998); "Global Reach: The Threat of International Drug Trafficking," by Rensselaer Lee, *Current History* (May 1995); and "Passing Grades: Branding Nations Won't Resolve the U.S. Drug Problem," by Mathea Falco, *Foreign Affairs* (September/October 1995). Christina Jacqueline Johns's book *Power, Ideology, and the War on Drugs: Nothing Succeeds Like Failure* (Praeger, 1992) describes the pitfalls of an international approach to addressing drug-related problems.

ISSUE 3

Should Congress Impose a Lower Blood Alcohol Concentration Limit for Drunk Driving?

YES: Paul D. Wellstone et al., from "Should Congress Pass a .08 Blood-Alcohol Concentration (BAC) Drunk Driving Standard? Pro," *Congressional Digest* (June–July 1998)

NO: Trent Lott et al., from "Should Congress Pass a .08 Blood-Alcohol Concentration (BAC) Drunk Driving Standard? Con," *Congressional Digest* (June–July 1998)

ISSUE SUMMARY

YES: U.S. senator Paul D. Wellstone and his colleagues argue that the federal government should support a law establishing .08 as the national blood alcohol concentration (BAC) level for drunk driving. Prompted by the thousands of deaths caused annually by people driving under alcohol's influence, they contend that there are fewer fatal automobile crashes in states with a .08 BAC standard.

NO: U.S. senator Trent Lott and his colleagues maintain that establishing BAC standards should be left to individual states, not to the federal government. They argue that their opponents' desire to mandate a national standard for BAC is another example of the federal government overstepping its boundaries.

When discussions of drinking and driving arise, many people justifiably express concern. Too many people die needlessly because of others' poor judgment regarding whether or not they can safely operate a motor vehicle after drinking. However, the news is not all bad. In the last 20 years, the number of alcohol-related driving fatalities in the United States has decreased significantly. In the early 1980s about 26,000 people died each year because of drivers under the influence of alcohol. In 1998 the number of people killed in automobile accidents on American highways because of drunk drivers was around 17,000. This represents a 30 percent decline. Despite this significant reduction, few would argue against further improvement.

The figure of 17,000 alcohol-related automobile fatalities represents the number of people who were killed by a driver who was legally intoxicated at the time of the accident. Missing from this figure is the number of people who were killed by drivers who may have been drinking but who were not legally drunk. However, one does not need to be drunk to be impaired. A number of studies have demonstrated that driving ability is impaired with a blood alcohol concentration (BAC) level as low as .04.

The BAC is the amount of alcohol that is in a person's body as measured by the weight of the alcohol in a certain volume of blood. A person's BAC can be measured by testing the blood, breath, urine, or saliva. In most of the United States, a BAC of .10 is considered legally intoxicated, although, as this debate indicates, many people do not consider that level low enough.

The U.S. senators representing the two sides of this issue are debating whether or not the federal government should impose a national blood alcohol concentration standard of .08 for drunk driving. Preliminary research indicates that lowering the BAC limit from .10 or higher to .08 reduces the number of people who get behind the wheel of a car after drinking. However, the senators are not debating whether a lower standard like .08 is desirable but what the role of the federal government should be in this matter. As of 1998, 15 states have implemented a BAC standard of .08, and 5 more are considering adopting a similar standard.

The current proposal before Congress would require states to adopt a .08 BAC limit or risk losing a percentage of the highway funds allotted by the federal government. The precedent for this type of action was set in the early 1980s when President Ronald Reagan threatened to withdraw highway funds from states that did not raise the drinking age to 21. That situation, like the current issue, raises a fundamental question: Should the federal government have the right to dictate to individual states what is an acceptable BAC standard? Is the role of government to conduct research in order to allow states to make informed decisions? If, as Senator Jack Reed (D-Rhode Island) has indicated, a .08 BAC saves between 500 and 600 lives a year, shouldn't the federal government take a more strident stand?

In the following selections, Senators Paul D. Wellstone et al. argue that Congress should enact a national blood alcohol concentration standard of .08 for driving while intoxicated to save lives and to prevent serious injuries. They support withholding highway funds from states that do not comply with this standard. Senators Trent Lott et al. also want to reduce alcohol-related driving offenses, but they feel that Congress would be overstepping its boundaries by enacting this law. They favor allowing individual states the autonomy to make their own decisions.

YES

Paul D. Wellstone et al.

SHOULD CONGRESS PASS A .08 BLOOD-ALCOHOL CONCENTRATION (BAC) DRUNK DRIVING STANDARD?

PAUL D. WELLSTONE, UNITED STATES SENATOR, MINNESOTA, DEMOCRAT

I am pleased to add my voice to those of my colleagues in support of this amendment to require States to pass .08 blood-alcohol content (BAC) laws.

People who drive while they are impaired are placing all of us in harm's way. The real issue is whether or not a person should be driving after consuming alcohol. There is no good reason that this should be accepted as a standard practice in our society.

Opponents of this amendment will argue such things as, "this means that a 120-pound woman could not drive after drinking two glasses of wine." I believe they are missing the point. The point is that if a person is impaired by alcohol, he or she should not be driving—period. The point is that someone's BAC might reach .08 after consumption of a certain amount of alcohol, and that BAC level might just be indicative of physical impairment that would affect driving ability. We are not talking about someone being fallen-down drunk, but perhaps a young woman whose reaction time might be slowed, so that as a young child darts out into the street in front of her car, she is unable to react quickly enough to hit the brakes in time to stop the car from hitting the child. Was this woman "drunk"? No. But the alcohol in her body slowed her reaction time.

Here are some facts from the National Institute on Alcohol and Alcohol Abuse at NIH [National Institutes of Health] that help to explain the issue:

The brain's control of eye movements is highly vulnerable to alcohol. In driving, the eye must focus briefly on timing. The eye must focus briefly on important objects and track them as they and the vehicle being driven move. BACs of .03 to .05 can interfere with these eye movements.

Steering is a complex task in which the effects of alcohol on eye-to-hand reaction time are superimposed upon the effects on vision. Studies have shown that significant impairment in steering ability may begin at a BAC as low as .04.

Alcohol impairs nearly every aspect of information processing by the brain. Alcohol-impaired drivers require more time to read a street sign or to respond to a traffic signal than unimpaired drivers.

Research on the effects of alcohol on performance by both automobile and aircraft operators shows a narrowing of the attention field, starting at a BAC of approximately .04. The National Public Services Research Institute reports the following:

Approximately 10 percent of miles driven at BACs of .08 and above are at BACs between .08 and .10. Every year, crashes that involve drivers at BACs of .08 to .99 kill 660 people and injure 28,000.

Driving with a BAC of .08 is very risky. They estimate that crash costs average $5.80 per mile driven with a BAC of .10 or higher, $2.50 a mile for a BAC between .08 and .99, and only 11 cents a mile for each mile driven while sober.

The preliminary evaluation of the .08 legislation by the National Highway Traffic Safety Administration indicates that this law will reduce alcohol-related fatalities by 5 to 8 percent. This is at least comparable to the impact of other laws, such as zero-tolerance for youth, administrative license revocation, or graduated licensing.

The evidence is clear. There is no good argument against the .08 legislation. In fact, responsible alcohol distributors and manufacturers should favor it.

There is no excuse not to implement a law that could decrease traffic fatalities by 600 each year and decrease traffic-related injuries by many thousands. We need to be responsible and encourage the implementation of .08 legislation in

all States, and to provide incentives for doing so.

People who drive while they are impaired are placing all of us in harm's way. That is really the issue.

JACK REED, UNITED STATES SENATOR, RHODE ISLAND, DEMOCRAT

I rise today in support of the Lautenberg-DeWine amendment. It would establish a .08 blood-alcohol concentration level, or BAC level, as a threshold for driving under the influence throughout the United States.

As we all know, drunk driving is a scourge on the highways of the United States of America. It is something that we are all against. This legislation would take a very positive step to ensure that all States provide for a very rigorous .08 blood-alcohol content standard as their measure of driving under the influence of alcohol.

This law builds on previous success. Since 1986, alcohol-related fatalities on our roads have decreased by 28 percent. That is a result of the efforts of many, many people. It is the result of tougher laws, increased enforcement, public education, and particularly the work of Mothers Against Drunk Driving, who have done so much to illustrate this problem and reach policymakers throughout the United States. Although we are proud of this success, we can and must do more.

In 1996, more than 17,000 people were killed because of drunk driving. These deaths are not accidents, because these are tragedies that could have been avoided—many of them—if we had tougher laws and better enforcement.

That is what we are about today. We are trying to declare throughout this country that we have a tough standard for those who would drink and drive, a standard that would save lives throughout this country in every community.

I don't think any of my colleagues would like to say to a family who lost a loved one, "Well, the standard of .10 was okay," because in that situation it is not okay. We can do better. We know these laws work, and we want to make them work much better.

In essence, the .08 blood-alcohol concentration standard means fewer deaths on the roads of America, fewer driving fatalities, fewer young people cut down in the prime of their lives. And it means a safer America. That is what we should stand for today.

Currently, 15 States already have adopted a .08 blood-alcohol concentration standard. A recent study by Boston University showed that these States experienced a 16 percent decline in fatal driver crashes where the driver's BAC was .08 or greater. Already these States have shown that this standard saves lives. And we can do better.

It is estimated that, nationally, if we adopt the .08 standard, we can save between 500 and 600 lives a year. Those are impressive statistics. But lives alone are not at stake. Each year, drunk driving accidents cost this country $45 billion. That is six times more than we spend on Pell [higher education] grants. We can do better. We can save lives. We can save resources. We can make our world much, much safer.

There are those who argue that this would put a huge constraint on law-abiding Americans who occasionally will have a drink and then drive. That is something I don't think is true at all, because under this standard, a 170-pound man must consume more than four drinks in an hour on an empty stomach to reach this BAC. A woman of 135 pounds would have to consume three drinks. That is not social drinking. That is drinking irresponsibly and then getting into an automobile.

This law will not affect the reasonable, rational, careful, deliberate person who may have one social drink or two and then drive. In fact, the American Medical Association said that really the beginning of impairment is not .08, it is .05 blood-alcohol content. So this standard is far from what medical experts would argue is the beginning of deterioration of motor skills when one drives an automobile. We have to recognize today that we can do better.

There are those of my colleagues who have suggested that this proposal is an improper infringement on the prerogatives of the States. First of all, we have taken positive steps before in this land. For example, just a few years ago, we adopted, through congressional action, a zero-tolerance policy that would say for young people driving that the blood-alcohol content was basically zero, that they should have no drinks if they are driving an automobile, and we have seen success already.

We have already seen the success of our zero-tolerance policy throughout the United States, a policy that was promulgated through Congress and adopted by many States, where fatalities at night by younger drivers have dropped to 16 percent in States that are following the zero-tolerance policy.

So this law and this approach is not an impermissible imposition on the States. It is a rational, reasonable way to encourage what is the right thing to do. It is small comfort that if one State, such as my State of Rhode Island, adopts this standard but it is not adopted next door in Massachusetts or Connecticut, and someone in Massachusetts comes speeding into my State. That is not a States' rights issue. That is an issue of interstate commerce, of national economy, of national highways that reach every corner of this country regardless of State lines. We don't stop the national highways at the State lines. We shouldn't stop good, sensible bills that will control drunk driving in this country at the State lines.

I urge passage of this legislation.

MIKE DEWINE, UNITED STATES SENATOR, OHIO, REPUBLICAN

I appreciate some of the very eloquent comments that have been made this morning on the Senate floor. I appreciate the comments about States' rights. Let me say, though, that there are very few times when we, as Members of the Senate, can come to the floor and cast our votes when we know that the vote we cast will save lives. That is true in this case. There is absolutely no doubt about it. Lives will be saved and families will be spared the heartache of losing child or mother or father.

There are other things I think we clearly know and that are not in dispute. That is one. The second is that no one has come to the floor suggesting that a person who tests .08 has any business being behind the wheel of a car. That is not really in dispute at all. No doctor who has looked at this, no emergency room doctor who has looked at it, no police officer who is involved in testing people, pulling them over, and seeing what they test and looking at their reflexes, looking at how they act—everyone who has had that experience agrees—at .08, no one should be behind the wheel.

If anyone has a doubt about it, think of it this way: If you were at a party and someone had four beers in an hour and you watched him drink those four beers in an hour, and you observed he didn't have anything to eat, and he looked over after that time and said, "Let me take your little five-year-old daughter to the Tastee-Freeze and buy her an ice cream cone," how many of us would put her in that car? We would not do that. There is no doubt about it. So it is absolutely a reasonable standard.

Does it include social drinkers? We are not talking about one or two beers and a pizza. We are talking about people who have absolutely no business being behind the wheel of a car.

I think Ronald Reagan did say it best. I think he had it right in 1984. He supported a similar type concept, and that concept was that there should be a minimum standard across the country for the drinking age, and it should be 21, no matter where you were in the country. He supported that. The great champion of States' rights said, in this case, a national uniform standard will save lives and makes common sense. This is what Ronald Reagan said in 1984 when he signed the bill:

> This problem is much more than just a State problem. It's a national tragedy. There are some special cases in which the overwhelming need can be dealt with by prudent and limited Federal influence. In a case like this I have no misgivings about a judicious use of Federal inducements to save precious lives.

It is a minimum standard. It is a rational standard. Doesn't it make sense that when you get in your car and put your family in the car and go on a trip—many of us cross two or three State lines every week, every day, some of us—doesn't it make sense there should be some assurance that there is a minimum standard that exists, no matter where you drive your car in this country? I think it does.

It is a question of rights. The rights of families, the right to live, the right to have a fair chance on the highway not to have someone come at you who has been drinking and driving. That is what this is all about.

So I urge my colleagues to vote "yes" on this amendment. It is a rare opportunity, among all the things we debate, all the rhetoric, to save lives. I urge my colleagues to take this rare opportunity and spare a family, spare hundreds of families, life's greatest tragedy, the loss of a loved one.

FRANK R. LAUTENBERG, UNITED STATES SENATOR, NEW JERSEY, DEMOCRAT

I remind our colleagues, as I listen to the debate, about the issues being discussed. Frankly, it bewilders me, because I stand next to the picture of a child who was nine when a drunk driver took her life. I hear discussions of process, that the process is the issue. The process is not the issue. The issue is whether or not we want to say to every American parent: "We have done something more to save, perhaps, your child or your grandchild or your sister or your brother." That is the issue, and I hope the American people are going to say when they look at the vote count, "My senator stood up for life."

"My senator," on the other hand, they can brag, "proudly stood up for process."

Can you imagine in the homes across America, all the people who are going to be applauding because someone stood

up for process? It is outrageous. It cannot be that way.

In the balcony sit people I have come to know very well: Brenda, Randy, and Stephanie Frazier—mother, father, and sister of Ashley.

I wish I could ask them to speak about their view of process, whether or not they think that process is the thing that we ought to be talking about. Or should we be talking about the loss that they had, that they do not want anyone else to experience.

Before senators vote on this amendment, I ask them to think about their children and the pain that could come from the loss of a child they know and love. Today we can spare parents across this country, in all 50 States, the grief experienced by the Frazier family.

I hope that the happy hour is over for drunk drivers. Every year in this country, more people are killed in alcohol-related crashes than were killed in our worst year of fighting in Vietnam. And the country stood in national mourning at that time. By lowering to .08 the blood-alcohol level at which a person is considered legally drunk, we can save more than 500 lives each year.

Drunk driving is a crime, like assault, like shooting at someone, like murder; and it should be treated with the same severity as other crimes that bring harm or death to another person. We can prevent many injuries and deaths that result from drunk driving by making .08 the national alcohol limit, just like 21 is the drinking age limit across the country. And if we do that, we could save lots of lives, like other westernized countries —like Canada, Ireland, Great Britain,

Germany, and Switzerland. Poland has a .03 BAC, and Sweden .02.

We can make .08 work in America if we pass this amendment and declare our opposition to violence on our highways, because it is at .08 that a person's capacity to function is impaired. Their vision, balance, reaction time, judgment, self-control—this is the level at which they are medically drunk. And if they are medically drunk, we ought to deem them legally drunk, in every State, no matter where they live.

The alcohol lobby is trying to bottle up this bill. We are not targeting social drinkers. We are targeting drunk drivers. When you get drunk, it is your business. But when you get drunk and drive, it is our business. We are not asking people to stop drinking. We are not running a temperance society here. We are asking them not to drive if they are drunk.

NO

Trent Lott et al.

SHOULD CONGRESS PASS A .08 BLOOD-ALCOHOL CONCENTRATION (BAC) DRUNK DRIVING STANDARD?

TRENT LOTT, UNITED STATES SENATOR, MISSISSIPPI, REPUBLICAN

The [Lautenberg-DeWine] amendment would require States to enact the .08 alcohol content legislation instead of the present .10 level of alcohol. That has to be done by September 30, 2000. Noncompliant States would lose 5 percent of highway funding on October 1, 2000, and then 10 percent thereafter.

Currently, 15 States already have the .08 level of alcohol content to be considered drunk in drunk driving cases.

I think we should encourage people not to drink. We should encourage all people not to drink excessively. We should do all that we can to get the States to pass the lower level of .08. I support that. We need to combat the problem of drunken driving.

I understand the tragedy and the ravages of people that drink and drive. My father was killed in just such an accident. So this is not an issue that I take lightly. But I will oppose this amendment. This is a typical Federal Government attitude—not to encourage you to do right, not to say if you do the right thing there will be incentives in it for you.

No, you do it our way, or we will punish you. You will lose funds if you don't do it the way we say.

I am very much opposed to alcoholism and drinking and driving. But for us to stand here and pontificate about how you must do it our way, that this is the solution, or we are going to take your funds away. What about poor States like mine, where people are killed every week because of bad roads, potholes in the roads, dangerous bridges? What about safety?

If a State, for whatever reason, by mistake or obviously for the wrong reasons, doesn't do it, we take a big chunk of money away from them. Is that going to save lives? No. As a matter of fact, it may lead to more lives being lost.

So while I know this is well-intentioned, and while I support the intent of the goals of this legislation, the idea that we are going to punish States because you don't do it our way I think is the wrong thing to be doing.

I hope my colleagues will think about this very, very seriously before they cast a vote in favor of this amendment.

DON NICKLES, UNITED STATES SENATOR, OKLAHOMA, REPUBLICAN

Regretfully, I rise in opposition to this amendment. I say regretfully because if I were in the State Senate of Oklahoma, I would vote in favor of this amendment. Presently, there is no Federal standard or Federal law for blood-alcohol level —none. So we have an effort now to federalize a national problem. I don't think we should do that.

I led the effort years ago that would allow the States to set speed limits. I thought the States should set the speed limits, not the Federal Government. I didn't say that I thought every State should increase their speed limits. I thought States should set the speed limit.

What about the alcohol level? Again, if I were a State legislator, I would support the lower level. Fifteen States have this level—.08. Maybe it should be lower. Let the States make that decision. I hate to federalize problems, and I hate to tell the States that if they don't do such and such we are going to withhold 5 percent of their money in the first few years and 10 percent thereafter.

Whose money is it? Is that Federal money? No. That money is paid for by our constituents, by our consumers, and by people who are on the road. They pay that money. It comes to Washington, D.C.,

and now we start putting strings on it. We basically tell the States, if you do not pass a law that we have determined is best— and I don't know anything about blood-alcohol limits. I have heard three beers, I have heard four beers. I don't know. I have not done the homework. I will take their word for it. But really, should we be dictating or mandating that on the States? I don't think so.

We are talking about hundreds of millions of dollars. In a few years, it will be 10 percent. So it is a heavy penalty if they don't subscribe to our Federal dictate. I just disagree with that. That money came from the States. It came from individuals. This is not Federal money. For us to put on these strings I think is a mistake.

I am very sympathetic to the goal of the authors of the amendment, and I want to compliment them for trying to say we want to reduce drunken drivers on the streets. I want to do the same thing. I just do not agree with their tactics.

The Commerce Committee amendment has some incentives to encourage States to lower levels, and if the States lower those levels, they can get more money. In other words, a little bit of carrot. This is a heavy stick. As a matter of fact, this is more than a heavy stick. This is a dagger. This says you have to do it. I think we should encourage it.

Again, I go back to the Constitution. Sometimes we ignore the Constitution. But the Tenth Amendment to the Constitution says: "The powers not delegated to the United States by the Constitution, not prohibited by it to the States, are reserved to the States respectively, or to the people."

Time and time again, we come to this body and we find a problem. And drunk driving is a real serious problem. But we want to have a Federal solution. The Federal Government knows best. I think the framers of the Constitution were right when they said we should reserve those powers to the States and to the people, and encourage the States —maybe even give them a little bonus— if they make some moves that we think would positive. But to federalize it and now, for the first time in history, have a blood-alcohol content which has always been the prerogative of the States, in my opinion, is wrong.

I think we are trampling on States' rights. We are also encouraging this idea that if there is a problem, we need a Federal solution, and we will not give back your money.

I resented the fact that when we sent our highway moneys to Washington, D.C., from our State, we only got about 80 cents back. We would only get about 80 cents on the dollar back.

Then, not only that, when we got the 80 cents back, we got all the strings attached: You have to have the Federal highway speed limit; you have to have all of these other Federal requirements; you have to have the Davis-Bacon [an act that affects the construction industry] standard. You have to pass all of these rules. By the time we complied with those rules, that dollar would only buy about 60 some cents' worth of road. It wasn't a very good deal for our State.

So I would like to not put more punitive actions on the States if they don't comply with what we think— Government knows best.

One of the reasons I rise in opposition to the amendment is the penalty is too hard. I care just as much about wanting to eliminate drunk driving as anybody in this chamber. The penalty under this bill is too harsh. And 10 percent of the

highway funds is—looking at any State —the State of Texas is $1 billion over six years. That is a pretty big penalty. The penalty in my State of Oklahoma is $200 million. That is a pretty big penalty.

The reason why I was asking or inquiring is it amenable is that maybe we should change the penalty from 5 percent and 10 percent to half of a percent and 1 percent. You are still talking about real money that would be a real incentive, but 10 percent is too high. In other words, we want to encourage States.

The Commerce Committee amendment has an incentive program. It is not a lot. I think $25 million. Not much of a carrot. So we encourage States to do it. Maybe that should be enhanced a little bit.

But I look at the draconian penalties in this thing. This is really a dagger at the highway program to take 10 percent of the funds. In Michigan, you are talking about $477 million. That is a lot of money. It is too much of a gun at the head of the States, saying, "You have to do this or you're going to lose hundreds of millions of dollars."

For the State of California, it would be $1.3 billion over a six-year period of time.

So I understand the desire that some people want to federalize alcohol-content crimes. That, I believe, should be left in the States' jurisdiction. I kind of wonder, if you have States that are not complying —maybe the States are going to change their law, but do not really enforce it. Are we going to have the Federal Government come in and say, "Wait a minute. Now you're going to have to monitor the amount of enforcement?"

We cannot have the State of Rhode Island say they are going to change the law but not really enforce it until you get over the .10. I do not know that would happen, but I question the wisdom of federalizing blood-alcohol content. It has not been a Federal crime. If this provision is going to be in, I think we should reduce the penalties.

It is far too harsh. It is too much of a dictate, too much of a mandate, too much of the Federal Government saying, "Before you get your money back, you must do the following. Before you get your highway money back, we're going to put an additional string on it, an additional penalty, up to 10 percent, which is hundreds of millions of dollars." I think it goes too far.

One other comment. My colleagues alluded to the fact that in 1984 we did something comparable, and we had a national drinking age of 21. Now it might surprise some of my colleagues on the other side. I supported that. And the reason is, I live very close to the border in Oklahoma. And Oklahoma had a 21; Kansas had an 18. And we had people running back and forth across the State line to take advantage of that situation. Not a very safe situation. So I supported it.

I saw some differences in that provision, although the penalty was still very high. It was too high then, in my opinion. This, I think, is a little bit different. Now we are federalizing blood-alcohol content, and I seriously doubt the wisdom of doing that.

Again, for those of us that read the Constitution and say all of the rights and powers are reserved to States and the people, I think some of our colleagues and proponents, who have very good intentions, are saying there is a problem and, therefore, we have to have a Federal solution. We are going to use the heavy hand of the Federal Government and withhold funds that come from the States, from the people, and say, you cannot have that money back unless you do as we determine. I think that is a mistake.

CRAIG THOMAS, UNITED STATES SENATOR, WYOMING, REPUBLICAN

We are here again talking about an issue that seems to come up every time there are highway bills and highway funds to be distributed. We always come up with this question of process, of who has the responsibility to make the kinds of laws that would be there.

I am disappointed that some of the speakers have indicated they don't think the States have the ability to make the decisions, that they don't think the State legislatures feel as passionately about drunk driving as we do. I think they do. I have been there. To say, "Well, this is something the States simply can't do, or aren't capable of doing, or don't care about," is not fair or balanced.

I think we ought to talk about the process here. And the process is, how do we best deal with States as a Federal entity, in this case, with highway funding? This isn't the first kind of mandate that has been applied. Every time this comes up we have mandates, whether it be highways, helmets, speed limits—which, by the way, were put on in a similar kind of process and were changed later because it didn't work very well.

There is no one in this place or no one that I know of in the whole country who doesn't want to do more about preserving safety in driving. There is no one here who cares more about the losses that we have. That is not the issue here. The issue is process, procedure, and what is the proper role in doing it. I think we ought to consider incentives, and we have done that: $25 million on incentives here for the States to do this. But instead we move towards penalties.

We have been through this a number of times, and we are back at it again. I think we ought to give the leadership, and the President wants to give leadership on this issue. Why doesn't he do that as President? We can't do that. If this is the proper level, and I do not disagree with it, I would support it in my State legislature. But the process is what we are talking about. Should this body say to the States, "Look. If you want the money that your people pay into the fund, if you want it back, then you have to do what the Congress prescribes"? It is not as if the money came from somewhere else. This money came from the States.

I do think the system is important. The process is important, and we ought to really consider it over a period of time, as to how much of this sort of thing we do. We do it each time this arises. So I think we ought to put on all the pressure that we can. I think we ought to have all the incentives that are possible to move toward safer driving, to move toward doing something about drunk driving losses. But I think we also ought to ask ourselves about where do we stop in this idea of penalizing the States if they do not properly adhere to what this body proclaims they ought to do.

So I appreciate the opportunity for us to debate this. I am a great supporter of this bill, and I hope we can move forward with it. I hope we can do it without encumbering it with mandates of any kind. I thought we were going to be able to do that this year. The fact is, the committee, I think it is fair to say, probably wasn't in support of doing it and therefore it did not come out of the committee that way. But now, of course, we are continuing to work on it. So I hope we can find additional ways, incentives to move toward .08. I have no objection to that. On the contrary, I support it.

On the other hand, I do think it is necessary for us, over time, to take a strong look at the kinds of processes and procedures that we impose on the States. I am sorry I cannot make as light of States' rights as has been made on the floor this morning, as if it does not pertain. It does, in fact, pertain. And we have different kinds of conditions.

LARRY E. CRAIG, UNITED STATES SENATOR, IDAHO, REPUBLICAN

I share the concern of my colleagues from New Jersey and Ohio [Senators Lautenber and DeWine] and all the cosponsors of this amendment.

I am in complete agreement with the view that there should be a no-tolerance policy for drinking and driving. That kind of irresponsibility is inexcusable. The senseless human tragedy it produces is unpardonable.

Our laws should be severe enough to deter anyone who thinks he or she can abuse alcohol and drive without impairment.

Our law enforcement officials should have the tools they need to locate and stop these accidents waiting to happen.

My State of Idaho adopted a blood-alcohol content standard of .08 percent. They believed this was a reasonable standard, based on sound data, that would help save lives. Other States have come to the same conclusion and made the same choice.

And that brings me to my point.

While I would support a strong resolution from this Senate, denouncing drunk driving or even recommending the adoption of this particular blood-alcohol content standard, I cannot endorse this amendment.

The Federal Government should leave this decision to the States, where it constitutionally belongs in the first place. I am confident, if the facts truly support it, this standard will be adopted voluntarily by every State.

However, I am not willing to say today that this is the one and only way to solve the terrible problem of drunk driving, nor that it is the best way.

We've heard a lot on this floor and from the Administration about how our States are "laboratories of ideas." Instead of burdening them with new Federal mandates, we should be ensuring they have the maximum freedom and flexibility to work out effective solutions for local problems, especially problems of this magnitude.

In short, transportation dollars that are critical to public safety should not be threatened in order to force States into compliance with the "solution of the day," no matter how well intended.

While I strongly agree with the goal of stopping drunk driving in America, I strongly disagree with the path this amendment would take to achieve that goal. For all these reasons, I have no alternative but to vote against this amendment.

POSTSCRIPT

Should Congress Impose a Lower Blood Alcohol Concentration Limit for Drunk Driving?

An important follow-up question to the discussion of whether or not the federal government should withhold highway dollars from states that do not adopt a national BAC standard of .08 for driving while intoxicated is, Is the government unreasonably superseding the rights of state governments? Should individual states have the prerogative to establish their own policies regarding BAC levels for drunk driving? Is the federal government being presumptuous in trying to implement a policy that it feels is best for its citizens, despite the positions of individual states? On the other hand, if it has been shown that a .08 BAC limit lowers the rate of alcohol-related accidents, doesn't the federal government have a moral and ethical obligation to prevent these accidents?

Alcohol abuse is a serious problem. Although restricting a person from drinking and driving may not reduce the incidence of alcohol abuse, it may reduce other problems. Driving a motor vehicle after drinking alcohol is clearly dangerous. Not only are the drinker and the drinker's passengers endangered, but anyone else who may be driving a car in the vicinity of the drunk driver is at risk. Thousands of people, including pedestrians, are killed or maimed each year by drunk drivers. Lowering the BAC limit to .08 may not reduce alcohol abuse, but it may reduce the risks faced by others.

Balancing the rights of individual states to establish their own laws against the need of the federal government to implement a policy that it believes is right is a recurring issue. There is a lack of consistency in the matter of federal and state laws. During the oil crisis of the 1970s, for example, the federal government required states to have speed limits no higher than 55 miles per hour. Yet each state has its own laws regarding the sale of alcohol. Who decides when the position of the federal government takes precedence over the position of state governments?

Several excellent articles and reports examine the issue of drinking and driving. See "Drinking and Driving: Factors Influencing Accident Risk," by the National Institute on Alcohol Abuse and Alcoholism, *Alcohol Alert No. 31* (January 1996); the National Highway Traffic Safety Administration report *Zero-Tolerance Laws to Reduce Alcohol-Impaired Driving by Youth* (January 1998); and *Drunk Driving: Should Each State Be Required to Enact a 0.08 Blood Alcohol Concentration (BAC) Law?* by Paul F. Rothberg (January 12, 1998), published by the Library of Congress's Congressional Research Service.

ISSUE 4

Should Needle Exchange Programs Be Supported?

YES: David Vlahov and Benjamin Junge, from "The Role of Needle Exchange Programs in HIV Prevention," *Public Health Reports* (June 1998)

NO: Office of National Drug Control Policy, from "Needle Exchange Programs: Are They Effective?" *ONDCP Bulletin No. 7* (July 1992)

ISSUE SUMMARY

YES: In their review of various studies, professor of epidemiology and medicine David Vlahov and Benjamin Junge, evaluation director for the Baltimore Needle Exchange Program, found that needle exchange programs successfully reduced the transmission of the virus that causes AIDS. In addition, many people who participated in needle exchange programs reduced their drug use and sought drug abuse treatment.

NO: The Office of National Drug Control Policy, an executive agency that determines policies and objectives for the U.S. drug control program, sees needle exchange programs as an admission of defeat and a retreat from the ongoing battle against drug use, and it argues that compassion and treatment are needed, not needles.

Both selections presented here refer to intravenous drug use as a factor in the escalating incidence of AIDS (acquired immunodeficiency syndrome). One point needs to be clarified: Any type of drug injection, whether it is intravenous (mainlining), intramuscular, or just below the surface of the skin (skin popping), can result in the transmission of AIDS. Technically, what is transmitted is not AIDS but the human immunodeficiency virus (HIV), which ultimately leads to the development of AIDS.

Until a cure for AIDS is found or a vaccine against HIV has proven to be effective, the relationship between AIDS and injecting drugs will remain a cause of great concern. According to the Centers for Disease Control, approximately one-third of AIDS cases in the United States are directly or indirectly associated with drug injection, and half of all new HIV infections occur among users of injected drugs.

No one disagrees that the spread of AIDS is a problem and that the number of people who inject drugs is a problem. The issue that needs to be addressed is, What is the best course of action to take to reduce drug injection and the transmission of AIDS? Is it better to set up more drug treatment facilities, as the Office of National Drug Control Policy (ONDCP) suggests, or to allow people who inject drugs access to clean needles?

One concern of needle exchange opponents is that endorsement of these programs convey the wrong message concerning drug use. Instead of discouraging drug use, they feel that such programs merely teach people how to use drugs or encourage drug use. Needle exchange advocates point to studies showing that these programs have not resulted in an increase of intravenous drug users. Other studies indicate that many drug users involved in needle exchange programs drop out and that drug users who remain in the programs are not as likely to share needles in the first place.

Proponents of needle exchange programs argue that HIV is easily transmitted when needles are shared and that something needs to be done to stem the practice. Opponents argue that whether or not needle exchange programs are available, needles will be shared. Three reasons cited by drug users for sharing needles are (1) they do not have access to clean needles, (2) they do not own their own needles, and (3) they cannot afford to buy needles. If clean needles were readily available, would drug addicts necessarily use them? Some studies show that people who inject drugs are concerned about contracting AIDS and will alter their drug-taking behavior if presented with a viable alternative.

Although needle exchange programs may result in the use of clean needles and encourage people to obtain treatment, they do not get at the root cause of drug addiction. Drug abuse and many of its concomitant problems stem from inadequate or nonexistent employment opportunities, unsafe neighborhoods, underfunded schools, and insufficient health care. Some argue that until these underlying causes of drug abuse are addressed, stopgap measures like needle exchange programs should be implemented. Needle exchange programs, however, may forestall the implementation of other programs that could prove to be more helpful.

Needle exchange programs generate a number of legal and social questions. Since heroin and cocaine are illegal, giving needles to people for the purpose of injecting these drugs contributes to illegal behavior. Should people who are addicted to drugs be seen as criminals or as victims who need compassion? Should drug users, especially drug addicts, be incarcerated or treated? The majority of drug users involved with needle exchange programs are members of minority groups. Could needle exchange programs promote the continuation of drug use and, hence, the enslavement of minorities?

In the following selections, David Vlahov and Benjamin Junge address the benefits of needle exchange programs and respond to criticisms of these programs. The ONDCP points out the inadequacies of previous research regarding needle exchange programs and argues that these programs exacerbate drug abuse problems by facilitating drug use.

YES

David Vlahov and Benjamin Junge

THE ROLE OF NEEDLE EXCHANGE PROGRAMS IN HIV PREVENTION

SYNOPSIS

Injecting drug users (IDUs) are at high risk for infection by human immunodeficiency virus (HIV) and other blood-borne pathogens. In the United States, IDUs account for nearly one-third of the cases of acquired immunodeficiency syndrome (AIDS), either directly or indirectly (heterosexual and perinatal cases of AIDS where the source of infection was an IDU). IDUs also account for a substantial proportion of cases of hepatitis B (HBV) and hepatitis C (HCV) virus infections. The primary mode of transmission for HIV among IDUs is parenteral, through direct needle sharing or multiperson use of syringes. Despite high levels of knowledge about risk, multiperson use of needles and syringes is due primarily to fear of arrest and incarceration for violation of drug paraphernalia laws and ordinances that prohibit manufacture, sale, distribution, or possession of equipment and materials intended to be used with narcotics. It is estimated that in 1997 there were approximately 110 needle exchange programs (NEPs) in North America. In part, because of the ban on the use of Federal funds for the operation of needle exchange, it has been difficult to evaluate the efficacy of these programs. This [selection] presents data from the studies that have evaluated the role of NEPs in HIV prevention.

Evidence for the efficacy of NEPs comes from three sources: (1) studies originally focused on the effectiveness of NEPs in non-HIV blood-borne infections, (2) mathematical modeling of data on needle exchange on HIV seroincidence, and (3) studies that examine the positive and negative impact of NEPs on HIV and AIDS. Case-control studies have provided powerful data on the positive effect of NEPs on reduction of two blood-borne viral infections (HBV and HCV). For example, a case-control study in Tacoma, Washington, showed

From David Vlahov and Benjamin Junge, "The Role of Needle Exchange Programs in HIV Prevention," *Public Health Reports* (June 1998). Washington, DC: U.S. Government Printing Office, 1998. References omitted.

that a six-fold increase in HBV and a seven-fold increase in HCV infections in IDUs were associated with nonuse of the NEP.

The first federally funded study of needle exchange was an evaluation of the New Haven NEP, which is legally operated by the New Haven Health Department. Rather than relying on self-report of reduced risky injection drug use, this study utilized mathematical and statistical modeling, using data from a syringe tracking and testing system. Incidence of HIV infection among needle exchange participants was estimated to have decreased by 33% as a result of the NEP.

A series of Government-commissioned reports have reviewed the data on positive and negative outcomes of NEPs. The major reports are from the National Commission on AIDS; the U.S. General Accounting Office; the Centers for Disease Control/University of California; and the National Academy of Sciences. The latter two reports are used in this [selection].

The aggregated results support the positive benefit of NEPs and do not support negative outcomes from NEPs. When legal restrictions on both purchase and possession of syringes are removed, IDUs will change their syringe-sharing behaviors in ways that can reduce HIV transmission. NEPs do not result in increased drug use among participants or the recruitment of first-time drug users.

* * *

Injecting drug users (IDUs) are at risk for human immunodeficiency virus (HIV) and other blood-borne infections. The principal mode of transmission is parenteral through multiperson use of needles and syringes. The mechanism of contamination is through a behavior called registering, whereby drug users draw back on the plunger of a syringe after venous insertion to ensure venous placement before injecting drug solutions. Strategies to prevent or reduce parenteral transmission of HIV infection need to focus on reducing, if not eliminating altogether, the multiperson use of syringes that have been contaminated. The principle underlying these strategies has been stated clearly in the recommendations of the 1995 National Academy of Sciences Report on preventing HIV infection as follows: "For injection drugs the once only use of sterile needles and syringes remains the safest, most effective approach for limiting HIV transmission." This principle was echoed in the 1996 American Medical Association's booklet *A Physician's Guide to HIV Prevention* and in 1995 in the booklet of the U.S. Preventive Services Task Force *Guide to Clinical Preventive Services*. More recently, this principle has been codified in a multiagency *HIV Prevention Bulletin*.

The first line of prevention is to encourage IDUs to stop using drugs altogether. However, for drug users who cannot or will not stop drug use, owing to their addiction, other approaches are needed. Two major approaches have been developed to provide sufficient sterile needles and syringes to drug users to reduce transmission of HIV and other blood-borne infections. The first is needle exchange programs (NEPs), and the second is modification of syringe prescription and paraphernalia possession laws or ordinances. Hereafter, we will refer to the latter as deregulation of prescription and paraphernalia laws.

NEPs There are now more than 110 NEPs in the United States. By comparison, there are 2000 or more outlets in Australia and hundreds in

Great Britain. The exchange programs are varied in terms of organizational characteristics. Some operate out of fixed sites; others are mobile. Some are legally authorized; others are not. Funding, staffing patterns, policies, and hours of operation vary considerably among the different programs.

Despite different organizational characteristics, the basic description and goals of NEPs are the same. They provide sterile needles in exchange for contaminated or used needles to increase access to sterile needles and to remove contaminated syringes from circulation in the community. Equally important, needle exchanges are there to establish contact with otherwise hard-to-reach populations to deliver health services, such as HIV testing and counseling, as well as referrals to treatment for drug abuse.

Over time, numerous questions have arisen about NEPs, such as whether these programs encourage drug use and whether they result in lower HIV incidence. These questions have been summarized and examined in a series of published reviews and Government-sponsored reports. The Government-sponsored reports include those from the National Commission on AIDS in 1991, the U.S. General Accounting Office in 1993, the University of California and Centers for Disease Control (CDC) Report in 1993, and the National Academy of Sciences in 1995.

As to whether NEPs increase drug use among participants, the 1993 California report examined published reports that involved comparison groups (Table 1). Because the sampling and data collection methods varied considerably among studies, the summary has been reduced here to show whether needle exchange was associated with a beneficial, neutral, or adverse effect. Of the eight reports that examined the issue of injection frequency, three showed a reduction in injection frequency, four showed a mixed or neutral effect (no change), and one initially recorded an increase in injection frequency.

In terms of attracting youth or new individuals into NEPs in the United States, programs that have no minimum age restriction have reported that recruitment of participants who are younger than 18 years old was consistently less than 1%; this low rate of use was noted in studies that were conducted in San Francisco and New Haven and in our recent studies in Baltimore. However, recent studies also have shown that new injectors who are adolescent or young adults also are at extremely high risk for HIV infection. In response to this problem, Los Angeles has recently developed an NEP specifically directed at new initiates into injection drug use (P. Kerndt, personal communication, February 10, 1996).

Another question is whether the presence of NEPs in a community conveys a message to youth that condones and encourages drug use. This issue is particularly difficult to study. In 1993, the authors of the University of California-CDC report examined longitudinal national drug use indicator data (data from the DAWN Project), which monitors emergency-room mentions of drug-abuse-related admissions. Comparisons of data before and after the opening of needle exchanges and between cities with and without NEPs showed no significant trends.

The only systematic study to date of trends in drug use within a community following the opening of a needle exchange comes from Amsterdam. Using data on admissions to treatment for drug

Table 1
Summary of Studies of Behavioral Change Within NEPs

Outcome measures	Beneficial NEP effect	Mixed or neutral NEP effect	Adverse NEP effect
Drug risk:			
Sharing frequency	10	4	–
Give away syringes	3	1	1
Needle cleaning	3	1	–
Injection frequency	3	4	1
Sex risk:			
Number of partners	2	1	–
Partner choice	1	1	–
Condom use	1	1	1

abuse, Buning and colleagues noted that the proportion of drug users younger than 22 declined from 14% in 1981 to 5% in 1986; the NEP opened in 1984. The opening of the needle exchange increased neither the proportion of drug users overall nor the proportion of those younger than 22 years. Thus, the currently available data argue against the belief that needle exchange encourages drug use.

Another issue is whether needle exchanges will result in more contaminated syringes found on the street. If a needle exchange is designed as a one-for-one exchange, the answer is no. In Baltimore, a carefully designed systematic street survey showed no increase in discarded needles following the opening of an NEP. An update following two years of surveys has shown a similar trend of no increase.

Findings of behavioral change associated with needle exchange are varied. A number of published studies have compared levels of risky behavior among IDUs participating and those not participating in needle exchange. As the University of California-CDC report noted, methods varied considerably among these published reports, so that the summary here (Table 1) sorts the studies into

whether and how the needle exchange has shown an effect—risk reduction, no effect, or adverse effect.

In terms of drug risks, Table 1 shows that there were 14 studies that looked at the frequency of needle sharing, the most dangerous behavior in terms of drug-related risk of HIV transmission. In those studies, 10 showed a reduction in needle sharing frequency, four had no effect, and none showed any increase in needle sharing.

Similar trends were noted for the practice of giving away syringes: three showed a reduction in this practice, one no effect, and one an increase. Three out of four studies reporting on this needle cleaning showed a positive effect. Finally, in terms of sexual risk behavior, few studies overall have examined the impact of needle exchange on sexual risks. Sexual transmission among IDUs is an important area that merits further investigation.

The next question about NEPs is whether such programs actually reduce the incidence of HIV infection in IDUs. While the idea of using only sterile needles makes the question of efficacy seem obvious, the real question centers on how effective the programs are in practice and how subject such programs are to the ubiquitous "law of unintended consequences."

Studies of the impact of needle exchange on the incidence of HIV infection in the United States are few, primarily because funding for such evaluations is relatively recent and sample size requirements are large. The first study (shown in Table 2) was conducted by Hagan and colleagues in Tacoma, Washington. In that city, the prevalence and, therefore, the incidence of HIV were extremely low. A needle exchange was initiated with the goal of maintaining HIV incidence at a low level. Two case-controlled analyses used hepatitis B and hepatitis C virus infection as outcome variables because the epidemiology of these two viruses is similar to HIV, although transmission of hepatitis is more efficient than HIV. In these studies, needle exchange participation was associated with more than an 80% reduction in the incidence of hepatitis infection. Over time, HIV prevalence has not risen.

In terms of HIV studies, Kaplan and Heimer at Yale utilized information about HIV test results of washes from syringes returned to the New Haven Needle Exchange Program by constructing an elegant statistical model to estimate that needle exchange reduced HIV incidence by 33%. This model has been reviewed by three independent statistical reviewers who have judged the model sound in estimates as reasonable or even conservative.

More recently, Des Jarlais and colleagues from New York City published a prospective study of seroconversion between attendees and nonattendees of needle exchange. In this study, they estimated a 70% reduction in HIV incidence. Several other studies are ongoing in San Francisco, Chicago, and Baltimore, but their findings are too preliminary to present at this time.

In terms of HIV seroconversion studies from needle exchanges with comparison groups from outside the United States, data are available from Amsterdam and Montreal. In Amsterdam, data from a case-control study nested within an ongoing cohort study identified a slightly increased risk of HIV seroconversion with needle exchange use. However, when the analyses were examined by calendar time, the needle exchange was initially protective, but the association reversed over time. The authors attributed their results to the needle exchange losing lower risk users to pharmacy access over time, leaving a core of highest risk users within the exchange.

More recently a study was published using a case-control analysis nested within a cohort study in Montreal. Of 974 HIV-seronegative subjects followed an average of 22 months, 89 subjects seroconverted. Consistent use of needle exchange compared with nonuse was associated with an odds ratio for HIV seroconversion of 10.5, which remained elevated even during multivariate adjustment. The authors concluded that NEPs were associated with higher HIV rates and speculated that the exchange may have facilitated formation of new social networks that might have permitted broader HIV transmission. In an accompanying commentary, Lurie criticized the Montreal study saying that the more likely explanation for the findings was that powerful selection forces attracted the most risky IDUs as evidenced by substantial differences in the baseline

Table 2
Impact of NEPs on Incidence of Blood-Borne Infections in the United States

Author	City	Design	Outcome	Percent reduction
Hagan et al.	Tacoma	Case-control	HBV HCV	83 86
Kaplan et al.	New Haven	Mathematical modeling based on testing of syringes returned to NEP	HIV	33
Des Jarlais et al.	New York	Prospective study of seroconversion; NEP is external cohort and IDUs in neighboring regions	HIV	70

data for the exchangers *vs.* nonexchangers: exchangers had higher injection frequencies, were less likely to have a history of drug abuse treatment, were more likely to share needles and use shooting galleries, and had a high HIV prevalence. Lurie attributed the differences to the hours and locations of the exchange (late night in the red-light district) attracting only a select subset of users.

In Vancouver, Strathdee reported on HIV incidence in a cohort of IDUs of whom 92% were enrolled in needle exchange. The incidence of 18.6 (100 person-years) was associated with low education, unstable housing, commercial sex, borrowing needles, injecting with others, and frequent use of needle exchange. The related study by Archibald and colleagues demonstrates a selection of higher risk individuals into needle exchange in Vancouver.

The point to consider is what accounts for the discrepancy between the U.S. and non-U.S. studies. From a methodological perspective, selection factors could be operating. For example, in Vancouver, a study compared characteristics of exchangers with those of nonexchangers, or high frequency *vs.* low frequency exchangers; this study showed that the high frequency exchangers were more likely to engage in high risk activities. While the Vancouver study showed that self-selection into needle exchange results in leaving a comparison group that is not similar in other respects, the data do suggest that needle exchange has been successful in recruiting high risk users.

At another level, the U.S. studies involve evaluation of a needle exchange in comparison with people who do not have access to an NEP or to sterile needles through other sources. In contrast, the Canadian and Dutch studies have involved comparisons that do have an alternative source for sterile needles, principally through pharmacies; their studies may have selected into the needle exchange the people who cannot get needles from pharmacies. The effectiveness of NEPs depends on understanding who constitutes the comparison group.

More recently, an ecological analysis was published with serial HIV seroprevalence data for 29 cities with NEPs and 52 cities without such programs. The results, although subject to a possible ecological fallacy, indicated a 5.8% decline in HIV prevalence per year in cities with NEPs and a 5.9% increase in cities without exchange.

Deregulating syringe prescription and paraphernalia laws   In 1992, Connecticut changed the state laws to permit sale and possession of up to 10 syringes at a time. The CDC, in conjunction with the state of Connecticut, conducted initial studies that examined whether IDUs utilized pharmacies and discovered that they did. The CDC and the state of Connecticut then examined how pharmacy utilization affected needle-sharing behaviors in the two samples of IDUs that were interviewed: 52% reported sharing needles before the law changed, and 31% did so after the law changed. While these data are encouraging, data on needle disposal and HIV incidence are not yet available.

SUMMARY

Access to sterile needles and syringes is an important, even vital, component of a comprehensive HIV prevention program for IDUs. The data on needle exchange in the United States are consistent with the conclusion that these programs do not encourage during use and that needle exchanges can be effective in reducing HIV incidence. Other data show that NEPs help people stop drug use through referral to drug treatment programs. The studies outside of the United States are important for reminding us that unintended consequences can occur. While changes in needle prescription and possession laws and regulations have shown promise, the identification of organizational components that improve or hinder effectiveness of needle exchange and pharmacy-based access are needed.

NO

Office of National Drug Control Policy

NEEDLE EXCHANGE PROGRAMS: ARE THEY EFFECTIVE?

When President Bush took office, most Americans regarded the use of illegal drugs as the most serious problem confronting the Nation. Since that time, the Nation has made substantial progress in reducing drug use. But now, in response to the AIDS epidemic, there are those who are ready to sound a retreat in the war against drugs by distributing clean needles to intravenous drug users in the hope that this will slow the spread of AIDS. I believe this would be a serious mistake. We must not lose sight of the fact that illegal drugs still pose a serious threat to our Nation. Nor can we allow our concern for AIDS to undermine our determination to win the war on drugs.

In 1988, 14.5 million Americans and nearly two million young people, aged 12–17, were using drugs. In response to the devastation caused by drug use, the President boldly announced the first National Drug Control Strategy in a televised address to the Nation in 1989. That Strategy was a landmark document. Not only did it establish a coherent, coordinated policy for the national effort against drugs, but it committed unprecedented new resources for fighting drug use.

The Strategy is working; the use of illegal drugs by Americans is declining. Between 1988 and 1991, almost two million fewer Americans were using drugs, a drop of almost 13 percent. And by 1991, about half a million fewer young people were current users of drugs, a drop of 27 percent. Since 1985, the number of Americans using drugs has fallen by over 10 million.

Key to the success of the Strategy has been increasing Americans' intolerance of illicit drugs. But, for those already caught in the deadly web of addiction, we must act with compassion. The Administration therefore vigorously supports efforts to provide effective drug treatment to those who want it and can benefit from it, and has increased finding for drug treatment from $1.1 billion in 1989 to a proposed $2.1 billion for 1993.

Our gains against drug use have been hard-won, and this is no time to jeopardize them by instituting needle exchange programs. Despite all the arguments made by proponents of needle exchange, there is no getting around

From Office of National Drug Control Policy, Executive Office of the President, "Needle Exchange Programs: Are They Effective?" *ONDCP Bulletin No. 7* (July 1992). Some notes omitted.

the fact that distributing needles facilitates drug use and undercuts the credibility of society's message that using drugs is illegal and morally wrong. And just as important, there is no conclusive evidence that exchange programs reduce the spread of AIDS.

The Administration's concerns about needle exchange are widely shared. Recently, for example, the Congress extended a prohibition on the use of most Federal drug treatment funds to support needle exchange programs. And in June 1992, the National Association of State Alcohol and Drug Abuse Directors informed every member of Congress of its support for continuing this prohibition. Also, in February 1992, the National District Attorneys Association passed an official policy position condemning needle exchange.

The Administration will continue to work with the Congress, and with State and local officials to support alternatives to needle exchange, including expanded and improved drug treatment and aggressive outreach programs. These efforts will provide addicts with something that needle exchange programs cannot: hope and a chance for real recovery from drug addiction.

NEEDLE EXCHANGE PROGRAMS IN THE UNITED STATES

Intravenous drug use and HIV/AIDS.[1] Intravenous drug users in the United States are one of the groups most at risk for contracting AIDS. AIDS prevention and education programs, which have had a measurable effect on the behavior of other high-risk groups, have not been so successful with intravenous drug users. In fact, the Centers for Disease Control estimates that about 32 percent of the diagnosed AIDS cases in this country, involving nearly 70,000 individuals, resulted from intravenous drug use or sexual contact with intravenous drug users. In addition, intravenous drug use is responsible for half of the AIDS cases among women.

AIDS is spread among intravenous drug users primarily through the sharing of hypodermic syringes, or "needles," and other drug-using paraphernalia (e.g., cotton and water) that have been contaminated with the AIDS virus, and secondarily by high-risk sexual behavior. Thus, intravenous drug users pose a threat not only to themselves, but to their sexual partners and offspring as well. In fact, 58 percent of all reported pediatric AIDS cases are associated with intravenous drug use.

Faced with the growing link between intravenous drug use and AIDS, some cities and communities have instituted or are contemplating programs to provide clean needles to addicts in the hope that this will help reduce the sharing of needles, and hence, the spread of the HIV virus.

Needle exchange programs. Needle exchange programs provide free, clean needles to intravenous drug users in an attempt to reduce the likelihood that they will share needles with other users. Some programs operate from fixed locations such as city government offices or pharmacies. Others are mobile, using outreach workers in vans, on foot, and at temporary sites. Some programs provide a new needle only in exchange for an old one, while others provide at least one "starter" needle. Most programs limit the number of needles that can be exchanged at any one time. Some programs provide needles to persons only if they have a verifiable history of drug injection, and most have age limits. Most programs are privately funded; others are supported with State or municipal government funds.[2]

Needle exchange programs also differ in scope. Some only exchange needles, while others are more comprehensive and provide counseling, referral to testing and drug treatment, bleach to clean needles, and safer sex information.

Needle exchange and the law. In 39 States and the District of Columbia, sterile needles can be purchased inexpensively without a prescription in many pharmacies.[3] In most of the remaining 11 States, a prescription is required. However, four of the 11 are considering legislation that would broaden access to needles. Only one State, Alabama, is considering legislation that would restrict accessibility by making it a criminal offense for those other than licensed pharmacists or practitioners to sell needles.

Forty-nine States, the District of Columbia, and numerous local jurisdictions have laws to prohibit the sale and distribution of drug paraphernalia. The majority of these laws conform with the Model Drug Paraphernalia Act, which was released by the Drug Enforcement Administration in August 1979. The Model Drug Paraphernalia Act would make it a crime to possess, deliver, or manufacture needles with the intent to violate anti-drug laws. Therefore, operating needle exchange programs may be a violation of the law in many States and local jurisdictions. Furthermore, operating such programs may subject municipalities to civil liability in some jurisdictions.

What the research shows. Several studies on the efficacy of needle exchange programs have been conducted in the United States and abroad. Some of these studies have been cited by proponents of needle exchange as evidence that such programs work. However, all of the needle exchange programs studied have yielded either ambiguous or discouraging results. Moreover, the methodology used to conduct these studies has been flawed. For example:

- Many studies make long-term projections of addict behavior based on short-term results;
- Many use a small or insufficient sample size and then project results to larger populations;
- Despite claims that needle sharing was reduced, none of the studies conducted objective tests (e.g., analysis of blood types on returned needles) to determine whether needles were shared;
- Most do not use valid comparison or control groups; and
- Most have program staff, rather than independent evaluators, conduct client interviews on which the findings of the studies are based.

There are four other significant problems with the research. First, needle exchange programs are plagued by high levels of attrition. Programs may have initial contact with intravenous drug users who are at the highest risk of sharing needles and contracting AIDS, but only as few as 20 percent may return for a second or third visit.

Second, needle exchange programs tend to attract and retain a self-selecting group of older, long-term intravenous drug users who are less likely to share needles than less experienced, more promiscuous users. Therefore, positive reports on the effectiveness of exchange programs may be due *more* to the behavior of this less risky subset of the intravenous drug using population and *less* to the availability of clean needles.

Third, programs offering needle exchange often provide bleach for cleaning needles, referrals to testing and treatment, and other services. However, the research conducted to date has not isolated the specific impact that exchanging needles has had on reducing the transmission of AIDS compared with these other factors. Most researchers have simply attributed positive results to needle exchange.

The fourth weakness with the research relates to the dynamics of addiction. No matter what addicts promise when they are not on drugs, they may still share needles when they shoot up heroin or cocaine. In many cases it is simply part of the ritual of taking drugs. More often, a drug-induced state overwhelms rational thinking. Many addicts know that they can get AIDS from dirty needles. Yet hazards to their health—even deadly ones—do not weigh heavily on their minds. Rather, they are primarily concerned with the instant gratification of drugs.

To expect an individual locked in the grip of drug addiction to act responsibly by not sharing needles is unrealistic. Such a change in behavior requires self-discipline and a willingness to postpone gratification and plan for the future—all of which are contrary to the drug-using lifestyle. The fact that addicts can purchase clean needles cheaply, without prescription, in many pharmacies in most States, but often fail to do so, is evidence of their irresponsible behavior.[4] In fact, the only proven way to change an addict's behavior is through structured interventions, such as drug treatment.

The New Haven study. A 1991 interim study of a needle exchange program in New Haven, Connecticut, is cited by many needle exchange advocates as evidence of the benefits of needle exchange.[5] The study asserts numerous positive findings, most of which are not supported by the data.

The study states that retention rates stabilized after a high attrition rate early in the program. But, of the 720 addicts who initially contacted the New Haven program over an eight-month period, only 288 (40 percent) returned at least once to exchange a used needle (Figure 1). The New Haven study defines the 288 returning intravenous drug users as "program participants," but does not distinguish between those who exchanged needles once and those who exchanged needles more frequently.[6] The loose definition of "program participation" exaggerates the program's reported retention rate and calls into question the claim that participation in the program stabilized. In addition, the study does not provide information on the 288 individuals who remained in the program and whether they shared needles before the program started. In fact, the study reports that of the 720 addicts who contacted the program, 436 (61 percent) reported never sharing needles before the program began (Table 1).

The study also states that about half of the 10,180 needles distributed by the program between November 1990 and June 1991 were returned, and that an additional 4,236 "street" or nonprogram needles were brought in for exchange. However, the study fails to account for the 4,917 needles—50 percent of those given out—that were not returned. Based on this information, the study claims that the circulation time for needles was

Figure 1

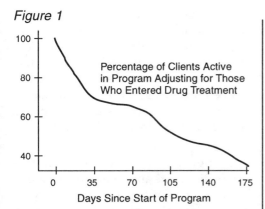

Percentage of Clients Active
in Program Adjusting for Those
Who Entered Drug Treatment

Days Since Start of Program

Source: The New Haven Study, July 1991.

Table 1

Extent of Needle Sharing Reported at Initial Contact With Program

How Often Shared Works		
Always (100%)	16	(2%)
Almost Always (67–99%)	16	(2%)
Half the Time (34–66%)	43	(6%)
Sometimes (1–33%)	196	(27%)
Never (0%)	436	(61%)
(Missing)	13	(2%)

Source: The New Haven Study, July 1991.

reduced and that fewer contaminated needles were appearing in public places. However, no data are presented to directly support such conclusions.

The authors also report that 107 intravenous drug users (about 15 percent of those who contacted the program) entered treatment over an eight-month period through contact with the New Haven program, but there are no data on how many of these individuals were "program participants" (e.g., had exchanged needles more than once). Therefore, the study does not present any basis for correlating the *exchange* of needles to entry into drug treatment. Also, no data on treatment retention or completion are presented.

The study also claims that intravenous drug use in the community did not increase. Although this may be true, it is not supported by convincing data. The study indicates that 92 percent of those who initially contacted the program were experienced users who had been injecting drugs for one year or more. The study uses this statistic to demonstrate that the availability of free needles did not entice individuals to begin using intravenous drugs. However, there is no evidence to

verify that experienced users did not use needles distributed by the program to initiate new users. The study also cites an unchanged rate in drug arrests as evidence that no increase in intravenous drug use occurred due to the program. However, the New Haven program had only been in operation for two months and had been contacted by fewer than 200 addicts at the time statistics on drug arrests were recorded. Therefore, it is unlikely that the program could have had any impact on the rate of drug arrests.

The most striking finding of the New Haven study—that the incidence of new HIV infections was reduced by one-third among those participating in the program—is based on tenuous data. The study indicates that 789 needles—581 from the program, 160 from the street, and 48 from a local "shooting gallery"[7] —were tested for the presence of HIV.[8] The tests found that program needles were much less likely to be HIV positive than street or gallery needles. The tests also indicated that "dedicated" program needles (e.g., those returned by the original recipient) were much less likely to be HIV positive than other program needles. Based on this information, the study concludes that "dedicated" needles were not shared, *although no tests were conducted to determine if different blood types appeared on the needles or the blood type on the needle matched that of the program participant.* Without conducting such tests, accurate conclusions as to whether needles were shared cannot be drawn, and a reduction in the spread of HIV cannot be attributed to needle exchange.

Finally, the study projects that expanding the availability of clean needles to New Haven's entire intravenous drug using population would also reduce the incidence of new HIV infections by one-third. The projection is based on a highly complex mathematical model involving eight different factors that are supported by numerous assumptions, estimates, probabilities, and rates. While the model may be valid, its projections are based on the tenuous assumption that the 288 intravenous drug users "participating" in the New Haven program are representative of the general intravenous drug using population. However, the high attrition rate of the New Haven program demonstrates that such an assumption cannot be made.

FOREIGN NEEDLE EXCHANGE PROGRAMS

In recent years, other countries—most notably the Netherlands and the United Kingdom—have established needle exchange programs. Studies of these programs have also produced mixed results. Most reflect the problems noted in existing research on needle exchange. Many report anecdotal or other unquantified information. Furthermore, some base "success" on the number of needles distributed.

In Amsterdam, a program started in 1984 reported that the number of participants grew more than tenfold in four years. The program also reported that during the first four years participants shared fewer needles, the HIV prevalence rate among intravenous drug users stabilized, and instances of Hepatitis B decreased.

In England, about 120 exchange programs distribute approximately four million needles annually. These programs reportedly reach users who have not been in contact with drug treatment services, decrease needle sharing, and increase contact with other social services by participants.

Sweden's three needle exchange sites reported after three years that no project participant had become infected with HIV, that needle sharing had declined, and that many users not previously in contact with drug treatment had been attracted to the program.

Although generally positive, the reports on these programs are scientifically weak and present very few objective indicators of success. All claim that needle exchange reduced the number of needles shared, but none of the programs conducted the tests (e.g., blood-type tests) necessary to make that determination.

In addition, the attrition rates in foreign programs are extremely high. A 1989 study of 15 needle exchange programs in England and Scotland reported that only 33 percent of intravenous drug users who initially contacted the programs returned up to five times. As in the United States, needle exchange programs in other countries are more likely to attract and retain intravenous drug users who are already predisposed not to share needles, and who therefore are at lower risk of contracting AIDS than other, less cautious, users.

ALTERNATIVES TO NEEDLE EXCHANGE

The challenges to society presented by drug use and HIV/AIDS require the steady development of scientific understanding and the promotion of effective interventions. Requested Federal funding for AIDS prevention, treatment, research, and income maintenance in 1993 is $4.9 billion—a 69 percent increase since 1990 (Figure 2). The President's National Drug Control Strategy supports using a portion of these funds for research, experiments, and demonstrations to seek out high-risk drug users; to encourage and support their entry into drug treatment; and to provide them with information on the destructiveness of their behavior and ways to change it. The Strategy also supports efforts to expand the capacity and effectiveness of drug treatment for intravenous drug users.

Outreach programs.   The most effective method of reducing the spread of AIDS among intravenous drug users is to treat successfully their drug addiction. However, Federal studies estimate that more than 40 percent of intravenous drug users have never been in treatment, even though many have used drugs intravenously for more than 10 years. Therefore, it is essential to continue efforts to aggressively recruit intravenous drug users into treatment.

Since 1987, the Department of Health and Human Service's National Institute on Drug Abuse has funded projects in more than 40 cities to help identify intravenous drug users and persuade them to enter treatment. In these cities, squads

Figure 2

Federal Funding for HIV/AIDS, 1990–1993

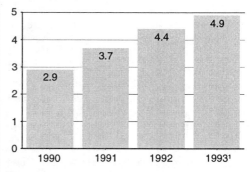

[1]Requested

Source: Office of Management and Budget, 1992

of outreach workers contact addicts and encourage them to avoid sharing needles and other risky behaviors and to enter treatment. Outreach workers also provide addicts with information on the threat of AIDS and dispense materials (e.g., bleach and condoms) to reduce the risk of HIV infection.

Between 1987 and 1992, outreach workers contacted approximately 150,000 intravenous drug users. Of these, 45,000 addicts (54 percent of whom reported regularly sharing needles) and 9,500 sexual partners were provided with information on treatment, counseling and methods for reducing the risk of infection. Program participants were assigned to standard and enhanced interventions. Follow-up surveys were conducted six months after the assignments were made, and the results of those surveys indicated that:

- 31 percent of the intravenous drug users had enrolled in formal drug treatment programs;
- 38 percent were sharing needles less frequently;

- 44 percent had begun to always clean their needles, always use a new needle, or had stopped injecting completely; and
- 47 percent had stopped injecting or reduced their frequency of injection.

The success of this effort demonstrates that outreach programs are highly effective in persuading intravenous drug users to avoid sharing needles and to seek treatment. By comparison, only 15 percent of those who contacted the New Haven program entered treatment. The Federal government will continue to support outreach programs by awarding approximately 60 grants in 1992 and 1993.

The Centers for Disease Control also administers an extensive outreach program for preventing the spread of the HIV virus among intravenous drug users. This program, which is operated through State departments of health and community-based organizations, offers intravenous drug users counseling, testing, and referral to treatment. An evaluation of the program will be completed in about two years.

Expanding treatment capacity. The Federal government continues to support expanded treatment capacity for intravenous drug users, primarily through the Alcohol, Drug Abuse and Mental Health Services Block Grant program, which requires States to use at least 50 percent of their drug allotment for outreach and treatment of these drug users. Also, the Capacity Expansion Program, which was created by the Bush Administration in Fiscal Year 1992, will increase the number of drug treatment slots for areas and populations in the greatest need of treatment, including intravenous drug users. If Congress fully funds this pro-

gram in Fiscal Year 1993 (the Administration has requested $86 million), an additional 38,000 addicts—many of whom will be intravenous drug users—will be provided with drug treatment.

Medications development. The Federal government is continuing its efforts to develop medications to treat heroin addiction. New pharmacological therapies, such as LAAM (a longer-acting alternative to methadone), depot naltrexone, and buprenorphine, are showing considerable promise in treating heroin addiction and should be available within the next few years.[9] In addition, performance standards and clinical protocols are being developed for methadone treatment programs to enhance their safety and effectiveness in treating heroin addiction.[10]

CONCLUSION

The rapid spread of AIDS has prompted officials of some of America's cities to institute programs that distribute clean needles to intravenous drug users. Such programs are questionable public policy, however, because they facilitate addicts' continued use of drugs and undercut the credibility of society's message that drug use is illegal and morally wrong. Further, there is no compelling research that needle exchange programs are effective in preventing intravenous drug users from sharing needles, reducing the spread of AIDS, or encouraging addicts to seek drug treatment.

Research does show, however, that aggressive outreach efforts are an effective way to get intravenous drug users to end their high-risk behavior and seek treatment. Therefore, the National Drug Control Strategy will continue to support such outreach programs. It also will continue to support expanded treatment capacity for high-risk populations, including intravenous drug users; the development of medications for treating heroin addiction; and the exploration of other options that may offer intravenous drug users a real chance for recovery.

NOTES

1. Human Immunodeficiency Virus/Acquired Immunodeficiency Syndrome.

2. Federal law prohibits the use of Alcohol, Drug Abuse, and Mental Health Services Block Grant funds—the major source of Federal support for drug treatment—to pay for needle exchange programs.

3. In some States, such as California, needles may be sold without prescription for the administration of insulin or adrenaline if the pharmacist can identify the purchaser and records the purchase.

4. Syringes cost about $.30 each. For example, in a recent study of pharmacies in St. Louis, Compton et al. found the cost of a package of 10, 28-gauge, 100-unit insulin syringes to range from $1.92 to $4.28.

See Compton, W., et al. "Legal Needle Buying in St. Louis," *American Journal of Public Health*, April 1992, Vol. 82, No. 4.

5. In Fiscal Year 1992, the National Institute on Drug Abuse awarded a grant to Yale University to conduct a rigorous evaluation of the New Haven program over a three-year period. Results of the evaluation will be available in 1995.

6. Researchers estimate that intravenous heroin users on average inject two or more times a day, heavy users four to six times a day. Intravenous cocaine users invariably inject more frequently. There is very little data yet available on the number of injections an average user gets from a needle before it is discarded, although a 1989 California survey of 257 users found a mean of 22.5 uses (with 27 reporting one use and 15 reporting over 100).

7. A "shooting gallery" is a communal injection site notorious for inadequate sterilization of injection equipment.

8. The study does not specify the method used to select program and street needles or whether they are considered random or representative samples.

9. LAAM is a longer-acting alternative to methadone, depot naltrexone is a long-acting heroin blocker, and buprenorphine is being investigated for treating individuals addicted to both heroin and cocaine.

10. Methadone is a synthetic medication used to treat heroin addicts by relieving withdrawal symptoms and craving for heroin for 24 hours. Methadone is only administered as part of a supervised treatment program.

POSTSCRIPT

Should Needle Exchange Programs Be Supported?

The implementation of needle exchange programs arouses several ethical and practical concerns. Opponents challenge the wisdom of giving drug addicts needles to inject themselves with illegal drugs. They ask, What might impressionable adolescents think if the government funds programs in which drug addicts are given needles? Some people reason that those who inject drugs into their bodies know the risks and should live with the consequences of their actions. Others wonder whether the distribution of needles will lead to an increase or a decrease in drug use.

Whether or not needle exchange programs will help slow down the spread of AIDS is extremely relevant because people who inject drugs are the primary sources for heterosexual transmission of AIDS to sexual partners. Also, many pregnant drug users end up infecting their fetuses either through their own or their sexual partners' drug use. Individuals who inject cocaine are more likely to infect sexual partners than heroin users because cocaine heightens perceptions of sexual arousal. Also, the immune systems of drug addicts are impaired not only by their addictions but by their typically poor environment as well. With a weakened immune system, one can contract HIV more easily.

One potential advantage of needle exchange programs is that needles may be safely discarded after they have been used. Unsafely discarded needles may accidentally prick someone (including nonusers) and lead to HIV transmission. A second potential benefit is that when people come to needle exchange sites, they can be encouraged to enter drug treatment programs. It is difficult to reach the drug-injecting population; one place to reach these individuals is where they exchange needles.

Despite the difficulties of studying people who inject drugs, long-term studies are needed to determine the impact of needle exchange programs on (1) the incidence of AIDS, (2) the continuation or reduction of drug use, (3) whether or not these programs attract new users to the drug culture, (4) the likelihood of program participants entering drug treatment programs, and (5) the impact on other high-risk behaviors. Preliminary studies into the effectiveness of needle exchange programs are contradictory. One such program was introduced in Tacoma, Washington, and needle sharing declined 30 percent. Programs in New York City and New Haven, Connecticut, resulted in fewer reports of HIV infection without an increase in drug use. Conversely, in a program in Louisville, Kentucky, nearly two-thirds of people who inject drugs continued to share needles. In Louisville, however, needles are obtained through a prescription, which may have a different effect in the long run than receiving needles through an exchange program. If needle exchange programs are implemented, who should organize and finance them? Is this the responsibility of government? Should public funds be used? Would these programs save taxpayers money in the long run?

Despite the absence of federal funding, Denise Paone et al., in "Syringe Exchange in the United States, 1996: A National Profile," *American Journal of Public Health* (January 1999), report that needle exchange programs are increasing. In "Prevention of HIV/AIDS and Other Blood-Borne Diseases Among Injection Drug Users: A National Survey on the Regulation of Syringes and Needles," *JAMA* (January 1, 1997), Lawrence Gostin et al. discuss how needle exchange programs may reduce the spread of AIDS with little impact on crime. In "Needed: A Zero-Tolerance Policy on AIDS," *Drug Policy Letter* (Summer 1995), Peter Lurie argues that thousands of lives are sacrificed due to the government's policy of denying funds for needle exchange programs. In "Clean Needles May Be Bad Medicine," *The Wall Street Journal* (April 22, 1998), David Murray writes that needle exchange programs are a bad idea because they legitimize drug abuse and because addicts will continue to get ill from contaminated drugs.

ISSUE 5

Should Pregnant Drug Users Be Prosecuted?

YES: Paul A. Logli, from "Drugs in the Womb: The Newest Battlefield in the War on Drugs," *Criminal Justice Ethics* (Winter/Spring 1990)

NO: Sue Mahan, from *Crack Cocaine, Crime, and Women: Legal, Social, and Treatment Issues* (Sage Publications, 1996)

ISSUE SUMMARY

YES: Paul A. Logli, an Illinois prosecuting attorney, argues that it is the government's duty to enforce every child's right to begin life with a healthy, drug-free mind and body. Logli maintains that pregnant women who use drugs should be prosecuted because they may harm the life of their unborn children.

NO: Writer Sue Mahan asserts that the prosecution of pregnant drug users is unfair because poor women are more likely to be the targets of such prosecution. Mahan argues that instead of treating these women as criminals, both society and these women would be better served by the provision of adequate prenatal care and treatment. Fear of prosecution may dissuade some women from seeking prenatal care.

The effects that drugs have on a fetus can be mild and temporary or severe and permanent, depending on the extent of drug use by the mother, the type of substance used, and the stage of fetal development at the time the drug crosses the placental barrier and enters the bloodstream of the fetus. Both illegal and legal drugs, such as cocaine, crack, marijuana, alcohol, and nicotine, are inreasingly found to be responsible for incidents of premature births, congenital abnormalities, fetal alcohol syndrome, mental retardation, and other serious birth defects. The exposure of the fetus to these substances and the long-term involuntary physical, intellectual, and emotional effects are disturbing. In addition, the medical, social, and economic costs to treat and care for babies who are exposed to or become addicted to drugs while in utero (in the uterus) warrant serious concern.

An important consideration regarding the prosecuting of pregnant drug users is whether this is a legal problem or a medical problem. In recent years, attempts have been made to establish laws that would allow the incarceration of drug-using pregnant women on the basis of "fetal abuse." Some cases have been successfully prosecuted: mothers have been denied custody of their infants until they enter appropriate treatment programs, and criminal charges have been brought against mothers whose children were born with drug-related complications. The underlying presumption is that the unborn fetus should be afforded protection against the harmful actions of another person, specifically the use of harmful drugs by the mother.

Those who profess that prosecuting pregnant women who use drugs is necessary insist that the health and welfare of the unborn child is the highest priority. They contend that the possibility that these women will avoid obtaining health care for themselves or their babies because they fear punishment does not absolve the state from the responsibility of protecting the babies. They also argue that criminalizing these acts is imperative to protect fetuses and newborns who cannot protect themselves. It is the duty of the legal system to deter pregnant women from engaging in future criminal drug use and to protect the best interests of infants.

Others maintain that drug use and dependency by pregnant women is a medical problem, not a criminal one. Many pregnant women seek treatment, but they often find that rehabilitation programs are limited or unavailable. Shortages of openings in chemical dependency programs may keep a prospective client waiting for months, during which time she will most likely continue to use the drugs to which she is addicted and prolong her fetus's drug exposure. Many low-income women do not receive drug treatment and adequate prenatal care due to financial constraints. And women who fear criminal prosecution because of their drug use may simply avoid prenatal care altogether.

Some suggest that medical intervention, drug prevention, and education —not prosecution—are needed for pregnant drug users. Prosecution, they contend, drives women who need medical attention away from the very help they and their babies need. Others respond that prosecuting pregnant women who use drugs will help identify those who need attention, at which point adequate medical and social welfare services can be provided to treat and protect the mother and child.

In the following selections, Paul A. Logli, arguing for the prosecution of pregnant drug users, contends that it is the state's responsibility to protect the unborn and the newborn because they are least able to protect themselves. He charges that it is the prosecutor's responsibility to deter future criminal drug use by mothers who he feels violate the rights of their potential newborns to have an opportunity for a healthy and normal life. Sue Mahan asserts that prosecuting pregnant drug users is counterproductive to improving the quality of infant and maternal health. The threat of arrest and incarceration may decrease the likelihood that pregnant drug users will seek out adequate prenatal care.

YES

Paul A. Logli

DRUGS IN THE WOMB: THE NEWEST BATTLEFIELD IN THE WAR ON DRUGS

INTRODUCTION

The reported incidence of drug-related births has risen dramatically over the last several years. The legal system and, in particular, local prosecutors have attempted to properly respond to the suffering, death, and economic costs which result from a pregnant woman's use of drugs. The ensuing debate has raised serious constitutional and practical issues which are far from resolution.

Prosecutors have achieved mixed results in using current criminal and juvenile statutes as a basis for legal action intended to prosecute mothers and protect children. As a result, state and federal legislators have begun the difficult task of drafting appropriate laws to deal with the problem, while at the same time acknowledging the concerns of medical authorities, child protection groups, and advocates for individual rights.

THE PROBLEM

The plight of "cocaine babies," children addicted at birth to narcotic substances or otherwise affected by maternal drug use during pregnancy, has prompted prosecutors in some jurisdictions to bring criminal charges against drug-abusing mothers. Not only have these prosecutions generated heated debates both inside and outside of the nation's courtrooms, but they have also expanded the war on drugs to a controversial new battlefield—the mother's womb.

A 1988 survey of hospitals conducted by Dr. Ira Chasnoff, Associate Professor of Northwestern University Medical School and President of the National Association for Perinatal Addiction Research and Education (NAPARE) indicated that as many as 375,000 infants may be affected by maternal cocaine use during pregnancy each year. Chasnoff's survey included 36 hospitals across the country and showed incidence rates ranging from 1 percent to 27 percent. It also indicated that the problem was not restricted to urban populations

From Paul A. Logli, "Drugs in the Womb: The Newest Battlefield in the War on Drugs," *Criminal Justice Ethics*, vol. 9, no. 1 (Winter/Spring 1990), pp. 23–29. Copyright © 1990 by *Criminal Justice Ethics*. Reprinted by permission of The Institute for Criminal Justice Ethics, 899 Tenth Avenue, New York, NY 10019-1029. Notes omitted.

or particular racial or socio-economic groups. More recently a study at Hutzel Hospital in Detroit's inner city found that 42.7 percent of its newborn babies were exposed to drugs while in their mothers' wombs.

The effects of maternal use of cocaine and other drugs during pregnancy on the mother and her newborn child have by now been well-documented and will not be repeated here. The effects are severe and can cause numerous threats to the short-term health of the child. In a few cases it can even result in death.

Medical authorities have just begun to evaluate the long-term effects of cocaine exposure on children as they grow older. Early findings show that many of these infants show serious difficulties in relating and reacting to adults and environments, as well as in organizing creative play, and they appear similar to mildly autistic or personality-disordered children.

The human costs related to the pain, suffering, and deaths resulting from maternal cocaine use during pregnancy are simply incalculable. In economic terms, the typical intensive-care costs for treating babies exposed to drugs range from $7,500 to $31,000. In some cases medical bills go as high as $150,000.

The costs grow enormously as more and more hospitals encounter the problem of "boarder babies"—those children literally abandoned at the hospital by an addicted mother, and left to be cared for by the nursing staff. Future costs to society for simply educating a generation of drug-affected children can only be the object of speculation. It is clear, however, that besides pain, suffering, and death the economic costs to society of drug use by pregnant women is presently enormous and is certainly growing larger.

THE PROSECUTOR'S RESPONSE

It is against this backdrop and fueled by the evergrowing emphasis on an aggressively waged war on drugs that prosecutors have begun a number of actions against women who have given birth to drug-affected children. A review of at least two cases will illustrate the potential success or failure of attempts to use existing statutes.

People v. Melanie Green   On February 4, 1989, at a Rockford, Illinois hospital, two-day-old Bianca Green lost her brief struggle for life. At the time of Bianca's birth both she and her mother, twenty-four-year-old Melanie Green, tested positive for the presence of cocaine in their systems.

Pathologists in Rockford and Madison, Wisconsin, indicated that the death of the baby was the result of a prenatal injury related to cocaine used by the mother during the pregnancy. They asserted that maternal cocaine use had caused the placenta to prematurely rupture, which deprived the fetus of oxygen before and during delivery. As a result of oxygen deprivation, the child's brain began to swell and she eventually died.

After an investigation by the Rockford Police Department and the State of Illinois Department of Children and Family Services, prosecutors allowed a criminal complaint to be filed on May 9, 1989, charging Melanie Green with the offenses of Involuntary Manslaughter and Delivery of a Controlled Substance.

On May 25, 1989, testimony was presented to the Winnebago County Grand Jury by prosecutors seeking a formal indictment. The Grand Jury, however, declined to indict Green on either charge. Since Grand Jury proceedings in the State of Illinois are secret, as are the jurors' deliberations and votes, the reason for the decision of the Grand Jury in this case is determined more by conjecture than any direct knowledge. Prosecutors involved in the presentation observed that the jurors exhibited a certain amount of sympathy for the young woman who had been brought before the Grand Jury at the jurors' request. It is also likely that the jurors were uncomfortable with the use of statutes that were not intended to be used in these circumstances.

It would also be difficult to disregard the fact that, after the criminal complaints were announced on May 9th and prior to the Grand Jury deliberations of May 25th, a national debate had ensued revolving around the charges brought in Rockford, Illinois, and their implications for the ever-increasing problem of women who use drugs during pregnancy.

People v. Jennifer Clarise Johnson On July 13, 1989, a Seminole County, Florida judge found Jennifer Johnson guilty of delivery of a controlled substance to a child. The judge found that delivery, for purposes of the statute, occurred through the umbilical cord after the birth of the child and before the cord was severed. Jeff Deen, the Assistant State's Attorney who prosecuted the case, has since pointed out that Johnson, age 23, had previously given birth to three other cocaine-affected babies, and in this case was arrested at a crack house. "We needed to make sure this woman does not give birth to another cocaine baby."

Johnson was sentenced to fifteen years of probation including strict supervision, drug treatment, random drug testing, educational and vocational training, and an intensive prenatal care program if she ever became pregnant again.

SUPPORT FOR THE PROSECUTION OF MATERNAL DRUG ABUSE

Both cases reported above relied on a single important fact as a basis for the prosecution of the drug-abusing mother: that the child was born alive and exhibited the consequences of prenatal injury.

In the Melanie Green case, Illinois prosecutors relied on the "born alive" rule set out earlier in *People v. Bolar.* In *Bolar* the defendant was convicted of the offense of reckless homicide. The case involved an accident between a car driven by the defendant, who was found to be drunk, and another automobile containing a pregnant woman. As a result, the woman delivered her baby by emergency caesarean section within hours of the collision. Although the newborn child exhibited only a few heart beats and lived for approximately two minutes, the court found that the child was born alive and was therefore a person for purposes of the criminal statutes of the State of Illinois.

The Florida prosecution relied on a live birth in an entirely different fashion. The prosecutor argued in that case that the delivery of the controlled substance occurred after the live birth via the umbilical cord and prior to the cutting of the cord. Thus, it was argued, that the delivery of the controlled substance occurred not to a fetus but to a person who enjoyed the protection of the criminal code of the State of Florida.

Further support for the State's role in protecting the health of newborns even against prenatal injury is found in the statutes which provide protection for the fetus. These statutes proscribe actions by a person, usually other than the mother, which either intentionally or recklessly harm or kill a fetus. In other words, even in the absence of a live birth, most states afford protection to the unborn fetus against the harmful actions of another person. Arguably, the same protection should be afforded the infant against intentional harmful actions by a drug-abusing mother.

The state also receives support for a position in favor of the protection of the health of a newborn from a number of non-criminal cases. A line of civil cases in several states would appear to stand for the principle that a child has a right to begin life with a sound mind and body, and a person who interferes with that right may be subject to civil liability. In two cases decided within months of each other, the Supreme Court of Michigan upheld two actions for recovery of damages that were caused by the infliction of prenatal injury. In *Womack v. Buckhorn* the court upheld an action on behalf of an eight-year-old surviving child for prenatal brain injuries apparently suffered during the fourth month of the pregnancy in an automobile accident. The court adopted with approval the reasoning of a New Jersey Supreme Court decision and "recognized that a child has a legal right to begin life with a sound mind and body." Similarly, in *O'Neill v. Morse* the court found that a cause of action was allowed for prenatal injuries that caused the death of an eight-month-old viable fetus.

Illinois courts have allowed civil recovery on behalf of an infant for a negligently administered blood transfusion given to the mother prior to conception which resulted in damage to the child at birth. However, the same Illinois court would not extend a similar cause of action for prebirth injuries as between a child and its own mother. The court, however, went on to say that a right to such a cause of action could be statutorily enacted by the Legislature.

Additional support for the state's role in protecting the health of newborns is found in the principles annunciated in recent decisions of the United States Supreme Court. The often cited case of *Roe v. Wade* set out that although a woman's right of privacy is broad enough to cover the abortion decision, the right is not absolute and is subject to limitations, "and that at some point the state's interest as to protection of health, medical standards and prenatal life, becomes dominant."

More recently, in the case of *Webster v. Reproductive Health Services,* the court expanded the state's interest in protecting potential human life by setting aside viability as a rigid line that had previously allowed state regulation only after viability had been shown but prohibited it before viability. The court goes on to say that the "fundamental right" to abortion as described in *Roe* is now accorded the lesser status of a "liberty interest." Such language surely supports a prosecutor's argument that the state's compelling interest in potential human life would allow the criminalization of acts which if committed by a pregnant woman can damage not just a viable fetus but eventually a born-alive infant. It follows that, once a pregnant woman has abandoned her right to abort and has decided to carry the fetus to term, society can well impose a duty on the mother to insure that the fetus is born as healthy as possible.

A further argument in support of the state's interest in prosecuting women who engage in conduct which is damaging to the health of a newborn child is especially compelling in regard to maternal drug use during pregnancy. Simply put, there is no fundamental right or even a liberty interest in the use of psycho-active drugs. A perceived right of privacy has never formed an absolute barrier against state prosecutions of those who use or possess narcotics. Certainly no exception can be made simply because the person using drugs happens to be pregnant.

Critics of the prosecutor's role argue that any statute that would punish mothers who create a substantial risk of harm to their fetus will run afoul of constitutional requirements, including prohibitions on vagueness, guarantees of liberty and privacy, and rights of due process and equal protection....

In spite of such criticism, the state's role in protecting those citizens who are least able to protect themselves, namely the newborn, mandates an aggressive posture. Much of the criticism of prosecutorial efforts is based on speculation as to the consequences of prosecution and ignores the basic tenet of criminal law that prosecutions deter the prosecuted and others from committing additional crimes. To assume that it will only drive persons further underground is to somehow argue that certain prosecutions of crime will only force perpetrators to make even more aggressive efforts to escape apprehension, thus making arrest and prosecution unadvisable. Neither could this be accepted as an argument justifying even the weakening of criminal sanctions....

The concern that pregnant addicts will avoid obtaining health care for themselves or their infants because of the fear of prosecution cannot justify the absence of state action to protect the newborn. If the state were to accept such reasoning, then existing child abuse laws would have to be reconsidered since

they might deter parents from obtaining medical care for physically or sexually abused children. That argument has not been accepted as a valid reason for abolishing child abuse laws or for not prosecuting child abusers....

The far better policy is for the state to acknowledge its responsibility not only to provide a deterrant to criminal and destructive behavior by pregnant addicts but also to provide adequate opportunities for those who might seek help to discontinue their addiction. Prosecution has a role in its ability to deter future criminal behavior and to protect the best interests of the child. The medical and social welfare establishment must assume an even greater responsibility to encourage legislators to provide adequate funding and facilities so that no pregnant woman who is addicted to drugs will be denied the opportunity to seek appropriate prenatal care and treatment for her addiction.

ONE STATE'S RESPONSE

The Legislature of the State of Illinois at the urging of local prosecutors moved quickly to amend its juvenile court act in order to provide protection to those children born drug-affected. Previously, Illinois law provided that a court could assume jurisdiction over addicted minors or a minor who is generally declared neglected or abused.

Effective January 1, 1990, the juvenile court act was amended to expand the definition of a neglected or abused minor....

> those who are neglected include... any newborn infant whose blood or urine contains any amount of a controlled substance....

The purpose of the new statute is to make it easier for the court to assert jurisdiction over a newborn infant born drug-affected. The state is not required to show either the addiction of the child or harmful effects on the child in order to remove the child from a drug-abusing mother. Used in this context, prosecutors can work with the mother in a rather coercive atmosphere to encourage her to enter into drug rehabilitation and, upon the successful completion of the program, be reunited with her child.

Additional legislation before the Illinois Legislature is House Bill 2835 sponsored by Representatives John Hallock (R-Rockford) and Edolo "Zeke" Giorgi (D-Rockford). This bill represents the first attempt to specifically address the prosecution of drug-abusing pregnant women. . . .

The statute provides for a class 4 felony disposition upon conviction. A class 4 felony is a probationable felony which can also result in a term of imprisonment from one to three years.

Subsequent paragraphs set out certain defenses available to the accused.

> It shall not be a violation of this section if a woman knowingly or intentionally uses a narcotic or dangerous drug in the first twelve weeks of pregnancy and: 1. She has no knowledge that she is pregnant; or 2. Subsequently, within the first twelve weeks of pregnancy, undergoes medical treatment for substance abuse or treatment or rehabilitation in a program or facility approved by the Illinois Department of Alcoholism and Substance Abuse, and thereafter discontinues any further use of drugs or narcotics as previously set forth.

. . . A woman, under this statute, could not be prosecuted for self-reporting her addiction in the early stages of the pregnancy. Nor could she be prosecuted under this statute if, even during the subsequent stages of the pregnancy, she discontinued her drug use to the extent that no drugs were present in her system or the baby's system at the time of birth. The statute, as drafted, is clearly intended to allow prosecutors to invoke the criminal statutes in the most serious of cases.

CONCLUSION

Local prosecutors have a legitimate role in responding to the increasing problem of drug-abusing pregnant women and their drug-affected children. Eliminating the pain, suffering and death resulting from drug exposure in newborns must be a prosecutor's priority. However, the use of existing statutes to address the problem may meet with limited success since they are burdened with numerous constitutional problems dealing with original intent, notice, vagueness, and due process.

The juvenile courts may offer perhaps the best initial response in working to protect the interests of a surviving child. However, in order to address more serious cases, legislative efforts may be required to provide new statutes that will specifically address the problem and hopefully deter future criminal conduct which deprives children of their important right to a healthy and normal birth.

The long-term solution does not rest with the prosecutor alone. Society, including the medical and social welfare establishment, must be more responsive in providing readily accessible prenatal care and treatment alternatives for pregnant addicts. In the short term however, prosecutors must be prepared to play a vital role in protecting children and deterring women from engaging in conduct which will harm the newborn child. If prosecutors fail to respond, then they are simply closing the doors of the criminal justice system to those persons, the newborn, who are least able to open the doors for themselves.

NO

Sue Mahan

CRIMINALIZATION OF PREGNANCY

ANALYSIS OF JUDICIAL ALTERNATIVES

Criminalization

A large number of criminal actions against cocaine-abusing pregnant women originate in Florida, reflecting a punitive approach to crack mothers. There are more pregnant women in prison in Florida than in any other state, and a number of babies are born while their mothers are incarcerated in the state (Maguire & Pastore, 1994).

Criminally prosecuting mothers who give birth to drug-dependent babies conflicts with the stated public policy underlying Florida's child welfare laws. The Florida legislature's paramount concern in providing comprehensive protective services for abused and neglected children is supposed to be "to preserve the family life of the parent and children, to the maximum extend possible, by enhancing the parental capacity for adequate child care." Instead, enforcing a punitive policy actually results in lower parental capacity to provide for adequate child care. Criminal prosecutions needlessly destroy the family by incarcerating the mother when alternative measures could both protect the child and stabilize the family (Spitzer, 1987).

This contradiction between goals and application of one state's policy on pregnant substance abusers is typical. Discrepancies among policies, legislation, and case law concerning crack babies in many states resulted from public confusion and hasty responses that accompanied the fear of the crack epidemic spreading across the United States in the late 1980s.

Public policy, procedure, and laws designed to control women who use drugs during their pregnancy can be classified into three types: narcotics laws, criminalization laws, and informant laws. All three types of law focus on punishing a mother for drug use so that the fetus will be protected.

Narcotics laws apply existing prohibitions against drug possession and distribution to pregnant women. Both men and women lose their liberty when they are convicted for illegal drug use; pregnant women may lose their liberty for longer. The intent of existing narcotics laws has been expanded so that women can be charged with delivering a controlled substance to a minor when the recipient is a fetus or newborn infant.

Criminalization laws are recently drafted statutes that specifically define behaviors such as fetal endangerment or fetal abuse. Many authors have called this fetal abuse path in policy a legal "slippery slope" (Bagley & Merlo, 1995). Fetal abuse laws have two important limitations. They define a fetus as a child, but court decisions have not supported the concept of a fetus as a separate entity. They also hold the rights of a fetus as above the rights of a pregnant woman to make decisions about her own body.

Informant laws are those most often used to take away the rights of the mother. Informant laws require health care workers or other treatment providers to report suspected or actual drug use by pregnant women. Women who are routinely subjected to drug testing or the testing of their newborns are likely to be poor and either black or Hispanic.

Fetal Abuse as Child Abuse

When pregnant mothers are charged with "child abuse" before their babies have been born, there may be some question about how the behavior is defined in the law. In most statutes, reference is made to nonaccidental harm inflicted on children by those responsible for their care. Three issues arise from thee statutes: the meaning of "nonaccidental," the proof of harm, and whether fetuses are to be considered as children.

Child abuse laws are enacted at the state level. Their purpose is to protect infants and children from abuse and neglect perpetrated by parents or guardians. When someone reports to a state's division of child protective services that a child is being abused or neglected, a worker usually will conduct a preliminary investigation. If abuse or neglect is substantiated, the worker may petition the court for temporary custody of the child.

In many states, child protective service agencies have petitioned the courts in order to get protective custody of fetuses. In these actions, it has been affirmed that the child (fetus) is or will be abused or neglected. The Supreme Court, however, upheld that for state child protection laws to apply to the unborn fetus, the laws must specifically define a "fetus" as a "child," or it must be clear that the state legislature intended an unborn fetus to be considered a child under the child abuse and neglect laws (*Webster v. Reproductive Health Services*, 1989).

Some state divisions of child protective services have tried to obtain protective custody of a fetus in order to get custody of the child upon birth. New Jersey enacted a child protection statute that is applicable to an unborn fetus. The statute provides,

> Whenever it shall appear that any child within this state is of such circumstances that his welfare will be endangered unless proper care or custody is provided, an application *may be filed* seeking that the Bureau of Children's Services accept and provide such care or custody of such child as the circumstances may require. The provisions of this section shall be deemed to include an application on behalf of an unborn child. (NJ Stat. Ann. §30:4C-11)

When a charge of improper parenting or delivery of a controlled substance is based on using illicit substances while pregnant, the question that must be addressed by the court is whether fetal abuse is child abuse. Most states do not recognize fetal abuse as child abuse (Kantrowitz, 1989). The following is Florida's statute (1993) with regard to child abuse; many states have similar statutes.

> Whoever, willfully or by culpable negligence, deprives a child of, or allows a child to be deprived of, necessary food, clothing, shelter, or medical treatment, or who, knowingly or by culpable negligence, permits physical or mental injury to a child, and in so doing causes great bodily harm, permanent disability, or permanent disfigurement to such child, shall be guilty of a felony of the third degree. (Sec. 827.04(1))

At the district level, some courts of appeal have held that a child abuse statute does not include a fetus and, therefore, that the defendant cannot be prosecuted for child abuse based on introduction of drugs into her own body during gestation (*State v. Gethers*, 1991). A New York City court also held that a defendant cannot be charged with endangering the welfare of a child based on acts that endanger the unborn (*The People of the State of New York v. Melissa A. Morabito*, 1992). The Kentucky Supreme Court decided that the offense of criminal child abuse does not extend to the defendant's use of drugs while pregnant (*Commonwealth v. Welch*, 1993).

Many cases of drug-exposed and drug-addicted infants reach the dependency side of the juvenile court. The first point of entry of drug-exposed infants and their families into the juvenile court system is often immediately after birth. Many hospitals routinely perform neonatal toxicology screens when maternal substance abuse is suspected. Based on a positive toxicology test, the hospital may report the results to the child protective services agency, which in turn may ask the juvenile court to prevent he child's release to the parents while an investigation takes place. Child neglect is an issue with "boarder babies" being abandoned by their parents. Crack addiction is said to have led to the creation of a large number of babies being boarded in maternity, pediatric, and other settings because they have been abandoned by, or taken away from, their parents (Levy & Rutter, 1992). Babies being abandoned may be directly related to threats of civil and criminal action and to fear of authorities on the part of childbearing addicts. Threat of court action against pregnant drug users may also be indirectly responsible for harm inflicted from unprofessional abortions and lack of adequate care during pregnancy.

Courts have ruled that the use of drugs during pregnancy is by itself sufficient basis to trigger a child-abuse report and to support juvenile court dependency jurisdiction (Sagatun, 1993).

Such cases, however, seldom are upheld on appeal. For example, the Court of Appeals of Ohio decided that the juvenile court has no jurisdiction to regulate the conduct of a pregnant adult for the purpose of protecting the health of her unborn child (*Cox v. Court of Common Pleas*, 1988).

Although the sate may justify coercion of cocaine mothers on the basis of its interest in protecting the fetus, it does not undertake any duty to ensure the necessary care for the woman's body. Instead, when pregnant addicts are handled by the court, the duty for protecting the fetus is imposed entirely on the pregnant woman. A wide variety of acts or conditions on the part of a pregnant woman could pose some threat to her fetus, including failure to eat well; using nonprescription, prescription, or illegal drugs; engaging in sexual intercourse; exercising or not exercising; smoking; drinking alcohol; and even ingesting something as common as caffeine. Other threats, such as physical harm resulting from accident or disease and working or living near toxic substances, also are significant when it comes to imposing responsibility (Kasinsky, 1993).

Harm and danger to a potential life may be greatest from an environment over which the mother has little control. The perils of pollution and ecological damage to unborn children, which are the responsibility of the state, remain unconsidered in child abuse and neglect issues (Mariner, Glantz, & Annas, 1990).

These environmental risks are likely to be high for those pregnant women who also are at the greatest risk of being criminalized for substance abuse.

Delivery of a Controlled
Substance to a Minor

Women can be charged with delivery of a controlled substance to a minor when blood test results are positive for cocaine at the moment of birth. This action presumes that health care personnel will provide information and that the mother has no right to privacy. The state can require a physician to administer a toxicology test to a pregnant women without her consent if there is a compelling interest that outweighs her Fourth Amendment right to privacy from government intrusion. The state statute, however, must be strictly worded for the protection of infant rights over the rights of the mother (Appel, 1992).

The state of Missouri has one such strictly worded statute. Its wording includes the following:

[N]eglect also includes prenatal exposure to a controlled substance ... used by the mother for a non-medical purpose, as evidenced by withdrawal symptoms in the child at birth, results of a toxicology test performed on the mother at delivery or the child at birth, or medical effects or developmental delays during the child's first year of life that medically indicate prenatal exposure to a controlled substance.

In addition any

person with responsibility for the care of children, [who] has reasonable cause to suspect that a child has been or may be subjected to conditions or circumstances which would reasonably result in abuse or neglect, including the use of a controlled substance by a pregnant women for a non-medical purpose, ... shall immediately report or cause a report to be made to the Missouri division of family services. (Missouri Senate Bill No. 756, 1990)

Many medical and legal experts criticize the practice of administering toxicology tests to nonconsenting pregnant women. These experts believe that toxicology tests given without the knowledge or consent of the patient violate their professional trust (Appel, 1992). Such tests raise the issues of discrimination, consent, and confidentiality. They often target women who cannot afford prenatal care or who can afford only to go to public hospitals or clinics. These women are labeled "high risk" and are tested routinely without their consent. Those who can afford private care remain effectively insulated from this form of state intrusion (Robin-Vergeer, 1990).

Hair analysis also has been used in some studies to detect gestational cocaine exposure. Samples of hair are collected from the mothers, and meconium, urine, and hair are also collected from newborns ("Best Way," 1992; Marques, Tipetts, &

Branch, 199). Intrusiveness and right to privacy issues are important with hair analysis, as with urine and blood testing.

Florida, along with many other states, passed a statute in 1987 calling for state intervention when infants are born drug dependent. It was argued that although legislators may not have the right to protect the unborn, they must make an effort to protect the quality of life for children born to drug-dependent mothers. Hospital workers are required to notify the state department of Health and Rehabilitative Services immediately whenever babies are born with drugs in their systems. Child dependency proceedings can then be initiated to remove the child from parental custody (Spitzer, 1987). Throughout the United States, special prosecutors handling child abuse cases have made it clear that no woman, whether she is pregnant or not, has the right to use cocaine. In this area, they see no reason for concern about legal rights (Curriden, 1990).

Jennifer Johnson was the first woman in the United States to be convicted for delivery of a controlled substance to a minor on the birth of a baby with traces of cocaine in her system. The Florida Supreme Court did not uphold the conviction.

Likewise, the circuit court in Michigan held that the use of cocaine by pregnant women, which may result in postpartum transfer of cocaine through the umbilical cord to their infants, is not the type of conduct that the legislature intended to be prosecuted under the *delivery of cocaine* statutes (*People v. Hardy*, 1991).

The court decisions are, no doubt, a reaction to the obvious limits of the criminal approach to the problem of cocaine pregnancies. In order to have proof of delivery of a controlled substance to the new-born child, the child must be born alive. In addition, evidence of delivery of cocaine must rest on blood tests done at the moment of birth. Positive results indicate cocaine use very close to the delivery. There is no way to prove delivery of cocaine to the fetus in the first or second trimester of pregnancy, although the damage to the developing child from drug use may be great during the early stages and long before the moment of birth.

Medical personnel may avoid reporting cocaine use by pregnant women because they believe that, out of fear of prosecution, mothers will stay away from prenatal care (Mills & Bishop, 1990). Some prosecutors disagree. Those who favor criminal sanctions say that the fear of pregnant addicts avoiding prenatal care is not a sufficient concern to interfere with the action of the state to protect the unborn. From this perspective, if laws against crack mothers should not be enforced because they might keep pregnant addicts from seeking prenatal care, then child abuse laws should not be enforced either. Child abuse penalties may deter parents from obtaining medical care for abused children out of fear of criminal consequences in the same ways that crack abuse penalties may deter mothers from seeking medical care for themselves while pregnant (Logli, 1990).

Although the state's motive in prosecuting pregnant women may be to provide an incentive for them to stop using drugs, drug treatment is largely unavailable to them. Their pregnancy acts as a disqualifying factor for most programs (Kasinsky, 1993).

Manslaughter

Pregnant drug users may be charged with manslaughter even though the statutes were intended for third party criminal culpability. For example, the Florida criminal code makes the willful killing of an unborn quick child, by any injury *to the mother* of such child that would be murder if it resulted in the death of such mother, to be deemed manslaughter, a felony in the second degree (Florida Criminal Code 782.09, 1992). The law does not mention injury done *by the mother* to herself, yet there have been cases after the second trimester in which infants were stillborn and their mothers were charged with manslaughter. The court must decide that the death resulted from cocaine use for a crack mother to be convicted of manslaughter.

Attributing the stillbirth of an infant to cocaine abuse and considering this to be manslaughter comes from a "reasonable person" perspective about the law. The rationale behind this approach is that pregnant women are being asked only to act reasonably. If a women elects to have unprotected sex, and once pregnant elects not to have an abortion, she takes on the additional responsibilities to see that, as far as possible, the child will be born healthy (Curriden, 1990). This may not seem so reasonable to a pregnant crack user.

The pregnant addict may not realize that she is pregnant until far into the first trimester and after significant risk of damage to the fetus already has been incurred. She may expect that if she uses cocaine, she is likely to have a spontaneous abortion. Although the numbers of spontaneous miscarriages among cocaine-abusing pregnant women are high, using the drug may not bring about the results she sought, and instead an unhealthy infant may result.

Finally, holding responsible for the health birth of the child the pregnant mother who carries her fetus to full term, rather than electing to have an abortion, assumes that safe, no-cost abortions are available to all women in the first few weeks of pregnancy. Legal, medically authorized abortions are not free to any female who wants to have one. Adequate prenatal health care is not easily available to all pregnant women, either. Without them, pregnant addicts in the throes of a lifestyle of compulsion are not likely to take care of their own health and well-being or to be responsible for that of their unborn children.

It is doubtful whether manslaughter charges would ever result in a conviction for a cocaine mother if tested in a jury trial. It is even more unlikely that the charge would be upheld in an appeal to a higher court. The case law is clear: The legal conception of "person" does not include a fetus (Spitzer, 1987). The Supreme Court has held that at no state of development is a fetus a "person" with legal rights separate from those of the mother (Paltrow, 1990). When cocaine mothers have been convicted of manslaughter, it was the result of their guilty pleas without the deliberation of public trials.

Involuntary Detention

Punishment, rehabilitation, and deterrence all have been used to justify involuntary detention of pregnant addicts, along with education and protection for the "infant" (Mills & Bishop, 1990). For some, detention is the key element in treating pregnant cocaine addicts to reduce the severity of the effects of cocaine use on the fetus (New York Senate Committee on Investigations, Taxation and Government Operations, 1989). According to *The New York Times*, when medical doctors who were maternal-fetal specialists were surveyed in 1986, more than half of them agreed that pregnant women who refuse medical advice and endanger the life of the fetus should be detained in hospitals and forced to follow their physicians' orders (Lewin, 1987). Some law enforcement agents and state prosecutors have justified the detention of pregnant cocaine addicts in jails and lock-up facilities for this reason, not necessarily because of punishment or retributive goals.

In effect, the state has taken custody of a child before it is born (Gest, 1989). In other words, the mother-fetus relationship can cause conflict because the treatment of one involves the mistreatment of the other. There is an understood obligation to the mother's health and well-being, but with involuntary detention, the health and well-being of the fetus comes first, although this is not a legally recognized obligation (Nelson & Milliken, 1988).

Some public officials and researchers have suggested that drug users can be civilly committed to a drug treatment program while they are pregnant. Involuntary civil commitment is a process whereby an individual is found to pose a danger to herself or others and is forced to undergo care. Conditions that usually subject a person to civil commitment include mental illness, developmental retardation, mental retardation, alcoholism, drug dependency, or some combination of these factors. Approximately 75% of the states have some statutory provision governing the involuntary commitment of drug-dependent persons (Garcia & Keilitz, 1990). In these states, the laws limit involuntary civil commitments to drug-dependent persons in need of treatment and care, who are likely to be dangerous to themselves or others, or who are unable to meet their basic needs for sustenance, shelter, and

self-protection. Pregnant drug users may be subject to laws that find them to be dangers to themselves because of their actions, or maternal addiction may be deemed to endanger an "other" with protectable rights. Addicts may lose their maternal rights as well as their rights to liberty in civil proceedings because they are considered dangerous, even though no criminal charge can be made.

When pregnant drug users are charged with any offense, they can be subject to the discretionary orders of the judge before whom they appear. For example, judges throughout the country are sentencing pregnant drug offenders to enter drug treatment facilities. Prosecutors are also arguing successfully that release from jail or prison be made conditional on completion of drug treatment. Judicial discretion also can affect the length of sentence imposed. Sometimes judges impose longer sentences on pregnant drug users. In 1993, 489 pregnant women were being held in state corrections institutions (in 47 states for which there were reports), and 105 pregnant inmates were in federal custody. During that year, there were 789 reported births in inmates (Maguire & Pastore, 1994). Many more went uncounted because inmates delivered in community facilities and then returned to the state or federal prison to complete their sentences. These are only a small proportion of the pregnant women being detained. The number of pregnant inmates serving terms in county jails and local facilities is not available. It is likely that most crack addicts are sentenced to misdemeanor terms in local corrections facilities to detain them until their babies are born.

Jailing pregnant drug users may not reduce harm to the fetus at all. In jail, where the mother may be experiencing extreme stress, there actually may be an increased chance of fetal distress. In addition, pregnant women may not get adequate medical care. Health care providers within the criminal justice system are neither well equipped nor prepared to handle obstetrics.

When judges tailor a woman's sentence to her reproductive status, the resulting harsher treatment has an impact not only for the individual being sentenced but for all women in general. Women who suffer from drug or alcohol dependency and AIDS do not exist in a social, political, and economic vacuum, yet when policy calls for criminalization and medicalization for these problems, each individual is treated without consideration of her environmental concerns. The conditions of poverty, discrimination, unemployment, inadequate health care services, and violence against women are not addressed. General social problems underlying the symptoms confronted in criminal courts and crisis health care treatment are ignored (Bagley & Merlo, 1995).

Women who do seek help for drug addiction during pregnancy cannot get it. Two-thirds of the hospitals surveyed by the House Select Committee reported they had not drug treatment programs to which their pregnant patients could be referred; none reported the availability of special programs geared to providing comprehensive drug treatment and prenatal care (Kasinsky, 1993). Without treatment, prosecutions are simply punitive stopgaps, and reporting laws force poor women of minority groups to surrender their children (Humphries, 1993).

Fetal Endangerment

Fundamental rights. The use of narcotics and cocaine already is illegal. Many states have found it sufficient simply to enforce already existing laws rather than add penalties for pregnant women. When laws make actions criminal that only women can commit, the laws are, by their nature, discriminatory.

Prosecutions by the criminal justice system for drug use have been of predominantly poor women of minority backgrounds who have given birth to drug-exposed babies. Between 1987 and 1991, at least 165 women in 26 states were arrested on criminal charges because of their drug behavior during pregnancy. Tens of thousands more women have had their children removed from them and taken into custody by welfare agencies. Poor women have been prosecuted by a largely white social welfare establishment; more than half of all the recent prosecutions of pregnant women were of women of color (Kasinsky, 1993).

Women are being prosecuted for behavior that *may be* harmful without proof that the behavior *has been* harmful. The failed duty of these women is failure to avoid risk, not failure to avoid harm (Reed, 1993).

Rights of women. There has been increasingly outspoken opposition of public health organizations to prosecutions of cocaine-addicted pregnant women (Paltrow, 1990). The very nature of the problem mandates that whatever action criminal justice authorities may take will be possible only with the cooperation and support of health care providers.

Health care providers are being asked to supply information to legal and criminal authorities if pregnant patients are using cocaine. It is not clear by what judicial standard a mother may have her acts of commission and omission while pregnant made subject to state scrutiny (Paltrow, 1990). Health care providers are being asked to take on a role outside the purview of their professions. As informants for the state, they are also acting in potential violation of patients' rights.

Rather than a focus on criminalization of pregnant addicts, a more comprehensive and complex policy is needed. Instead of filtering pregnant substance abusers through the costly process of criminalization, women in need of care can be identified by outreach workers in their neighborhoods. Some drug treatment programs have employed former addicts as outreach workers. Workers go to laundromats, grocery stores, and crack houses searching for pregnant women on drugs. These neighborhood workers are more likely than others to be effective in encouraging pregnant women to seek care and helping them find appropriate drug treatment, health care, and family services (Appel, 1992).

When compared with that of other industrialized countries, the infant mortality rate is high in the United States, and the rate of infant death has climbed since the 1970s. Despite a high standard of living, the United States ranks low on this significant indicator of quality of life. Improving the status of the nation in this important area will come only when all pregnant women are provided with quality prenatal care and assistance before and throughout their pregnancies. Making infant mortality a priority for change means addressing the multiple health care problems of all childbearing women (Merlo, 1993).

Structural issues. To some, laws relating to family life are important because of their direct effect in coercing compliance. The real importance of these laws is that they set the outer limits of what the community regards as morally tolerable (Johnson, 1990). Prohibitory laws show that concern is not really focused on the well-being of infants, nor that of their mothers. Drastic action toward cocaine mothers and other substance abusers reflects public fear and loathing toward crack cocaine. The risks faced by pregnant women in the workplace and in substandard housing without adequate health care are not considered; instead, responsibility for the fetus is made a personal responsibility.

In assessing blame, criminal law focuses on the past. A wiser approach is to look toward the future, in which the well-being of both the mother and the child should be of equal importance to a society that has an interest in producing future generations of healthy people.

POSTSCRIPT

Should Pregnant Drug Users Be Prosecuted?

Babies born with health problems as a result of their mothers' drug use is a tragedy that needs to be rectified. The issue is not whether or not this problem needs to be addressed but what course of action is best. The need for medical intervention and specialized treatment programs serving pregnant women with drug problems has been recognized. The groundwork has been set for funding and developing such programs. The Office of Substance Abuse Prevention is funding chemical dependency programs specifically for pregnant women in several states.

Mahan argues that drug use by pregnant women is a medical problem that requires medical, not criminal, attention. She supports the notion that pregnant drug users and their drug-exposed infants are victims of drug abuse. She also feels that there is an element of discrimination in the practice of prosecuting women who use drugs during pregnancy because these women are predominantly low-income, single, members of minorities, and recipients of public assistance. Possible factors leading to their drug use—poverty, unemployment, poor education, and lack of vocational training—are not addressed when the solution to drug use during pregnancy is incarceration. Moreover, many pregnant women are denied access to treatment programs.

Prosecution proponents contend that medical intervention is not adequate in preventing pregnant women from using drugs and that criminal prosecution is necessary. Logli argues that "eliminating the pain, suffering and death resulting from drug exposure in newborns must be a prosecutor's priority." He maintains that the criminal justice system should protect newborns and, if legal cause does exist for prosecution, then statutes should provide protection for the fetus. However, will prosecution result in more protection or less protection for the fetus? If a mother stops using drugs for fear of prosecution, then the fetus benefits. If the mother avoids prenatal care because of potential legal punishment, then the fetus suffers.

If women can be prosecuted for using illegal drugs such as cocaine and narcotics during pregnancy because they harm the fetus, then should women who smoke cigarettes and drink alcohol during pregnancy also be prosecuted? The evidence is clear that tobacco and alcohol place the fetus at great risk; however, most discussions of prosecuting pregnant drug users overlook women who use these drugs. Also, the adverse health effects from secondhand smoke are well documented. Should people be prosecuted if they smoke around pregnant women?

Two articles that address the effects of prenatal exposure to cocaine are "The Impact of Maternal Cocaine Use on Neonates in Socioeconomic Disadvantaged Population," by Wei Yue Sun and William Chen, *Journal of Drug Education* (vol. 27, no. 4, 1997) and "Hope for Snow Babies," by Sharon Begley, *Newsweek* (September 29, 1997). In "Punishment, Treatment, Empowerment: Three Approaches to Policy for Pregnant Addicts," *Feminist Studies* (Spring 1994), Iris Marion Young contends that punishing pregnant addicts may be both racist and sexist. In "Alcohol-Induced Cell Death in the Embryo," *Alcohol Health and Research World* (vol. 21, no. 4, 1997), Susan M. Smith describes the effects of alcohol on the embryo.

Two additional articles that examine this issue are "Crack in the Cradle: Social Policy and Reproductive Rights Among Crack-Using Females," by John Lieb and Claire Strek-Elifson, *Contemporary Drug Problems* (Winter 1995) and "How Social Policies Make Matters Worse: The Case of Maternal Substance Abuse," by Maureen Norton-Hawk, *Journal of Drug Issues* (Summer 1994).

ISSUE 6

Should Young People Be Taught How to Use Marijuana?

YES: **Marsha Rosenbaum,** from " 'Just Say Know' to Teenagers and Marijuana," *Journal of Psychoactive Drugs* (April–June 1998)

NO: **Wayne Hall and Nadia Solowij,** from "Adverse Effects of Cannabis," *The Lancet* (November 14, 1998)

ISSUE SUMMARY

YES: Marsha Rosenbaum, director of the Lindesmith Center in San Francisco, California, supports teaching young people how to use marijuana responsibly in order to reduce the potential problems of marijuana use. She argues that telling young people that they should not use marijuana and relating horror stories connected to its use have not reduced marijuana use.

NO: Writers Wayne Hall and Nadia Solowij maintain that marijuana causes numerous medical, psychological, perceptual-motor, and academic problems and that its use should be discouraged.

The authors of both selections presented here recognize that marijuana use is not desirable. Although opinions on the severity of the problems associated with marijuana vary, there is little debate that marijuana use entails potential harm. The question debated in this issue is, What is the best strategy for reducing the potential physical, psychological, intellectual, and social problems resulting from marijuana use? Is it more desirable to make young people aware of all the dangers that can be caused by marijuana or to teach young people how to use marijuana in a way that reduces its potential problems?

Surveys of 8th-, 10th-, and 12th-grade American students have shown that usage rates of marijuana and other drugs during the 1990s rose significantly for all three grade levels. It is apparent that efforts to reduce drug use, including the use of marijuana, have been ineffective. One is left with the question of whether more effective strategies for reducing or stopping drug use need to be implemented or whether a program needs to be developed that would teach young people who do use marijuana how to use it without hurting themselves.

A critical point in this debate revolves around whether or not it is even possible to teach young people how to use marijuana responsibly. Are American teens mature enough to comprehend a message of responsible use? In one sense this point is oxymoronic because how can someone be taught to use a substance responsibly (in this case marijuana) if the substance is illegal? Because marijuana is illegal, any use could be construed as irresponsible. Of course, hundreds of thousands of teenagers are using marijuana already, and it is unlikely that they will stop if they are told that it is illegal and unhealthy.

In the following selection, Marsha Rosenbaum states that, because thousands of young people currently use marijuana, and because almost 90 percent have access to it, merely advocating abstinence will not be effective. A nonuse message has been promoted for several decades, yet levels of marijuana use remain high. Rosenbaum maintains that a normal part of adolescence is taking risks and that if young people are going to engage in risk-taking behavior, then they need to be given accurate and nonjudgmental information. She feels that American teenagers are not given enough credit for being able to make wise decisions or for being able to use marijuana safely and moderately.

Rosenbaum considers her approach to educating teenagers about the potential problems of marijuana pragmatic. She feels that too many drug education programs emphasize the dangers of marijuana only. Consequently, teenagers who use marijuana and do not have terrible experiences with it may disregard *any* information about marijuana. In the long run, argues Rosenbaum, providing incorrect or misleading information can be counterproductive. Educators need to be viewed as credible sources of information.

In the second selection, Wayne Hall and Nadia Solowij discuss many problems that may arise from marijuana use. They point out that marijuana impairs short-term memory, attention, motor skills, and reaction time. Thus, marijuana use may have a negative impact on one's ability to operate a motor vehicle. Hall and Solowij also describe how anxiety and panic are the most common side effects among occasional users. They estimate that 1 in 10 users develops a dependency on marijuana, and they describe a wide variety of health problems that have been linked with marijuana use. Hall and Solowij recommend that people refrain from using marijuana.

YES

"JUST SAY KNOW" TO TEENAGERS AND MARIJUANA

Abstract—Despite increasing expenditures on prevention, government survey after survey indicates that marijuana use—which comprises 90% of illicit drug use—has not been eradicated among teenagers. Today's adolescents have been exposed to the largest dose of prevention in our history. After three decades of such efforts, one must ask why young people continue to use marijuana, and why drug education has failed to bring about a marijuana-free teenage America. Drug education falls short because it is based on a "no-use" premise, scare tactics and top-down teaching. Such programs do not educate, and may even be counterproductive for those who choose to say "maybe" or "sometimes," or "yes." Moreover, drug education, as has been the case since its advent, is based on politics rather than science—an enormous taxpayer drain with few demonstrative results. A new strategy for drug education requires a pragmatic view that accepts the ability of teenagers, if educated honestly and in ways they trust, to make wise decisions leading, if not to abstinence, to moderate, controlled, and safe use.

The sprawled body of a young girl lay crushed on the sidewalk the other day after a plunge from the fifth story of a Chicago apartment house. Everyone called it suicide, but actually it was murder. The killer was a narcotic known to America as marijuana, and to history as hashish. It is a narcotic used in the form of cigarettes, comparatively new to the United States and as dangerous as a coiled rattlesnake.

How many murders, suicides, robberies, criminal assaults, holdups, burglaries, and deeds of maniacal insanity it causes each year, especially among the young, can be only conjectured. The sweeping march of its addiction has been so insidious that, in numerous communities, it thrives almost unmolested largely because of the official ignorance of its effects.

From Marsha Rosenbaum, " 'Just Say Know' to Teenagers and Marijuana," *Journal of Psychoactive Drugs*, vol. 30, no. 2 (April/June 1998). Copyright © 1998 by Haight Ashbury Publications, 612 Clayton Street, San Francisco, CA 94117. Reprinted by permission of *Journal of Psychoactive Drugs*.

Here indeed is the unknown quantity among narcotics. No one can predict its effect. No one knows, when he places a marijuana cigarette to his lips, whether he will become a philosopher, a joyous reveler in a musical heaven, a mad insensate, a calm philosopher, or a murderer.

That youth has been selected by the peddlers of this poison as an especially fertile field makes it a problem of serious concern to every man and woman in America. (Anslinger & Cooper 1937)

In 1937, Harry Anslinger, then America's Commissioner of the Federal Bureau of Narcotics, warned, as in the above quotation, that marijuana use would lead to the destruction of American youth. Those warnings begot the Marijuana Tax Act of 1937, effectively prohibiting marijuana cultivation, possession, use, sale and distribution. For some thirty years the vast majority of young people in America did not, in fact, use marijuana. Some never heard of it, most never saw or smelled it—until the 1960s when, for social and political reasons, white middle-class students began using marijuana. Since then, beginning with Richard Nixon's war on drugs and continuing through the Clinton administration, marijuana has been associated with the downfall of American youth and prompted massive prevention efforts in the form of drug education.

Drug education programs of the 1960s, derived from the "scare tactics" dating back to the Women's Christian Temperance Movement, were designed to frighten young people out of using marijuana, as well as LSD, heroin and methamphetamine (Beck 1998; Rosenbaum 1996). The programs of the early 1970s carried a more ambivalent mes-

sage, that "... the mere use of addictive drugs was not necessarily bad, that children had to be encouraged to learn all they could about the favorable and unfavorable effects of drugs in order to be able to make their own decisions about drug use." (Goldstein 1994). This "soft" approach, produced by the Drug Abuse Council, the Do It Now Foundation and even the federal government, did not endure. By 1973 the White House Special Action Office for Drug Abuse Prevention stopped producing such materials. During the late 1970s and early 1980s drug education programs proliferated, with the explicit goal of "primary prevention." By 1983 any materials construed as neutral were prohibited. For example, perhaps the most thorough and informative book for teenagers, *Chocolate to Morphine: Understanding Mind-Active Drugs,* by Andrew Weil, M.D. and Winifred Rosen (1983) was hastily removed from drug education curricula shortly after its publication because it stressed the importance of nonabusive relationships with drugs rather than total abstinence.

Still, post-1980 drug education programs were seen as more sophisticated than the old scare tactics. Students were given information about the dangers of drugs as well as concrete psychosocial techniques for countering "peer pressure." Mrs. Reagan instructed inner city children on how to "just say no," while drug education programs gave them heavy doses of self-esteem and self-control to fill the void that rendered them "at risk" to the lure of mind-altering drugs such as marijuana (Rosenbaum 1996).

Despite increasing expenditures on prevention, government survey after survey indicated that marijuana use—which comprises 90% of illicit drug use—was not being eradicated among teenagers. Usage went up and down and then up again, but never disappeared completely. According to the 1996 National Institute on Drug Abuse [NIDA] Household Survey, 16% of teenagers (aged 12 to 17) has used marijuana at some point in their lives (Substance Abuse and Mental Health Services Administration 1997). And according to the Monitoring the Future Survey (Johnston, Bechman & O'Malley 1997), nearly half (49.6%) of high school students had tried marijuana by the time they were seniors. With 7% of teenagers using it monthly (Substance Abuse and Mental Health Services Administration 1997), marijuana use may not be epidemic nor chronic, but it would seem that neither slick advertising, drug education programs, nor punishment has brought about a marijuana-free teenage America.

Drug education is in full-force today, with the federal government spending $2.4 billion annually on such programs (U.S. General Accounting Office 1997). Today's teenagers, as a result of such expenditures, have been exposed to the largest dose of prevention in America's history.

WHY TEENAGERS STILL USE MARIJUANA

After three decades of serious prevention efforts, one must ask why young people continue to use marijuana. Defined loosely, "theories" abound as to why teenagers use marijuana and experiment with drugs in general. Some researchers define marijuana use as "deviant," aberrant behavior caused by a personality problem. Other explanations suggest a "proneness" on the part of certain teenagers to problem behavior such as unconventionality (e.g., sagging pants) and willingness to take risks (e.g., driving too fast). Sociological explanations include lack of ties to family, religion and school, "peer pressure" and membership in drug-using groups. Each of these theories contributes to a partial understanding of teenage marijuana use, but does not tell the whole story (Goode 1993).

Alternative explanations present a more normative view, one which seems more grounded in a society in which nearly half of all teenagers experiment with marijuana. First, the United States is a drug culture. The American people and their children are perpetually bombarded with messages that encourage them to imbibe and medicate with a variety of substances. We routinely alter our states of consciousness through conventional means such as alcohol, tobacco, caffeine, and prescription medications. In this context, and acknowledging that legal-illegal distinctions are irrelevant to many adolescents, experimentation with mind-altering substances such as marijuana could be defined as "normal" (Shedler & Block 1990; Newcomb & Bentler 1988).

Americans are not alone in our drug-taking patterns. Drug use is but one way to alter consciousness, and according to Andrew Weil (1972), the quest to change consciousness may be innate and a universal drive. About children, he says:

> We seem to be born with a drive to experience episodes of altered consciousness. This drive expresses itself at very early ages in all children in activities designed to cause loss or major disturbance of ordinary awareness [spinning around, causing dizziness]. As children grow, they explore many ways of inducing similar changes in consciousness and usually discover chemical methods be-

fore they enter school.... older children come to understand that social support is available for chemical satisfaction of this need by means of alcohol. Today's youth, in the continuing experimentation with methods of changing awareness, have come across a variety of other chemicals which they prefer to alcohol. Thus, use of illegal drugs is nothing more than a logical continuation of a developmental sequence going back to early childhood. It cannot be isolated as a unique phenomenon of adolescence, of contemporary America, of cities, or of any particular social or economic class.

Risk-taking is a normal part of adolescence. Many teenagers feel immortal, and as a consequence take part in activities that strike fear in the hearts of adults (especially their parents). For example, it is no wonder that teenagers learn to drive so easily. They are able to learn how to operate a motor vehicle while oblivious to the dangers of the road (watch a 35-year-old learning how to drive and moving painfully slowly and you'll understand the difference). If marijuana use is defined as risky, it becomes attractive rather than unattractive to teenagers, and in this context its use is predictable.

Despite America's efforts to reduce supply, marijuana is readily available to teenagers. Eighty-five percent of high school seniors report that illegal drugs are "fairly easy" or "very easy" to get (Johnston, Bechman & O'Malley 1996). The ease with which teenagers can buy marijuana is exemplified by the following story. My friend's 75-year-old mother (an Orange County Republican), was recently (after passage of Prop. 215, California's medical marijuana initiative) diagnosed with glaucoma. She asked her physician whether medical marijuana might help. He balked at the suggestion,

saying, "Oh come on now, you don't want to go down that road." She insisted she wanted to try it if it might help prevent blindness. The physician argued, "Well even if I did recommend it, where would you find the marijuana?" To which my friend's mother replied, "Doctor, I've got six teenage grandchildren—I'll have no trouble getting marijuana!" Anecdotes aside, nine in 10 high school seniors report that marijuana is easy to obtain. (Johnston, Bechman & O'Malley 1997).

In America, the desire to change one's level of awareness is anything but deviant. Instead, it is normal, and differs only methodologically. For teenagers, risk-taking goes with the territory. Couple this with availability and it should come as no surprise that teenagers are continuing to use marijuana, despite efforts at deterrence such as drug education.

WHAT'S WRONG WITH DRUG EDUCATION?

Drug education is based on the conviction that marijuana and other illegal drug use is inherently pathological, deviant, and dangerous, and can be explained by disconnection from conventional ties and pressure from marijuana-using friends. Furthermore, advocates of traditional programs (and parents as well) believe that if teenagers are using marijuana, they have a personality problem. Given the right approach, it is argued, it is possible to deter teenagers from its use. Programs are designed, then, to impart information about the dangers of marijuana that will deter students from its use, as well as the social skills to resist peer pressure.

Certainly conventional drug education has had a role in preventing marijuana use among some teenagers. While abstinence-only programs may be useful for those teenagers who choose to abstain, such programs do nothing and may even be counterproductive for those who choose to say "maybe" or "sometimes," or "yes." There are three basic problems with the conventional approach: an abstinence-only-or-else posture; the utilization of misinformation and scare tactics to deter students from using marijuana; and top-down, non-interactive teaching methods.

Government-funded drug education programs in the United States are mandated to teach teenagers to abstain completely from the use of illegal drugs. As noted above, the human desire to alter consciousness may be universal, and is certainly integral to American culture. It should not, therefore come as a surprise that teenagers would experiment with marijuana. In addition, experimentation with marijuana is part of a composite of "deviant" activities that comes with adolescence. The expectation that teenagers, at a time in their lives when they are most amenable to risk-taking, will be inoculated from experimentation with consciousness change is unreal at best (U.S. General Accounting Office 1993). In fact, as noted earlier, nearly half of all American teenagers will have tried marijuana by the time they graduate from high school, and four out of five will use alcohol. The insistence on complete abstinence has meant the inevitable failure of programs which make this their primary goal (Ching 1981).

Perhaps the single most important premise of prevention is that if children knew the *dangers* of marijuana, they would not try it (Bechman, Johnston & O'Malley 1990). The majority of programs are based on the following mis-

conceptions, or "scare tactics" pertaining specifically to marijuana that are designed to frighten teenagers (and their parents): Marijuana *use,* by definition, is equivalent to *abuse* and often leads to addiction; marijuana is the gateway to "harder" drugs such as cocaine and heroin (Gabany & Plummer 1990; Kandel 1975); marijuana use causes a host of health problems, including arrested development, hormonal change, and infertility (National Institute on Drug Abuse 1998; American Council for Drug Education 1997).

Regarding use, abuse, and addiction, some programs use the terms interchangeably; others utilize an exaggerated definition of use that defines anything other than one-time experimentation as abuse. There is no evidence that marijuana use leads to addiction. In fact, the 1996 NIDA Household Survey indicates that although 17% of teenagers (12 to 17 years old) reported they had used marijuana at some point in their lives, less (13%) reported using it during the past year, and still fewer (7%) had used it during the past month (Substance Abuse and Mental Health Services Administration 1997). Programs that do not differentiate between marijuana use and abuse are ineffective because they are inconsistent with students' observations and experiences. (D'Emidio-Caston & Brown 1998; U.S. General Accounting Office 1993; Duncan 1991). Teenagers see for themselves that others can and do use marijuana without serious negative consequence that would constitute "abuse," thus claims of addiction do not fit their experience. The danger of making unsubstantiated claims of possible addiction, and that occasional use of marijuana constitutes abuse, is that teenagers may ignore the message entirely and doubt the credibility of the source. This is illustrated by the comments of a heroin addict I interviewed over twenty years ago. She, like myself at the time, was a "nice Jewish girl" who came from an upper middle-class suburb in a large metropolitan area. Genuinely intrigued by her situation, I asked how she had ended up in jail and addicted to heroin. I will never forget what she told me: "When I was in high school they had these so-called drug education classes. They told us if we used heroin we would become addicted. They told us if we used marijuana we would become addicted. Well, we all tried marijuana and found we did *not* become addicted, so we figured the entire message was b.s. I then tried heroin, got strung out, and here I am."

The "gateway" or "stepping stone" theory is another assertion that is not grounded in scientific evidence or teenagers' experience. The fear, and subsequent claim, is that even if marijuana itself is physiologically less dangerous than alcohol, its use will open the door to more deleterious substances. From marijuana, it is claimed, teenagers will progress to cocaine and heroin. There is no evidence that the use of marijuana causes one to use other drugs, and several researchers have found that the vast majority of marijuana smokers do not go on to become abusers of other substances (Zimmer & Morgan 1997; Brown & Horowitz 1993). For example, based on the NIDA Household Survey, [Lynn] Zimmer and [John P.] Morgan calculate that for every 100 people who have tried marijuana, one is a current user of cocaine (Zimmer & Morgan 1997). Teenagers know from their own experience and observation that marijuana use does not inevitably lead to the use of harder drugs. Therefore when such information is given, they discount both the message and the messenger.

Regarding health problems such as arrested development, hormone change and infertility, Zimmer and Morgan (1997:92) say:

> There is no evidence that marijuana causes infertility in men or women. In animal studies, high doses of THC diminish the production of some sex hormones and can impair reproduction. However, most studies of humans have found that marijuana has no impact on sex hormones. In those studies showing an impact, it is modest, temporary, and of no apparent consequence for reproduction. There is no scientific evidence that marijuana delays adolescent sexual development, has a feminizing effect on males, or a masculinizing effect on females.

Students may not be aware of the scientific evidence, but they do know from their own observations that marijuana smokers do not exhibit opposite-sex characteristics.

Some methods for deterring teenagers are so absurd that teenagers see them as ludicrous and do not take them seriously. The advertisements comparing a brain on drugs to a fried egg ("This is your brain, this is your brain on drugs") are a prime example. These ads, sponsored by the Partnership for a Drug-Free America, became a joke, and fodder for an entire line of anti-drug T-shirts. They did little, however, to prevent adolescent marijuana use.

There are many good reasons why teenagers should refrain from using marijuana: some studies indicate that early use can precede abuse (Yamaguchi & Kandel 1984; Kandel & Yamaguchi 1993); there is potential for lung damage as a result of smoking; intoxication can led to the inability to work, study, drive or play sports; and there can be social and legal ramifications of detection. All of these factors are consistent with what young people see and experience. It is unnecessary to exaggerate or fabricate information in an effort to scare them.

A final critique of drug education is that information is often presented "top down," with the belief that teenagers have little, if anything (short of role playing in "groups"), to contribute to lessons about marijuana and other drugs. Although many of the more sophisticated programs today overtly stress decision-making skills, in reality they are being taught that only one decision is appropriate—abstinence. According to [Joel H.] Brown (1997:40): "When young people recognize that they are being taught to follow directions, rather than to make decisions, they feel betrayed and resentful. As long as federal mandates force this charade, drug education programs and policies will continue to fail."

A common complaint about Drug Abuse Resistance Education (DARE), the most widely-used, federally-funded drug education program, according to [Earl] Wysong, [Richard] Aniskiewicz and [David] Wright (1994:459), was from students who did not believe their opinions were taken into account: "It's like nobody cares what we think. . . . The DARE cops just wanted us to do what they told us and our teachers never talked about DARE . . . It seems like a lot of adults and teachers can't bring themselves down to talk to students . . . so you don't care what they think either."

In fact, in California the Department of Education's evaluation revealed that of 5,000 fifth through twelfth graders interviewed, only 15% felt drug education had a "large effect" on their choice of whether to use drugs, and 45% said they were "not affected at all" (Brown, D'Emidio-Caston & Pollard 1997).

The combination of a zero-tolerance, no-use message, coupled with top down teaching has the effect of cutting off dialogue. Those students who persist in using marijuana therefore have no context in which to become truly educated. Thus drug education is not really education at all, but indoctrination, which frustrates students and many teachers alike. A county-funded drug educator reported to me that he would like to give his students (who he knew smoked marijuana) information that might help them minimize its dangers (e.g., not to smoke and drive). But to admit that they might use it at all would violate the abstinence-only policy dictated by federal funding regulations. He believed his hands were tied, and he could not really *educate* his students about marijuana.

What's really wrong with drug education, as has been the case since its advent, is that it is based on politics rather than science. Ita Kreft and Joel Brown (1998), in a special issue of *Evaluation Review* argue that "zero tolerance" programs not only fall short on preventing teenagers from using illegal drugs such as marijuana, they are evaluated by methods which are oversimplistic. They measure attitude rather than ability to make wise decisions, and tend to report findings indicating a positive result while ignoring or even covering up those which question the effectiveness of "no use" prevention education. Brown and his colleagues conclude that methodological flaws in the way programs are evaluated would have us believe that drug education is effective. It is, in fact, an enormous taxpayer drain with few demonstrable "results" (Kreft & Brown 1998). In a comprehensive evaluation of several of the most popular programs, [D. M.] Gorman (1998) concludes:

> The evidence presented herein, from both national surveys and program evaluations, shows that we have yet to develop successful techniques of school-based drug prevention. The claims made on behalf of the aspect of the nation's drug control policy are largely unsupported by empirical data. Evidence is cited selectively to support the use of certain programs, and there is virtually no systematic testing of interventions developed in line with competing theoretical models of adolescent drug use.

The blatant political nature of drug education becomes obvious when researchers who criticize the program are discredited. Such was the case with researchers who criticized DARE, America's largest prevention program. The critical findings of a Research Triangle Institute meta-analysis funded by the National Institute of Justice were suppressed by that agency, but later published in the *American Journal of Public Health* (Ennett et al. 1994). Since then, other researchers such as Dennis Rosenbaum (no relation) at the University of Illinois have found higher rates of drug use among DARE graduates than among their peers (Rosenbaum & Hanson 1998). When rigorous methodological evaluations are applied, the vast majority of other programs fare no better in terms of outcome (Gorman 1998).

A NEW STRATEGY: EDUCATION

A new strategy for drug education requires a substitute set of basic assumptions and goals. Since total abstinence, though preferred, is not a realistic alternative, we must take a pragmatic rather than moralistic view of marijuana use.

Such use is likely to happen, so instead of becoming indignant and punitive, we ought to assume the existence of drug use and strategize to minimize its negative effects. Harm reduction should replace zero tolerance.

There are concrete risks and dangers in the use of marijuana. To deny this fact would be tantamount to producing falsehoods similar to those perpetrated in the name of achieving total abstinence. We must separate real and imagined dangers of marijuana and other drug use, and impart this information along with the knowledge that a key variable regarding risk is context of use.

The use of mind-altering substances does not necessarily constitute abuse. It is important to make distinctions between use and abuse in order to impart them in a practical way to students (Duncan & Gold 1983). The vast majority of individuals who use drugs (with the exception of nicotine, which is the most addictive of all substances, including crack cocaine and heroin) do not form an addictive or abusive relationship with them. Instead, 80% to 90% of users *control* their use of psychoactive substances (Nicholson 1992; Winick 1991; Rosenbaum 1989).

It is not surprising that responsible marijuana use is an invisible phenomenon. As a consequence of its illegal status, the vast majority of marijuana users are secretive and underground. Those with a "stake in conventional life" have the most to lose from exposure (Waldorf, Reinarman & Murphy 1991). What marijuana user with a good job and otherwise satisfactory life would admit to using an illegal drug? Instead, their use of substances, legal and illegal, happens in discreet ways that insure their conventional status (and keeps them out of jail).

To assume from the nonvisibility of controlled marijuana users that they do not exist is a mistake. Students who persist in their use of marijuana need to understand that it is possible to control their use by setting limits to use, such as never using marijuana at school or work, or while participating in sports or driving. Such "responsible use" messages are now being introduced to alcohol education as an alternative to zero-tolerance (Oldenberg 1998; Milgram 1996).

Perhaps nothing is more crucial regarding marijuana use than context. In his seminal work, *Drug, Set and Setting* (1984), the late Norman Zinberg imparted the notion that there were three elements essential to understanding drug use. The pharmacology of the drug itself is important, as is the dosage level. The "set," or psychological state of the user at the time of use, is the second ingredient to be understood. Finally, the setting—including geography, social group and even the weather—affect one's experience of a particular drug. All of these form the context of use, and it is within these contexts that educational efforts must be placed (Grob & Dobkin de Rios 1992). Without encouraging or condoning marijuana use (as sexual activity and alcohol use are not encouraged or condoned) teenagers need to be made aware of the importance of context in order to make wise decisions and to control their use.

Today's teenagers know much about marijuana through direct experience, and information from family, friends and the media. It is part of youth culture. They are also much more thoughtful, intelligent and concerned about their own well-being than we acknowledge. When asked in a confidential setting, many report that their choice of marijuana over other substances is for health and safety reasons. Many believe marijuana to be a natural herb that is less debilitating to their bodies than alcohol or cocaine. An effective drug education program will emphasize and encourage responsibility (Martin, Duncan & Zunich 1983). Peer education (in which the students themselves direct the program) and confluent education (in which the dissemination of information is coupled with personal experiences of the students themselves) are two vehicles for effective drug education (Brown & Horowitz 1993; Cohen 1993).

The above assumptions and goals lead to a new drug education approach based on harm reduction, which acknowledges the inevitability of marijuana experimentation. Rather than fight futilely to end what cannot be changed (drug use) the possibility of controlled use and the ability of teenagers, if educated honestly and in ways they trust, to make wise decisions are assumed. In this way programs can reduce problems associated with the use of psychoactive substances. Most important, those teenagers who persist, even as we urge them to remain abstinent, will at least be equipped to make responsible choices based on accurate information. As [J. E.] Beck (1998) says:

> Drug education programs should focus on preventing problems associated with drug use. For some students, that may mean the ability to develop decision-making skills that lead them to avoid alcohol, tobacco, and illegal drugs completely; for other students, that might mean being more careful than they previously were when they were experimenting with substances; for others, that might mean making the decision to get

help for a substance abuse problem. A harm-reduction program does not advocate substance use, but it does advocate the health of youth.

REFERENCES

American Council for Drug Education. 1997. *Drug Awareness Series.* New York: American Council for Drug Education.

Anslinger, H.J. & Cooper, C.R. 1995 [1937]. Marijuana: Assassin of youth. In: J. Inciardi & K. McElrath (Eds.) *The American Drug Scene.* Los Angeles: Roxbury.

Bachman, J.G.; Johnston, L.D. & O'Malley, P.M. 1990. Explaining the recent decline in cocaine use among young adults: Further evidence that perceived risks and disapproval lead to reduced drug use. *Journal of Health and Human Social Behavior* 31 (2): 173–84.

Beck, J.E. 1998. 100 years of "just say no" versus "just say know": Reevaluating drug education goals for the coming century. *Evaluation Review* 22 (2): 39.

Brown, J. 1997. Listen to the kids. *American School Board Journal* December: 38–47.

Brown, J.H.; D'Emidio-Caston, M. & Pollard, J. 1997. Students and substances: Social power in drug education. *Educational Evaluation and Policy Analysis* 19: 65–82.

Brown, J.H. & Horowitz, J.D. 1993. Deviance and deviants: Why adolescent substance use prevention programs do not work. *Evaluation Review* 17 (5). [An excellent discussion on confluent education.]

Ching, C.L. 1981. The goal of abstinence: Implications for drug education. *Journal of Drug Education* 11 (1): 13–18.

Cohen, J. 1993. Achieving a reduction in drug-related harm through education. In: N. Heather; A. Wodak; E.A. Nadelman & P. O'Hare (Eds.) *Psychoactive Drugs and Harm Reduction: From Faith to Science.* London: Whurr. [An excellent discussion of peer education.]

D'Emidio-Caston, M. & Brown, J.H. 1998. The other side of the story: Student narratives on the California drug, alcohol and tobacco education programs. *Evaluation Review* 22 (1):95–117.

Duncan, D.F. 1991. Problems associated with three commonly used drugs: A survey of rural secondary school students. *Psychology of Addictive Behavior* 5 (2):93–6.

Duncan, D. & Gold, R.S. 1983. Cultivating drug use: A strategy for the eighties. *Bulletin of the Society of Psychologists in Addictive Behaviors* 2 (3): 143–47.

Ennett, S.T.; Tobler, N.S.; Ringwalt, C.L. & Flewelling, R. 1994. How effective is drug abuse resistance education? A meta-analysis of project DARE outcome evaluations. *American Journal of Public Health* 84 (9): 1394–401.

Gabany, S.G. & Plummer, P. 1990. The marijuana perception inventory: The effects of substance abuse instruction. *Journal of Drug Education* 20 (3): 235–45.

Goldstein, A. 1994. *Addiction. From Biology to Drug Policy.* New York: W.H. Freeman and Company.

Goode, E. 1993. *Drugs in American Society. 4th Ed.* New York: McGraw-Hill.

Gorman, D.M. 1998. The irrelevance of evidence in the development of school-based drug prevention policy, 1986–1996. *Evaluation Review* 22 (1): 118–46.

Grob, C. & Dobkin de Rios, M. 1992. Adolescent drug use in cross-cultural perspective. *Journal of Drug Issues* 22 (1): 121–38. [An interesting discussion of the role of context in cross-cultural settings.]

Johnston, L.; Bechman, J. & O'Malley, P. 1997. *National Survey Results from the Monitoring the Future Study.* Washington, D.C.: National Institutes of Health.

Johnston, L.; Bechman, J. & O'Malley, P. 1996. *National Survey Results from the Monitoring the Future Study.* Washington, D.C.: National Institutes of Health.

Kandel, D. 1975. Stages in adolescent involvement in drug use. *Science* 190: 912–14.

Kandel, D. & Yamaguchi, K. 1993. From beer to crack: Developmental patterns of drug involvement. *American Journal of Public Health* 83: 851–55.

Kreft, I.G. & Brown, J.H. 1998. Introduction to the special issue: Zero effects of drug prevention programs: Issues and solutions. *Evaluation Review* 22 (1): 3–14.

Martin, C.E.; Duncan, D.F. & Zunich, E.M. 1983. Students motives for discontinuing illicit drug taking. *Health Values: Achieving High Level Wellness* 7 (5): 8–11.

Milgram, G.G. 1996. Responsible decision making regarding alcohol: A re-emerging prevention/education strategy for the 1990s. *Journal of Drug Education* 26 (4): 357–65.

National Institute on Drug Abuse. 1998. Available on the Internet at www.nida.nih.gov/nida home.html/marijuana information.

Newcomb, M. & Bentler, P. 1988. *Consequences of Adolescent Drug Use: Impact on the Lives of Young Adults.* Newbury Park, California: Sage.

Nicholson, T. 1992. The primary prevention of illicit drug problems: An argument for decriminilization and legalization. *Journal of Primary Prevention* 12 (4): 275–88.

Oldenberg, D. 1998. Kids and alcohol: A controversial alternative to "Just Say No." *Washington Post* March 10: B6.

Rosenbaum, M. 1996. *Kids, Drugs and Drug Education: A Harm Reduction Approach.* San Francisco: National Council on Crime and Delinquency.

Rosenbaum, M. 1989. *Just Say What? An Alternative View on Solving America's Drug Problem.* San Francisco: National Council on Crime and Delinquency.

Rosenbaum, D.P. & Hanson, G.S. 1998. *Assessing the Effects of School-based Drug Education: A Six-year Multi-level Analysis of Project D.A.R.E.* Chicago: Department of Criminal Justice and Center for Research in Law and Justice, University of Illinois at Chicago.

Schedler, J. & Block, J. 1990. Adolescent drug use and psychological health: A longitudinal inquiry. *American Psychologist* 45: 612–30.

Substance Abuse and Mental Health Services Administration (SAMHSA), Office of Applied Studies. 1997. *Preliminary Results from the 1996 National Household Survey on Drug Abuse.* Rockville, Maryland: SAMHSA, Office of Applied Studies.

U.S. General Accounting Office. 1997. *Substance Abuse and Violence Prevention: Multiple Programs Raise Questions of Efficiency and Effectiveness.* Washington, D.C.: U.S. GAO.

U.S. General Accounting Office, 1993. *Drug Use among Youth: No Simple Answers to Guide Prevention.* Washington, D.C.: U.S. GAO.

Waldorf, D.; Reinarman, C. & Murphy, S. 1991. *Cocaine Changes.* Philadelphia: Temple University Press.

Weil, A. 1972. *The Natural Mind: A New Way of Looking at Drugs and the Higher Consciousness.* Boston: Houghton Mifflin Company.

Weil, A. & Rosen, W. 1983. *Chocolate to Morphine; Understanding Mind-Active Drugs.* Boston: Houghton Mifflin Company.

Winick, C. 1991. Social behavior, public policy and nonharmful drug use. *The Milbank Quarterly* 69 (3): 437–57.

Wysong, E.; Aniskiewicz, R. & Wright, D. 1994. Truth and DARE: Tracking drug education to graduation and as symbolic politics. *Social Problems* 41 (3): 448–72.

Yamaguchi, K. & Kandel, D. 1984. Patterns of drug use from adolescence to youth adulthood. III: Predictors of progression. *American Journal of Public Health* 74: 673–81.

Zimmer, L. & Morgan, J. 1997. *Marijuana Myths, Marijuana Facts: A Review of the Scientific Evidence.* New York: The Lindesmith Center.

Zinberg, N. 1984. *Drug, Set and Setting.* New Haven: Yale University Press.

NO

Wayne Hall and Nadia Solowij

ADVERSE EFFECTS OF CANNABIS

Cannabis is the most widely used illicit drug in many developed societies. Its health and psychological effects are not well understood and remain the subject of much debate, with opinions on its risks polarised along the lines of proponents' views on what its legal status should be. An unfortunate consequence of this polarisation of opinion has been the absence of any consensus on what health information the medical profession should give to patients who are users or potential users of cannabis. There is conflicting evidence about many of the effects of cannabis use, so we summarise the evidence on the most probable adverse health and psychological consequences of acute and chronic use. This uncertainty, however, should not prevent medical practitioners from advising patients about the most likely ill-effects of their cannabis use. Here we make some suggestions about the advice doctors can give to patients who use, or are contemplating the use of, this drug.

In many western societies, cannabis has been used by a substantial minority, and in some a majority, of young adults, even though its use is prohibited by law. Debate about the justification for continuing to prohibit cannabis use has polarised opinion about the seriousness of its adverse health effects. In addition, the possible therapeutic effects of cannabinoids have become entangled in the debate about prohibition of recreational cannabis use.... The health effects of cannabis use, especially of long-term use, remain uncertain because there is very little epidemiological research and because of disagreements about the interpretation of the limited epidemiological and laboratory evidence. Here we summarise the evidence on the most probable adverse health effects of cannabis use acknowledging where appropriate the uncertainty that remains.

CANNABIS THE DRUG

Cannabis preparations are largely derived from the female plant of Cannabis sativa. The primary psychoactive constituent is d-9-tetrahydrocannabinol

(THC). The THC content is highest in the flowering tops, declining in the leaves, lower leaves, stems, and seeds of the plant. Marijuana (THC content 0.5–5.0%) is prepared from the dried flowering tops and leaves; hashish (THC content 2–20%) consists of dried cannabis resin and compressed flowers; and hashish oil may contain between 15% and 50% THC. Sinsemilla and Netherwood varieties of cannabis may have a THC content of up to 20%.

Cannabis may be smoked in a "joint," which is the size of a cigarette, or in a water pipe. Tobacco may be added to assist burning. Smokers typically inhale deeply and hold their breath to maximise absorption of THC by the lungs. Marijuana and hashish may also be eaten, but cannabis is mostly smoked because this is the easiest way to achieve the desired psychoactive effects.

A typical joint contains between 0.5 g and 1.0 g of cannabis. The THC delivered varies between 20% and 70%, its bioavailability ranging from 5% to 24%. As little as 2–3 mg of available THC will produce a "high" in occasional users, but regular users may smoke five or more joints a day.

Cannabinoids act on a specific receptor that is widely distributed in the brain regions involved in cognition, memory reward, pain perception, and motor coordination. These receptors respond to an endogenous ligand, anandamide, which is much less potent and has a shorter duration than THC. The identification of a specific cannabinoid antagonist promises to improve our understanding of the role of cannabinoids in normal brain function.

PATTERNS OF CANNABIS USE

Cannabis has been tried by many European young adults and by most young adults in the USA and Australia. Most cannabis use is intermittent and time-limited: most users stop in their mid to late 20s, and very few engage in daily cannabis use over a period of years. In the USA and Australia, about 10% of those who ever use cannabis become daily users, and another 20–30% use the drug weekly.

Because of uncertainties about THC content, heavy cannabis use is generally defined as daily or near daily use. This pattern of use over years places users at greatest risk of adverse health and psychological consequences. Daily cannabis users are more likely to be male, to be less well educated, to use alcohol and tobacco regularly, and to use amphetamines, hallucinogens, psychostimulants, sedatives, and opioids.

ACUTE EFFECTS OF CANNABIS

Cannabis produces euphoria and relaxation, perceptual alterations, time distortion, and the intensification of ordinary sensory experiences, such as eating, watching films, and listening to music. When used in a social setting it may produce infectious laughter and talkativeness. Short-term memory and attention, motor skills, reaction time, and skilled activities are impaired while a person is intoxicated.

The most common unpleasant side-effects of occasional cannabis use are anxiety and panic reactions. These effects may be reported by naive users, and they are a common reason for discontinuation of use; more experienced users may occasionally report these effects after receiving a much larger than usual dose of THC.

Cannabis smoking or ingestion of THC increases heart rate by 20–50% within a few minutes to a quarter of an hour; this effect lasts for up to 3 h. Blood pressure is increased while the person is sitting, and decreased while standing. These effects are of negligible clinical significance in healthy young users because tolerance develops to them.

The acute toxicity of cannabinoids is very low. There are no confirmed published cases worldwide of human deaths from cannabis poisoning, and the dose of THC required to produce 50% mortality in rodents is extremely high compared with other commonly used drugs.

PSYCHOMOTOR EFFECTS AND DRIVING

Cannabis produces dose-related impairments in cognitive and behavioural functions that may potentially impair driving a motor vehicle or operating machinery. These impairments are larger and more persistent for difficult tasks that depend on sustained attention. The most serious possible consequence of acute cannabis use is a road-traffic accident if a user drives while intoxicated.

The effects of recreational doses of cannabis on driving performance in laboratory simulators and standardised driving courses have been reported by some researchers as being similar to the effects when blood alcohol concentrations are between 0.07% and 0.10%. However, studies of the effects of cannabis on driving under more realistic conditions on roads have shown much more modest impairments, probably because cannabis users are more aware of their impairment and less inclined to take risks than alcohol users.

Results of epidemiological studies of road-traffic accidents are equivocal because most drivers who have cannabinoids in their blood also have high blood alcohol concentrations. In two studies with reasonable numbers of individuals who had only used cannabis, there was no clear evidence of increased culpability in these drivers. The separate effects of alcohol and cannabis on psychomotor impairment and driving performance in laboratory tasks are roughly additive, so the main effect of cannabis use on driving may be in amplifying the impairments caused by alcohol, which is often used with the drug.

EFFECTS OF CHRONIC CANNABIS USE

Cellular Effects and the Immune System

Cannabis smoke may be carcinogenic; it is mutagenic in vitro and in vivo. Cannabinoids impair cell-mediated and humoral immunity in rodents, decreasing resistance to infection, and noncannabinoids in cannabis smoke impair alveolar macrophages. The relevance of these findings to human health is uncertain because the doses of THC used in animal studies have been very high, and tolerance may develop to the effects on immunity in human beings.

A few studies that have pointed to the adverse effects of cannabis on human immunity have not been replicated. There is no conclusive evidence that consumption of cannabinoids impairs human immune function, as measured by numbers of T lymphocytes, B lymphocytes, or macrophages, or immunoglobulin concentrations. Two prospective studies of HIV-positive homosexual men have shown that cannabis use is not associated with an increased risk of progression to AIDS concentrations.

Respiratory System

Chronic heavy cannabis smoking is associated with increased symptoms of chronic bronchitis, such as coughing, production of sputum, and wheezing. Lung function is significantly poorer and there are significantly greater abnormalities in the large airways of marijuana smokers than in non-smokers. Tashkin and colleagues have reported evidence of an additive effect of marijuana and tobacco smoking on histopathological abnormalities in lung tissue.

Bloom and colleagues reported similar additive effects on bronchitic symptoms in an epidemiological study of the respiratory effects of smoking "non-tobacco" cigarettes in 990 individuals aged under 40 years in Tucson, Arizona, USA. Non-tobacco smokers reported more coughing, phlegm production, and wheeze than non-smokers, irrespective of whether they also smoked tobacco. Those who had never smoked any substance had the best respiratory functioning, followed in order of decreasing function by current tobacco smokers, current non-tobacco smokers, and current smokers of both tobacco and non-tobacco cigarettes. Non-tobacco smoking alone had a larger effect on respiratory function than tobacco smoking alone, and the effect of both types of smoking was additive.

In 1997, Tashkin and colleagues reported that the rate of decline in respiratory function over 8 years among marijuana smokers did not differ from that in non-smokers. This finding contrasted with that of a follow-up of the Tuc-

son cohort, in which there was a greater rate of decline in respiratory function among marijuana-only smokers than in tobacco-only smokers and additive effects of tobacco and marijuana smoking. Both studies showed that long-term cannabis smoking increased bronchitic symptoms.

In view of the adverse effects of tobacco smoking, the similarity between tobacco and cannabis smoke, and the evidence that cannabis smoking produces histopathological changes that precede lung cancer, long-term cannabis smoking may also increase the risks of respiratory cancer. There have been reports of cancers in the aerodigestive tract in young adults with a history of heavy cannabis use. These reports are worrying since such cancers are rare among adults under the age of 60, even those who smoke tobacco and drink alcohol. Case-control studies of the role of cannabis smoking in these cancers are urgently needed.

Reproductive Effects

Chronic administration of high doses of THC to animals lowers testosterone secretion, impairs sperm production, motility, and viability, and disrupts the ovulatory cycle. Whether cannabis smoking has these effects in human beings is uncertain because the published evidence is small and inconsistent.

Cannabis administration during pregnancy reduces birthweight in animals. The results of human epidemiological studies have been more equivocal. The stigma of using illicit drugs during pregnancy discourages honest reporting, and when associations are found, they are difficult to interpret because cannabis users are more likely than non-users to smoke tobacco, drink alcohol, and use other illicit drugs during pregnancy, and they differ in social class, education, and nutrition. Several studies have suggested that cannabis smoking in pregnancy may reduce birthweight. In the best controlled of these studies, this relation has persisted after statistical control for potential confounding variables, but other studies have not shown any such association. The effect of cannabis on birthweight in the studies that have found an association has been small compared with that of tobacco smoking.

That cannabis use during pregnancy increases the risk of birth defects is unlikely. Early case reports have not been supported by large well-controlled epidemiological studies. For example, the study by Zuckerman et al. included a large sample of women with a substantial prevalence of cannabis use that was verified by urine analysis, and there was no increase in birth defects.

There is suggestive evidence that infants exposed in utero to cannabis have behavioural and developmental effects during the first few months after birth. Between the ages of 4 and 9 years, children who were exposed in utero have shown deficits in sustained attention, memory, and higher cognitive functioning. The clinical significance of these effects remains unclear since they are small compared with the effects of maternal tobacco use.

Three studies have shown an increased risk of non-lymphoblastic leukemia, rhabdomyosarcoma, and astrocytoma in children whose mothers reported using cannabis during their pregnancies. None of these was a planned study of the association; cannabis use was one of many potential confounders included in statistical analyses of the relation between the exposure of interest and childhood cancer. Their replication is a priority.

Behavioural Effects in Adolescence

There is a cross-sectional association between heavy cannabis use in adolescence and the risk of leaving high-school education and of experiencing job instability in young adulthood. However, the strength of this association is reduced in longitudinal studies when statistical adjustments are made for the fact that, compared with their peers, heavy cannabis users have poor high-school performance before using cannabis.

There is some evidence that heavy use has adverse effects on family formation, mental health, and involvement in drug-related crime. In each case, the strong associations in cross-sectional studies are more modest in longitudinal studies after statistical control for associations between cannabis use and other pre-existing characteristics that independently predict these adverse outcomes.

A consistent finding in the USA has been the regular sequence of initiation into drug use in which cannabis use has typically preceded involvement with "harder" illicit drugs such as stimulants and opioids. The interpretation of this sequence remains controversial. The less compelling hypothesis is that cannabis use directly increases the use of other drugs in the sequence. There is better support for two other hypotheses—namely, that there is a selective recruitment into cannabis use of non-conforming adolescents who have a propensity to use other illicit drugs, and that once recruited to cannabis use, social interaction with drug-using peers, and greater access to illicit-drug markets, they are more likely to use other illicit drugs.

Dependence Syndrome

Animals develop tolerance to the effects of repeated doses of THC, and studies suggest that cannabinoids may affect the same reward systems as alcohol, cocaine, and opioids. Heavy smokers of cannabis also develop tolerance to its subjective and cardiovascular effects, and some report withdrawal symptoms on the abrupt cessation of cannabis use.

There is evidence that a cannabis dependence syndrome occurs with heavy chronic use in individuals who report problems in controlling their use and who continue to use the drug despite experiencing adverse personal consequences. There is some clinical evidence of a dependence syndrome analogous to that for alcohol. In the USA, cannabis dependence is among the most common forms of illicit-drug dependence in the population. About one in ten of those who ever use cannabis become dependent on it at some time during their 4 or 5 years of heaviest use. This risk is more like the equivalent risk for alcohol (15%) than for nicotine (32%) or opioids (23%).

Cognitive Effects

The long-term heavy use of cannabis does not produce the severe or grossly debilitating impairment of memory, attention, and cognitive function that is found with chronic heavy alcohol use. Electrophysiological and neuropsychological studies show that it may produce more subtle impairment of memory, attention, and the organisation and integration of complex information. The longer cannabis has been used, the more pronounced the cognitive impairment. These impairments are subtle, so it remains unclear how important they are for everyday functioning, and whether they are reversed after an extended period of abstinence. Early studies that suggested gross structural brain damage with heavy use have not been supported by better controlled studies with better methods. Research in animals has shown that chronic cannabinoid administration may compromise the endogenous cannabinoid system (its function is unclear, but it has roles in memory, emotion, and cognitive functioning, as mentioned above). These results are consistent with the subtlety of the cognitive effects of chronic cannabis use in human beings.

Psychosis

Large doses of THC produce confusion, amnesia, delusions, hallucinations, anxiety, and agitation. Such reactions are rare, occurring after unusually heavy cannabis use; in most cases they remit rapidly after abstinence from cannabis.

There is an association between cannabis use and schizophrenia. A prospective study of 50,000 Swedish conscripts found a dose-response relation between the frequency of cannabis use by age 18 and the risk of a diagnosis of schizophrenia over the subsequent 15 years. A plausible explanation is that cannabis use can exacerbate the symptoms of schizophrenia, and there is prospective evidence that continued use predicts more psychotic symptoms in people with schizophrenia. A declining incidence of treated cases of schizophrenia over the period when cannabis use has increased suggests, however, that cannabis use is unlikely to have caused cases of schizophrenia that would not otherwise have occurred. This observation suggests that chronic use may precipitate schizophrenia in vulnerable individuals, an effect that would not be expected to change incidence.

Premature Mortality

There have been two prospective epidemiological studies of mortality among cannabis users. A Swedish study of mortality during 15 years among male military conscripts showed an increased risk of premature death among men who had smoked cannabis 50 or more times by age 18. Violent and accidental death was the main contributor to this excess. However, the association between mortality and cannabis use disappeared after multivariate statistical adjustment for alcohol and other drug use.

Sydney and colleagues reported a 10-year study of mortality in cannabis users aged between 15 and 49 years among 65,171 members of the Kaiser Permanente Medical Care Program. The sample consisted of 38% who had never used cannabis, 20% who had used fewer than six times, 20% who were former users, and 22% who were current users. Regular cannabis use had a small association with premature mortality (RR 1.33), which was wholly explained by increased deaths from AIDS in men, probably because marijuana use was a marker for male homosexual behaviour in this cohort. It is too early to conclude from the study that marijuana use does not increase mortality because the average age at follow-up was only 43 years, and cigarette smoking and alcohol use were only modestly associated with premature mortality.

Possible Effects of Increased THC Content of Cannabis

The average THC content of cannabis has probably increased over the past several decades, but without good data by how much is unclear. This situation probably reflects a combination of an increased market for more potent cannabis products among regular users, and improved methods of growing high-THC-content. The net health consequences of any increase in potency are uncertain. Among naive users, higher THC content may increase adverse psychological effects, including psychotic symptoms, thereby discouraging some from continuing to use. Among those who continue to use cannabis, increased potency may increase the risks of developing dependence, having accidents if driving while intoxicated, and experiencing psychotic symptoms. If experienced users can regulate their dose of THC, the respiratory risks of cannabis smoking may be marginally reduced.

Health Advice for Cannabis Users

Uncertainty about the adverse health effects of acute, and especially chronic, cannabis use, should not prevent medical practitioners from advising patients who use cannabis about the most probable ill-effects of their cannabis use with emphasis on the uncertainty. In the absence of other risk factors, this should include advice about the possibility of being involved in a motor-vehicle accident if patients drive while intoxicated by cannabis; the higher risk of an accident if they drive when intoxicated by both alcohol and cannabis; the respiratory risks of long-term cannabis smoking, which are substantially increased if they also smoke tobacco; an increased risk of developing dependence if they are daily users of cannabis; and the possibility of subtle cognitive impairment if they use regularly over several years.

POSTSCRIPT

Should Young People Be Taught How to Use Marijuana?

Part of this debate concerns whether or not teaching young people how to use marijuana responsibly is rational and productive. Many people question whether or not the purported benefits of a responsible use message would outweigh the potential risks. Those who support teaching young people about the responsible use of marijuana argue that the drug is used extensively already and that efforts to prevent its use have failed miserably. And because its use is already rampant, teaching young people how to use marijuana responsibly is pragmatic.

Opponents of the responsible use message contend that the potential problems that may be caused by marijuana use justify their position. Physical problems include reduced lung functioning, impaired reproductive ability, and cancer. Academically, marijuana interferes with short-term memory, the ability to maintain attention, and the desire to succeed. Also, for people with existing psychological problems, marijuana may exacerbate those problems. Is it reasonable to expect that people with psychological problems can learn to use marijuana responsibly?

Another area that is clearly adversely affected by marijuana use is the ability to operate a motor vehicle. Critics note that thousands of people die on American highways because of people who drive their cars, trucks, and motorcycles after drinking alcohol. This sad fact occurs even though many efforts have been made to reduce drinking and driving. Similarly, there are serious concerns that despite attempts to educate young people about how to use marijuana use responsibly, many will attempt to drive after smoking marijuana.

Proponents of the responsible use message argue that previous prevention efforts have been unsuccessful. They feel that marijuana-related problems would be reduced greatly if a responsible use approach were implemented. Despite potential risks, advocates believe that a responsible use message is worth considering. They note that in many European cities, young people can use marijuana without penalty. Ironically, marijuana use rates among young people in these cities are lower than use rates in the United States.

Using alcohol and tobacco as examples, opponents say that a responsible use approach is not workable. They point out that many teenagers are taught how to use alcohol responsibly, yet binge drinking among young people is extremely high. Alcohol abuse is epidemic in the United States. Critics are concerned that if young people are told that marijuana can be used responsibly, marijuana abuse may escalate.

In addition to the potential physical, psychological, social, and academic problems of marijuana use, there are moral considerations as well. If young people are told how to use marijuana responsibly, is the wrong message being sent out? Might teenagers get the impression that marijuana is not harmful? Another concern is that young people may generalize their thinking in that if marijuana can be used responsibly, perhaps drugs like LSD and heroin can also be used responsibly. A fundamental question is, Are teenagers mature enough to comprehend a message teaching the responsible use of marijuana?

Numerous articles and books examine the effects of marijuana. One book that provides a comprehensive review of marijuana is *The Health Effects of Cannabis* edited by H. Kalant et al. (Addiction Research Foundation, 1998). An article that looks at the psychological impact of marijuana is "Early Onset Cannabis Use and Psychosocial Adjustment in Young Adults," by D. M. Fergusson and L. J. Horwood, *Addiction* (vol. 92, no. 3, 1997). And the effects of marijuana on mortality are discussed by S. Sidney et al. in "Marijuana Use and Mortality," *American Journal of Public Health* (vol. 87, no. 4, 1997).

ISSUE 7

Is Harm Reduction a Desirable National Drug Control Policy Goal?

YES: Robert J. MacCoun, from "Toward a Psychology of Harm Reduction," *American Psychologist* (November 1998)

NO: Robert L. DuPont and Eric A. Voth, from "Drug Legalization, Harm Reduction, and Drug Policy," *Annals of Internal Medicine* (vol. 123, 1995)

ISSUE SUMMARY

YES: Robert J. MacCoun, an associate professor in the Graduate School of Public Policy at the University of California, Berkeley, supports efforts to minimize problems associated with drugs. He states that a harm reduction approach will not resolve all drug problems, but he feels that reducing those problems is a desirable goal.

NO: Clinical professor of psychiatry Robert L. DuPont and clinical assistant professor Eric A. Voth argue that there is insufficient evidence that a policy of harm reduction is beneficial and that the notion of harm reduction is just another way for some people to rationalize legalizing drugs.

There is little debate as to whether or not drug use has the potential to cause adverse physical and psychological effects upon the user. Moreover, the families and communities of drug users are affected as well. It would be desirable if people always did that which was good for themselves, their families, and their communities. However, people do not always act in health-promoting ways. Tens of millions of people engage in unhealthy behaviors such as ingesting cocaine, smoking marijuana, chewing tobacco, drinking large quantities of alcohol, inhaling solvents, smoking cigarettes, and injecting heroin. The question is not whether drug use is harmful to the individual or whether drug use is the cause of many of the problems in our society. Rather, one needs to ask, What strategy is most likely to limit or reduce problems resulting from drug use? Is it better to teach people how to use drugs in order to reduce or minimize the personal and social hazards associated with drugs, or is it better to strive for drug abstinence and limit access to drugs?

There are various approaches that can be taken to address drug use. One approach focuses on harm reduction. Another approach focuses on supply reduction. The harm reduction approach attempts to minimize the dangers of drug use. The premise behind this approach is that since millions of people take drugs and that many will continue to take drugs regardless of whether or not they are legal, it is logical to teach people how to lessen the problems associated with using drugs. A harm reduction approach attempts to curtail drug-related problems while also trying to diminish drug use. Reducing the demand for drugs is an important component of this approach. The concept of harm reduction applies not only to the individual but to society as well.

Even if individuals do cause harm to themselves, are there policies that can be enacted to limit the risks that drugs pose to other members of society? Harm reduction opponents argue that all members of society would be better served by improving and expanding enforcement of existing drug laws. Harm reduction advocates maintain that current restrictive policies that strive for supply reduction by emphasizing drug enforcement, prosecution, and interdiction have been ineffective and that alternatives need to be explored.

Some of the goals of harm reduction include reducing violence related to the drug trade, lowering death rates directly attributable to drugs, reducing infectious diseases caused by drug use, and preventing the ravages of drugs from affecting family members. Another benefit may be economical in that less money would go for enforcement and prosecution, although more funds would be needed for drug prevention, education, and treatment. On the other hand, harm reduction may result in greater drug use and more people seeking drug treatment. Harm reduction opponents maintain that stiff drug laws act as important deterrents. Moreover, many people arrested for drug-related offenses receive treatment for their drug abuse while incarcerated.

Opponents of harm reduction feel that its advocates are hypocritical and point out that its advocates demand more stringent policies regarding tobacco advertising, smoking restrictions, and driving while under the influence of alcohol, while calling for a reduction in the penalties for illegal drug use. It is true that tobacco and alcohol cause more deaths and disabilities than illegal drugs do. However, it is not known whether or not a policy of harm reduction would increase the number of deaths and disabilities from illegal drugs.

Using the Netherlands to illustrate their point, drug prohibition proponents state that, following the decriminalization of marijuana in that country, there was an increase in shootings, robberies, and car thefts, as well as a rise in the rate of drug addiction. Even if the evidence demonstrated that decriminalization of marijuana in the Netherlands had beneficial effects, would it mean that marijuana decriminalization in the United States would have the same effects? Can the experience in the Netherlands be generalized to the United States?

The following selections debate whether or not a policy of harm reduction would lessen the adverse health and social effects that come from using illegal drugs. Robert J. MacCoun contends that a harm reduction approach should be expanded because it has been shown to be effective. Robert L. DuPont and Eric A. Voth maintain that a policy of harm reduction would increase the negative consequences of drugs and that restrictive policies are necessary because they deter drug use.

YES

Robert J. MacCoun

TOWARD A PSYCHOLOGY
OF HARM REDUCTION

This article discusses 3 different strategies for dealing with the harmful consequences of drug use and other risky behaviors: We can discourage people from engaging in the behavior (prevalence reduction), we can encourage people to reduce the frequency or extent of the behavior (quantity reduction), or we can try to reduce the harmful consequences of the behavior when it occurs (harm reduction). These strategies are not mutually exclusive; this article offers a framework for integrating them. The framework is useful for examining frequent claims that harm reduction "sends the wrong message." Opposition to harm reduction is based in part on a recognition of potential trade-offs among the strategies, but it is also fueled by several more symbolic psychological factors. Strategies for successfully integrating prevalence reduction, quantity reduction, and harm reduction are explored.

During the 1980s, a grassroots movement called *harm reduction* (or harm minimization) emerged in Amsterdam, Rotterdam, and Liverpool as a response to pervasive drug-related public health problems (Heather, Wodak, Nadelmann, & O'Hare, 1993). The movement gradually spread to many other European cities, eventually influencing the policies of several nations (MacCoun, Saiger, Kahan, & Reuter, 1993). Harm reduction is not yet a well-developed approach. Rather, it is a set of programs that share certain public health goals and assumptions. Central among them is the belief that it is possible to modify the behavior of drug users, and the conditions in which they use, in order to reduce many of the most serious risks that drugs pose to public health and safety. Examples of specific harm reduction interventions for drug use include needle and syringe exchange, low-threshold methadone maintenance, "safe-use" educational campaigns, and the use of treatment as an alternative to incarceration for convicted drug offenders.

From Robert J. MacCoun, "Toward a Psychology of Harm Reduction," *American Psychologist*, vol. 53, no. 11 (November 1998). Copyright © 1998 by The American Psychological Association. Adapted with permission. References omitted.

THE ENDS OF DRUG CONTROL

Table 1 lists and briefly defines six overlapping drug control strategies. The first two have dominated the American drug policy debate, centered on the appropriate balance between *supply reduction* (interdiction, source country control, domestic drug law enforcement) and *demand reduction* (treatment, prevention) in the federal budget. But despite their disagreements, demand-side and supply-side advocates share a common allegiance to what might be called the use reduction paradigm—the view that the highest, if not the exclusive, goal of drug policy should be to reduce (and hopefully eliminate) psychoactive drug use. In both practice and rhetoric, use reduction usually means *prevalence reduction*. That is, the goal has been to reduce the total number of users by discouraging initiation on the part of nonusers, and by promoting abstinence for current users. Table 1 introduces three newer terms—*quantity reduction, micro harm reduction,* and *macro harm reduction*—that are described in more detail below. These terms add more jargon to an already jargon-laden domain, but I hope to show that they make it possible to think more strategically about options for effective drug control.

The harm reduction critique of the enforcement-oriented U.S. drug strategy is twofold. First, prevalence-reduction policies have failed to eliminate drug use, leaving its harms largely intact. Second, these harsh enforcement policies are themselves a *source* of many drug-related harms, either directly or by exacerbating the harmful consequences of drug use (Nadelmann, 1989). Although many drug-related harms result from the psychopharmacologic effects of drug consumption, many others are

Table 1
Overlapping Drug Control Strategies

Strategy	Goal
Supply reduction	Reduce total supply of drugs
Demand reduction	Reduce total demand for drugs
Prevalence reduction	Reduce total number of drug users
Quantity reduction	Reduce total quantity consumed
Micro harm reduction	Reduce average harm per use of drugs
Macro harm reduction	Reduce total drug-related harm

mostly attributable to drug prohibition and its enforcement (MacCoun, Reuter, & Schelling, 1996). These harms would be greatly reduced, if not eliminated, under a regime of legal availability. The acknowledgment that prohibition is a source of harm does not imply that legalizing drugs would necessarily lead to a net reduction in harm; as we shall see, much depends on the effects of legal change on levels of drug use (MacCoun, 1993; MacCoun & Reuter, 1997). But by almost exclusively relying on use reduction—especially drug law enforcement—as an indirect means of reducing harm, we are foregoing opportunities to reduce harm directly. We are even increasing some harms in the process.

AMERICAN RESISTANCE TO HARM REDUCTION

With remarkable consistency, the U.S. government has aggressively resisted harm reduction (Kirp & Bayer, 1993; Reuter & MacCoun, 1995). For example, there are probably more than 1 million injecting drug users in this country, and injection drug use accounts for about one third of all AIDS cases. Though the evidence is not unanimous, a considerable body of evidence demonstrates that needle exchange programs can bring about significant reductions in HIV transmission (Des Jarlais, Friedman, & Ward, 1993; General Accounting Office, 1993; Hurley, Jolley, & Kaldor, 1997; Lurie & Reingold, 1991).[1] Lurie and Drucker (1997) recently estimated that between 4,394 and 9,666 HIV infections could have been prevented in the United States between 1987 and 1995 if a national needle exchange program had been in place. Yet there are fewer than 100 needle exchange programs operating in the United States. Why? Because prescription laws, paraphernalia laws, and local "drug-free zone" ordinances ban needle exchange programs in most of the country. Indeed, almost half of the existing programs are operating under an illicit or quasi-legal status. Despite the fact that these programs have been endorsed by the Centers for Disease Control, the National Academy of Sciences, and various leading medical journals and health organizations, drug policy officials in the federal government and most state governments have actively opposed needle exchange. In 1998, Department of Health and Human Services (DHHS) Secretary Donna Shalala publicly endorsed needle exchange on scientific grounds, but subsequently announced that the administration had decided that federal funding of needle exchanges would be unwise. A *Washington Post* story claimed that DHHS officials had arranged her press conference in the mistaken belief that the President would support needle exchange funding; Secretary Shalala's memo of talking points announcing his support was reported to say "the evidence is airtight" and "from the beginning of this effort, it has been about science, science, science" (J. F. Harris & Goldstein, 1998).

Our almost exclusive emphasis on use reduction rather than harm reduction probably has many causes (Reuter & MacCoun, 1995). One is the fear that harm reduction is a Trojan horse for the drug legalization movement (e.g., McCaffrey, 1998). Another factor might be that whereas harm reduction focuses on harms to users, drug-related violence and other harms to *nonusers* are more salient in the United States than in Europe. In addition, prevalence is more readily measurable than harms, and few harm-reduction programs, with the notable exception of needle exchange, have been rigorously evaluated—though political opposition to harm reduction is itself a major cause of the lack of relevant data. But other objections involve beliefs about behavior. For example, it may seem only logical that reducing use is the best way to reduce harm. But this logic holds only if the elimination of drug use is nearly complete, and if efforts to reduce use do not themselves cause harm. Unfortunately, many prevalence-reduction policies often fail on one or both counts. Although it is true that abstinence from drugs (or teenage sex, or drinking among alcoholics) is "100% effective" at reducing harm, the key policy question is whether we are 100% effective at convincing people to *become* abstinent. Finally, the most frequent objection to harm reduction is the claim that harm reduction programs will "send the wrong message." The logic by which harm reduction "sends the wrong message" is rarely articulated in any detail, suggesting that for its proponents, the proposition is self-evident. It seems likely that harm-reduction advocates will continue to face opposition in the United

States until they successfully address this concern.

HARM REDUCTION IN OTHER POLICY DOMAINS

The tension between preventing a behavior and reducing the harmfulness of that behavior is not unique to the debate about illicit drugs. Table 2 lists some intriguing parallels in other contemporary American policy debates. Despite many superficial differences, each domain involves a behavior that poses risks to both the actor and others. And each raises the question about the relative efficacy of policies that aim to reduce the harmful consequences of a risky behavior (harm reduction) versus policies designed to discourage the behavior itself (prevalence or quantity reduction).

The first row of Table 2—safety standards for consumer products—is notable for its relative lack of controversy outside of the halls of Congress. Even though these safety regulations clearly have a harm-reduction rationale—albeit one generally not recognized as such—recent Congressional efforts to scale them back have received a remarkably lukewarm public response. But in the other domains listed in Table 2, a debate centers on the fear that an intervention to reduce harm—harm reduction in spirit if not in name—will in some way "send the wrong message," encouraging the risky behavior. The parallels to drugs are particularly striking for the topic of condom distribution in schools (and to a lesser degree, sex education). Advocates argue that condom distribution is needed to reduce the risks of unplanned pregnancies and sexually transmitted diseases, whereas opponents vociferously argue that distribution programs and other safe

sex interventions actually promote sexual activity (Mauldon & Luker, 1996). On the other hand, recent U.S. debates about welfare and immigration benefits may seem to have little to do with concepts like risk regulation or harm reduction. But at an abstract level, the issues are similar. Assertions are made that policies designed to mitigate the harmful consequences of being unemployed, or of immigrating to the United States, actually encourage people to become (or remain) unemployed, or to immigrate to the United States. Aside from brief excursions into the lessons of motor vehicle safety standards and tobacco and alcohol policy, this article focuses almost exclusively on harm reduction for illicit drugs. But it seems possible that the analysis might provide insights for other domains of risk reduction—in part because my arguments were often informed by those literatures but also because it seems unlikely that the underlying behavioral questions are unique to the drug domain.

OVERVIEW

The remainder of this [selection] explores critics' concerns about harm reduction. This [selection] does not attempt a comprehensive review of the evaluation literature on harm reduction or on the specifics of interventions at the clinical level (see Des Jarlais, Friedman, & Ward, 1993; Heather et al., 1993). Instead, the [selection] has four goals: (a) to demonstrate the value of distinguishing microlevel harm from macrolevel harm, and prevalence of a behavior from the quantity or frequency of that behavior; (b) to identify potential trade-offs between prevalence reduction, quantity reduction, and micro harm reduction; (c) to explore some nonconsequentialist psy-

Table 2
Policies Aimed at Reducing Harms Associated With Risky Behaviors

Policy	Risky behavior	Harms that policy tries to reduce
Mandated safety standards for motor vehicles, toys, sports equipment, food, pharmaceuticals, and so on	Driving, participation in sports, consumption of products, and so on	Physical injury, illness, death
Needle exchange	Intravenous drug use	HIV transmission
Teaching of controlled drinking skills	Drinking by diagnosed alcoholics	Social, psychological, and physical harms of alcohol abuse
School condom programs	Unprotected sexual contact among teens	Sexually transmitted diseases, unwanted pregnancies
Welfare	Becoming or remaining unemployed	Poor quality of life (housing, health, education), especially for children
Provision of benefits for illegal immigrants	Illegal immigration to the United States	Poor quality of life (housing, health, education), especially for children

chological bases for opposition to harm reduction; and (d) to offer some tentative suggestions for successfully integrating harm reduction into our national drug control strategy. The next section examines two different senses in which harm reduction might "send the wrong message," either directly through its rhetorical effects or indirectly by making drug use less risky. I offer a theoretical framework for integrating prevalence-reduction and harm-reduction policies. I believe it offers a way of thinking about harm reduction that might reduce some of the barriers to a more flexible public health orientation to U.S. drug policy. But not necessarily. The tone of the harm-reduction debate suggests that at-

titudes toward drug policies—on both sides—are influenced by deeply rooted and strongly felt symbolic factors that are largely independent of concerns about policy effectiveness per se. These factors are explored in a later section.

USE REDUCTION AND HARM REDUCTION: AN INTEGRATIVE FRAMEWORK

Micro Versus Macro Harm Reduction
The efficacy of harm reduction depends on behavioral responses to policy interventions. In explaining this point, it is important to make a distinction between levels of analysis that is sometimes ob-

scured in the harm-reduction literature. Let me begin with a truism that is largely overlooked in the harm-reduction debate: *Total Harm = Average Harm per Use × Total Use*, where total use is a function of the number of users and the quantity each user consumes, and average harm per use is a function of two vectors of specific drug-related harms, one involving harms to users (e.g., overdoses, addiction, AIDS), and the other involving harms to nonusers (e.g., HIV transmission, criminal victimization; MacCoun & Caulkins, 1996; Reuter & MacCoun, 1995).

Figure 1 depicts this relationship graphically using a causal path diagram. Links *a* and *b* depict the intended effects of harm-reduction and use-reduction policies, respectively. Links *c*, *d*, and *e* depict the ancillary harmful effects—unintended and often unanticipated—these policies might have. Link *c* denotes the unintended harms caused by prohibiting a risky behavior (e.g., the lack of clean needles, lack of drug quality control, violence associated with illicit markets, inflated prices that encourage income-generating crime, and so on; Nadelmann, 1989). This category of unintended harms is of central concern to any assessment of alternative legal regimes for drug control (MacCoun, Reuter, & Schelling, 1996). But here I focus on a second set of unintended consequences, those resulting from harm-reduction policies, to see whether objections to harm reduction have merit. If a harm-reduction strategy reduces harm per incident but leads to increases in drug use (links *d* and *e*), the policy might still achieve *net* harm reduction; on the other hand, a sufficiently large increase in use could actually result in an *increase* in total harm. There are two potential mech-

anisms for such an unintended consequence, one direct and one indirect. For reasons to be explained, link *d* can be conceptualized as the direct *rhetorical* effect (if any) of harm reduction on total use; link *e* is an indirect *compensatory behavior* effect. Either might be interpreted as "sending the wrong message."

Direct Version: Does Harm Reduction Literally Send the Wrong Message?
The rhetorical hypothesis is that irrespective of their effectiveness in reducing harms, harm-reduction programs literally communicate messages that encourage drug use. As noted earlier, those who espouse this rhetorical hypothesis rarely explain how it is supposed to work. The most plausible interpretation is that without intending to do so, harm reduction sends tacit messages that are construed as approval—or at least the absence of strong disapproval—of drug consumption.

If harm reduction service providers *intend* to send a message, it is something like this: "We view drugs as harmful. We discourage you from using them, and we are eager to help you to quit if you've started. But if you will not quit using drugs, we can help you to use them less harmfully." Is that the only message? Psycholinguistic theory and research do suggest that people readily draw additional inferences that are *pragmatically implied* by an actor's conduct, regardless of whether those inferences were intended, or even endorsed, by the actor (R. J. Harris & Monaco, 1978; Wyer & Gruenfeld, 1995). Thus if we provide heroin users with clean needles, they might infer that we don't expect them to quit using heroin— if we did, why give them needles? Arguably, this perception could undermine their motivation to quit.

Figure 1

Use Reduction and Harm Reduction: An Integrative Framework

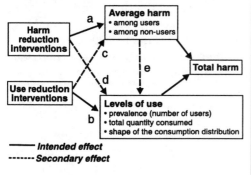

——— *Intended effect*
------- *Secondary effect*

But would users infer that we believe heroin use is *good*, or at least "not bad"? It is not obvious how harm reduction might actually imply *endorsement* of drug use. Ultimately, whether any such rhetorical effects occur is an empirical question. It would be useful to assess the kinds of unintended inferences that users and nonusers draw from harm-reduction messages, and from the mere existence of harm-reduction programs. But in the absence of such evidence, the rhetorical hypothesis that harm-reduction conveys approval of drug use is purely speculative.

Moreover, it is difficult to reconcile this notion with the secondary prevention and treatment efforts that frequently accompany actual harm-reduction interventions. Through such efforts, users are informed that their behavior is dangerous to themselves and others and that assistance and support are available to help them if they wish to quit drug use. Braithwaite's (1989) research on *reintegrative shaming* indicates that it is possible simultaneously to send a social message that certain acts are socially unacceptable while still helping the actors to repair their lives. Braithwaite suggests that this

approach is integral to Japanese culture, but it is also reflected in the Christian tradition of "hating the sin but loving the sinner."

Indirect Version: Does a Reduction in Harm Make Drugs More Attractive?
Even if no one took harm reduction to imply government endorsement of drugs, harm reduction might still influence levels of drug use *indirectly* through its intended effect, that is, by reducing the riskiness of drug use. This is a second interpretation of "sending the wrong message." Though there are ample grounds for being skeptical of a pure "rational-choice" analysis of drug use (MacCoun, 1993), the notion that reductions in risk might influence drug use is certainly plausible and would be consistent with a growing body of evidence of compensatory behavioral responses to safety interventions. Thus we should be mindful of potential trade-offs between harm reduction and use reduction.

Risk assessors have known for some time that engineers tend to overestimate the benefits of technological improvements in the safety of traffic signals, automobiles, cigarettes, and other products. The reason is that engineers often fail to anticipate that technological improvements lead to changes in behavior. When technological innovations successfully reduce the probability of harm given unsafe conduct, they make that conduct less risky. And if the perceived risks were motivating actors to behave somewhat self-protectively, a reduction in risk should lead them to take fewer precautions than before, raising the probability of their unsafe conduct to a higher level. This notion has been variously labeled *compensatory behavior, risk compensation, offsetting behavior,* or in its most extreme form, *risk homeostasis*—a term that implies efforts to maintain a constant level of risk (Wilde, 1982). Although some find this general idea counterintuitive, one economist has noted that, on reflection, it is hardly surprising that "soldiers walk more gingerly when crossing minefields than when crossing wheat fields," and "circus performers take fewer chances when practicing without nets" (Hemenway, 1988).

Compensatory behavioral responses to risk reduction have been identified in a variety of settings. For example, everything else being equal, drivers have responded to seat belts and other improvements in the safety of automobiles by driving faster and more recklessly than they would in a less safe vehicle (Chirinko & Harper, 1993). Similarly, filters and low-tar tobacco each reduce the harmfulness per unit of tobacco, yet numerous studies have demonstrated that smokers compensate by smoking more cigarettes, inhaling more deeply, or blocking the filter vents (Hughes, 1995). In both domains, some of the safety gains brought about by a reduction in the probability of harm given unsafe conduct have been offset by increases in the probability of that conduct. Though early correlational studies were criticized on methodological grounds, the compensatory behavioral hypothesis has received important support from recent controlled laboratory experiments (Stetzer & Hofman, 1996).

The compensatory behavioral mechanism suggests that if reductions in average drug-related harm were to motivate sufficiently large increases in drug use, micro harm reduction would actually increase macro harm. Blower and McLean (1994) offer a similar argument based on epidemiological simulations that suggest that an HIV vaccine, unless perfectly prophylactic, could actually exacerbate the San Francisco AIDS epidemic, provided that individuals behaved less cautiously in response to their increased sense of safety. But to date, research on compensatory responses to risk reduction provides little evidence that behavioral responses produce net increases in harm, or even the constant level of harm predicted by the "homeostatic" version of the theory. Instead, most studies find that when programs reduce the probability of harm given unsafe conduct, any increases in the probability of that conduct are slight, reducing but not eliminating the gains in safety (Chirinko & Harper, 1993; Hughes, 1995; Stetzer & Hofman, 1996). As a result, in our terms, micro harm reduction produces macro harm reduction.

Do Drug Interventions Achieve Macro Harm Reduction?

It is impossible to calculate total drug harm in any literal fashion, or to rigorously compare total harm across alternative policy regimes (MacCoun, Reuter, & Schelling, 1996). Many of the harms are difficult to quantify, and observers will differ in their weighting of the various types of harm. Thus at the strategic level of national policy formation, macro harm reduction is not a rigid analytical test but rather a heuristic principle: Are we reducing drug harms, and reducing drug use in ways that do not increase drug harm? But at the level of specific interventions, macro reduction of *specific* harms is a realistic evaluation criterion, as illustrated by the compensatory behavioral research just cited. Unfortunately, few drug policy programs are evaluated with respect to both use reduction and harm reduction. Prevention and treatment programs are generally evaluated with respect to changes in abstinence or relapse rates, whereas harm reduction evaluators tend to assess changes in crime, morbidity, and mortality rates. As a result, researchers are unable to determine whether many programs achieve macro harm reduction.

The empirical literature on needle exchange is a notable and exemplary exception. There is now a fairly sizable body of evidence that needle exchange programs produce little or no measurable increase in injecting drug use (Lurie & Reingold, 1993; Watters, Estilo, Clark, & Lorvick, 1994). Because it significantly reduces average harm, needle exchange provides both micro and macro harm reduction. But the empirical success record for needle exchange does not constitute blanket support for the harm reduction movement. Each intervention must be assessed empirically on its own terms.

Let me offer a few cautionary tales. One harm reduction intervention that has been tried and rejected is the "zone of tolerance" approach tried by Zurich officials in the Platzspitz—or, as the American press labeled it, "Needle Park." By allowing injecting drug users to congregate openly in this public park, and to shoot up without police interference, city officials were able to make clean needles and other health interventions readily available at the time and place of drug use. Even sympathetic observers agree that these benefits were ultimately offset by increases in local crime rates and in the prevalence of hard drug use in the city (Grob, 1992). Another example involves bongs and water pipes. Though these devices have been touted as a means of reducing the health risks of marijuana smoking,

a recent test found that they actually increase the quantity of tars ingested. The apparent reason harkens back to the compensatory behavioral mechanism. Water pipes filter out more THC than tar, so users smoke more to achieve the same high, thereby increasing their risk (Gieringer, 1996). The Zurich case and the bong study suggest that harm-reduction strategies can fail, but it is important to note that neither failure resulted from increasing rates of *initiation* to drug use. In the Zurich case, the prevalence of drug use rose because the park attracted users from other Swiss cities and neighboring countries. Arguably, the program might have been successful had other European cities adopted the idea simultaneously. In the bong case, the filtering benefits were offset by increases in consumption levels among users, but I am unaware of any evidence that bongs and water pipes have ever encouraged nonusers to start smoking marijuana.

One can imagine hypothetical examples of how a harm-reduction strategy might plausibly attract new users. For example, from a public health perspective, we are better off if current heroin injectors switch to smoking their drug. Imagine a public information campaign designed to highlight the relative health benefits of smoking. If some fraction of nonusers have resisted heroin because of an aversion to needles (for anecdotal evidence, see Bennetto, 1998), our campaign might indeed end up encouraging some of them to take up heroin smoking, despite our best intentions. Of course, no one has seriously proposed such a campaign. But the example demonstrates that concerns about increased use are plausible in principle.

Quantity Reduction as a Middle Ground?

As noted earlier, American drug policy rhetoric is dominated by concerns about the number of users, drawing a bright line between "users" and "nonusers." This is illustrated by our national drug indicator data. Most available measures of drug use are *prevalence* oriented: rates of lifetime use, use in the past year, or use in the past month. But drug-related harms may well be more sensitive to changes in the *total quantity consumed* than to changes in the total number of users. One million occasional drug users may pose fewer crime and health problems than 100,000 frequent users. Our nation's recent cocaine problems provide an illustration. After significant reductions in casual use in the 1980s, total consumption has become increasingly concentrated among a smaller number of heavy users. At an individual level, these heavy users are at much greater risk than casual users with respect to acute and chronic illness, accidents, job- and family-related problems, and participation in criminal activities. Thus although cocaine prevalence has declined, total cocaine consumption and its related harms have remained relatively stable (Everingham & Rydell, 1994).

This suggests that *quantity reduction* (reducing consumption levels) holds particular promise as a macro harm reduction strategy. Quantity reduction occupies a point halfway between prevalence reduction and micro harm reduction. Like prevalence reduction, quantity reduction targets use levels rather than harm levels. But like harm reduction, quantity reduction is based on the premise that when use cannot be prevented, we might at least be able to mitigate its harms.

What is less clear is the optimal targeting strategy for quantity reduction. Consider the distribution of users across consumption levels, which for most psychoactive drugs (licit and illicit) is positively skewed, with a long right tail indicating a small fraction of very heavy users. One strategy is to target those heaviest users—to "pull in" the right tail of the distribution. The marginal gains in risk reduction should be greatest at the right tail, and only a small fraction of users need be targeted.

This approach has received considerable attention—and notoriety—in the alcohol field under the rubric "controlled drinking." Few public health experts dispute the notion that problem drinkers are better off drinking lightly than drinking heavily. But there has been an extraordinary furor surrounding the notion of controlled drinking as a treatment goal. The evidence suggests that (a) although abstinence-based treatment programs experience high relapse rates, many of the relapsing clients successfully reduce their drinking to relatively problem-free levels; (b) it is possible to *teach* controlled drinking skills to many, but not all, problem drinkers; (c) we cannot yet predict which problem drinkers will be able to control their drinking at moderate levels; and (d) most treated problem drinkers fail to achieve either abstinence or controlled levels of drinking (Marlatt, Larimer, Baer, & Quigley, 1993). But opponents assert that, irrespective of any benefits to be derived from controlled drinking, the very notion undermines the goal of abstinence and discourages drinkers from achieving it. The small-scale studies conducted to date do not support that claim, but the evidence is not yet decisive.

In addition to the abstinence–moderation debate, a second quantity-reduction debate has emerged among alcohol experts. Are problem drinkers even the appropriate intervention target? An alternative quantity-reduction strategy targets the middle of the alcohol consumption distribution. For some years, many experts have argued that the total social costs of alcohol might be better reduced by lowering average consumption levels rather than concentrating on the most problematic drinkers at the right tail (Rose, 1992; Skog, 1993). If so—and this is a matter of ongoing debate in the pages of *Addiction* and other journals—broad-based efforts to reduce total drug use might indeed be the best way to achieve total harm reduction, at least for alcohol consumption. The controversy here has been more purely technical and less emotional than the controlled drinking debate, in part because few people still champion the notion of abstinence for casual drinkers. Many Americans seem quite willing to accept the notion of "non-problem" alcohol consumption yet reject the notion of "nonproblem" marijuana or cocaine consumption.

In fact, the viability of "lower-risk" drug consumption, and the relative efficacy of the "pull in the tail" and the "lower the average" strategies, will depend on a variety of factors. One factor is the degree of skew of the consumption distribution: The greater the probability mass in the right tail, the greater the efficacy of targeting heavy users. A second is the dose-response curve for risks, which is usually S-shaped for those drug-risk combinations that have been studied. (We know a great deal more about dose-response functions for health and public safety risks involving licit drugs than for comparable risks involving illicit drugs.) When this function is very steep, even moderate consumption levels are very risky, making the "shift-the-distribution" strategy more efficacious. A third factor involves the possibility that individuals with a higher propensity for danger self-select higher consumption levels. The latter effect will spuriously inflate the quantity–risk relationship. To the extent that this effect predominates, convincing right-tail users to cut back may yield fewer benefits than anticipated.

THE PUBLIC ACCEPTABILITY OF HARM REDUCTION

Whereas American citizens and policy-makers have embraced drug strategies that promote prevalence reduction, harm reduction and some forms of quantity reduction are often greeted with considerable hostility—when they are not ignored altogether. In this section, I offer a number of hypotheses about this negative reaction. The opposition to harm reduction surely has multiple causes, so these explanations are not mutually exclusive. They vary along a continuum ranging from *consequentialist* to *symbolic* grounds for opposition. Many people probably hold both kinds of views. Harm reduction opponents might be placed along this continuum based on their responses to the following hypothetical questions:

1. If new evidence suggested that needle exchange (or some other harm-reduction strategy) reduced total harm, would you still be opposed?

2. If the answer is "yes": If new evidence suggested a reduction in harm, *with no increase in use*, would you still be opposed?

3. If the answer is "yes": Would you be opposed to drug use even if it were made *completely* harmless?

Those who would say "no" to the first question are pragmatic or consequentialist in their opposition to harm reduction. Those who say "yes" to the third question are at the other extreme; for them, drug use is intrinsically immoral, irrespective of its consequences—what philosophers call a *deontological* stance. Those who would support harm reduction only if there were no increase in drug use fall somewhere in between. Their views might reflect a complex mix of instrumental and symbolic concerns.

Consequentialist Grounds

The consequentialist grounds for opposing harm reduction are the easiest to describe. They are characterized primarily by the belief that harm reduction will be counterproductive, either by failing to reduce average harm or by increasing drug use enough to increase total harm. Those who oppose harm reduction on truly consequentialist grounds should change their mind and support it if the best available facts suggest that an intervention reduces harm without producing offsetting increases in use. In recent years, the favorable evidence for needle exchange has received increasing publicity in the mass media. This media coverage may explain why a 1996 poll found that 66% of Americans endorsed needle exchange as a means of preventing AIDS —a dramatic increase over earlier surveys (The Henry J. Kaiser Family Foundation, 1996). Of course, this may be an over-optimistic reading of the impact of empirical research (MacCoun, 1998). Program evaluations rarely yield unequivocal verdicts; even when effects are statistically reliable, they are usually open to multiple interpretations. Expert consensus on the effects of high-profile policy interventions is rare, even when the accumulated body of research is large. And the vehemence of the opposition to harm reduction suggests that attitudes toward these interventions are based on something more than purely instrumental beliefs about the effectiveness of alternative drug policies.

Attitudes toward the death penalty are instructive in this regard. Attitude research indicates that many citizens overtly endorse a *deterrence* rationale for the death penalty, believing that "it will prevent crimes." Yet most do not change their views when asked how they would feel if there were unequivocal evidence that execution provided no marginal deterrence above and beyond life imprisonment. The evidence suggests that ostensibly instrumental views are actually masking deeper retributive motives (Ellsworth & Gross, 1994). As a result, support for capital punishment is relatively impervious to research findings (Lord, Ross, & Lepper, 1979).

The nonconsequentialist grounds for opposing harm reduction are more complex than the consequentialist grounds. There are a number of distinct psychological processes that might play a role in shaping these views.[2]

The Need for Predictability and Control

Harmonious social relations require a minimal level of predictability because we must routinely relinquish control to other people—automobile drivers, surgeons, airline pilots, our children's teachers, and so on. The notion that others are using drugs can be threatening because it suggests that they've lost some self-control. Although harm reduction can minimize the consequences of diminished control, it may be more reassuring to believe that others are completely abstinent. When we are unable to control aversive stimuli, any signal that helps us to anticipate danger will significantly reduce our anxiety (Miller, 1980). Perhaps the belief that others are abstinent from drugs works like a "safety signal" to free us from worrying about their conduct.

Our fears about others are augmented by a robust bias in risk perceptions. Most people—adults as well as adolescents—perceive themselves to be less vulnerable than the average person to risks of injury or harm (e.g., Weinstein & Klein, 1995). An apparent corollary is that most of us believe we are surrounded by people less cautious or skillful than ourselves. We may think we can control our own use of intoxicants (most of us feel that way about alcohol), but we find it harder to believe that others will do the same. Indeed, this might explain why a sizable minority of regular cannabis users opposes the complete legalization of that drug (Erickson, 1989).

Aversion to Making Value Trade-Offs

Our attitudes toward public policy involve more than simple judgments about effectiveness and outcomes. They are symbolic expressions of our core values. Unfortunately, most difficult social problems bring core values into conflict. Drug problems are no exception; they bring personal liberty into conflict with public safety, compassion into conflict with moral accountability. Contemplating harm reduction brings these conflicts into strong relief. According to [Philip E.] Tetlock's *value pluralism model*, acknowledging such conflicts is psychologically aversive, and so many people avoid ex-

plicit trade-off reasoning, preferring simpler mental strategies (Tetlock, Peterson, & Lerner, 1996). The easiest is to deny that there is a conflict, by ignoring one value or the other. If that doesn't work, we may adopt a simple "lexicographic" ranking. Many of us engage in complex multidimensional trade-off reasoning only when we can't avoid it, as when the conflicting values are each too salient to dismiss or ignore.

In a recent content analysis of op-ed essays debating the reform of drug laws, my colleagues and I found that legalizers and decriminalizers (all of whom were harm-reduction advocates, though the converse is not necessarily true) used significantly more complex arguments than prohibitionists (MacCoun, Kahan, Gillespie, & Rhee, 1993). The reform advocates were less likely to view the drug problem in terms of a simple good–bad dichotomy; they identified multiple dimensions to the problem and were more likely to acknowledge trade-offs and counterarguments to their own position. It may be hard to persuade others to acknowledge the full complexity of harm-reduction logic unless the values that support it become more salient in drug policy discourse.

The Propriety of Helping Drug Users

Of course, there is little basis for value conflict if one feels that drug users *should* suffer harm when they use drugs. There are a number of reasons why some people might hold this view. One is authoritarianism, a complex trait defined as a chronic tendency to cope with anxiety by expressing hostility toward outgroup members; intolerance of unconventional behavior; and submissive, unquestioning support of authority figures. Authoritarianism is strongly correlated with support for punitive drug policies (Peterson, Doty, & Winter, 1993). Indeed, several items from the Right Wing Authoritarianism Scale—a leading research instrument for measuring this trait—seem to equate authoritarianism with opposition to harm-reduction interventions almost by definition (Christie, 1991). According to Item 7, "The facts on crime, sexual immorality, and the recent public disorders all show we have to crack down harder on deviant groups and troublemakers if we are going to save our moral standards and preserve law and order." Item 12 states, "Being kind to loafers or criminals will only encourage them to take advantage of your weakness, so it's best to use a firm, tough hand when dealing with them." And authoritarians are more likely to disagree with Item 19: "The courts are right in being easy on drug offenders. Punishment would not do any good in cases like these."

But scoring high in authoritarianism is probably not a prerequisite for hostility toward drug users. There is a general antagonism to hard drug users among U.S. citizens, partly stemming from the strong association between drugs and street violence in American cities. It is much easier to see harshness as the appropriate response in the United States than in Europe, where drug use is more likely to be perceived as a health problem. Race and social distance may play a role here as well; arguably, Americans were more tolerant of drug users in the 1970s, when the mass media's prototypical drug user was an Anglo-American student in a college dorm instead of a young African American man on a city street corner (Kirp & Bayer, 1993). As a result, Americans have supported (or at least tolerated) sentencing policies that tend to disproportionately burden minority and

poor offenders relative to those who are Anglo-American or middle class (Tonry, 1995).

But irrespective of race and class, the mere fact that someone uses drugs will often be sufficient to categorize them as "the other," particularly if we don't already know them. Citizens with a friend or family member who is an addict may embrace micro harm reduction, whatever its aggregate consequences, but those who don't know any addicts may prefer a strategy of isolation and containment.

Even in the absence of malice, many people may feel that addicts should suffer the consequences of their actions. Addiction is widely viewed as a voluntary state, regardless of many experts' views to the contrary (Weiner, Perry, & Magnusson, 1988). Many Americans, especially conservatives, are unwilling to extend help to actors who are responsible for their own suffering; such actors are seen as undeserving (Skitka & Tetlock, 1993). The retributive view that bad acts require punishment is deeply rooted in the Judeo-Christian tradition, particularly in Protestant fundamentalist traditions. In light of the possibility that opposition to harm reduction traces back to our nation's strong Puritan and Calvinist roots, it is quite ironic that the Dutch and the Swiss have championed such an approach in Europe.

Disgust and Impurity

A final ground for opposing harm reduction might be the vague, spontaneous, and nonrational sense that drug use defiles the purity of the body and hence that anything that comes in contact with drug users becomes disgusting through a process of contagion. Stated so bluntly, this may sound utterly implausible; such concepts are quite alien to Western moral discourse. Nevertheless, this kind of thinking is quite explicit in other cultures, and anthropologists argue that it often lurks below the surface of our own moral judgments (Douglas, 1966; Haidt, Koller, & Dias, 1993). I know of no direct evidence that such reactions influence attitudes toward drug policy, but the hypothesis is testable in principle and worthy of further investigation.

CONCLUSION

In this [selection], I have tried to take a frank look at the arguments against harm reduction, and I have suggested that, like most policy interventions, the approach has potential pitfalls. Not every harm-reduction intervention will be successful, and some might even increase aggregate harm. We are still woefully ignorant about the complex interplay between formal drug policies and informal social and self-control factors (MacCoun, 1993). Still, the evidence to date on harm reduction is encouraging (as the success of needle exchange programs makes clear), and I believe that we have much to gain by integrating harm-reduction interventions and goals into our national drug control strategy. I conclude by offering five hypotheses about how harm reduction might be more successful—successful both in reducing aggregate harm and in attracting and retaining a viable level of political support.

1. Harm-reduction interventions should have the greatest political viability when they can demonstrate a reduction in average harm—especially harms that affect nonusers—without increasing drug use levels. Interventions that lead to increases in drug use are likely to encounter stiff opposition, even if they yield demonstrable net reductions in aggregate harm. Thus, harm-reduction interventions need to be rigorously evaluated with respect to four types of outcome: effects on targeted harms, "side effects" on untargeted harms (especially harms to nonusers), effects on participants' subsequent use levels, and effects on local nonparticipants' use levels.

2. Because the compensatory behavioral mechanism is triggered by perceived changes in risk, harm-reduction efforts seem least likely to increase drug use when those harms being reduced were already significantly underestimated, discounted, or ignored by users and potential users (see Wilde, 1982). At one extreme, if perceptions of risk are serious enough, few people will use the drug in the first place. (Witness the almost complete disappearance of absinthe after its dangers became apparent in the late 19th century.) At the other extreme, those who are either ignorant of, or indifferent to, a drug's risks, seem unlikely to escalate their use when an intervention lowers those risks.

3. Similarly, interventions involving safe-use information or risk-reducing paraphernalia should be less likely to increase total use, and hence be more politically viable, when they are highly salient for heavy users but largely invisible to potential initiates to drug use. Maintenance interventions, which provide drugs or drug substitutes for addicts, should be less likely to encourage use if the program has few barriers to entry for heavy users but high barriers to entry for casual users. (The risk of these targeting

strategies is that new initiates may fail to obtain the benefits of the interventions.)

4. Reducing users' consumption levels should generally provide harm reduction, an important strategy for achieving use reduction when heavy users refuse to become abstinent.

5. Whenever feasible, harm-reduction interventions should be coupled with credible primary and secondary prevention efforts, as well as low-threshold access to treatment.

This last point is a truism among many harm-reduction providers. Still, a few in the harm-reduction movement are uncomfortable with the notion that harm-reduction programs should urge users to stop their drug use. Some take that position on libertarian grounds, but others associate traditional use-reduction efforts with dishonesty ("reefer madness"), hypocrisy ("what about alcohol and tobacco?"), or an apparent willingness to jeopardize user health (e.g., the U.S. decision to spray Mexican marijuana crops

with paraquat in the 1970s). But harm-reduction advocates who categorically reject the opposition risk undermining their own cause. Americans who oppose harm reduction are unlikely to change their views until they feel their fears have been taken seriously.

NOTES

1. This finding is not universal; participation in needle exchanges was associated with elevated HIV risk in recent studies in Vancouver (Strathdee et al., 1997) and Montreal (Bruneau et al., 1997), though the authors caution that this association might reflect features that distinguish these evaluations from others in the literature; for example, they were conducted at the peak of the HIV epidemic, their clients were heavily involved in cocaine injection, and the number of needles dispersed fell well short of the amount needed to prevent needle sharing (Bruneau & Schechter, 1998). A broader comparison of 81 U.S. cities estimated a 5.9% increase in HIV seroprevalence in 52 cities without needle exchange, and a 5.8% decrease in 29 cities with needle exchange during the period 1988 to 1993 (Hurley, Jolley, & Kaldor, 1997).

2. Note that these psychological accounts by themselves do not constitute evidence for or against the wisdom of opposition to harm reduction, nor are they meant to imply that such views are somehow pathological.

NO

Robert L. DuPont
and Eric A. Voth

DRUG LEGALIZATION, HARM REDUCTION, AND DRUG POLICY

BACKGROUND

Two alternative policy options shape the current debate about how to move forward in addressing the Nation's problems with drug use(1). One school of thought, broadly labeled as *prohibition,* supports widening interdiction, treatment and prevention efforts while keeping drugs such as marijuana, cocaine, LSD, and heroin illegal. A conflicting viewpoint labeled *legalization* supports the elimination of restrictive drug policy while trying to limit the harms associated with non-medical drug use. Understanding the history of drug control in the United States places into perspective today's debate about drug policy options, which include legalization and the related policy called *harm reduction*(2).

Modern drug prohibition began in the 19th century when medicinal chemistry began to produce an enormous array of potent and habituating drugs. This array included heroin, which was first sold in the United States in 1898. These drugs were sold as ordinary items of commerce along with a popular new drink, cocaine-containing Coca-Cola. Physicians at that time prescribed addicting drugs freely to their patients producing a large group of medical addicts. The use of drugs such as cocaine originated with legitimate medical indications. Drug use by the public later grew rapidly to include the compulsive use, illegal activity to support the non-medical use, and consumption despite clear medical and social consequences.

This era of indiscriminate sale and use of addictive drugs ended during the first two decades of the 20th century with a new social contract embodied in the Pure Food and Drug Act of 1906(3), which dealt with the labeling of drugs. In 1914, The Harrison Narcotics Act(4), prohibited the sale of narcotics. The Volstead Act along with the 18th Amendment to the Constitution in 1919 prohibited the sale of alcohol. These laws were part of a broad reform movement in the United States which also included the rights of women to vote.

From Robert L. DuPont and Eric A. Voth, "Drug Legalization, Harm Reduction, and Drug Policy," *Annals of Internal Medicine,* vol. 123 (1995), pp. 461–465. Copyright © 1995 by The American College of Physicians. Reprinted by permission.

Under this new social contract, habituating drugs were not available except through a physician's prescription, and then they were used sparingly in the treatment of illnesses other than addiction. In 1933 alcohol was removed from the group of strictly controlled or prohibited substances. In 1937 marijuana was added to the list of prohibited substances because of a sudden increase in the use of the drug(5). The patent drug epidemic had begun with morphine and heroin in the final decade of the 19th century and ended with an explosive increase in the use of cocaine during the first decade of the 20th century.

The social contract for drugs of abuse and supporting laws served the country well by virtually ending the first drug abuse epidemic. The American drug control laws proved to be a model throughout the world during the first two-thirds of the 20th century. The use of habituating drugs, which had been out of control at the end of the 19th century, was dramatically reduced in the United States from 1920–1965(5).

The nation was lulled into complacency by the great and prolonged success of this drug abuse policy. American public and policy leaders entered a period of amnesia for the tragic consequences of widespread drug use. By the 1960's, most Americans had no personal memory of the earlier American addiction epidemic. Strict non-alcohol drug prohibition was respected broadly until the ascendant youth culture integrated drugs as a central element of its new lifestyles.

Marijuana, the hallucinogens, and cocaine became widely defined as *marginally addictive* or *soft* drugs.(6) Their use grew to be the focus of a call for legalization based on unsubstantiated claims that they were *no worse than alcohol and tobacco*. The substantial health and addiction problems currently recognized to result from the use of crack cocaine and marijuana, and extensive research now available on the harmful effects of many drugs are testimony to how society was misled in the 1960's(7). These effects include but are not limited to addiction, vehicular trauma, disease, suicide, and specific negative physical effects of drugs themselves(8–15).

LEGALIZATION OF ILLEGAL DRUGS

During recent years, the drug legalization movement has gained modest public support by attempting to associate opponents of drug legalization with the negative public perceptions of alcohol prohibition and by labeling the opponents of legalization as prohibitionists. For purposes of this discussion, prohibition is a restrictive policy which maintains legal restrictions against non-medical use or sale of addicting drugs as covered under the Controlled Substances Act(16).

Drug legalization is neither a simple nor singular public policy proposal. For example, drug legalization could at one extreme involve a return to wide-open access to all drugs for all people as was seen at the end of the 19th century. Partial legalization could entail such changes in drug policy as making currently illegal drugs available in their crude forms to certain types of medical patients. It might include the maintenance of addicts on heroin or their drug of choice, handouts of needles to addicts without the requirement of cessation of drug use, or marked softening in sentencing guidelines for drug-related offenses short of frank legalization.

The evidence of the negative global experience with the legal substances tobacco and alcohol is overlooked by most supporters of drug legalization. The data on alcohol and tobacco support the view that legalization of drugs leads to large increases in the use of the legalized drugs and to higher total social costs. These added costs are mostly paid in lost productivity, illness, and death. About 125,000 deaths annually in the United States are attributed to alcohol, while tobacco is estimated to cause 420,000 deaths annually. The deaths resulting from all illicit drugs combined total less than 10,000 annually. The social costs from alcohol use in the United States are estimated at $86 billion, while the costs of prohibiting illegal drug use (including enforcement and incarceration) are annually $58 billion(17,18). The social costs of smoking tobacco are estimated to be $65 billion annually(17). If one of the goals of a drug policy is to reduce the harm to society resulting from drug use, then alcohol and tobacco must be a top priority within this strategy.

Considering the numbers of users of illegal and legal drugs in the United States and the trends in the rates of use from 1985 to 1991 (Table 1), it becomes apparent that prohibitive drug policy actually has maintained lower levels of use compared to relatively widely available habituating substances. Equally important are the rates of use of illicit drugs which have fallen faster in comparison to the rates of legal drug use(19).

Substantial progress was made in the reduction of adolescent drug use from 1978 to 1992 (Table 2). That success was due to a relatively clear national message and broad-based anti-drug efforts in both the public and private sectors. Since 1992, a recent rise in adolescent drug use and more accepting attitudes toward drug use(20) has occurred. While the causes are multifactoral, the reduction of government and media anti-drug efforts coupled with increases in pro-drug media campaigns have played a role.

HARM REDUCTION

While reducing the harm caused by drug use is a universal goal of all drug policies, policy proposals which are currently termed *harm reduction* include a creative renaming for the dismantling of legal restrictions against drug use and sale. The essential components of legalization policies are couched within the concept termed *harm reduction*. Much of the driving force behind the harm reduction movement also centers around personal choice and *safe* drug use habits.(21)

Paradoxically, some public policy attempts at reducing the harms associated with use of alcohol and tobacco involve tightening restrictions on events such as intoxicated driver legislation and smoking restrictions(22), while current harm reduction proposals involving illegal drugs, to the contrary, generally involve softening the restrictions on use of illegal drugs.

The current proposals for harm reduction focus heavily on reduction or elimination in criminal penalties for drug offenses, softening of sentencing guidelines, addict maintenance programs, needle exchange programs for intravenous drug users, and removal of workplace drug testing programs(23). The efficacy of any of these modalities is yet to be established.

Table 1

Drug Use in the United States Prior 30 Days (in Millions)

	1985	1993	Decline
Drugs Legal for Adults			
Alcohol	113	103	9%
Cigarettes	60	50	17%
The Most Widely Used Drugs That Are Illegal for All Ages			
Marijuana	18	9	50%
Cocaine	6	1.3	78%

Source: U.S. Department of Health and Human Services, Public Health Service, National Institutes of Health. *National Survey Results on Drug Use, from the Monitoring the Future Study 1975–1993.* NIH Publication No. 94–3809, 1994.

Harm reduction policy as it is represented in the current policy debate, also attempts to mitigate the negative effects of non-medical drug use without reducing the use of illegal drugs. It is based on the assumption that most of the harm caused by non-medical drug use is the result of the societal efforts to stop drug use rather than the result of drug use itself. Those harms are considered generally to be associated with arrests and legal consequences from illegal behavior and incarceration(24). While harm reductionists contend that essentially innocent drug users are targeted by prohibition, only 2% of federal inmates are incarcerated for possession-related crime while 48% are incarcerated for trafficking. Despite the clear deterrent effect of legal penalties, some positive outcomes can be attributed to the criminal justice system. For example, 35% of drug-related inmates obtain treatment while incarcerated(25).

The Netherlands has been the international model for decriminalization and harm reduction. Their experience with decriminalization has included an increase in crime and drug use associated with decriminalization. From 1984 to 1992 cannabis use among pupils in

the Netherlands has increased 250%. Between 1988 and 1993, the number of registered addicts has risen 22%. Reflecting the decriminalization of marijuana, the number of marijuana addicts has risen 30% from 1991 to 1993 alone. As we see in the United States, the harms of increased drug use go beyond the user alone. Since the onset of tolerant drug policy in that country, shootings have increased 40%, hold ups have increased 69%, and car thefts have increased 62%(26).

In the United States we experimented briefly with the decriminalization of marijuana. That temporary softening of drug policy resulted in a statistically significant increase in emergency room drug mentions as compared to metropolitan areas not having decriminalization(27).

The current and still dominant drug policy seeks to curb drug use and the associated harms by using the legal system and other means such as workplace drug testing and treatment to reduce non-medical drug use in society. In contrast to the advocates of harm reduction or legalization, supporters of the current restrictive drug policy emphasize that most drug-related harm

Table 2

Drug Use Rates: Marijuana

	Percent of High School Seniors Use of Marijuana							
	1978	1986	1987	1988	1991	1992	1993	1994
Last 12 Mos	50.2	39.0	36.0	33.1	23.9	21.9	26.0	30.7
Last 30 Days	37.1	23.4	21.0	18.0	13.8	11.9	15.5	19.0
Daily	10.7	4.0	3.3	2.7	2.0	1.9	2.4	3.0

Source: U.S. Department of Health and Human Services, Public Health Service, National Institutes of Health. *National Survey Results on Drug Use, from the Monitoring the Future Study 1975–1993*. NIH Publication No. 94–3809, 1994.

is the result of drug use and not simply the result of the prohibition of drugs(28).

The legalizers and the prohibitionists find some common ground in the support of drug education and treatment. Supporters of restrictive drug policy teach avoidance of non-medical drug use entirely, and harm reductionists support teaching *responsible use* of currently illegal drugs. Many harm reductionists admit that they seek the ultimate legalization of illegal drugs, especially marijuana. A distinct subset of harm reductionists support harm reduction because of the element of decriminalization which takes legal pressure off of their own drug use. Those individuals seek to manipulate drug policy to justify their own drug using behaviors.

Clearly, all forms of legalization, including harm reduction, are strategies ultimately aimed at softening public and governmental attitudes against non-medical drug use and the availability of currently illegal drugs.

COSTS OF DRUG POLICY

Those who support legalization correctly point out that prohibiting the use of our currently illegal drugs is an expensive strategy. Table 3 demonstrates the sources of overall costs produced by the use of legal drugs as compared to illegal drugs. These data also illustrate the fact that restrictive drug policy shifts the costs of drug use related to health and productivity to the criminal justice system.

Augmenting a restrictive drug policy by broadening the drug treatment available to addicts may be a beneficial and cost-effective policy decision. A recent study by Rand estimates that the current societal costs and actual costs of controlling cocaine use alone total $42 billion annually ($13 billion for control costs and $29 for societal costs). Rand also estimated that the net control and societal costs related to cocaine could be reduced to $33.9 billion(29) by maintaining our current enforcement policies and adding to it treatment for all addicts. The Rand study further concluded that treatment is effective in reducing the costs to society not only by reducing the demand for drugs, but in removing the addict from drugs for sustained periods of time.

The supporters of restrictive drug policy must acknowledge that prohibition alone does not end either the use of prohibited drugs or the high cost to society resulting from the use of these drugs. Furthermore, drug prohibition achieves its goals at a substantial cost in the form of

Table 3

Economic Costs of Addiction in the United States 1990

	Illicit Drugs	Alcohol	Tobacco
Total Cost (Billions)	$66.9	$98.6	$98.6
Medical Care (%)	3.2 (4.8)	10.5 (10.7)	20.2 (28)
Lost Productivity (%)	8.0 (11.9)	36.6 (37.1)	6.8 (9.0)
Death (%)	3.4 (5.1)	33.6 (34.1)	45 (63.0)
Crime (%)	46.0 (68.8)	15.8 (16.0)	0.0 (0.0)
AIDS (%)	6.3 (9.4)	2.1 (2.1)	0.0 (0.0)

Source: Institute for Health Policy, Brandeis University. *Substance Abuse: The Nation's Number One Health Problem—Key Indicators for Policy.* Prepared for the Robert Wood Johnson Foundation, Princeton, NJ, 1998.

maintaining the criminal justice system and some restriction of personal choice. Prohibiting the use of some drugs is undeniably costly, but it is well worth the cost given the fact that the overall level and the total societal costs of drug use are reduced.

DRUG POLICY OPTIONS

Recognizing the range of options available within legalization and drug prohibition policies, it is important to look at the big picture of drug policy. We must ask if prohibiting the consumption of some drugs is effective in reducing social costs, or *harm,* and if restrictive policy is cost-effective. Two models for drug policy exist which help provide answers to these questions.

The first model looks back at life in the United States one hundred years ago to a time when habituating drugs were sold like toothpaste or candy. The problems with freely available habituating drugs at the end of the 19th century were judged by Americans at that time to be unacceptable. In the context of today's debate on drug policy, recall that prohibition policies were the result of a nonpartisan out-

cry over the serious negative effects of uncontrolled drug use. In other words, the prohibition of marijuana, heroin, and cocaine did not cause widespread drug use in the United States. Rather, widespread use of those drugs caused their prohibition. Furthermore, non-alcohol drug prohibition was successful in reducing drug use, and it was almost universally supported by all political parties in the United States and throughout the world for half a century.

To a large extent, alcohol prohibition was also successful from a health perspective while it lasted. As examples, deaths from cirrhosis of the liver fell from 29.5 per 100,000 in 1911 to 10.7 in 1929. Admissions to state mental hospitals for alcohol psychosis fell from 10 per 100,000 in 1919 to 4.7 in 1928 (30). The main failure of alcohol prohibition was in attempting to remove availability of alcohol from the public after it had been legal, accepted, and deeply integrated into society for many years. Our currently illegal drugs do not share that same level of acceptance and integration.

The second model compares the costs generated by the drugs which are now legal for adults to those which are not.

This entails comparing the social costs resulting from the use of alcohol and tobacco (legal drugs), to marijuana, cocaine, heroin, and other illegal drugs. Alcohol and tobacco produce more harm than all of the illegal drugs combined because they are so widely used. They are more widely used because they are legal. Being legal substances, they enjoy greater social acceptance, widespread advertising, and glorification. The national experience with alcohol and tobacco does not represent an attractive alternative to the prohibition of drug use as it is currently practiced in the United States and other countries throughout the world.

Because of the deep integration of alcohol and tobacco into society, prohibiting their use is unrealistic politically. However, major constraints on their use such as total elimination of advertising, high taxation, restriction on smoking locations, designated drivers programs, and product liability by manufacturers and distributors of these products show some promise in reducing the harm produced by these legal drugs(23).

RECOMMENDATIONS

The relevant policy question is whether legalization or reducing the restrictions on the availability of drugs would increase the number of drug users and total social harm produced by the use of currently illegal drugs. The available data demonstrate that legalization would increase the use of currently prohibited drugs(3,20,26,27).

Legalization or decriminalization creates a particular risk among young people whose social adaptation and maturation are not yet complete. This fact can be illustrated by comparing the levels of the use of currently legal drugs by young

Table 4

Prevalence of Drug Use in the United States High School Seniors, 1993 (Percent)

Drug	Lifetime Use	Last 30 Days
Any Illicit Drug	43	18
Marijuana	35	16
Cocaine	6	1.3
Alcohol	87	51
Cigarettes	62	30

Source: U.S. Department of Health and Human Services, Public Health Service, National Institutes of Health. *National Survey Results on Drug Use, from the Monitoring the Future Study 1975–1993.* NIH Publication No. 94–3809, 1994.

people (alcohol and tobacco) to the levels of illegal drugs. The use of all or these drugs is illegal for youth, yet the drugs that are legal for adults are more widely used by youth than the drugs which are illegal for both adults and youth (Table 4).

What is needed today is not the dismantling of restrictive drug policies. Instead, a strong national policy with the goal of reducing the harm of drug use through harm prevention (implementing drug prevention programs) and harm elimination through broader interdiction and rehabilitation efforts(31,32,33). This new policy should strengthen efforts to reduce the use of alcohol and tobacco as well as currently illegal drugs. In so doing, this policy should take aim at the especially vulnerable parts of the community with a special emphasis on the young.

If those who seek to reform drug policy and harm reduction are sincere in their intent, they would focus their efforts on alcohol and tobacco where there exists an abundant need for harm reduction and leave the currently illegal drugs illegal.

Unless those who subscribe to the notion of harm reduction move ahead to harm prevention and harm elimination, the global costs associated with any form of drug use will continue to rise. Relaxation of the restrictive policies surrounding the use of currently illegal drugs should only be considered in the context of programs which can first prove drastic and lasting reductions in alcohol and tobacco use. Real harm reduction involves prohibiting illegal drugs while concurrently working to prevent and treat their use. We do not need new experiments to tell us what we already have learned from legal alcohol and tobacco. Those experiments have already been done at the cost of great human suffering.

REFERENCES

1. DeLeon G, Some Problems with the Anti-Prohibitionist Position on Legalization of Drugs. *Journal of Addictive Diseases*, 1994;13:35–57.

2. U.S. General Accounting Office, General Government Division. *Confronting the Drug Problem—Debate Persists on Enforcement and Alternative Approaches*, GAO/GGD-93-82. Report to the Chairman, Committee on Government Operations, House of Representatives. Washington, D.C.: United States General Accounting Office, General Government Division, 1993.

3. Pure Food and Drug Act of 1906, Public Law 59-384.

4. Harrison Narcotics Act. Public Law 63-47.

5. Musto DF, *The American Disease—Origins of Narcotic Control*. New York, Oxford University Press, 1987.

6. Brecher EM, ed. *Licit and Illicit Drugs*. Boston, Little, Brown, and Co, 1972:267–306, 335–451

7. U.S. Department of Health and Human Services. *Drug Abuse and Drug Abuse Research—The Third Triennial Report to Congress from the Secretary*, Department of Health and Human Services. Washington, D.C.: Superintendent of Documents, U.S. Government Printing Office, DHHS Publication no. (ADM) 91–1704, 1991.

8. Berman AL, Schwartz RH, Suicide Attempts Among Adolescent Drug Users. *AJDC*, 1990; 144:310–314.

9. Rivara FP, Mueller BA, Fligner CL, Luna G, Raisys VA, Drug Use in Trauma Victims. *The Journal of Trauma*, 1989; 29:462–470.

10. Soderstrom CA, Dischinger PC, Sinith GS, McDuff DR, Hebel JR, Gorelick DA, Psychoactive Substance Dependence Among Trauma Center Patients. *JAMA*, 1992;267: 2756–2759.

11. Committee on Drug Abuse of the Council on Psychiatric Services, Position Statement on Psychoactive Substance Use and Dependence: Update on Marijuana and Cocaine. *Am J Psychiatry*, 1987;144:698–702.

12. Polen MR, Sidney S, Tekawa IS, Sadler M, Friedman GD, Health Care Use by Frequent Marijuana Smokers Who Do Not Smoke Tobacco. *Western Journal of Medicine*, 1993;158:596–601.

13. Nahas GG, Latour C, The Human Toxicity of Marijuana. *The Medical Journal of Australia*, 1992; 156:495–497.

14. Schwartz RH, Marijuana: An Overview. *Pediatric Clinics of North America*, 1987;34: 305–317.

15. Council of Scientific Affairs, American Medical Association. Marijuana: Its Health Hazards and Therapeutic Potentials. *JAMA*, 1981;246:1823–1827.

16. Controlled Substances Act, 21 U.S.C. 811.

17. Institute for Health Policy, Brandeis University. *Substance Abuse: The Nation's Number One Health Problem—Key Indicators for Policy*. Princeton, NJ: Robert Wood Johnson Foundation, October, 1993.

18. U.S. Department of Justice, Bureau of Justice Statistics. Chapter III, Section 5—The Costs of Illegal Drug Use. In *Drugs, Crime, and the Criminal Justice System*, NCJ-133652, 126–127. U.S. Department of Justice, Bureau of Justice Statistics, 1992.

19. U.S. Department of Health and Human Services, Substance Abuse and Mental Health Services Administration. *National Household Survey on Drug Abuse: Main Findings 1991*, DHHS Publication No. (SMA) 93-1980. Rockville, MD: U.S. Department of Health and Human Services, Substance Abuse and Mental Health Services Administration, Office of Applied Studies, 1993.

20. U.S. Department of Health and Human Services, Public Health Service, National Institutes of Health. *National Survey Results on Drug Use, from the Monitoring the Future Study 1975–1993*. NIH Publication No. 94-3809, 1994.

21. Erickson PG, Prospects of Harm Reduction for Psychostimulants. In Nick Heath, ed. *Psychoactive Drugs and Harm Reduction: From Faith to Science*. London: Whurr Publishers, 1993:196.

22. Gostin LO, Brandt AM, Criteria for evaluating a ban on the advertisement of cigarettes. *Journal*

of the American Medical Association, 1993;269:904–909.

23. Nadelman E., Cohen P, Locher U, Stimson G, Wodak A, and Drucker E, Position Paper on Harm Reduction. *The Harm Reduction Approach to Drug Control: International Progress.* The Lindesmith Center, 888 Seventh Ave, New York, NY 10106. 1994.

24. Kleiman MAR, *The Drug Problem and Drug Policy: What Have We Learned from the Past Four Years.* Testimony to the United States Senate Committee of the Judiciary, April 29, 1993.

25 Maguire K, ed. *Sourcebook of Criminal Statistics,* Bureau of Justice Statistics, U.S. Department of Justice. 1992:491.

26. Gunning KF, Dutch National Committee on Drug Prevention. Personal Communication. September 22, 1993.

27. Model KE, The Effect of Marijuana Decriminalization on Hospital Emergency Room Drug Episodes: 1975–1978. *Journal of the American Statistical Association*, 1993; 88: 737–747.

28. Kleber HD, Our Current Approach to Drug Abuse—Progress, Problems, Proposals. *NEJM*, 1994;330:361–365.

29. Rydell CP, Everingham SS, *Controlling Cocaine: Supply Versus Demand Programs.* Santa Monica, Ca.:Rand 1994.

30. Gold MS, *The Good News About Drugs and Alcohol.* New York, Villard Books, 1991: 245.

31. Board of Trustees, The American Medical Association. Drug Abuse in the United States: Strategies for Prevention. *JAMA*, 1991;265: 2102–2107.

32. Romer D, Using Mass Media to Reduce Adolescent Involvement in Drug Trafficking. *Pediatrics*, 1994;93: 1073–1077.

33. Voth E, Drug Policy Options. Letter to the Editor in *JAMA*, 1995;273:459.

POSTSCRIPT

Is Harm Reduction a Desirable National Drug Control Policy Goal?

One could argue against the concept of harm reduction on the grounds that it is immoral. The question is, Is it moral to encourage people to use illegal drugs in such a way that their dangers are minimized? If a drug is illegal, then any use could be construed as harmful. By virtue of the illegality of drugs, the only way to minimize both personal and social risk is simple: do not use drugs. Another concern regarding the harm reduction approach is that some people, especially children and young adults, may get the wrong impression or receive a mixed message regarding drug use. If the federal government promotes the concept of harm reduction, young people may feel that, in the end, drug use is not that harmful.

In his selection, MacCoun does not argue in favor of drug use. He contends, however, that many of the personal and social problems emanating from drug use can be curtailed by developing a policy of harm reduction. Another point is that focusing on a program in which the primary goal is to eliminate access to drugs is inadequate because it overlooks differences among drugs, the extent of drug use, and the different types and groups of people who are using drugs. One could argue, for example, that persuading a person to switch from injecting drugs to a less dangerous form of drug use is more important than persuading an occasional marijuana user to cease use.

DuPont and Voth feel that the evidence does not support a policy of harm reduction. They contend that lessening or abolishing criminal penalties for drug offenses, promoting needle exchange programs, and eliminating work-place drug testing has not been proven to diminish drug-related problems. Deviating from a course of action that emphasizes reducing the supply of drugs and prohibiting their use is wrong, according to DuPont and Voth. They feel that a harm reduction approach would exacerbate the problems.

For an overview of the federal government's drug policy in the United States, read the *National Drug Control Strategy,* published annually by the Office of National Drug Control Policy. This publication outlines efforts that have been enacted toward reducing drug use and lists future goals. Several chapters in the book *Drug Policy and Human Nature: Psychological Perspectives on the Prevention, Management, and Treatment of Illicit Drug Abuse* edited by Warren K. Bickel and Richard J. DeGrandpre (Plenum Press, 1996) examine the debate over the harm reduction model. Finally, an article that advocates the harm reduction approach is "Harm Reduction: An Emerging New Paradigm for Drug Education," by David Duncan et al., *Journal of Drug Education* (vol. 24, 1994).

ISSUE 8

Should Tobacco Products Be More Closely Regulated?

YES: Edward L. Koven, from *Smoking: The Story Behind the Haze* (Nova Science Publishers, 1996)

NO: John Hood, from "Anti-Smoking War Could Deny Consumers Choice," *Consumers' Research* (June 1994)

ISSUE SUMMARY

YES: Writer Edward L. Koven asserts that current restrictions on tobacco products are minimal compared to restrictions on other products. He also contends that the negative effects of smoking tobacco, especially secondhand smoke, justify more restrictive regulations, such as banning tobacco use in public places.

NO: John Hood, vice president of the John Locke Foundation in Raleigh, North Carolina, argues that the tobacco industry is already heavily regulated, that smokers should have the freedom to choose to smoke, and that the Food and Drug Administration is attempting to intrude too much into the lives of individuals.

Most people, including those who smoke, recognize that tobacco is a dangerous product. Because of tobacco's reputation as an addictive substance that jeopardizes people's health, many activists are requesting that more stringent restrictions be placed on it. As it stands now, cigarette packages are required to carry warnings describing the dangers of tobacco products. Tobacco products cannot be advertised on television or radio. And laws that prevent minors from purchasing tobacco products are being more vigorously enforced than they have ever been before. The U.S. Food and Drug Administration (FDA), however, feels that enforcement needs to be tightened even more.

Defenders of the tobacco industry point to benefits associated with nicotine, the mild stimulant that is the chief active chemical in tobacco. In previous centuries, for example, tobacco was used to help people with a variety of ailments, including skin diseases; internal and external disorders; and diseases of the eyes, ears, mouth, and nose. Tobacco and its smoke was often employed by Native Americans for sacramental purposes. For users, nicotine provides a sense of euphoria, and smoking is a source of gratification that does not impair thinking or performance. One can drive a car, socialize, study for a test, and engage in a variety of activities while smoking. Nicotine can relieve anxiety and stress, and it can reduce weight by lessening one's appetite and by increasing metabolic activity. Many smokers assert that smoking cigarettes enables them to concentrate better and that abstaining from smoking impairs their concentration.

Critics paint a very different picture of tobacco products, citing some of the following statistics: Tobacco is responsible for about 30 percent of deaths among people between ages 35 and 69, making it the single most prominent cause of premature death in the developed world. The relationship between cigarette smoking and cardiovascular disease, including heart attack, stroke, sudden death, peripheral vascular disease, and aortic aneurysm, is well documented. Even as few as one to four cigarettes daily can increase the risk of fatal coronary heart disease. Cigarettes have also been shown to reduce blood flow and the level of high-density lipoprotein cholesterol, which is the beneficial type of cholesterol.

Cigarette smoking is strongly associated with cancer, accounting for over 85 percent of lung cancer cases and 30 percent of all deaths due to cancer. Cancer of the pharynx, larynx, mouth, esophagus, stomach, pancreas, uterus, cervix, kidney, and bladder have been related to smoking. And studies have shown that smokers have twice the rate of cancer than nonsmokers.

According to smokers' rights advocates, the majority of smokers are already aware of the potential harm of tobacco products; in fact, most smokers tend to overestimate the dangers of smoking. Adults should therefore be allowed to smoke if that is their wish. Many promote the idea that the FDA and a number of politicians are attempting to deny smokers the right to engage in a behavior that they freely choose. On the other hand, tobacco critics maintain that due to the addictiveness of nicotine—the level of which some claim is manipulated by tobacco companies—smokers really do not have the ability to stop their detrimental behavior. That is, it is not really freely chosen behavior. Respondents note that the level of tar and nicotine in cigarettes has dropped almost 70 percent since the 1950s. Moreover, 40 million Americans have stopped smoking since 1964.

There is an economic element associated with this issue. Should taxpayers financially assist smokers who need medical help as a result of their use of tobacco products? Much money is collected on taxes paid by smokers, but several billion dollars go out every year to cover Medicaid costs for smoking-related illnesses. Should such illnesses be covered by government-funded medical programs?

In the following selections, Edward L. Koven argues that the scientific evidence demonstrating that tobacco use is harmful to both smokers and nonsmokers is indisputable and that greater restrictions on tobacco products are warranted. John Hood argues that the goal of the FDA is not to restrict tobacco products but to prohibit them altogether. Hood maintains that individuals should have the freedom to choose whether or not they want to smoke and that the government has no right to interfere in this matter.

YES

Edward L. Koven

BAN SMOKING IN PUBLIC PLACES

Most Americans spend a substantial portion of each day in public places such as worksites, day-care centers, schools and universities, military and educational living quarters, restaurants, public buildings, malls and athletic arenas and stadiums. Many children and adults are exposed to high levels of poisonous secondary tobacco smoke up to eight hours a day in these facilities.

Think of those unpleasant experiences in restaurants where smoke was blowing in your face for two to three hours at a time. And how about the baseball or football game where the person next to you was blowing smoke in your face for more than three hours while you were supposed to be enjoying the fresh air and sunshine. And have you ever worked at a position where a co-worker was spreading the carcinogens and toxins of secondary tobacco smoke 40 hours a week into your eyes, nose, and lungs.

It is a crime for a person to physically assault another person. It should be illegal for a person to chemically assault a person in a public facility with the carcinogens and toxins of poisonous secondary tobacco smoke. Smoking in a public facility should be at least a misdemeanor punishable by a large fine. Clearly, it is a much more serious offense against human beings than illegal parking or parking at a meter whose time has expired.

The spark that recently stimulated a great concern about the adverse health impact of secondhand tobacco smoke was the report released by the Environmental Protection Agency on January 7, 1993 containing strong evidence that secondary tobacco smoke poses a serious cancer threat to adults and a major health threat to children. The report warns that each year environmental tobacco smoke causes 3,000 lung cancer deaths, contributes from 150,000 to 300,000 respiratory infections in babies, triggers 8,000 to 26,000 new asthma cases in previously unaffected children, and exacerbates symptoms in 200,000 to a million asthmatic children.

The Environmental Protection Agency (EPA) announced guidelines on smoking in public buildings on July 21, 1993 to help curb illness from secondhand tobacco smoke reinforcing the EPA's stand six months earlier when the agency declared that secondhand tobacco smoke caused cancer and respiratory disease and should be regulated. The EPA's voluntary guidelines urged that all restaurants, schools, day-care centers, and other places where children spend time prohibit smoking or establish practices to insure that air from smoking areas is not recirculated to the rooms occupied by children. The guidelines urged parents not to smoke in their homes and nonsmokers should be protected from secondhand smoke in public areas and in the workplace.

The extent of America's exposure to environmental tobacco smoke [ETS] is not easy to fully comprehend. The EPA in its June 1989 pamphlet "Indoor Air Facts No. 5" entitled "Environmental Tobacco Smoke" succinctly explained why environmental tobacco smoke is so abundant and harmful.

The EPA pointed out that "ETS comes from secondhand smoke exhaled by smokers and sidestream smoke emitted from the burning end of cigarettes, cigars, and pipes." Environmental tobacco smoke is a "mixture of irritating gases and carcinogenic tar particles." The EPA report goes on to point out that these gases and carcinogenic tar particles are a known cause of lung cancer, respiratory symptoms, and have been linked to heart disease.

As of June 1989, the EPA pointed out that there were 50 million American smokers annually smoking 600 billion cigarettes, four billion cigars, and the equivalent of 11 billion pipefuls of tobacco annually. Since people spend approximately 90 percent of their time indoors, about 467,000 tons of tobacco are burned indoors each year. Over a 16-hour day, the average smoker smokes about two cigarettes per hour taking about ten minutes per cigarette. The EPA points out that it only takes a few smokers in a given space to release a more-or-less steady stream of environmental tobacco smoke into the indoor air.

The EPA points out that because the organic material in tobacco does not burn completely, cigarette smoke contains more than 4,700 chemical compounds including carbon monoxide, nicotine, carcinogenic tars, sulfur dioxide, ammonia, nitrogen oxides, vinyl chloride, hydrogen cyanide, formaldehyde, radio-nuclides, benzene, and arsenic. There are 43 carcinogenic compounds in tobacco cells. In addition, some substances are mutagenic which means they can cause permanent, and often harmful, changes in genetic materials of cells.

Smoking in the home, according to the EPA, includes serious respiratory changes in children with asthmatic children particularly at risk. The risk of cancer and heart disease is much greater.

The EPA concluded in June 1989 that environmental tobacco smoke can be totally removed from the indoor air only by removing the main source—cigarette smoking. The agency points out that separating smokers and nonsmokers in the same room as in some restaurants may reduce, but will not eliminate nonsmokers' exposure to harmful tobacco smoke since they are on the same ventilation system. The EPA points out that research indicates that total removal of tobacco smoke through ventilation is both technically and economically impractical.

Surprisingly, a 1987 Gallup opinion poll found that 55% of all persons interviewed, including both nonsmokers and smokers, favored a total ban on smoking in public places. A 1994 New York Times/CBS News poll revealed that 67% of the persons interviewed favored such a ban, up from 61% in a November 1991 Gallup poll.

The tobacco company spin control spokespersons have attempted to poke flaws in the methodology of the EPA studies. However, I have not heard of one reputable scientist or physician supporting the tobacco industry position or maintaining that smoking and secondary tobacco smoke are not harmful to human beings. As recently reported in the Journal of the American Medical Association, smoking by physicians declined from 18.8% in the mid-1970s to 3.3% in 1990 and 1991. Apparently the tobacco industry is attempting to persuade the American public that it is all right to smoke unless the government can show "beyond a reasonable doubt," the standard for criminal guilt, that tobacco smoke and secondary tobacco smoke are harmful to the smokers and the nonsmokers. Such a high standard is not utilized for recall of potentially dangerous children's toys, a potentially dangerous car defect, where contaminated food is found, when a few bottles of a medication such as Tylenol has been contaminated, or when a few bottles of Perrier has been found to contain benzene, one of the compounds contained in secondary tobacco smoke. Unlike other industries, the tobacco industry has been given a free ride to poison American children and adults with the 43 carcinogens and toxins in secondary tobacco smoke and thus endanger the health and lives of more than 200 million American nonsmokers.

It is imperative to the health of our nation that we eradicate our workplaces, restaurants, public buildings, malls, athletic facilities, schools, day-care centers, and public transportation vehicles from the harmful tobacco smoke by banning smoking in all these facilities. Steps have been taken at the local, state and federal levels to eliminate smoking in public facilities, but more needs to be done. For example, as of March 1992 over 500 communities in the United States have enacted ordinances restricting smoking in workplaces, restaurants and other public places, 19 completely eliminated smoking in workplaces, and 25 eliminated smoking in all restaurants. Since environmental tobacco smoke meets the criteria of the Occupational Safety and Health Administration for classifying substances potentially occupational carcinogens, both the EPA and the National Institute of Occupational Safety and Health recommend that smoking be eliminated in all workplaces, or be restricted to private rooms that have a separate ventilation system which is exhausted directly outside.

The private sector, whether because of concerns for its employees or because of fear of lawsuits, has voluntarily established total smoking bans in 34% of workplaces as of March 1992 compared with 2% in 1986. Another 34% restrict smoking in all common areas. Caring parents, concerned employers, and responsible elected officials are coming to the same conclusion—smoking in public facilities should be banned. The only groups opposing these bans besides the smokers are the tobacco industry and those related businesses who believe that profits are more important than human lives.

RESTAURANTS

... There is little question that waiters, bartenders, and other food service workers face a significantly elevated risk of lung cancer from breathing customers' smoke. Dr. Michael Siegel, whose research was conducted during his residency at the University of California at Berkeley, reviewed studies of indoor air quality in restaurants, bars, offices and homes containing at least one smoker as well as several epidemiology studies of mortality among food service workers published between 1977 and 1993.

Dr. Siegel found that levels of secondhand smoke in restaurants were 1.6 to 2 times higher than in offices and 1.5 times higher than in homes with at least one smoker. The level of secondhand smoke in bars which tend to have more smokers and poorer ventilation than restaurants was 3.9 to 6.1 times higher than offices and about 4.5 times higher than in homes containing a smoker. Dr. Siegel estimates that restaurant workers face a 50% greater risk of developing lung cancer than the general population. This conclusion is consistent with the EPA report released in January 1993 estimating that about 3,000 nonsmokers die annually of lung cancer caused by secondhand smoke. Moreover, Dr. Siegel points out that while being seated for an hour or two in a restaurant nonsmoking section may help customers, nonsmoking sections do not help employees who work eight-hour shifts since tobacco smoke tends to diffuse to fill all areas, a basic law of physics.

In a related study, Dr. Siegel found that California waitresses and waiters are twice as likely to die of lung cancer as people in other occupations because they inhale their customers' secondhand cigarette smoke. Waitresses have the highest mortality rate of any predominantly female occupation in California.

By industry estimates as many as 25% of fast food customers are under 18, 10% are under age 10, and as many as 40% of the employees in fast food restaurants are under 18. The overwhelming majority of fast food restaurants permit smoking on the premises.

A group of 15 state Attorney Generals in May 1993 formed a working group to study tobacco-related issues, with a focus on passive smoke and children. The study was sparked by the EPA January 1993 report concluding passive tobacco smoke is carcinogenic. The report concluded that nonsmokers who inhale passive smoke face increased risks of lung cancer, respiratory track infections, asthma attacks and coughing, with children at particular risk. Since millions of American children spend time eating and playing in designated areas in fast food restaurants and working behind counters, the 15 Attorney Generals have developed a series of recommendations to the fast food industry to facilitate the development of smoke free restaurant environments.

The Attorney Generals made the following observations:

1. Most fast food companies would ultimately like to go smoke free;
2. Many companies would prefer to wait until legislative smoking bans are enacted before ordering a smoke free policy for their customers;
3. The companies would not oppose legislation to ban smoking in restaurants and some even indicated a willingness to support such legislation;
4. The companies are concerned that they may lose business if they implement a smoke free policy before their competitors do;
5. The companies want to operate on a level playing field with respect to smoking policies.

Of course, it is anticipated that tobacco companies, tobacco industry PACs [political action committees] and their lobbyists will do everything legally possible to thwart such legislation banning smoking in restaurants and especially fast food chains. They are aware that tobacco smoke and secondary tobacco smoke kills, but they are more concerned about tobacco company and industry profits than the health and lives of children and restaurant workers. . . .

The 15 State Attorney Generals made the following preliminary recommendations for implementing smoke free policies in fast food restaurants:

1. Implement a corporate smoke free policy in all corporate locations immediately, and a minimum of 10% of all corporately owned fast food restaurants initially and expand this policy by an additional 20% in each quarter thereafter;
2. Implement a smoke free policy in all newly opened corporate restaurants;
3. Require a smoke free policy as part of all new franchise agreements;
4. Encourage all franchise operators to implement a smoke free policy immediately;
5. Remove cigarette vending machines from all fast food restaurants;
6. Support legislation to ban smoking in restaurants;
7. Post a warning in corporate and franchise operated restaurants that are not smoke free of the dangers of smoking, especially to children.

The State Attorney General recommendations are sound food for thought suggestions. Parents and especially their children deserve a break today and every day from being exposed to the carcinogens and toxins of poisonous secondary tobacco smoke. Parents should be warned that a Big Mac attack may be the precursor of a smoking-induced asthma attack. Perhaps ample "cynical menus" to persuade state and local legislators to vote for smoking bans in restaurants could contain items such as carcinogen burgers, toxin burgers, poison dogs and a benzene shake. Dining and working in restaurants may be a sure fast track to Marlboro Country, the local cemetery, unless smoking is banned.

Word has gotten around to the big restaurant chains. For example, effective June 1, 1995, Dunkin' Donuts has banned smoking in its 3,000 shops. Other large restaurant chains have and will follow the Dunkin' Donuts example.

SMOKING IN THE WORKPLACE

There is no question that smoking in the workplace is harmful. A health physicist who has specialized in indoor air pollution examined portions of two buildings containing federal offices in a large city downtown area where smoking was not permitted. When asked what would happen if smoking were to be initiated in these office spaces, the physicist said that the work areas would be turned into "gas chambers" in one building because of the age and the shape and ventilating problems and in the other building because of serious air flow obstructions resulting from remodeling. The health physicist noted that the buildings he had examined were not atypical. It is unfortunate that many workers have to spend at least 40 of the 168 hours in a week in such unhealthy work environments.

The National Institute for Occupational Safety and Health (NIOSH) concluded in June 1991 that cigarette smoke causes cancer and possibly heart disease. NIOSH recommended that employers "should minimize occupational exposure to environmental tobacco smoke by using all available preventive measures." The purpose of the report was to persuade many employers to impose or toughen smoking restrictions in the workplace and to assist the Occupational Safety and Health Administration (OSHA) to establish regulations for smoking in the workplace. OSHA has been reluctant to take meaningful steps to regulate passive smoking in the workplace. Finally, in March 1994 OSHA took the first steps towards banning smoking in almost all workplaces.

A study in the Journal of the American Medical Association concluded that where there were limited bans on smoking, nonsmokers in workplaces were 2.8 times more likely to be exposed to environmental tobacco smoke than those working in a smoke free environment. The author of this 1990 California Tobacco Survey conducted by the University of California-San Diego indicated "that the only way to protect non-smokers' health is with a smoke-free work site."

Aside from the health and humanitarian reasons, it makes sense from a business economics standpoint to ban smoking in the workplace. Dr. William Weiss, Chairman of the Accounting Department of the University of Seattle Business School, estimates that a smoker costs an employer $4,611 each year broken down as [in Table 1].

In April 1994 Lockheed Aeronautical Systems followed a small group of companies such as Turner Broadcasting and Northwest Airlines that will no longer hire smokers. A spokesman for the Marietta-based subsidiary of Lockheed Corp., a 10,000 person unit affected by this new policy, pointed out the policy will help cut health costs since smokers cost more on a long-term basis. The company cited a study finding that 77% of Lockheed's employees who are cardiac patients also smoke. Hopefully, other companies will follow the lead of Turner Broadcasting, Northwest Airlines, and Lockheed in an effort to both hold down health care costs and improve the health of the American worker by not hiring smokers. Such a step will be an important additional incentive for the nation's 46 million smokers to stop.

A growing number of insurance companies offer premium reductions for life, health, fire and casualty policies for companies that have smoke-free workplaces. Smoking in the workplace may result in higher worker's compensation case recoveries. Absenteeism for smokers is generally higher than nonsmokers. There is every reason from a health standpoint to have a smoke-free work environment.

It is surprising that it took so long for many hospitals to eliminate smoking. Day-care centers where parents entrust the safety and health of their children should have similar restrictions. Whether day-care center workers smoke should be high on the list of questions asked by any parent seeking a place to care for his or her children each workday.

With approximately three fourths of workers being nonsmokers, the quarter minority subjecting the overwhelming majority to the carcinogens and toxins of secondary tobacco smoke is liable to create a great deal of resentment and animosity in the workplace. In a country where the majority rules, why should a minority be permitted to subject the overwhelming majority, including pregnant employees at particular risk, to major health risks? There is no excuse, even a union contract provision, for a working condition that subjects three quarters of the employees who care about the quality of the air they breathe

Table 1

On the job time spent smoking	$1,820
Morbidity/Early Mortality	765
Property Damage	500
Maintenance	500
Effects on nonsmokers (secondhand smoke)	486
Medical care	230
Absenteeism	220
Insurance (excluding health)	90

to increased lung cancer, heart disease, emphysema, and other health risks.

Senator Frank Lautenberg from New Jersey and Representative Henry Waxman from California proposed legislation banning smoking in all public facilities to protect nonsmokers from exposure to poisonous secondary tobacco smoke. The legislation was suggested not only by the American Lung Association, the Coalition on Smoking or Health, and the American Academy of Pediatrics, but also the Building Owners and Managers Association International which manages or owns more than five billion square feet of North American office space. The nation's more than 200 million nonsmokers should ascertain how their representatives stand on the bill or similar bills and how much tobacco PAC and industry money their representatives receive, if any. The voters should not be fooled by someone like New York Congressman Edolpus Towns who when questioned about how the $8,100 he got from the tobacco industry influenced his vote against the airline smoking ban, he glibly replied, "Not at all, I don't know who contributes to my campaign." ...

ATHLETICS

It is annoying and unhealthy to go to a baseball game and other athletic events and sit through both the pre-game festivities and the game with cigarette,

cigar and pipe smoke blowing in one's face for three to four hours. ...

Since experiencing over three hours of tobacco smoke blowing in my face at a 1991 Northwestern-Notre Dame football game at smoky Soldier Field in Chicago, I have refused to go to any athletic stadium where smoking is permitted. Hopefully many of the other over 200 million nonsmokers will follow suit. ...

More than half of the major league baseball stadiums have 100% smoke free seating. As of the fall of 1993, the Atlanta Braves, the Boston Red Sox, the Chicago Cubs, the Chicago White Sox, the Florida Marlins, the Kansas City Royals, the Milwaukee Brewers, the New York Mets, the New York Yankees, the Pittsburgh Pirates, the St. Louis Cardinals, and the San Francisco Giants had 100% smoke free seating. A number of stadiums are also tobacco ad free. Hopefully pressure by the paying public to all athletic events will result in all stadiums being 100% smoke free, including eating and restroom areas, and tobacco ad free. Parents with asthmatic children should consider keeping their children away from smoky sports facilities.

Many athletic events, including tennis and automobile racing, are sponsored by tobacco companies. There is no rational relationship between athletics, good health, and smoking. The nation's over 200 million nonsmokers should boycott all tobacco-sponsored sporting events, just for the health of it.

Some unions have obstructed the enactment of a health and safety measure designed to benefit their bargaining unit members—banning smoking. As of June 15, 1993, tobacco use was banned in the minor leagues. The ban applies to players, coaches, and umpires anywhere in the ballpark or on team buses. While officials can unilaterally put the ban into effect in the minor leagues, such a ban must be subject to collective bargaining with the major league union, the Major League Baseball Players Association. For the sake of the health of major league ballplayers, their families, and the youth of this country who frequently emulate athletes, the major league union should be urged to follow the minor league ban.

Many years and decades ago athletics were supposed to encompass everything that is healthy about life. The multi-million dollar contracts, the influence of television, and the huge endorsement money for athletes has made the "health" aspect of athletics a myth. . . .

Bowling alleys are a nonsmoker's horror. Although I enjoyed bowling, I quit in my late teens because I could not stand the smoke-filled bowling alleys. It is amazing that one's lungs can survive until the fifth or beer frame. Local ordinances curtailing smoking in bowling alleys would protect youngsters as well as adults from the horrors of smoking.

OTHER PUBLIC PLACES

Most commercial airline flights in the United States have been smokefree since 1990 thanks to the courageous testimony of flight attendants who passed on their horror stories of colleagues being struck down by lung cancer from working in smoke-filled gas chamber type environments. Their stories were so emotionally overwhelming that tears were seen in the eyes of several members of Congress during the hearings leading up to the airline smoking ban. The tobacco companies and PACs were unable to prevent passage of the legislation in this highly emotional atmosphere. The International Civil Aviation Organization has recommended that all international flights be smoke free. The Clinton administration is reportedly attempting to speed up the process by revising its agreement with other nations directly.

During the April 1992 National Collegiate Athletic Association final-four basketball weekend in Minneapolis the only motel available to me at the last minute was a recently refurbished dive that reeked of tobacco smoke compounded by an antique ventilation system. I should have slept outside in a sleeping bag. It would have been much healthier. Fortunately hotels are designating nonsmoking floors and rooms since tobacco smoke gets into the carpeting, curtains, and blankets and smells up the rooms. Hopefully in the foreseeable future all hotels and motels will be designated 100% smokefree.

A friend similarly complained of a rental car that made her ill from the residues of tobacco smoke. A renter frequently has an option of requesting a nonsmoking car.

Banks and other financial institutions have begun to institute total bans on smoking. One of the largest downtown banking institutions in Chicago, the Northern Trust Company, initiated a total smoking ban on July 1, 1993, for health and economic reasons.

The railroads in this country have frequently been slow to modernize and stay up to date with the times. Amtrak in 1993 finally decided to ban smoking on all trains with scheduled running time of less than $4^1/_2$ hours and on selected routes 6 hours or less, as well as trains within California and selected sleeping cars. This came more than three years after similar bans on domestic airline flights.

A parent assumes when sending his or her son or daughter to college that the child is going to get a sound education in a healthy environment. All too frequently the son or daughter gets assigned to a smoking roommate and thereby finds himself or herself in an unhealthy indoor air environment a significant portion of the time.

The Columbia University Center on Addiction and Substance Abuse chaired by former HEW Secretary Joseph A. Califano, Jr., issued a report in August 1993 urging the nation's colleges to create smoke free campuses, including a ban on the sale, advertising, and distribution of tobacco products on the nation's 3,535 college campuses containing 14 million students with almost 25% who smoke. The report points out that since "virtually all Americans who smoke begin in their teens or early twenties" higher educational institutions should take steps to limit the opportunities to buy and consume cigarettes. Besides calling for a ban on smoking in all campus facilities, vehicles, and dormitories, the report encouraged universities to offer treatment programs to help students quit smoking. The report said that besides improving the health of faculty and students, a smoke free campus would protect universities from possible future lawsuits from graduates asserting damages from secondary tobacco smoke and would reduce health care and cleaning costs.

A number of universities have already implemented no smoking policies. Indiana University at Bloomington was scheduled to become smokefree as of November 1, 1993. Smoking was banned in all indoor air space on campus including faculty, staff, student, and administrative offices, as well as University owned and leased housing.

The lead by universities such as Indiana should be followed by high school, grade school, nursery school, and day-care center faculties and support staff by banning smoking on school and center premises. Adults should lead by example.

Starting in the 1950s shopping malls sprouted up throughout the country. With the indoor malls, came the proliferation of smokers. With about a quarter of today's adult population smokers, one out of every four adult visitors to a shopping mall is a potential spreader of the carcinogens and toxins of secondary tobacco smoke. Those parents who have an asthmatic child or child with other bronchial problems, might be advised to boycott those indoor malls that permit smoking.

Many malls have banned smoking. The International Council of Shopping Centers has reported that many of the nation's 38,966 shopping centers visited by 179.4 million customers each month have announced plans to go smoke free. The huge Mall of America in Bloomington, Minnesota, has had a no-smoking policy since it opened on August 11, 1992, which did not deter 35 million people from visiting it during the first year.

Of the nation's 38,966 shopping centers, 1,835 are enclosed malls containing at least 400,000 square feet. Of the enclosed malls as of December 1993, 93 in New York, all centers in Houston, Fulton and DeKalb Counties in Georgia, Howard and Anne Arundel County in Maryland, and a few in New Jersey are smoke free. The 103 centers operated by JMP were scheduled to become smoke free January 1, 1994.

The shopping centers are visited by 179.4 million adults each month or 94% of the country's population of which 13% are 15 to 19 years olds. Clearly, banning smoking in the nation's nearly 39,000 shopping centers will help make them a healthier place for all child and adult visitors.

NO

John Hood

ANTI-SMOKING WAR COULD DENY CONSUMERS CHOICE

Are tobacco products regulated? The average person would no doubt answer yes. In the past two decades, at least 600 local laws have been passed across the country to require non-smoking areas in workplaces, schools, government buildings, public facilities, and restaurants. Every state legislature has taken action against smoking in one form or another. On the federal level, tobacco advertising is heavily regulated—banned from broadcast and saddled with labeling requirements in print. Manufacturers must also live with significant reporting requirements for ingredients and additives. And the Occupational Safety and Health Administration [OSHA] proposed a new rule in March that would ban smoking in virtually all indoor workplaces, including bars and restaurants.

But to many regulators and anti-smoking activists, these numerous restrictions seem almost irrelevant. Former U.S. Surgeon General Antonia Novello once said that tobacco was "the least regulated consumer product" in the country. Tobacco is "a product that is virtually unregulated for health and safety," says Scott Ballin, vice president for public affairs at the American Heart Association. Ballin and other activists have been pressing the U.S. Food and Drug Administration (FDA) for years to assert regulatory authority over tobacco—a move that, given current FDA requirements about the "safety" of products, would almost certainly result in banning virtually all tobacco products. FDA Commissioner David Kessler has recently suggested to a congressional subcommittee that his agency does, indeed, have such authority, given so-called "new" information about the use of tobacco as a drug.

Naturally, tobacco companies, farmers, and smokers' rights groups will fight such a move tooth and nail. Indeed, cigarette manufacturer Philip Morris has already filed a multi-million-dollar libel suit against ABC-TV's "Day One" program for its allegations that tobacco companies add nicotine to cigarettes to foster addiction among consumers.

At stake, however, is not simply the survival of the tobacco industry or tobacco farmers. The real issue is freedom of choice by consumers of all products, not merely cigarettes. Kessler recognizes this implication and stated to Congress that "it is fair to argue that the decision to start smoking may be a matter of choice. But once they have started smoking regularly, most smokers are in effect deprived of their choice to stop smoking." The commissioner is arguing that he, as head of the FDA, must step in to help consumers who can't otherwise help themselves. His intention may be genuine benevolence, but the result of such new regulation would codify and extend the powers of an agency that already limits the freedom of individual consumers to make their own decisions.

A RISKY DECISION

Are smokers the prisoners of nicotine and therefore of the companies that supply their "fix"? Kessler reports that even smokers who develop serious health conditions, presumably as a result of their smoking, remain "in the grip of nicotine." After surgery for lung cancer, he says, almost half of smokers resume smoking. Among smokers who suffer a heart attack, 38% resume smoking while they are still in the hospital.

Overall, Kessler argues that 15 million of the 17 million Americans who try to stop smoking every year fail. But the fact remains that since 1964, more than 40 million people have stopped smoking permanently without any outside intervention or assistance. Over the past decade, domestic consumption of tobacco has dropped both in share (37% of Americans were smokers in 1981, 30% in 1991) and in products (U.S. smokers consumed 640 billion cigarettes in 1981, 500 billion in 1991). Perhaps one reason for this is that, according to statistics from the U.S. Department of Health and Human Services,

levels of tar and nicotine have *fallen* by almost 70% since the 1950s, in nicotine's case, from 2.5 milligrams per cigarette to less than 1 milligram. This fact is difficult to square with conspiracy theories about manufacturers spiking cigarettes with nicotine to keep smokers addicted.

Indeed, the evidence that manufacturers do this is essentially that manufacturers *could* do this. Kessler's case, and that of other anti-smoking partisans, centers almost entirely around patents obtained by tobacco companies for processes which replace nicotine lost during manufacturing. When confronted with strong industry denials that spiking has occurred—as well as evidence showing that there is less nicotine than in the original tobacco leaves from which they are made—Rep. Henry Waxman (D-Calif.) claimed that manufacturers were only playing semantic games. Deliberately restoring some of the nicotine lost during manufacturing is still "playing around with nicotine levels," he said. But tobacco industry officials reply that previous attempts to introduce nicotine-free cigarettes have flopped, and that the presence of the substance clearly affects a smoker's enjoyment of the product.

However, the crucial question in evaluating Kessler's argument is not just whether tobacco companies spike cigarettes, but what should be the operative definition of "addiction." Many of us use the term addiction in loose fashion. We sometimes say we're addicted to coffee, to chocolate, to Cajun cooking, to television. In every case, what we mean is that we value highly the experience of consuming a product or participating in an activity that provides us pleasure, and even that we would be willing to sacrifice other valuable goods—be they money or time—to continue our consumption.

Some of these addictions have a physical component, such as the caffeine in coffee. Others do not.

Using the broadest definition of addiction, most Americans might legitimately be termed "addicts." They could give up their addictions, but it would be distressing for them to do so. Not only are there millions of people who have tried and failed to quit smoking—there are also millions of people who have tried and failed to stop eating fatty foods and sweets, to give up coffee and sodas, to exercise regularly, or to limit the time they spend watching TV. In every case, one can argue that there are health issues at stake (in the case of TV, perhaps mental health issues). At most, tobacco's risks differ only by degree, not by kind; certainly the health risks of alcohol abuse, high-fat diets, and a sedentary lifestyle are themselves most serious. The Center for Science in the Public Interest claims that 445,000 Americans die prematurely each year from poor diet and lack of exercise, compared with 420,000 per year from tobacco use. Alcohol abuse kills around 100,000.

In *Smoking: Making the Risky Decision,* published in 1993, Duke University researcher Kip Viscusi challenges the notion that smokers, as distinguished from people who engage in other personally or socially destructive behavior, are not to be trusted to make their own decisions. "We make choices throughout our lives that are costly to reverse—getting married, choosing a profession, selecting a place to live, and purchasing a car. The fact that reversing such decisions is costly does not imply that such choices are incorrect." Viscusi's research has found that smokers tend to accept and tolerate higher levels of risk in other areas, such as choice of career. They also tend to overestimate, not underestimate, the risks associated with smoking, reflecting the effectiveness of decades of public service and campaigns on the evils of tobacco.

As long as there are lower-nicotine cigarettes, nicotine patches, chewing gum, and fortitude, some smokers will limit their risk, others will eliminate it altogether by quitting, and still others will choose to continue their habit, most of them knowing the risks they are assuming. Viscusi notes that survey data showing most smokers want to quit but can't are about as reliable as surveys showing that most people want to move to the country or change jobs, even though they never do: "Survey statements in which individuals indicate that they would like to quit smoking, for example, might mean that they would like to smoke without risk. However, the fact that they have continued to smoke even with the availability of chewing gum with nicotine suggests that these statements . . . should not always be taken at face value."

Obviously, the debate on smoking regulation would change dramatically with the introduction of solid evidence that significant numbers of *nonsmokers* are harmed by tobacco smoke. But . . . such evidence does not yet exist. Indeed, if the risk the consumption of a substance poses on innocent bystanders is to be the criterion for banning the substance, then bringing back the prohibition of alcohol would be a much higher priority than banning cigarettes, given the former's undeniable role in many of the 44,000 traffic fatalities each year. So far, the highest number of second-hand smoke fatalities the EPA can come up with —by massaging the data well beyond believability—is 3,000 a year. (See also,

"Facts Catch Up With 'Political' Science," *CR*, May 1993.)

So, the new war against tobacco, predicated on the idea that cigarettes are nothing more than the delivery system for a highly addictive drug, must be waged on behalf of paternalism, not concern for bystanders. To justify a major expansion of federal regulatory authority, Kessler and the Congress should have to prove that smokers cannot help themselves and do not recognize the risks associated with their behavior—and that regulation would resolve these problems.

MUZZLING INFORMATION

Unfortunately, Kessler does not really have to prove these points. Once Congress decides that the FDA has authority to regulate cigarettes, the burden of proof for all health and safety issues shifts to manufacturers and consumers. The government doesn't have to prove that tobacco kills innocent bystanders, or that nicotine can be reduced without affecting the quality of tobacco products, or that new tobacco products are unsafe, to make rulings. Instead, tobacco companies will have to prove that their products are "safe," which under the FDA definition means essentially risk-free, an admittedly impossible standard to meet for these products.

Based as it is on the "guilty until proven innocent" standard, the FDA's scrutiny of new pharmaceuticals has already deprived consumers of products from which they might have obtained great benefit. The average cost of developing a new drug approaches $360 million, according to the U.S. Office of Technology Assessment. A good amount of this cost reflects regulatory compliance. Firms have to file separate ap-

plications, running up to 1,000 pages each, for different treatments by the same drug. The approval process can last up to 12 years. In recent years, the FDA has stymied efforts to bring drugs to market that could have treated patients suffering from Alzheimer's disease, angina, hypertension, gastric ulcers, heart conditions, and AIDS.

The agency has also limited or prohibited advertising of health claims that it doesn't believe are conclusively proven by scientific research. So, despite the fact that many researchers think the regular ingestion of aspirin may help prevent heart attacks, the FDA forbids aspirin manufacturers from telling consumers this. The agency has made similar rulings regarding health claims for vitamins, nutritional supplements, and foods. It even allows health claims for some *foods* containing vitamins—such as vitamin E, vitamin C, and betacarotene—but not for *supplements* containing the same vitamins. These restrictions prevent many consumers from discovering and evaluating information that could help them make healthier choices. As former Federal Trade Commission economist Paul Rubin says, "the FDA behaves as if it has a general aversion to provision of information to consumers by manufacturers."

The FDA "is charged with regulating 'false and misleading' advertising and product labeling. However, the agency has substantial discretion in fulfilling this mission," Rubin adds. "While advertising which is clearly false should be eliminated, the agency uses its mandate to enforce an extremely broad interpretation of misleading [advertising] and thereby muzzles the flow of valuable information to consumers."

Kessler says that because extension of the FDA's authority to tobacco would likely result in an immediate ban, Congress should impose stiff regulations directly on the industry that stop short of an outright ban.

But even enacting legislation to give the FDA specific powers to regulate nicotine content, the manufacturing process, and the introduction of new tobacco products would represent a massive increase in the agency's power over the average American. Once let loose on tobacco, the FDA will probably never be restrained by subsequent legislation, as the drafter of the current anti-smoking bill, Rep. Mike Synar (D-Okla.), has admitted. "We wanted to get the jurisdiction over tobacco into the FDA," he says. "It was simple politics. Once we got the product in there, we wouldn't have to do anything legislatively again."

The question must be asked: Where do we stop? Will the FDA also regulate the fat content of steaks, or require that caffeine be removed from all soft drinks (obviously this can be done, given the prevalence of caffeine-free brands today)? And it's not just the FDA that will be emboldened by congressional action here. Efforts by OSHA, EPA, and other regulators will intensify. Regulatory scrutiny of personal behavior will move beyond the workplace as well. Already courts in 11 states have ordered parents to stop smoking or risk losing custody of their children. Will parents next be forced to comply with diet, exercise, or other behavioral guidelines?

At the core of the new war on tobacco is the notion that federal agencies must not only provide information about the risks of what consumers choose to do, but also substitute their judgment to prevent consumers from choosing the "wrong" things.

Health and safety issues are not so cut and dried. Many popular activities have varying levels of risks and benefits, and consumers differ dramatically in how tolerant they are of risk and how highly they value pleasure or satisfaction. No team of regulators is qualified to make blanket judgments about what is and isn't a good choice for consumers. And when government makes such judgments, the consequences can be significant—ranging from lost satisfaction and pleasure to, in the case of drug approvals, lost lives.

The FDA should become less intrusive, not more. Consumers have good reason to make decisions for themselves, given their disparate interests and needs in a marketplace of one-quarter billion Americans. Given the opportunity and accurate, timely information, most consumers will make choices that maximize their happiness. The FDA's role, like that of other federal agencies, should be to provide such information and let individual Americans, even smokers, take it from there.

POSTSCRIPT

Should Tobacco Products Be More Closely Regulated?

Much data indicates that smoking cigarettes is injurious to human health. For example, more than 400,000 people die from tobacco-related illnesses each year, costing the U.S. health care system more than $80 billion annually. Hood, however, questions the accuracy of that data. How the data are presented and interpreted may affect how one feels about the issue of placing more restrictions on tobacco products. There is currently a great deal of antismoking sentiment in society. Even Hood does not *recommend* that people use tobacco products; he states only that the consequences linked to it may be exaggerated.

Despite the reported hazards of tobacco smoking, many proponents of smokers' rights assert that smoking is a matter of choice. However, former U.S. Food and Drug Administration (FDA) commissioner David Kessler argues that smoking is not a matter of choice because smokers become addicted to nicotine. Kessler agrees that the decision to start smoking is a matter of choice, but that once dependency occurs, "most smokers are in effect deprived of the choice to stop smoking." Nevertheless, says Hood, people make all types of choices, and if the choices that people make are ultimately harmful, then that is their responsibility.

Several times a year the SmokeFree Educational Services publishes *Smoke-Free Air*, a newsletter describing actions that have been taken to limit smoking in public locations. In "Prying Open the Door to the Tobacco Industry's Secrets About Nicotine," *JAMA* (October 7, 1998), Richard D. Hurt and Channing R. Robertson describe actions taken by states to get the tobacco industry to admit that it covered up industry documents revealing that nicotine is an addictive drug and that industry strategies utilized this knowledge to increase cigarette sales. In a similar article, "The Defeat of Philip Morris' California Uniform Tobacco Control Act," *American Journal of Public Health* (December 1997), Heather MacDonald, Stella Aguinga, and Stanton A. Glantz discuss the techniques used by Philip Morris and other tobacco companies to prevent tobacco control by local municipalities.

On the Internet . . .

http://www.dushkin.com

The Addiction Research Foundation (ARF)
Located in Toronto, Canada, the Addiction Research Foundation conducts workshops and publishes reports on topics ranging from pharmacology to drug treatment, the incidence of drug use, and drug prevention.
http://www.arf.org

The National Center on Addiction and Substance Abuse at Columbia University (CASA)
The National Center on Addiction and Substance Abuse at Columbia University provides access to information, research, and commentary on tobacco, alcohol, and drug abuse issues, including prevention, treatment, and cost data.
http://www.casacolumbia.org

Drug Watch International
Drug Watch International is a volunteer, nonprofit information network and advocacy organization that promotes the creation of healthy drug-free cultures in the world and opposes the legalization of drugs.
http://www.drugwatch.org

Action on Smoking and Health (ASH)
Action on Smoking and Health is a national, nonprofit legal action and educational organization that fights for the rights of nonsmokers and addresses the problems associated with smoking. *http://ash.org*

National Clearinghouse for Alcohol and Drug Information (NCADI)
The National Clearinghouse for Alcohol and Drug Information, a service of the Substance Abuse and Mental Health Services Administration, publishes thousands of government publications and resource materials from several government agencies. *http://www.health.org*

PART 2

Drugs and Social Policy

Except for the debate over legalizing marijuana for medicinal use, each debate in this section focuses on drugs that are already legal. Despite concerns over the effects of illegal drugs, the most frequently used drugs in society are legal drugs. Because of their prevalence and legal status, the social, psychological, and physical impact of drugs like tobacco, alcohol, and prescription drugs are often minimized or discounted. However, tobacco and alcohol cause far more death and disability than all illegal drugs combined.

The recent trend toward medical self-help raises questions of how much control one should have over one's own health. The current tendency to identify nicotine as an addictive drug and to promote the moderate use of alcohol to reduce heart disease has generated controversy. In the last several years the increase in prescriptions for the antidepressant drug Prozac and the stimulant Ritalin has also created much concern. Lastly, should marijuana be prescribed for people with certain illnesses for which some have suggested the drug could be beneficial?

■ Should Marijuana Be Legal for Medicinal Purposes?

■ Should Doctors Promote Alcohol for Their Patients?

■ Is Nicotine Addictive?

■ Are Too Many Children Receiving Ritalin?

■ Is Prozac Overprescribed?

ISSUE 9

Should Marijuana Be Legal for Medicinal Purposes?

YES: Lester Grinspoon and James B. Bakalar, from *Marihuana, the Forbidden Medicine,* rev. and exp. ed. (Yale University Press, 1997)

NO: Robert L. DuPont, from *The Selfish Brain: Learning from Addiction* (American Psychiatric Press, 1997)

ISSUE SUMMARY

YES: Professor of psychiatry Lester Grinspoon and law lecturer James B. Bakalar argue that anecdotal evidence indicates that marijuana has medical benefits for patients suffering from chemotherapy nausea, AIDS, glaucoma, chronic pain, epilepsy, and migraine headaches. They assert that the federal government is prohibiting its use without justification.

NO: Robert L. DuPont, a clinical professor of psychiatry, contends that the medicinal value of marijuana is questionable and inconclusive. He maintains that the many people who support marijuana use for medical purposes are ultimately looking for a way to establish marijuana use for nonmedical purposes.

Since the mid-1990s voters in California, Arizona, Oregon, Colorado, and other states have passed referenda to legalize marijuana for medical purposes. Despite the position of these voters, however, the federal government does not support the medical use of marijuana, and federal laws take precedence over state laws. A major concern of opponents of these referenda is that legalization of marijuana for medicinal purposes will lead to its use for recreational purposes.

Marijuana's medicinal qualities have been recognized for centuries. Marijuana was utilized medically as far back as 2737 B.C., when Chinese emperor Shen Nung recommended marijuana, or cannabis, for medical use. By the 1890s some medical reports had stated that cannabis was useful as a pain reliever. However, despite its historical significance, the use of marijuana for medical treatment is still a widely debated and controversial topic.

Marijuana has been tested in the treatment of glaucoma, asthma, convulsions, epilepsy, and migraine headaches, and in the reduction of nausea, vomiting, and loss of appetite associated with chemotherapy treatments. Many medical professionals and patients believe that marijuana shows promise in the treatment of these disorders and others, including spasticity in amputees and multiple sclerosis. Yet others argue that there are alternative drugs and treatments available that are more specific and effective in treating these disorders than marijuana and that marijuana cannot be considered a medical replacement.

Because of the conflicting viewpoints and what many people argue is an absence of reliable, scientific research supporting the medicinal value of marijuana, the drug and its plant materials remain in Schedule I of the Controlled Substances Act of 1970. This act established five categories, or schedules, under which drugs are classified according to their potential for abuse and their medical usefulness, which in turn determines their availability. Drugs classified under Schedule I are those that have a high potential for abuse and no scientifically proven medical use. Many marijuana proponents have called for the Drug Enforcement Administration (DEA) to move marijuana from Schedule I to Schedule II, which classifies drugs as having a high potential for abuse but also having an established medical use. A switch to Schedule II would legally allow physicians to utilize marijuana and its components in certain treatment programs. To date, however, the DEA has refused.

Currently, marijuana is used medically but not legally. Most of the controversy surrounds whether or not marijuana and its plant properties are indeed of medical value and whether or not the risks associated with its use outweigh its proposed medical benefits. Research reports and scientific studies have been inconclusive. Some physicians and many cancer patients say that marijuana greatly reduces the side effects of chemotherapy—it has antiemetic qualities that are greater than other, legally prescribed chemotherapy buffers. Many glaucoma patients believe that marijuana use has greatly improved their conditions. In view of these reports by patients and the recommendations by some physicians to allow inclusion of marijuana in treatment, expectations have been raised with regard to marijuana's worth as a medical treatment.

Marijuana opponents argue that the evidence in support of marijuana as medically useful suffers from far too many deficiencies. The DEA, for example, believes that studies supporting the medical value of marijuana are scientifically limited, based on biased testimonies of ill individuals who have used marijuana and their families and friends, and grounded in the unscientific opinions of certain physicians, nurses, and other hospital personnel. Furthermore, marijuana opponents state that the safety of marijuana has not been established by reliable scientific data weighing marijuana's possible therapeutic benefits against its known negative effects.

In the following selections, Lester Grinspoon and James B. Bakalar assert that the federal government has set up needless political roadblocks to prevent needy individuals from receiving the medicinal benefits of marijuana. Robert L. DuPont argues that marijuana should not be used for legal medical purposes because the current research on marijuana's medicinal benefits is insufficient, unreliable, and poorly conducted.

YES

Lester Grinspoon and
James B. Bakalar

IN DEFENSE OF ANECDOTAL EVIDENCE

It is often objected, especially by federal authorities, that the medical usefulness of marihuana has not been demonstrated by controlled studies. We have
[elsewhere] discussed the several experiments with large numbers of subjects
suggesting an advantage for marihuana over oral THC and other medicines.
But such studies have their limitations. They can be misleading if the wrong
patients are studied or the wrong doses used. The focus of the studies is
a statistically significant effect on a group, but medicine has always been
concerned mainly with the needs of individual patients. Idiosyncratic therapeutic responses to a drug can be obscured in group experiments, where there
is often little effort to identify the features of patients that affect responses.

Today drugs must undergo rigorous, expensive, and time-consuming tests
to win approval by the Food and Drug Administration [FDA] for marketing
as medicines. The purpose of the testing is to protect the consumer by establishing both safety and efficacy. Because no drug is completely safe (nontoxic)
or always efficacious, a drug approved by the FDA has presumably satisfied a
risk-benefit analysis. When physicians prescribe for individual patients, they
conduct an informal analysis of a similar kind, taking into account not just
the drug's overall safety and efficacy but its risks and benefits for a given
patient and a given condition. The formal drug-approval procedures help to
provide physicians with the information they need to make this analysis.

First, the drug's safety (or rather, limited toxicity) is established through
animal and then human experiments. Next, double-blind controlled studies
are conducted to determine whether the drug has more than a placebo effect
and is more useful than an available drug. As the difference between drug
and placebo may be small, large numbers of patients are often needed in
these studies for a statistically significant effect. Medical and governmental
authorities sometimes insist that before marihuana is made legally available
to patients, this kind of study should be performed for each of the [necessary]
indications.

But it is doubtful whether FDA rules should apply to marihuana. First, ...
there is no question about its safety. It has been used for thousands of years by

millions of people with very little evidence of significant toxicity. Similarly, no double-blind studies are needed to prove marihuana's efficacy. Any astute clinician who has experience with [certain] patients knows that it is efficacious to some degree for many people with various symptoms and syndromes. What we do not know is what proportion of patients with a given symptom will get relief from cannabis and how many will be better off with cannabis than with the best presently available medicine. Here large controlled studies will be helpful.

Physicians also have available evidence of a different kind, whose value is often underestimated. Anecdotal evidence commands much less attention than it once did, yet it is the source of much of our knowledge of synthetic medicines as well as plant derivatives. As Louis Lasagna, M.D., has pointed out, controlled experiments were not needed to recognize the therapeutic potential of chloral hydrate, barbiturates, aspirin, curare, insulin, or penicillin. He asks why regulators are now willing to accept the experiences of physicians and patients as evidence of adverse effects but not as evidence of therapeutic effects.[1]

There are many more recent examples of the value of anecdotal evidence. It was in this way that the use of propranolol for angina and hypertension, of diazepam for status epilepticus (a state of continuous seizure activity), and of imipramine for childhood enuresis (bedwetting) was discovered, although these drugs were originally approved by regulators for other purposes. A famous recent example is minoxidil, which was developed by the Upjohn Company to lower blood pressure. The company had no idea that topical application could restore lost scalp hair. But anecdotal evidence (later confirmed by controlled studies) was so persuasive that it is now marketed mainly as a treatment for baldness. Another drug, tretinoin (Retin-A), was originally marketed as an acne treatment. Anecdotal evidence that it had antiwrinkle properties led to formal studies proving its effectiveness for that purpose. Further studies have now been inspired by new anecdotal evidence that it can erase liver spots—brownish freckle-like blemishes on the hands and face of older people caused by exposure to sunlight.

As early as 1976 several small and methodologically imperfect studies, not widely known in the medical community, had shown that an aspirin a day could prevent a second heart attack. In 1988, a large-scale experiment demonstrated effects so dramatic that the researchers decided to stop the experiment and publish the life-saving results. On one estimate, as many as 20,000 deaths a year might have been prevented from the mid-1970s to the late 1980s if the medical establishment had been quicker to recognize the value of aspirin. The lesson is suggestive: marihuana, like aspirin, is a substance known to be unusually safe and with enormous potential medical benefits. There is one difference, however; it was impossible to be sure about the effect of aspirin on heart attacks without a long-term study involving large numbers of patients, but the reports we have presented show that cannabis often brings immediate relief of suffering, measurable in a study with only one subject. Anecdotes or case histories of the kind [we have studied] are, in a sense, the smallest research studies of all.

Anecdotes present a problem that has always haunted medicine: the anecdotal fallacy or the fallacy of enumeration of favorable circumstances (counting the hits and ignoring the misses). If many people suffering from, say, muscle spasms caused by multiple sclerosis take cannabis and only a few get much better relief than they could get from conventional drugs, those few patients would stand out and come to our attention. They and their physicians would understandably be enthusiastic about cannabis and might proselytize for it. These people are not dishonest, but they are not dispassionate observers.

Therefore, some may regard it as irresponsible to suggest on the basis of anecdotes that cannabis may help people with a variety of disorders. That might be a problem if cannabis were a dangerous drug, but, as we shall see, it is remarkably safe. Even in the unlikely event that only a few people get the kind of relief [we have] described, it could be argued that cannabis should be available for them because it costs so little to produce and the risks are so small.

In addition to anecdotal evidence, there is an experimental method known as the N-of-1 clinical trial, or the single-patient randomized trial. In this type of experiment, active and placebo treatments are administered randomly in alternation or succession to a patient. The method is often useful when large-scale controlled studies are impossible or inappropriate because the disorder is rare, the patient is atypical, or the response to the treatment is idiosyncratic.[2]

Following are excerpts from an N-of-1 study published in the British medical journal the *Lancet* in 1995:

After reading accounts in the press that smoking cannabis had improved the symptoms of other patients with multiple sclerosis, a forty-five-year-old man with multiple sclerosis persuaded his general practitioner to prescribe nabilone [the British equivalent of dronabinol]. Nabilone is a synthetic cannabinoid with powerful antiemetic effects licensed for short-term use in patients undergoing chemotherapy. He obtained immediate benefit from a small dose of the drug, reporting decreased pain from muscle spasm, cessation of nocturia [bedwetting], and an improvement in how he felt generally. Because nabilone is only available by hospital prescription, his general practitioner was unable to continue the drug and he was referred to the Wessex Neurological Centre.

The patient had been seen ... in 1974. At that time, symptoms and signs of right-sided sensory disturbance together with a history of unicular central visual loss and, on fundoscopy, pallor of both optic discs suggested a diagnosis of multiple sclerosis. Over the next twenty years, his disease had pursued a relapsing and remitting course, but his disability had gradually increased. He now has a severe paraparesis [a partial paralysis of the lower limbs] and is no longer independently mobile.

We were unsure whether the improvement in symptoms that this patient reported was due to a pharmacological effect of nabilone or a placebo response and suggested to him that we evaluate the treatment in an n-of-1 trial. He readily agreed. Nabilone 1 mg every second day or placebo was given for four successive periods each lasting four weeks. The starting treatment was randomly allocated, and thereafter treatments alternated [see figure 1]. The patient knew about the design of the study, but the capsules containing nabilone were indistinguishable from those containing placebo and neither he nor his doctors were aware which treatment periods had been allocated to the active drug. He evalu-

Figure 1

Symptoms of Multiple Sclerosis in Relation to Treatment with Nabilone (Tetrahydrocannabinol)

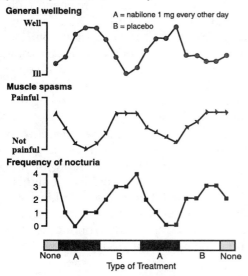

Reproduced from C. N. Martyn, L. S. Illis, and J. Thom, "Nabilone in the Treatment of Multiple Sclerosis," Lancet 345 (March 4, 1995): 579.

ated the effectiveness of treatment at the end of each week by noting frequency of nocturia on the previous night and by use of visual analogue scales to quantify pain and discomfort from muscle spasm and record how he felt generally.

The results of the trial are summarized in figure 1. The patient's reports show a striking reduction in frequency of nocturia and severity of muscle spasm and an improvement in mood and well-being that correspond to the periods of treatment with nabilone.

Transient feelings of euphoria are experienced by some patients taking nabilone. Our patient did not report such an effect, although he noticed a brief period of mild sedation after taking the active drug. This may have helped him distinguish between active drug and placebo, but it seems unlikely that the benefits he experienced derived from nabilone's mood-elevating effects.[3]

Donald Spear, Greg Paufler, Robert Randall, and Harvey Ginsburg—four of the patients who [have told us] their stories—carried out somewhat similar experiments on themselves when they alternated periods of cannabis use with periods of no use. In Paufler's case the target symptom was muscle spasms. In Spear's case it was severe and debilitating pruritus (itching), and in the cases of Randall and Ginsburg, it was loss of vision. Ginsburg, as we have seen, actually collected formal scientific data. Admittedly, in these experiments cannabis was not administered randomly in alternation with a placebo, but the psychoactive effects of marihuana are usually unmistakable, and few patients or observers would be deceived by a placebo. This kind of experiment, of course, has limitations. It can be used only for disorders that are stable and chronic, and the effect of the treatment must be both fairly rapid and quickly reversible on discontinuation. Nevertheless, it is certain that cannabis won its reputation as a medicine partly because many other patients around the world carried out the same kind of experiment.

A NOTE ON THE PHYSICIAN'S ROLE

We have seen repeatedly in these case histories that people who use cannabis as a medicine must suffer the anxiety, uncertainty, and risks associated with obtaining and using an illegal substance. The responses of physicians, as indicated in their stories, vary a great deal. A few are hostile or contemptuous, some are indifferent or unconvinced, and many offer at least some encouragement or moral support. Unfortunately, most are either afraid to do more because of the law or able to provide nothing more because they have been miseducated about cannabis and simply know too little about its therapeutic value.

But there are also signs in these stories and elsewhere that physicians are becoming more sophisticated about this drug. As several of the above accounts illustrate, they are learning about it in an unusual way—not from articles in medical journals or the advertisements of drug companies, but from their patients. In a typical case, a person with AIDS who has been wasting away despite everything he and his physician can do, discovers that cannabis slows down or even reverses his weight loss. On his next visit to the doctor he steps on the scale and proves it. Eventually the physician's incredulity is overcome, and he may tell other patients about it. As more and more physicians undergo this unusual form of drug education, medical societies and organizations will eventually have to change their official positions on cannabis.

That change may be on the way already. In 1995, fifty years after its editorial attacking the LaGuardia Commission, the American Medical Association [AMA] invited the authors of this book to write an editorial for the *Journal of the American Medical Association*. Its title was "Marihuana as Medicine: A Plea for Reconsideration." After reviewing some medical uses of marihuana and noting its safety, we concluded: "We are not asking readers for immediate agreement with our affirmation that marihuana is medically useful, but we hope they will do more to encourage open and legal exploration of its potential. The ostensible indifference of physicians should no longer be used as a justification for keeping this medicine in the shadows."[4]

Although the journal was careful to point out that our opinion did not represent the official position of the AMA, the decision to publish it signals a change in attitude that is ultimately driven, we believe, by the experiences of patients repeatedly coming to the attention of their physicians.

NOTES

1. L. Lasagna, "Clinical Trials in the Natural Environment," in *Drugs Between Research and Regulations*, ed. C. Stiechele, W. Abshagen, and J. Koch-Weser (New York: Springer-Verlag, 1985), 45–49.

2. E. B. Larson, "N-of-1 Clinical Trials: A Technique for Improving Medical Therapeutics," *Western Journal of Medicine* 152 (January 1990): 52–56; G. H. Guyatt, J. L. Keller, R. Jaeschke, et al., "The N-of-1 Randomized Controlled Trial: Clinical Usefulness," *Annals of Internal Medicine* 112 (1990): 293–299.

3. C. N. Martyn, L. S. Illis, and J. Thom, "Nabilone in the Treatment of Multiple Sclerosis," *Lancet* 345 (March 4, 1995): 579.

4. L. Grinspoon and J. B. Bakalar, "Marihuana as Medicine: A Plea for Reconsideration," Commentary, *JAMA* 73:23 (June 21, 1995): 1875–1876.

NO
Robert L. DuPont

MARIJUANA AS MEDICINE

Marijuana, like opium, coca leaves, and alcohol, has a long history as a folk medicine used to treat an endless variety of human miseries. Prescientific cultures, lacking modern purified, potent medicines, relied on commonly available natural psychoactive substances to reduce human suffering. The abused drugs, because of their effects on the brain's pleasure/pain centers, were attractive in this role. In addition, incorporating these abusable substances into folk medicines rather than making them available for personally controlled pleasure ensured that their use within the community would be controlled not merely by the user but by culturally responsible therapists. Thus, the use of folk medicines was not for recreational purposes but for medical purposes with strict cultural controls.

Until the middle of the 19th century, there were few chemically pure medicines, so the use of complex natural substances, such as opium and cannabis, was common. In the last half of the 19th century, modern chemistry purified chemicals used as medicines so that morphine was extracted from opium and cocaine was extracted from the coca leaf. Only in the late 1960s was purified THC extracted from marijuana leaves and resin and identified as the chemical that causes the high and many of the other effects of marijuana use.

Modern medicine, beginning in the first two decades of the 20th century, for the first time brought chemical science to the ancient art of medical therapeutics. Physicians from then on did not use unpurified and unstable natural products as medicines. They used chemically purified and stable pharmaceuticals to treat specifically diagnosed medical illnesses. For severe pain, for example, physicians prescribed morphine or, in more recent years, synthetic opiate substitutes, rather than prescribing a mixture of alcohol and opium, called *laudanum,* as occurred in the 19th century and earlier. By using a chemical that was pure and stable, physicians knew precisely what their patients were taking and could give their patients these substances free of a hodgepodge of inactive and potentially harmful substances. Physicians could be sure that the specific therapeutic substance was present in a known, controllable dose.

Marijuana, with over 420 chemicals, let alone marijuana smoke, with over 2,000 different chemicals, many of which are known to be harmful to the user's health, is not an attractive modern medicine. Nevertheless, marijuana smoke does have powerful effects on the brain and other parts of the body. Modern biomedical research into the effects of smoked marijuana has identified many effects, some of which may be found to have therapeutic potentials to treat specific illnesses.

Several years ago, dronabinol (Marinol), a synthetic THC, was approved by the FDA as a medicine in both capsule and suppository forms to treat the severe nausea and vomiting sometimes caused by cancer chemotherapy. When patients are treated with powerful medicines to kill cancer cells in their bodies, the medicines also are toxic to other rapidly dividing cells in the body, including those in the gastrointestinal tract and those that make both red and white blood cells. Some of these anticancer medicines also stimulate the brain's vomiting center. Nausea and vomiting after cancer chemotherapy are both extremely unpleasant and potentially dangerous, especially for people who are already seriously ill.

Doctors discovered that THC reduces nausea and vomiting for such patients. This led to strong political pressure from the promarijuana lobby to approve marijuana for medical treatment as a compassionate response to the suffering of cancer patients. Marijuana, or even purified THC, was not and never has been proposed as a treatment for cancer. The only proposed use for marijuana or THC in the treatment of cancer patients is to treat the nausea and vomiting associated with the use of chemotherapy.

Oncologists, the medical specialists who treat cancer, studied THC and found that it was helpful for some patients but that it had many unwanted side effects, including making it unsafe to drive a car and sometimes causing psychosis. Most cancer patients who were not previously drug addicted found the effects of THC to be extremely unpleasant. Oncologists did not want to use smoked crude marijuana as a medicine because it contained so many chemicals, some of which actually caused cancer and suppressed the immune system, and because the dose of THC reaching the patient could not be controlled accurately with smoking. In recent years, new synthetic medicines, unrelated to THC or marijuana, have been developed that have made THC obsolete in the treatment of nausea and vomiting from chemotherapy. Ondansetron (Zofran) is one example of these new, more effective, far safer, and more powerful antinausea medicines.

Marijuana has been proposed as a treatment for the wasting (loss of appetite and loss of weight, which can be life threatening) in AIDS because of marijuana's well-known tendency to produce "the munchies," or the desire to eat high-calorie foods. Not only is there no solid scientific evidence that marijuana or THC helps AIDS patients, but marijuana's well-known ability to depress the immune system and to cause cancer makes it extremely unattractive as a medicine for AIDS sufferers, who are literally dying from damaged immune systems. The fact that marijuana can cause some AIDS sufferers to feel high and therefore less upset is no more a reason to use marijuana as medicine for these sick patients than it is to give them alcohol or cocaine.

Marijuana has been proposed as a treatment for asthma, but, although THC does dilate the bronchi (which are closed down by asthma attacks) in the short run, the irritants in marijuana smoke actually cause lung pathology, including long-term bronchial constriction, after prolonged use. Therefore, marijuana is not likely to gain favor as an asthma treatment.

It has been proposed that marijuana can be used to treat glaucoma. THC does reduce the pressure in the eye for a few hours, as do many other substances, including alcohol. However, glaucoma is a 24-hour-a-day disease, so a person who is treated for glaucoma with marijuana has to smoke pot or take THC pills around the clock. Worse still, marijuana and THC are weak in their effects on pressure in the eyeball, so the person with glaucoma has to use not only around-the-clock marijuana smoke or THC but also routine glaucoma medicines. No controlled scientific studies have shown that THC or marijuana add anything useful to the other medicines routinely used in the treatment of glaucoma, all of which last longer, produce fewer unwanted side effects, and are more powerful in their effects in reducing eye pressure than is marijuana, or THC.

Marijuana has been proposed as a treatment for the spasticity of multiple sclerosis. No controlled studies have been conducted to show that THC helps with this serious problem, although cannabidiol, a nonpsychotropic cannabinoid found in marijuana, may prove effective. These preliminary results showing benefit from the use of cannabidiol have not been confirmed in controlled studies.

The National Institutes of Health recently completed a review of all the proposed medical uses of marijuana and THC and concluded that there was no longer any basis for the government to have a compassionate program to supply marijuana to sufferers from any illness whatsoever. None of the medical uses for marijuana so far proposed met even the minimal standards of safety and efficacy required of a proposed medicine. Thus, although THC capsules and suppositories remain available to doctors treating cancer patients for nausea and vomiting, there is no other approved use for THC, and there is no approved use for smoked marijuana as a medicine to treat any illness. When THC and marijuana have been used in experimental settings to treat various illnesses, doctors have found that the psychoactive effects—the high and the mental clouding—are unpleasant to most patients, except those who were previously drug abusers. Marijuana and THC are poorly tolerated and exceedingly unattractive to most medical patients.

Meanwhile, the promarijuana lobby has not been satisfied with the approval of purified, synthetic THC because they want to focus on very sick patients using smoked marijuana, the crude drug, as medicine. They want the public to see smoked marijuana as medicine— as a way of rehabilitating the negative image of marijuana. Promarijuana apologists insist on the use of crude, smoked marijuana, not THC or other purified chemicals for medical treatments. The marijuana-as-medicine controversy has become a political issue in North America.

The FDA and the National Institutes of Health oppose such proposals, as do the National Institute on Drug Abuse and the Drug Enforcement Administration. Virtually all of the medical organizations that speak up for the welfare of the patients in each of the proposed areas where marijuana might be used are also opposed to marijuana as medicine. Most of the proponents of marijuana as medicine are the same people who want to normalize and/or legalize illicit drugs, especially marijuana.

It is useful to remember that all abused drugs have powerful effects on the body It may someday be discovered that one or more of the individual chemicals in some of the commonly abused drugs will play a uniquely useful role in the medical treatments of some illnesses. The biomedical research now going on into the effects of abused drugs may identify important therapeutic effects of some of these specific chemicals.

Even the most antidrug activist needs to recall the nature of the modern social contract for drug use. It specifies that, under the careful supervision of a physician, abused drugs will be available in medical treatments of illnesses other than addiction. Thus, medical use is not an enemy of drug abuse prevention, as long as the medical use of potentially addictive medicines meets the standards set for other medicines and as long as the use is properly controlled to protect both the patient being treated and the community from the potential harm such medicines can cause when they leak out of the medical care system.

To this contract for medical treatments with abused drugs, I add one additional element. Substances that are of high abuse potential and substances that are currently widely used nonmedically in the society should be required to meet a higher standard than substances not widely abused. Not only should they be shown as safe and effective in specific medical applications, the standard that any medicine must meet, but they should also meet the standard that they provide a significant benefit not currently available from nonabused or less abused medicines.

Thus, before THC or heroin, two widely abused substances, are introduced as medicines, they should be shown to offer specific benefits not available with less socially risky substances. Although it is possible that in the future some of the chemicals in abused drugs will meet this higher standard, none does so today. Certainly, smoked marijuana will never be approved as a medicine, any more than smoked tobacco or, for that matter, alcohol, will be approved as an acceptable modern medicine.

The marijuana-as-medicine advocates have several advantages in the current political debates over medical use. The prodrug lobby is large and powerful in North America, and it has now concentrated on this issue because it has proved powerless in its earlier, more frontal assault on the prohibition against marijuana. To sharpen their attacks on prohibition and to gain supporters, promarijuana advocates have focused on the most feared illnesses that induce the greatest sympathy for their sufferers, such as terminal cancer, AIDS, and multiple sclerosis. They have exploited the widespread conviction that the government agencies that control the approval of medicines are too slow and too tradition-bound to approve many medicines that can help suffering patients with these illnesses, especially potential medicines that are controversial because they are abused drugs.

Finally, this lobby has capitalized on the interest in traditional medicines and on alternatives to modern scientific medicines, both of which have enjoyed a new vogue in recent years. Folk medicines have an appeal to many North

Americans who fear modern science. Thus, the fact that marijuana was used for centuries as a folk medicine is seen, in this highly romanticized view, as evidence that it should be available today as a prescribed or an over-the-counter remedy.

Recall the free-for-all days of the end of the 19th century when patent medicines did contain abused drugs. Although the promarijuana lobby can score some points today by talking about folk medicines in ancient China, the patent medicine debacle of a hundred years ago not only is closer to home but virtually impossible to romanticize. Americans tried the experiment of using cocaine, heroin, alcohol, and other abused drugs as folk medicines, as over-the-counter products, at the beginning of the 20th century. It was an unmitigated disaster. We do not need to repeat that experiment at the end of the 20th century.

The way medicines are approved in the United States today not only favors medicines that are developed and sponsored by large, sophisticated pharmaceutical companies, but the current path to approval by the FDA requires the issuing of a potentially lucrative patent that permits the recovery of the large costs of gaining approval. Because no one can patent ancient drug substances such as opium and marijuana, there is no money in such remedies for modern pharmaceutical companies.

Government agencies that often sponsor biomedical research, including research into the effects of abused drugs, seldom promote specific medicines, and when they do they have a hard time gaining FDA approval. Thus, if any of the chemicals in abused drugs were to show promise as more effective medicines than the medicines currently in use, it would not be easy to get approval within the current system. On the other hand, patents can be granted for specific chemicals in these crude, traditional drugs.

Today, more than 70 chemicals found in marijuana or related to chemicals found in marijuana smoke are under active investigation by pharmaceutical companies in all parts of the world. The normal profit motive will reinforce the desire of these companies to find more effective medicines for serious illnesses. It is possible that someday, perhaps soon, one or more of these chemicals will become widely useful in the modern treatment of a disease. If so, we can all be grateful for one more benefit from the modern scientific study of abused drugs, because that study will have been the basis of the new medicine.

A persistent fantasy of mine is that someday there will be a clear-cut positive medical use from one of the chemicals in abused drugs, and I will be able to join with my longtime foes in the drug prohibition battles and support approval for the medical use of the substance. This would please me greatly because it would add credibility to my claim all these years that I do not oppose the medical uses of these substances on a political, or even an emotional, basis, but simply because none of the chemicals in currently widely abused drugs has met the minimum standard of showing promise that it is better for the treatment of any illnesses than currently available medicines. When I see that evidence, I look forward to joining in the battle on the side of the medical use of these chemicals. So far I have waited 20 years without having that opportunity.

POSTSCRIPT

Should Marijuana Be Legal for Medicinal Purposes?

Grinspoon and Bakalar strongly advocate the legalization of marijuana for medical treatment. They believe that the delay in the medicalization of marijuana stems from arduous and restrictive procedures of the federal government and that the government blocks people in need from receiving medication that is both therapeutic and benign.

From DuPont's perspective, promoting marijuana as a medicinal agent would be a mistake because it has not been proven medically useful or safe. Moreover, he feels that the availability of marijuana should not be predicated on personal accounts of its benefits, and he asserts that studies showing that marijuana has medical value suffer from unscientific methodology and other deficiencies. The results of previous research, DuPont contends, do not lend strong credence to marijuana's medicinal value.

Some people have expressed concern about what will happen if marijuana is approved for medicinal use. Would it then become more acceptable for nonmedical, recreational use? There is also a possibility that some people would misinterpret the government's message and think that marijuana *cures* cancer when, in fact, it would only be used to treat the side effects of the chemotherapy.

A central question is, If physicians feel that marijuana use is justified to properly care for seriously ill patients, should they promote this form of medical treatment even though it falls outside the law? Does the relief of pain and suffering for patients warrant going beyond what federal legislation says is acceptable? Also, should physicians be prosecuted if they recommend marijuana to their patients? What about the unknown risks of using an illegal drug? Is it worthwhile to ignore the possibility that marijuana may produce harmful side effects in order to alleviate pain or to treat other ailments?

Many marijuana proponents contend that the effort to prevent the legalization of marijuana for medical use is purely a political battle. Detractors maintain that the issue is purely scientific—that the data supporting marijuana's medical usefulness are inconclusive and scientifically unsubstantiated. And although the chief administrative law judge of the Drug Enforcement Administration (DEA) made a recommendation to change the status of marijuana from Schedule I to Schedule II, the DEA and other federal agencies are not compelled to do so, and they have resisted any change in the law.

Several articles discuss whether or not marijuana should be legalized as a medication. These include "The War Over Weed," by Tom Morganthau, *Newsweek* (February 3, 1997); "Acceptance of Marijuana Therapy Prompts

Call for More Research," by Sally Lehrman, *Nature* (November 1996); and "The Battle for Medical Marijuana," by Sarah Ferguson, *The Nation* (January 6, 1997).

In a study conducted by Richard Doblin and Mark Kleiman, "Marijuana as Medicine: A Survey of Oncologists," in Arnold Trebach and Kevin Zeese, eds., *New Frontiers in Drug Policy* (Drug Policy Foundation, 1991), almost half of the oncologists surveyed recommended marijuana to their patients to help them deal with the side effects of chemotherapy. In "Should Marijuana Be Legalized as a Medicine? No, It's Dangerous and Addictive," *The World & I* (June 1994), Eric A. Voth writes that legalization of marijuana for medical reasons is a bad idea because it is capable of producing many negative effects.

ISSUE 10

Should Doctors Promote Alcohol for Their Patients?

YES: Stanton Peele, from "Should Physicians Recommend Alcohol to Their Patients? Yes," *Priorities* (vol. 8, no. 1, 1996)

NO: Albert B. Lowenfels, from "Should Physicians Recommend Alcohol to Their Patients? No," *Priorities* (vol. 8, no. 1, 1996)

ISSUE SUMMARY

YES: Psychologist Stanton Peele, an expert on alcoholism and addiction, asserts that physicians should recommend that their patients drink alcohol in moderate amounts. He maintains that numerous studies demonstrate the benefits of moderate alcohol use in reducing the risk of coronary heart disease, the leading cause of death in the United States.

NO: Albert B. Lowenfels, a professor at New York Medical College, contends that recommending moderate alcohol consumption is not prudent, especially since many people come from families with histories of alcohol abuse. He argues that it is inappropriate to extol the merits of moderate alcohol use to people who have abstained throughout their lives.

Heart disease is the leading cause of death in the United States, so it is reasonable to assume that people are interested in reducing the risks that lead to heart disease. Magazines are replete with articles describing ways to control factors that are linked with heart disease, such as minimizing the amount of saturated fats we consume, managing stress in our lives, controlling our blood pressure, and exercising to counter the effects of a sedentary lifestyle. It has been suggested that it is possible to diminish the likelihood of heart disease through the moderate consumption of alcohol. The relationship between alcohol and heart disease and whether or not physicians should recommend moderate alcohol consumption are the focus of this issue.

Discussions regarding the effects of alcohol usually center on the consequences associated with excessive alcohol use. Alcoholism is a devastating problem; an estimated 10–20 million people are affected by it. Individuals and families are sometimes ruined by the unhealthy use of alcohol. Despite a decline since the early 1980s in the number of fatalities linked to driving while intoxicated, about 17,000 people were killed in 1998 by drivers under the influence of alcohol. Alcoholism is often described as a national epidemic that poses a threat to every member of society. Is it therefore unwise for physicians to promote the moderate use of alcohol, even though such behavior may reduce the risk of heart disease?

An important aspect of this debate is what constitutes moderate alcohol use. The concept of moderation varies from one individual to another: To a social drinker, moderation may involve one, two, or three drinks per week. To an alcoholic, moderation is probably much more. To a college student, binge drinking may be viewed as moderate if it is limited to weekends and special occasions. Also, how much alcohol does one need to drink to reduce heart disease? How much is too much? Numerous studies show that two drinks per day are beneficial. However, due to individual and cultural differences, many experts feel that no one definition of moderation is adequate.

Health researcher Stanton Peele concurs that excessive alcohol use entails potential harm, but he contends that it is reasonable to advocate moderate alcohol consumption. Peele feels that educators and public health officials are preoccupied with discussing the negative effects of alcohol; thus, moderate alcohol use is not learned by young people. He also believes that researchers downplay the positive effects of alcohol because they fear that people would drink more than a moderate amount if alcohol's benefits were promoted. Peele contends that this fear is unfounded.

Professor of surgery Albert B. Lowenfels questions the value of promoting moderate alcohol consumption for individuals who have maintained a lifetime of sobriety. He concurs that research shows that moderate use is beneficial to people who drink, but he argues that there is no research supporting the benefits of moderate alcohol use for abstainers. Some experts maintain that the evidence demonstrating the benefits of moderate alcohol use over abstinence is misleading because these studies are based on self-reports, which are frequently inaccurate and nonrepresentative.

One major concern with regard to promoting moderate alcohol consumption to lessen the likelihood of heart disease is that some people may misconstrue the information. Heavy drinkers, for example, may rationalize their behavior, maintaining that their drinking is for health purposes. Also, if moderate alcohol use acts as a protective behavior against heart disease, some people may disregard warnings against behaviors that are clearly harmful, such as smoking, not getting enough exercise, and practicing poor nutrition. Furthermore, moderate alcohol consumption is clearly harmful in some situations, such as before driving, before operating dangerous equipment, while on medication, and during pregnancy.

In the following selections, Peele argues that there is strong evidence that two alcoholic drinks daily act to mitigate the risk of heart disease and that there may be other benefits from publicly advancing such a message. Lowenfels contends that the benefits of moderate alcohol use over abstinence are questionable. He also indicates that promoting a moderate-use message may lead to other problems, especially for individuals with a family history of heavy drinking.

YES

Stanton Peele

SHOULD PHYSICIANS RECOMMEND ALCOHOL TO THEIR PATIENTS? YES

Whenever I have visited a physician over the last decade, the following scenario has been replayed: We discuss my cholesterol levels (total, LDL and HDL). We review dietary guidelines and other medical recommendations. Then I say, "Don't forget to remind me to drink a glass or two of wine daily." Invariably, the doctor demurs: "That hasn't been proven to protect you against atherosclerosis."

My doctors, all of whom I have respected and liked, are wrong. Evidence has established beyond question that alcohol reduces coronary artery disease, America's major killer. This result has been found in the Harvard Physician and Nurse studies and in studies by Kaiser Permanente and the American Cancer Society (ACS). Indeed, the evidence that alcohol reduces coronary artery disease and mortality is better than the evidence for the statin drugs, the most potent cholesterol-reducing medications.

Drinking to excess does increase mortality from several sources, such as cancer, cirrhosis and accidents. But a series of studies in the 1990s—including those conducted in conjunction with Kaiser, ACS and Harvard—in the U.S., Britain and Denmark, have found that moderate drinking reduces overall mortality.

Nonetheless, many people object to the idea that doctors should inform their patients that moderate drinking may prolong life. They fear that such advice will justify the excessive drinking some patients already engage in, or they worry that encouragement from doctors will push people who cannot handle alcohol to drink.

The view that people are so stupid or malleable that they will become alcohol abusers because doctors tell them moderate drinking is good for them is demeaning and self-defeating. If people can't regulate their own diets, drinking and exercise, then doctors should avoid giving patients any information about their health behavior, no matter how potentially helpful.

Not only can people handle such information on lifestyle, it offers the primary and best way to attack heart disease. Of course, doctors may also prescribe medications. These medications rarely solve underlying problems,

From Stanton Peele, "Should Physicians Recommend Alcohol to Their Patients? Yes," *Priorities*, vol. 8, no. 1 (1996), pp. 24, 26, 28. Copyright © 1996 by The American Council on Science and Health. Reprinted by permission of *Priorities*, a publication of The American Council on Science and Health, 1995 Broadway, 2d Floor, New York, NY 10023-5860.

however, and they often cause adverse side effects that counterbalance their positive effects. Because they are not a cure, courses of medication, once begun, are rarely discontinued.

People are the best regulators of their own behaviors. Even those who drink excessively often benefit when doctors provide straightforward, accurate information. Clinical trials conducted by the World Health Organization around the world showed that so-called brief interventions, in which medical personnel advised heavy drinkers to reduce their drinking, are the most successful therapy for problem drinking.

But far more Americans drink less, not more, than would be most healthful for them. To fail to inform these patients about the benefits of moderate drinking is both counterproductive and dishonest. Physicians may ask, "How much alcohol do you drink," "Is there any reason that you don't drink (or that you drink so little)," and (to those without religious objections, previous drinking problems, etc.), "Do you know that one or two glasses of wine or beer a day can be good for your health if you can safely consume them?"

Here are the data about alcohol and mortality:

1. In 1995 Charles Fuchs and his colleagues at Harvard found that women who drank up to two drinks a day lived longer than abstainers. Subjects were 85,700 nurses.

2. In 1995, Morten Gronbaek and colleagues found that wine drinkers survived longer than abstainers, with those drinking three to five glasses daily having the lowest death rate. Subjects were 20,000 Danes.

3. In 1994, Richard Doll and his colleagues found that men who drank up to two drinks daily lived significantly longer than abstainers. Subjects were 12,300 British doctors.

4. In 1992 Il Suh and colleagues found a 40 percent reduction in coronary mortality among men drinking three and more drinks daily. The 11,700 male subjects were in the upper 10 to 15 percent of risk for coronary heart disease based on their cholesterol, blood pressure and smoking status. Alcohol's enhancement of high density lipoproteins was identified as the protective factor.

5. In 1990, Paolo Boffetta and Lawrence Garfinkel found that men who drank occasionally—up to two drinks daily —outlived abstainers. Subjects were over a quarter of a million volunteers enrolled by the American Cancer Society.

6. In 1990, Arthur Klatsky and his colleagues found that those who drank one or two drinks daily had the lowest overall mortality rate. Subjects were 85,000 Kaiser Permanente patients of both genders and all races.

These data—from large prospective studies of people of both sexes, different occupations, several nations and varying risk profiles—all point to alcohol's life-sustaining effects. This phenomenon is now so well accepted that the U.S. dietary guidelines released in January 1996 recognize that moderate drinking can be beneficial.

The levels of drinking at which alcohol lowers death rates are still open to dispute. The new U.S. guidelines indicate that men should not drink more than two drinks per day and women should not exceed one per day. But the British

Table 1

Temperance, Alcohol Consumption and Cardiac Mortality

Alcohol Consumption (1990)	Temperance Nations[a]	Non-Temperance Nations[b]
total consumption[c]	6.6	10.8
percent wine	18	44
percent beer	53	40
percent spirits	29	16
AA groups/million population	170	25
coronary mortality[d] (males 50–64)	421	272

[a]Norway, Sweden, U.S., U.K., Ireland, Australia, New Zealand, Canada, Finland, Iceland
[b]Italy, France, Spain, Portugal, Switzerland, Germany, Denmark, Austria, Belgium, Luxembourg, Netherlands
[c]Liters consumed per capita per year
[d]Deaths per 100,000 population

Source: Peele S. *Culture, alcohol, and health: the consequences of alcohol consumption among Western nations.* December 1, 1995. Morristown, NJ.

government has set its limits for "sensible drinking" at three to four drinks for men and two to three drinks for women. That abstemiousness increases the risk of death, however, can no longer be doubted. Moreover, alcohol operates at least as effectively as pharmaceuticals to reduce the risk of death for those at high risk for coronary disease.

At one point, researchers questioned whether people who had quit drinking due to previous health problems inflated the mortality rate among abstainers. But this position can no longer be maintained. The studies described above separated drinkers who had quit drinking and who had preexisting health problems from other non-drinkers. The benefits of drinking persisted with these individuals omitted.

At some point, ranging from three to six drinks daily, the negative effects of drinking for cancer, cirrhosis and accidents catch up to and surpass alcohol's beneficial cardiac impact. Moreover, women under 50—who have relatively low rates of heart disease and relatively high rates of breast cancer mortality—may not benefit from drinking.

That is, unless they have one or more cardiac risk factors. Even younger women with such risk factors benefit from light to moderate drinking. And, we must remember, most American women and men have such risk factors. (Fuchs et al. found about three quarters of the nurses in the Harvard study had at least one.) Remember, over all ages, American women are ten times as likely to die of heart disease (40 percent) as of breast cancer (4 percent).

Why, then, do Americans—physicians, public health workers, educators and political leaders—refuse to recognize alcohol's benefits? We might also ask why the United States banned the manufacture, sale and transportation of alcoholic beverages from 1920 to 1933. It is probably too obvious to mention that alcohol has never been banned—or prohibition even seriously discussed—in France, Italy, Spain and a number of other European nations.

What is it about America and some other nations that prevents them from considering that alcohol may be good for people? These so-called "temperance" nations see alcohol in a highly negative light. This is true even though nations with higher alcohol consumption have lower death rates from coronary heart disease (see Table 1). Oddly, temperance nations—despite concentrating on alcohol problem prevention and treatment—actually have more drinking problems than those in which alcohol is socially accepted and integrated.

This occurs even though temperance nations drink less alcohol. But they drink a higher percentage of their alcohol in the form of spirits. This drinking is more likely to take place in concentrated bursts among men at sporting events or in drinking establishments. This style of drinking contrasts with that in wine-drinking nations, which encourage socialized drinking among family members of both genders and all ages at meals and other social gatherings. These cultures do not teach people that alcohol is an addictive drug. Rather, moderate drinking is modeled for children and taught to them in the home. Furthermore, these cultures accept that drinking may be good for you. We should, too.

NO

Albert B. Lowenfels

SHOULD PHYSICIANS RECOMMEND ALCOHOL TO THEIR PATIENTS? NO

If physicians were to encourage their patients to drink alcohol, what patients would be the target group? Certainly not heavy drinkers, whose health, job and family may already suffer from alcohol abuse or addiction; the advice for these unfortunate individuals should be to reduce alcohol consumption or, preferably, to abstain entirely from alcohol.

Light and moderate drinkers need no encouragement to drink alcohol; instead, they need advice about safe levels for drinking, the dangers of drinking while driving or operating motorized equipment and, for females, the necessity for abstinence from alcohol prior to conception and during pregnancy.

The only target group, therefore, would be those patients who are nonconsumers of alcohol. Physicians would never advocate alcohol consumption for children, so our advice would be limited to nondrinking adults. The size of this group can be estimated as follows: There are currently about 200 million adults in the United States. Although the exact number of nondrinkers in that population is unknown, a good estimate is about 25 to 30 percent, or at least 50 million persons.

We know that this large group of nondrinkers includes many different subgroups. Some nonconsumers avoid alcohol because they already suffer from an alcohol-related disease. Others abstain because they have a chronic disease and have been advised to avoid alcohol. A third group may have an alcoholic parent and intuitively know they must avoid alcohol. A final group abstains from alcohol because of religious convictions. Clearly, it would be unwise to recommend light or moderate drinking to patients in any of these categories.

What about the residual group of nondrinkers who have no definite reason to avoid alcohol? Would their health improve if they began drinking? To give a thoughtful answer to this important question, we must first review the complex relationship between alcohol and health. What are the detrimental effects of alcohol consumption and what, if any, are its health benefits? This problem has attracted an enormous amount of interest: In the past few years thousands of articles have been published on alcohol and health.

From Albert B. Lowenfels, "Should Physicians Recommend Alcohol to Their Patients? No," *Priorities*, vol. 8, no. 1 (1996), pp. 25, 27, 29. Copyright © 1996 by The American Council on Science and Health. Reprinted by permission of *Priorities*, a publication of The American Council on Science and Health, 1995 Broadway, 2d Floor, New York, NY 10023-5860.

Alcohol consumers are known to have increased risks for many diseases. These include cirrhosis of the liver; digestive-tract diseases such as ulcers or pancreatitis; several painful and often lethal cancers such as throat cancer, esophageal cancer and liver cancer; and certain neurologic disorders such as blackouts and seizures. In addition, all types of accidents, including fatal car crashes, are more frequent in drinkers than in non-drinkers. Finally, fetal alcohol syndrome, now thought to be the most common cause of mental retardation, occurs only in children of alcohol consumers. While it is true that some of these health problems occur primarily in heavy drinkers, any amount of alcohol may be hazardous for other diseases such as fetal alcohol syndrome, for which a safe, lower limit is unknown.

There is only one well-recognized health "benefit" of alcohol consumption: Health professionals now agree that drinking small amounts of alcohol seems to reduce the risk of coronary heart disease. But is this single gain enough to balance the long list of alcohol-associated health problems?

We could find a convincing answer to the overall impact of alcohol on health if we were able to conduct the following experiment, a prospective randomized trial. Nondrinking adults would be randomly assigned to one of two groups: an alcohol-consuming group in which all the participants would be required to drink a daily glass of fruit juice spiked with about an ounce or two of alcohol, and a second "control" group who would drink only fruit juice without alcohol. The two groups would be followed for 10 to 20 years so that we could compare the death rates in alcohol consumers to the rates in nonconsumers.

For various ethical and practical reasons, this experiment—which would give us badly needed information about the potential health benefits of light or moderate drinking—will never be performed. Therefore, to answer the "to drink or not to drink" question, we're forced to rely upon indirect, weaker evidence from nonrandomized trials—retrospective studies that look back at past alcohol exposure and cross-cultural studies that compare drinking levels and health status among different groups. These types of studies can be plagued by confounding and bias.

If we accept the premise that alcohol protects against certain types of heart disease, will we gain or lose by telling our nondrinking patients they should drink? We know that there are already at least 100,000 alcohol-related deaths each year in the United States. It is difficult to predict the number of heart disease deaths caused by alcohol abstinence, but the number has been estimated to be approximately equal to the number of alcohol-related deaths. Thus a health policy of advocating light or moderate drinking for our abstinent patients would be unlikely to save many lives.

According to a report prepared for the Robert Wood Johnson Foundation, the cost of alcohol addiction for the year 1990 in the United States amounted to almost 100 billion dollars—higher than the estimated 67 billion dollars we spend for illicit drugs and the 72 billion dollars we spend for tobacco addiction. An unpredictable number of new alcohol consumers would eventually turn into heavy drinkers or become addicted to alcohol, requiring additional funds to cover the costs of their alcohol-related problems.

Advocates for moderate drinking often speak of the "French paradox." In the southwest of France—despite high consumption of foods rich in cholesterol, such as buttery sauces, various cheeses and goose liver—the risk of heart disease, particularly in men, appears to be lower than expected. According to moderate-drinking advocates, this "paradox" of a high-cholesterol diet and a low risk of heart disease can be explained by the beneficial, protective effect of copious amounts of alcohol—particularly red wine.

But men in France actually die about two years earlier than do men in Sweden or Norway, even though per capita alcohol consumption in Scandinavia is only about one third the consumption in France. Frenchmen, although they may not be dying of heart disease, are dying of other causes. Drinking alcohol does not guarantee longevity—and it certainly does not provide immunity against death!

And what has been the health experience of groups of individuals who have been lifelong abstainers? Do they die prematurely? Do they suffer from excess heart disease or other illnesses? Fortunately, such information is available from many reports reviewing the health of Seventh Day Adventists and Mormons—groups that abstain from alcohol on religious grounds. Their survival rates are generally higher than the American average. Avoiding alcohol does not interfere with an active, prolonged, healthy life.

From available statistics we know that there are more female than male nondrinkers. We also know that women are more likely to develop complications of alcohol, such as liver cirrhosis, at lower levels of alcohol intake than men. We therefore can predict that a policy of telling our nondrinking patients to begin drinking would be likely to yield more alcohol-related complications in women than in men.

There are many readily available non-addictive drugs that effectively reduce the risk of coronary-artery occlusion. Why, then, should we recommend a drug that we know leads to loss of control or alcohol addiction in about 10 percent of users? It makes little sense to recommend alcohol as a safeguard against coronary heart disease when there are so many much safer drugs already at hand.

As we focus on the problem of alcohol and public health, we can learn a great deal by reviewing recommendations from organizations with recognized expertise in this area.

In 1991 the World Health Organization assembled a special review group to formulate worldwide alcohol policy. The group's conclusion on drinking and heart disease was this: "Any attempt to put across a message which encourages drinking on the basis of hoped-for gains in coronary heart disease prevention would be likely to result in more harm than benefit to the population."

In the United States, the National Institute on Alcohol Abuse and Alcoholism warns us that vulnerability to alcoholism and alcohol-related pathologies varies among individuals and cannot always be predicted before a patient begins to drink.

Finally, the Christopher D. Smithers Foundations, the largest private philanthropic organization devoted to research on alcoholism in America, does not advocate light or moderate drinking as a public health measure.

Over 2,000 years ago Hippocrates, one of our wisest physicians, reminded us, "Above all, do no harm." Let us remember this prudent advice as we decide what we should tell our patients about alcohol and health.

POSTSCRIPT

Should Doctors Promote Alcohol for Their Patients?

Approximately 10 percent of adults in the United States are alcoholics. The social and economic burdens placed on society as a result of heavy alcohol use are immense. Heavy drinking leads to increased health care costs, accidents, premature death, and reduced productivity in the workplace. In view of the myriad of problems caused by excessive alcohol use, is it prudent to suggest that moderate alcohol consumption should be promoted?

Experts agree that heavy drinking is a problem in society; however, heart disease is also a grave concern. Numerous public health education programs strive to reduce the risk factors associated with heart disease. If it can be shown that moderate alcohol use lessens that risk, wouldn't it make sense for physicians to advocate moderate consumption?

An important point to consider is the effect of a program that promotes moderate alcohol use. Would such a program result in heavy drinkers' reducing their alcohol consumption? Or would nondrinkers start drinking and people who are predisposed to alcoholism become alcoholic? Peele feels that none of these effects are likely and, moreover, that promoting moderate use, especially among young people, will help them to develop a healthy attitude toward alcohol. Lowenfels questions whether or not nondrinkers would obtain lower rates of heart disease if they started drinking moderately.

There are numerous papers and studies that examine the issue of heart disease and moderate alcohol use. An excellent paper by Sally Casswell is "Population Level Policies on Alcohol: Are They Still Appropriate Given That Alcohol Is Good for the Heart?" *Addiction Suplement* (1997), S81–S90, which focuses on moderate alcohol use and the elderly. The effects of various types of alcoholic beverages are described in "Review of Moderate Alcohol Consumption and Reduced Risk of Coronary Heart Disease: Is the Effect Due to Beer, Wine or Spirits?" by Eric B. Rimm et al., *British Journal of Medicine* (vol. 312, 1996). Other good articles are "Do Drink and Thrive," by Emily Laurence Baker, *The Guardian* (December 9, 1997) and "Hazards and Benefits of Alcohol," by John D. Potter, *The New England Journal of Medicine* (December 11, 1997).

Finally, Jean Kinney warns of the potential dangers of moderate alcohol use in her book *Loosening the Grip: A Handbook of Alcohol Information*, 6th ed. (McGraw-Hill, 2000).

ISSUE 11

Is Nicotine Addictive?

YES: Janet Brigham, from *Dying to Quit: Why We Smoke and How We Stop* (Joseph Henry Press, 1998)

NO: Richard J. DeGrandpre, from "What's the Hook? Smoking Is More Than a Chemical Bond," *Reason* (January 1997)

ISSUE SUMMARY

YES: Janet Brigham, a research psychologist at SRI International in Menlo Park, California, maintains that nicotine is a powerfully addictive drug and that overcoming addiction to tobacco is as difficult as overcoming addiction to alcohol, heroin, or cocaine. She also argues that calling nicotine dependence a "habit" minimizes its addictiveness.

NO: Assistant professor of psychology Richard J. DeGrandpre contends that cigarette addiction is due to social, cultural, and economic factors and not because of physical dependence on nicotine. DeGrandpre asserts that nicotine replacement to help people stop smoking is not especially effective and that it is not just the nicotine that smokers desire when they light up a cigarette. He concludes that psychosocial factors are responsible for cigarette addiction.

Public health experts agree unanimously that cigarette smoking is dangerous to one's health; indeed, one does not need to be an expert to know that nicotine is harmful. Cigarette smoking is a major contributor to heart disease, lung cancer, and emphysema. This information is not breaking news. The perils associated with smoking were clearly identified in the first U.S. surgeon general's report on smoking and health, which was published in January 1964. Here, however, the issue being debated is not whether cigarette smoking is harmful. This issue focuses on whether or not nicotine causes physical dependence.

One argument against the notion that nicotine causes physical dependence is that millions of people have successfully stopped using nicotine. It can also be argued that smoking does not usually result in addiction. In a 1994 survey of American households, almost three-fourths of respondents indicated that they had smoked cigarettes at some time, but only slightly more than one-fourth responded that they had smoked within the previous 30 days of the survey. One can conclude from these results that not everyone who begins smoking gets hooked on it. According to Richard J. DeGrandpre in the second of the following selections, "50 percent of all Americans who have ever smoked no longer do." It is apparent, says DeGrandpre, that the potential for nicotine to cause dependency is exaggerated. Another argument against the addictiveness of nicotine is that most smokers who are trying to quit are not helped by nicotine replacement therapies, such as nicotine gum and nicotine patches.

Millions of people have been able to quit smoking, and many others have smoked without ever becoming dependent. Does this mean that nicotine does not produce dependency? Many people who have been addicted to alcohol, heroin, and cocaine have stopped using these drugs. Does this mean that these drugs do not produce dependency? Part of the problem rests with how the word *dependency* is defined. One could define dependency as "the inability, not unwillingness, to stop an unhealthy or undesirable behavior even though one wants to stop." By this definition, nicotine can be viewed as addictive because it is unhealthy to use it and many people are incapable of stopping its use despite sincere efforts to do so.

Many behaviors could be construed as addictive, from eating behaviors to exercise, watching television, gambling, and shopping. One characteristic of dependency to a substance or a behavior is the presence of withdrawal symptoms. Unlike alcohol and other depressants, the withdrawal symptoms from nicotine are not life-threatening. Nevertheless, nicotine withdrawal symptoms are very real, although the severity varies among individuals. Nicotine withdrawal symptoms include headaches, insomnia, drowsiness, anxiety, shortened attention span, tremors, aggressiveness, fatigue, and irritability. Moreover, the craving for nicotine may persist for years. In extreme cases, some people become so depressed when they give up smoking that their physicians recommend that they give up the idea of quitting.

Despite the consequences of smoking, people who smoke say that they derive certain benefits from smoking. Smoking helps some people to concentrate; other people like the idea of handling something; smoking may help reduce stress, sadness, and anxiety; some people smoke due to boredom; and some simply derive a sense of pleasure from smoking. Smoking behavior is often precipitated by certain cues. For example, many smokers enjoy a cigarette following a meal, when they drink coffee, when they study, or when they socialize with others. These examples suggest that social or emotional factors contribute to smoking.

In the following selections, Janet Brigham states that nicotine is an extremely addictive drug and that calling nicotine addiction a habit understates how addicting nicotine is. She maintains that because nicotine is addictive, most people who try to stop smoking are unsuccessful. DeGrandpre points to the fact that millions of people in the United States have been able to stop smoking and contends that nicotine's physical addictiveness is overstated. He argues that people smoke for reasons other than to satisfy their craving for nicotine.

YES

Janet Brigham

MYTHS AND MYSTERIES OF ADDICTION

THE ELUSIVE "ADDICTIVE PERSONALITY"

In Stephen Vincent Benet's epic *John Brown's Body*, the fictional belle Sally Dupré was like a forbidden fruit to young Clay Wingate, who fancied her. A soldier in the Civil War, Clay knew that if he so much as kissed her once before going off to fight, his heart would be unalterably turned toward her. "Your mouth is generous and bitter and sweet," Clay mused. "If I kissed your mouth, I would have to be yours forever." To a degree, this image depicts the fear of many people about addiction. They blame not the substance itself, but rather themselves for being addiction prone. They decide, with grim acceptance, that there must be something wrong with their personality.

A common cultural belief holds that some people are drawn like magnets to abusable substances and potentially compulsive behaviors. One drink, and they're alcoholic. One smoke, and they're addicted to nicotine. Whatever the substance, compulsion, vice, or temptation, it is supposedly the nature of their personality or their chemistry to be drawn toward it, to embrace it, and to be unable to abandon it. Believers in this notion apply the concept to an array of human behaviors. Those with this weakness, some believe, have an "addictive personality." It is their nature to be addicted easily and permanently.

Scientifically, however, this notion is unsupportable. At its core is a mis-application of several established, replicated research findings, including the following:

- Some people apparently are predisposed to developing addictive disorders such as alcoholism, amphetamine addiction, and dependence on the nicotine in tobacco. Even so, the predisposing factors differ between substances and life conditions, such that those predisposed toward alcoholism might not be predisposed to abuse cocaine or any other substance. This predisposition is not entirely ruled by genes, either. For instance, someone with a predisposition to alcoholism who has limited contact with alcohol might never develop the disorder.

- Substance-use disorders are more common in people with certain personality styles and personality disorders. However, no constellation of traits that could be identified as an "addictive personality" has ever been identified, despite major research efforts toward that end.
- Many behaviors can become compulsive, including such diverse actions as hand washing, counting holes in the tiles of ceilings, touching a certain object, gambling, performing mealtime rituals, cleaning doorknobs, and engaging in specific sexual practices. In short, most human behaviors can become compulsively driven, although they are not addictive. This is because, in some way or another, the behaviors are reinforced or are reinforcing. Some people may also eat compulsively, and some may engage in substance-*related* behaviors compulsively. This does not imply addiction, but rather may indicate some variant of a fixation or a compulsion, which are separate demons.
- Some people apparently are predisposed to developing compulsive behaviors. These are not necessarily the same people as those predisposed to developing alcoholism or drug abuse.

Despite heroic efforts and the expenditure of many research dollars, science has never been able to establish the existence of an addictive personality style that predisposes people to a variety of addictions and compulsions. Convincing the general public that this phenomenon does not exist may be difficult, since we have become accustomed to hearing about "chocoholics" and "foodaholics," and since the concept of an addictive personality offers a simplistic, intuitive explanation. In reality, the notion of the addictive personality remains unproven, undemonstrated, and most likely incorrect.

HAS SCIENCE EVER DEFINED ADDICTION?

Well, yes and no.

Facts exist independent of who is citing them or whether the person is using them correctly; it is the way they are cited that frames their interpretation and results in misapplied meanings. Few areas of substance abuse debate are as riddled with ambiguous meanings and syntactical nuances as is the word *addiction*.

Some tobacco-financed researchers and industry supporters have asserted that one reason for not believing that nicotine is addictive is their claim that science has no adequate, consistent definition of the term *addiction*. This claim surfaces in such diverse places as peer-reviewed scientific journal articles, newspaper columns, litigation, and testimony before Congress. To the contrary, scientists with no financial ties to the tobacco industry have argued that the question is not one of defining addiction, but rather one of defining the properties of nicotine itself. Whether or not we use the word *addiction*, does nicotine have traits in common with substances that we commonly identify as addictive?

Some scientists defined *addiction* to their satisfaction several decades ago, but the word was appropriated into other contexts and stripped of its precise meaning. The term was first applied to chronic use of opiates, including morphine and heroin. Originally, addiction was identified primarily by compulsive use, physical dependence, tolerance, and damage to the user and society.

Table 1
Gotcha!

50%	younger adult U.S. smokers who are nicotine dependent (addicted)
87%	older adult U.S. smokers who are nicotine dependent
three-fourths	U.S. smokers who say they are addicted
78%	U.S. smokers who say they could quit if they decided to
two-thirds	U.S. smokers who say they wish they could quit
four-fifths	U.S. smokers who say they wish they had never started

Readministration of the substance was found to relieve abstinence-related withdrawal symptoms, leading to the concept of physical dependence as a "central defining characteristic of addiction," as explained by pharmacologist Caroline Cohen, writing with colleagues Wallace Pickworth and Jack Henningfield.

When the term *drug addiction* became associated with pejorative images, the World Health Organization recommended using the term *drug dependence.* As Cohen explained, drug dependence is a "psychic and sometimes also physical" state marked by a compulsion to use a given substance continuously or periodically to experience its effects and sometimes to avoid the discomfort brought on by its absence. This state may or may not include tolerance. People can develop both tolerance to drugs and physical dependence on drugs that are not abused. Similarly, patients in experimental settings do not seek out some drugs despite having developed tolerance and physical dependence.

Cohen clarified: "Addictive agents have one common attribute: the creation of a behavioral response repertoire often referred to as 'psychic dependence.'" While some would claim that "psychic" dependence differs from physical dependence, this view denies the fact that psychological dependence has a physiological basis.

When it became fashionable to label as addictive such diverse activities as compulsive gambling, overeating, and frequent sex, the word *addiction* lost its moorings. Nonetheless, the term still can be applied to any drug use that involves "drug-seeking behaviors," compulsive use of the substance, denial of the consequences of using the substance, and relapse after cessation.

The scientific and medical communities have moved away from the term *addiction* and shifted instead toward the term *dependence* as a way to describe serious substance-use disorders, including addiction to nicotine. *Dependence* is a precise term with specific published criteria and implications. To meet criteria for dependence on a substance, someone must have experienced at least three of these symptoms:

- Tolerance.
- Withdrawal when the substance isn't used.
- Using more of the substance than was intended, or using it over a longer period of time.
- Persistent desire or unsuccessful efforts to cut down or to control the use.
- Spending considerable time obtaining the substance or recovering from its effects. In the case of smoking, this could refer to spending a lot of time smoking, rather than engaging in tobacco-seeking activities. It is also

possible that this criterion is not applicable to most use of nicotine.

These criteria, published in the fourth edition of the *Diagnostic and Statistical Manual* of the American Psychiatric Association and thus used for formal diagnosis, have become the basis for identifying and researching numerous substances of abuse, including hallucinogens, amphetamines, opiates, alcohol, and tobacco Although they are codified, they are by no means universally accepted by the scientific community or applied in research paradigms. Some researchers choose to define addiction and dependence much more simply: the inability to stop a drug-reinforced behavior when one wants to stop.

The concepts of *dependence* and its less severe cousin *abuse* provide a useful heuristic for understanding what constitutes nicotine addiction. Although they have become a gold standard of sorts, they are not the final word. For example, The National Household Survey on Drug Abuse included four key questions to determine nicotine dependence, as part of a much larger survey about overall substance use:

- Current smokers were asked whether they had felt that they needed cigarettes or were dependent on cigarettes during the previous year.
- Smokers were asked whether they had needed more cigarettes to get the same effect.
- Smokers who had tried to cut back were asked whether they felt unable to do so.
- These same smokers also were asked whether they had experienced withdrawal symptoms or felt sick when they stopped smoking or cut down on cigarettes.

These questions were not a comprehensive measure of nicotine addiction and did not measure all symptoms of nicotine withdrawal. Thus they probably underestimated the proportion of smokers who would qualify as dependent. A 1989 committee reporting to the Royal Society and to Health and Welfare Canada defined drug addiction as this: "a strongly established pattern of behaviour characterized by (1) the repeated self-administration of a drug in amounts which reliably produce reinforcing psycho-active effects, and (2) great difficulty in achieving voluntary long-term cessation of such use, even when the user is strongly motivated to stop."

Cohen and her colleagues added to this definition of dependence their summary of compelling research evidence that smoking is "a highly controlled or compulsive behavior." The control in smoking comes from the precision with which smokers obtain nicotine to maintain consistent blood levels. They cited as proof the consistent patterns of cigarette smoking; the gradual increase of cigarette intake over time until a stable level is achieved; and the findings that more than three-fourths of current smokers say they would like to quit, and two-thirds have made at least one serious attempt.

Additional evidence of nicotine's addictive nature is that it is considered rewarding by smokers, even to the point of being what Cohen and her colleagues called a "potent euphoriant."

ADDICTION OR HABIT?

Calling smoking merely a "habit" troubles many scientists who study the effects of nicotine and tobacco. "One of my linguistic pet peeves is the use of the word 'habit' in reference to smoking and tobacco use," wrote Ronald Davis, former director of the U.S. Office on Smoking and Health, now editor of the journal *Tobacco Control*. He decried the repeated use by the tobacco industry of the 1964 Surgeon General's report to justify their claims that nicotine is merely a habit. The 1964 document concluded: "The tobacco habit should be characterized as an habituation rather than an addiction." However, Davis noted, "[T]he industry invariably skips over the preceding paragraph," in which the report stated that habitual use was "reinforced and perpetuated" by nicotine's action on the central nervous system.

The 1964 report did not label nicotine as addictive, referring to it instead as a substance used habitually, like coffee. Those insisting that tobacco isn't strictly addictive latched onto this distinction. A smoker's morning cigarette, they said, was no different than a morning cup of coffee. It must have been disconcerting for them to read reports in respected medical journals in the mid-1990s that caffeine can also be addictive. Quitting caffeine use when one routinely has even a small amount per day can result in abstinence symptoms that often include a nasty headache that can last for days. However, this physical dependence usually is not accompanied by compulsive drug-seeking behavior.

Unlike the 1964 report, the 1988 Surgeon General's report (subtitled *Nicotine Addiction*) was devoted almost entirely to nicotine's addictive qualities. With the benefit of hindsight, the latter report explained the nuances of terminology and classification that had resulted in the 1964 report, and stated that the terms *drug addiction* and *drug dependence* are equivalent.

The debate about whether or not nicotine is addictive has centered on several assertions, as reiterated by R. J. Reynolds researchers John Robinson and Walter Pritchard, who have participated in scientific forums. Robinson and Pritchard argued:

- The scientific community lacks a precise definition of addiction, "apparently using the word to indicate any behavior that people engage in and may find difficult to stop."
- Classifying a drug or behavior as addictive "because some people may find it difficult to stop" is not in the best interest of scientific inquiry.
- Nicotine use can be seen as a habit, or as habituating (not referring, incidentally, to the precise meaning of that term as applied in the behavioral sciences).
- Because the use profile of nicotine differs from that of known addictive substances such as heroin, it should not be classed with them.
- Because nicotine is not "intoxicating" and does not impair motor performance (i.e., tasks requiring motor skills) or perception, it does not fit scientific criteria for addiction as established in the 1960s through 1980s.
- Nicotine has no "strong" euphoriant effect such as that of cocaine, although its use is "pleasurable."
- Research with laboratory animals suggests that nicotine self-administration in nonhumans is neither readily established nor robust. (Such self-administration is a standard research technique for studying drugs of abuse such as cocaine or heroin.)
- Since the "non-pharmacological aspects of smoking," such as how the smoke tastes, appear to drive smoking behavior, smoking is "more accurately

classified as habit than addiction." This is true, they claimed, because smoking is "a complex behavioral process involving both pharmacologic and non-pharmacologic factors."

Just how accurate are the tobacco industry's claims? Many scientists and policymakers are skeptical of arguments emanating from researchers on the payrolls of the tobacco industry, even if the arguments have validity and serve to nudge science toward a clearer definition of addiction. The 1988 Surgeon General's report compared nicotine addiction to that of the "hard" drugs, including the opiate heroin. It concluded that tobacco does have many addictive properties in common with other drugs of abuse. As a toxic substance, it often makes first-time users queasy, if not actually nauseated. With continued exposure, users develop a tolerance and can use increasingly larger quantities. When smokers are deprived of nicotine, they may experience measurable, unpleasant withdrawal symptoms. These characteristics, true of many hard drugs, are also well documented for nicotine use.

A small percentage of tobacco users continue to use nicotine at a low level for many years without developing tolerance or dependence. Their personalities, lifestyles, and metabolism of nicotine resemble those of smokers who are nicotine dependent. These low users are not naïve smokers, since they consume many thousands of cigarettes over the years that they smoke. However, they are anomalous smokers. They follow a daily use pattern that remains minimal, and they experience virtually no abstinence effects when they quit using tobacco.

Is the existence of such smokers, as described by Saul Shiffman in 1989, a valid argument against characterizing nicotine as an addictive substance? If nicotine were addictive, according to those arguing against that idea, shouldn't it be addictive for all users? That argument actually works against its proponents; the term *chippers*, which is often used to describe these low-use smokers, originated with the scientific and medical research on opiate use. The existence of chippers among opiate users does not call the addictiveness of opiates into question.

But staking the determination of nicotine's addictiveness on the slippery definition of *addiction* seems to beg the question. The imprecision of one term does not change the nature of the substance. No one has claimed that tobacco produces the same "high" as cocaine or the same intoxication as marijuana, at least in the doses commonly used by cigarette smokers. A more fundamental question is whether nicotine fits the profile of drugs known to be addictive, or carries a high risk for leading to chronic use. Thus, the questions addressed by the medical and mental health community are these: Do people become tolerant to higher and higher amounts of nicotine delivered over the course of the day? Do regular users of nicotine experience abstinence effects when they go without nicotine? If the answer is an overwhelming yes, it may indicate a physical dependence. Perhaps it matters little that common usage refers to people being "addicted" to Twinkies, or even that many tobacco-related behaviors can be labeled as habitual.

The nature of addiction is that each substance with a potential for abuse, including nicotine, has a unique profile of use. Each substance requires separate, specific examination. Why should the

Table 2
Chipping Away

fewer than 6	number of cigarettes smoked per day by the typical tobacco chipper
none	withdrawal symptoms experienced by chippers when they quit smoking
8.2%	Australian smokers who are chippers
15%	California smokers who are chippers
decades	how long the typical tobacco chipper smokes
tens of thousands	total cigarettes consumed over a chipper's lifetime of smoking
none	cigarettes per day considered safe to smoke

effects of inhaling nicotine have to be virtually identical to the effects of injecting heroin for the similarities to be worth noting? The commonalities provide evidence that both substances can be used deleteriously; the differences merely illuminate the complex nature of human addiction. . . .

IS ADDICTION A DISEASE?

It was not long ago that alcoholism was blamed on lack of character. And it was not long ago that smokers believed they could quit if only they had enough will power. Certainly, strength of character and strong will can boost attempts to overcome an addiction—or a habit, for that matter. Nevertheless, our present understanding of the biology of nicotine addiction offers both clarity and charity. In the last several decades, science has brought some humanity and compassion to our understanding of the conundrum of addiction by showing that human vulnerability to numerous drugs of abuse is widespread. Defining a substance as addictive and defining its overuse as a disorder or a disease have helped free users from the trap of labels. Some people argue that in using a disease model for understanding addictions, we have given substance users a convenient excuse for not changing behavior by hiding behind arguments that their problem is "genetic"

or is out of their control. While this claim may be accurate in part, it does not take into account the benefits that may come from biologically based explanations of addiction.

The first addiction to be recognized as a disease was alcoholism. In view of that, some have asked whether nicotine addiction is also a disease. Addressing this question requires that we consider the definition of *disease*. Whether or not nicotine addiction can be termed a disease depends on the answers to several questions. Is nicotine use under the control of the tobacco user? If nicotine use is addictive, then the onus is outside the individual smoker, even though the initial trials with cigarettes were the smoker's choice. As clinical researcher Norman Miller explained: "The primary foundation for considering nicotine addiction to be a disease rests on the acceptance of the loss of control by the nicotine addict."

Attributing the undesirable consequences of the addiction to "a disease concept" removes the weight of viewing smoking as a "moral dilemma" and thus facilitates the earliest steps toward cessation. Miller added: "[I]nsistence on correcting a weak character or treating an underlying psychiatric or emotional disorder will not initiate abstinence or prevent relapse to nicotine. Nicotine addicts are already filled with self-condemnation, and a further exaggeration of the guilt by making the addicts at fault for their smoking will further impede the addicts' accepting responsibility for treatment of the nicotine addiction and its consequences."

When Russell asked heroin users to rate drugs in terms of being "needed," they put cigarettes at the top of their list. They said that they perceived coping without cigarettes to be more difficult than coping without heroin. Russell concluded in a 1990 report that "cigarette withdrawal is no less difficult to achieve and sustain than is abstinence from heroin or alcohol." Additional evidence of nicotine's powerful pull is in the statistic that between 45 and 70 percent of smokers who survive a heart attack resume smoking again within a year. About half of all smokers who undergo lung cancer surgery take up smoking again.

WHERE THE ARGUMENT LEADS

Few scientists, and only a small percentage of smokers, doubt that nicotine is addictive, by some definition. Much is at stake in the addiction debate. The risk of the rhetoric is that the realities of tobacco use and the smoking experience will be lost in a terminology war. Discussions over the definition of addiction can become a smoke screen obscuring the more fundamental and burning question: What makes people smoke?

The question of addiction is at the heart of initiatives by the U.S. Food and Drug Administration (FDA) to exert more government controls over the manufacture and sale of cigarettes and other tobacco products. Former FDA commissioner David Kessler testified in unequivocal language that between 74 percent and 90 percent of all smokers were addicted. He summarized in 1994: "Accumulating evidence suggests that cigarette manufacturers may intend this result—that they may be controlling smokers' choice by controlling the levels of nicotine in their products in a manner that creates and sustains an addiction in the vast majority of smokers.... Whether it is a choice by cigarette companies to maintain addictive levels of nicotine in their cigarettes, rather than a choice by consumers to continue smoking, that in the end is driving the demand for cigarettes in this country."

Kessler recounted how the one-time "simple agricultural commodity" of tobacco eventually, evolved into the production and marketing industry for a "nicotine delivery system." To the surprise of many who heard his testimony, he explained that by reconstituting tobacco stems, scraps, and dust, cigarette makers began controlling and manipulating nicotine levels to achieve maximum addictive potential. He showed charts of patents in which tobacco companies added nicotine to tobacco rods, filters, and wrappers. Other patents indicated control of nicotine levels by extraction and utilization of new chemicals. Kessler stated: "Patents not only describe a specific invention. They also speak to the industry's capabilities, to its research, and provide insight into what it may be attempting to achieve with its products."

He cited the industry's achievements:

- Controlling the amount of nicotine to provide a desired psychological effect
- Increasing the amount of nicotine by manipulating nicotine levels
- Controlling the rate at which nicotine is delivered
- Transferring nicotine from one material to another

- Adding nicotine to other parts of the cigarette.

"Since the technology apparently exists to reduce nicotine in cigarettes to insignificant levels," Kessler asked, "why . . . does the industry keep nicotine in cigarettes at all?" And, similarly, "With all the apparent advances in technology, why do the nicotine levels found in the vast majority of cigarettes remain at addictive levels?" If nicotine is merely a flavorant, producing a burning in the throat to which smokers become accustomed, "why not use a substitute ingredient with comparable flavor, but without the addictive potential?"

Why not, indeed.

SO, IS NICOTINE ADDICTIVE?

On this question, some argue that the jury is still out. Others argue that the jury has never been presented with an adequate case. Others believe that the verdict was sealed more than a decade ago.

Here is a suggestion for those who aren't yet convinced. This winter, some day when it's 20 degrees Fahrenheit outside and snowing, look outside an office building in which smoking is prohibited. Note the smokers huddled outside in the doorways, braced against the weather. Ask yourself: Are they out there just for the pleasurable sensation of smoking?

NO

Richard J. DeGrandpre

WHAT'S THE HOOK? SMOKING IS MORE THAN A CHEMICAL BOND

During the presidential election campaign, Bill Clinton successfully cast Big Tobacco as a national enemy, with Bob Dole playing the role of collaborator by downplaying the addictiveness of nicotine. Meanwhile, the Food and Drug Administration has been asserting jurisdiction over cigarettes as "nicotine delivery devices," arguing that tobacco companies intend to hook their customers, just like schoolyard drug pushers. Hundreds of pending lawsuits, including class actions and cases filed by state governments, similarly allege a conspiracy to addict smokers. These developments represent important changes in our attitudes toward cigarettes. Though justified in the name of public health, the increasing emphasis on the enslaving power of nicotine may only make matters worse.

Understanding why requires careful consideration of the conventional wisdom about tobacco addiction, which recycles mistaken assumptions about illicit drugs. During the latter half of this century, the classical model of addiction, derived from observations of narcotic abuse, increasingly has been used to describe the cigarette habit. The classical model states that consumption of certain chemicals causes a physical dependence, either immediately or after prolonged use, characterized by withdrawal symptoms—symptoms that can be avoided or escaped only by further drug use. As Steven Hyman, director of the National Institute of Mental Health, opined recently in *Science*, "Repeated doses of addictive drugs—opiates, cocaine, and amphetamine—cause drug dependence and, afterward, withdrawal."

This cyclical model, in which the drug serves as both problem and solution, offers a simple, easy-to-grasp account of the addiction process, giving the concept great staying power in the public imagination. In the case of smoking, this view of addiction is central to the rationale for regulating tobacco and the concern that the cigarette companies have been doping their products with extra nicotine. But the classical model tends to conceal rather than elucidate the ultimate sources of addiction, and it is just as ill-suited to the cigarette habit as it has always been for understanding illicit drug use.

From Richard J. DeGrandpre, "What's the Hook? Smoking Is More Than a Chemical Bond," *Reason*, vol. 28, no. 8 (January 1997). Copyright © 1997 by The Reason Foundation, 3415 S. Sepulveda Blvd., Suite 400, Los Angeles, CA 90034. <www.reason.com> Reprinted by permission.

If a chemical compound can be addictive in the manner described by NIMH Director Hyman, we would expect anyone who regularly uses such a substance to become addicted. Yet only a minority of those who use illicit drugs—whether marijuana, cocaine, or heroin—ever develop a dependence on them. The prevalence of addiction, as defined by the *American Psychiatric Association's Diagnostic and Statistical Manual,* among users of alcohol and cocaine runs about 15 percent and 17 percent, respectively. Even in a sample of 79 regular crack users, Patricia Erickson and her colleagues at Toronto's Addiction Research Foundation found that only about 37 percent used the drug heavily (more than 100 times in their lives), and 67 percent had not used in the past month. A similar pattern holds for tobacco. In the 1994 National Household Survey on Drug Abuse, 73 percent of respondents reported smoking cigarettes at some time, but only about 29 percent reported smoking in the previous month, and not necessarily on a daily basis. Writing in the May/June *Mother Jones,* Jeffrey Klein manages to argue that nicotine enslaves its users and, at the same time, that Tobacco Inc. seeks to recruit young smokers to replace the 1.3 million Americans who quit each year. If nicotine is so relentlessly addictive, how can it be that 50 percent of all Americans who have ever smoked no longer do?

The classical model also suggests that the cigarette habit should be highly amenable to nicotine replacement therapy, such as the nicotine patch. Yet few of the tens of thousands of patch users have actually broken the habit (only about 10 percent to 15 percent succeed). In direct conflict with the classical model, most keep smoking while on the patch, continuing to consume the carcinogens in cigarette smoke while obtaining considerably higher blood levels of nicotine. A 1992 study of nicotine replacement therapy reported in the journal *Psychopharmacology* concluded that the "overall lack of effect [of the patch] on cigarette consumption is perhaps surprising and suggests that in regular smokers the lighting up of a cigarette is generally triggered by cues other than low plasma nicotine levels."

Most people who successfully quit smoking do so only after several failed attempts. If addiction is driven by physical dependence on a chemical—in this case, nicotine—relapse should occur during withdrawal, which for nicotine typically lasts a few weeks. Yet a sizable proportion of relapses occur long after the smoker has suffered through nicotine withdrawal. In fact, studies do not even show a relationship between the severity of withdrawal and the likelihood of relapse. As any former smoker could tell you, ex-smokers crave cigarettes at certain times and in certain situations for months, even years, after quitting. In these cases, the desire to smoke is triggered by environmental cues, not by withdrawal symptoms. This is one reason why people who overcome addiction to illicit substances such as heroin or cocaine often say they had more difficulty breaking the cigarette habit. Because regular tobacco users smoke in a wide array of circumstances (when bored, after eating, when driving) and settings (home, work, car), the cues that elicit the urge are more ubiquitous than for illicit drug use.

These failures of the classical model illustrate how conventional wisdom oversimplifies the dynamics of cigarette smoking. This reductionist view is dangerous because it ignores the psychosocial factors that underlie addiction. In coming to terms with cigarette addiction as a psychosocial process, rather than a simple pharmacological one, we need to distinguish between cigarette addiction and nicotine addiction. Certainly no one (except perhaps the tobacco companies) denies that cigarette smoking can be addictive, if by addiction one means a stubborn urge to keep smoking. But it is quite a different matter to say that nicotine accounts for the addictiveness of smoking. Nicotine withdrawal notwithstanding, nicotine alone is insufficient, and may even be unnecessary, to create cigarette addiction.

This claim can be clarified by two dramatic case studies reported in the *British Journal of Addiction* in 1973 and 1989. The earlier article described a 47-year-old woman with a two-and-a-half-year-long dependence on water, one of several such cases noted by the author. The woman reported a nagging withdrawal symptom—a dry, salty taste in her mouth—that was alleviated by the persistent drinking of water (up to 60 glasses per day). This case of dependence on a nonpsychoactive substance contrasts sharply with the second account, which described an 80-year-old woman who used cocaine without incident for 55 years. The authors reported that "she denies any feelings of euphoria or increased energy after [snorting] the cocaine nor any depression or craving for cocaine when her supplies run out. . . . She appears to have suffered no ill effects from the prolonged use of cocaine in physical, psychological or social terms." So we see that not every addiction involves drug use and not every instance of drug use involves an addiction.

To say that cigarette addiction is a psychosocial process means that social, cultural, and economic factors play a crucial role in acquiring and keeping a cigarette habit. In fact, the tendency to reduce the cigarette experience to chemical servitude may be one of the most powerful cultural factors driving addiction. Cigarette lore wrongly teaches smokers (and smokers-to-be) that they will suffer badly if they attempt to quit, while at the same time freeing them of responsibility for their drug use once they begin. Such beliefs also help romanticize cigarette smoking, elevating nicotine to a sublime abstraction. This not only reinforces the forbidden fruit effect, it helps transform the habit of smoking into a cult behavior. Smoking thus acquires the kind of meaning that the youth of America are most in search of: social meaning. As Richard Klein writes in *Cigarettes Are Sublime*, "smoking cigarettes is not only a physical act but a discursive one—a wordless but eloquent form of expression."

To counteract the forces that give momentum to drug use, the public meaning of addiction needs to be broadened to include the many, changing facets of the psychosocial realm in which we develop. "Putting people back in charge" of their addictions, as John Leo puts it in *U.S. News and World Report*, will not work if we focus only on the naked individual. Rather than pushing the pendulum of public policy between scapegoating the substance and scapegoating the individual, we should seek a middle ground. Realizing that the addiction process has at least three levels of complexity is a good place to start.

First, at the basic and most immediate level, are the short- and long-term biological processes that underlie the psychological experiences of drug use and drug abstinence. Even with the same drug, these experiences vary greatly across individuals. Scientists and journalists too easily forget that every psychological process is built on biology. Discoveries of biological mechanisms and processes underlying addiction are not proof that the problem is biological rather than social and psychological. Eating rich foods has powerful biological effects in both the short and long run, but we should not therefore conclude that the rise in obesity in the United States is a biological problem. Indeed, attempts to alter the addiction process that emphasize biochemistry (such as the nicotine patch) have met with little success.

At the next level are psychological processes (social, motivational, learning) that, although rooted in biology, are shaped by personal experience. Because each of us has unique life experiences, we do not necessarily interpret the same events in the same way. The reasons for one individual's addiction may be altogether different from the reasons for another's. As the recent Scottish film *Trainspotting* makes clear, stories of addiction are no less complex than any other personal stories. Still, intervention at this level has had some success with users of alcohol or illicit drugs, and several research and treatment institutions are examining methods for "matching" addicts with different treatment strategies based on their social and psychological characteristics.

Drug effects and drug addiction also vary greatly across time and place, impli-cating cultural factors as the third and most general aspect of drug addiction. These factors are rooted in but not reducible to psychological processes, just as psychological processes are not reducible to biology. Patterns of alcohol use around the world, which show that the prevalence of drinking problems cannot be predicted by consumption alone, illustrate the importance of culture. Italians, for example, historically have consumed large quantities of alcohol with relatively low rates of drunkenness and alcoholism. The effects of alcohol on human behavior—violence, boorishness, gregariousness—also have been shown to vary dramatically across cultures.

Given the cultural role in addiction and the radical changes that have occurred in attitudes about smoking, it is quite possible that the young smokers of today are not at all like the smokers of 50 years ago. Those who begin smoking now do so with the belief that it is addictive, causes poor health (and wrinkles!), and can be deadly. If individuals are willing to start smoking despite such knowledge, it is likely that they will acquire and keep the habit, seeming to confirm the current, politically correct image of addiction. And if this self-fulfilling prophecy is realized, chances are that interventions aimed at the social realm will continue to miss their target and fail to curtail addiction.

POSTSCRIPT

Is Nicotine Addictive?

In the United States, attitudes toward smoking have changed considerably over the last several decades. Smoking in public places used to be the norm, but smokers are now typically relegated to designated areas. At one time smoking was considered a rite of passage into adulthood. Today, the rate of adult smoking has declined and the rate of teenage smoking has increased. Smoking is becoming a rite of passage into adolescence. In the early part of the twentieth century, women who smoked were scorned and considered immoral. Some women now see smoking as a sign of their independence.

Brigham feels that the evidence supporting the contention that nicotine is addictive is overwhelming. Nicotine, like alcohol, opiates, and cocaine, affects neurotransmitters in the brain that regulate mood, attention, and memory. Because nicotine can alter emotional states in ways that smokers find desirable, smoking behavior is perpetuated. In the absence of nicotine, many smokers experience a decline in reasoning ability, memory, and attention. One way to overcome these cognitive impairments is by taking in nicotine.

It is possible that some people smoke because of depression. Compared to nonsmokers, smokers are twice as likely to suffer from major depression. Unfortunately, depressed individuals who would like to quit smoking have considerably less success than those who are not depressed; perhaps nicotine acts as an antidepressant. The fact that nicotine elevates mood contributes to the difficulty that smokers encounter when they attempt to stop.

DeGrandpre asserts that if nicotine is as physically addictive as many people believe, then why isn't everyone who has ever smoked addicted? To say that nicotine causes physical addiction, DeGrandpre states, oversimplifies the dynamics of cigarette smoking and ignores the psychosocial factors that contribute to cigarette addiction. The concept of cigarette addiction is acknowledged by DeGrandpre, but he does not agree with the idea that nicotine is addictive.

The internal workings of the tobacco industry are discussed in "Nicotine and Addiction: The Brown and Williamson Documents," by Lisa Bero et al., *JAMA* (July 19, 1995) and "Tobacco: Enemy Number 1," by Robert Dreyfuss, *Mother Jones* (May–June 1996). The relationship between nicotine and depression is studied in "Nicotine Dependence and Major Depression: New Evidence From a Prospective Investigation," by N. Breslau, M. M. Kilbey, and P. Andreski, *Archives of General Psychiatry* (January 1993). And in "Kicking Butts," *Psychology Today* (September/October 1994), Carl Sherman discusses the addictive nature of nicotine.

ISSUE 12

Are Too Many Children Receiving Ritalin?

YES: Richard Bromfield, from "Is Ritalin Overprescribed? Yes," *Priorities* (vol. 8, no. 3, 1996)

NO: Jerry Wiener, from "Is Ritalin Overprescribed? No," *Priorities* (vol. 8, no. 3, 1996)

ISSUE SUMMARY

YES: Harvard Medical School professor Richard Bromfield contends that physicians are often too eager to prescribe Ritalin for children with attention deficit/hyperactivity disorder (ADHD). Bromfield is concerned that Ritalin's long-term effects have not been adequately researched and that its overuse may be masking other childhood disorders.

NO: George Washington Medical School professor Jerry Wiener maintains that Ritalin has been proven to be safe and effective. Wiener argues that attention deficit/hyperactivity disorder is underdiagnosed in many instances and that children who could benefit from the use of Ritalin often do not receive it.

The number one childhood psychiatric disorder in the United States is attention deficit/hyperactivity disorder, which affects approximately 6 percent of all school-age children. The most commonly prescribed drug for ADHD is the stimulant Ritalin (the generic name is methylphenidate). About 2.5 million U.S. children, primarily boys between the ages of 5 and 12, receive Ritalin prescriptions for ADHD. In contrast, only 1 in 200 European children are diagnosed with ADHD. Ritalin is therefore much less likely to be prescribed in Europe. ADHD is characterized by inattentiveness, hyperactivity, and impulsivity. Many children are diagnosed as having only attention deficit disorder (ADD), which is ADHD without the hyperactivity.

The use of stimulants to treat such behavioral disorders dates back to 1937. The practice of prescribing stimulants for behavioral problems increased dramatically beginning in 1970, when it was estimated that 150,000 American children were taking stimulant medications. It seems paradoxical for physicians to be prescribing a stimulant such as Ritalin for a behavioral disorder that already involves hyperactivity. However, Ritalin appears to be effective with many children, as well as with many adults, who suffer from this condition. Looking at this issue from a broader perspective, one needs to ask whether or not behavioral problems should be treated as a disease. Also, does Ritalin really address the problem? Or could it be covering up other maladies that otherwise would be treated?

Ritalin enhances the functioning of the brain's reticular activating system, which helps one to focus attention and to filter out extraneous stimuli. The drug has been shown to improve short-term learning. Ritalin also produces adverse effects such as insomnia, headaches, irritability, nausea, dizziness, weight loss, and growth retardation. Psychological dependence may develop, but physical dependence is unlikely. The effects of long-term Ritalin use are unknown.

Since 1990 the number of children receiving Ritalin has increased 250 percent. This large increase in the number of children diagnosed with ADHD may be attributed to a broader application of the criteria for diagnosing ADHD, heightened public awareness, and changes in American educational policy regarding schools' identifying children with the disorder. Some people feel that the increase in prescriptions for Ritalin reflects an increased effort to satisfy the needs of parents whose children exhibit behavioral problems. Ritalin has been referred to as "mother's little helper." Regardless of the reasons for the increase, many people question whether Ritalin is overprescribed and children are overmedicated or whether Ritalin is a miracle drug.

One problem with the increased prevalence of Ritalin prescriptions is that illegal use of the drug has also risen. There are accounts of some parents getting prescriptions for their children and then selling the drugs illegally. On a number of college campuses there are reports of students using Ritalin to get high or to stay awake in order to study. Historically, illegal use of Ritalin has been minimal, although officials of the Drug Enforcement Administration (DEA) are now concerned that its illegal use is proliferating. Problems with its use are unlikely to rival those of cocaine because Ritalin's effects are more moderate than those of cocaine or amphetamines.

The fact is that children now receive prescriptions for Ritalin rather readily. Frequently, parents will pressure their pediatricians into writing the prescriptions. One survey found that almost one-half of all pediatricians spent less than an hour assessing children before prescribing Ritalin. On the other hand, if there is a medication available that would remedy a problem, shouldn't it be taken? If a child's academic performance can improve through the use of Ritalin, should that child be denied the drug? As indicated, Ritalin is effective for many children, although it works best if it is accompanied by behavioral therapy.

In the following selections, Richard Bromfield argues that despite the benefits of Ritalin, too many children are being given it inappropriately and that the long-term consequences of its use are unknown. Jerry Wiener maintains that ADHD is underdiagnosed and that more children should receive Ritalin. Wiener concedes that some children are misdiagnosed, but he argues that the benefits of Ritalin outweigh its risks.

YES   Richard Bromfield

IS RITALIN OVERPRESCRIBED? YES

Ritalin is being dispensed with a speed and nonchalance compati-
ble with our drive-through culture, yet entirely at odds with good
medicine and common sense. The drug does help some people pay
attention and function better; some of my own patients have bene-
fited from it. But too many children, and more and more adults, are
being given Ritalin inappropriately.

Psychiatry has devised careful guidelines for prescribing and monitoring this
sometimes-useful drug. But the dramatic jump in Ritalin use in the past five
years clearly suggests that these guidelines are being ignored and that Ritalin
is being vastly overprescribed. The problem has finally been recognized by
medical groups such as the American Academy of Child and Adolescent
Psychiatry, the American Psychiatric Association and the American Academy
of Pediatrics, which have written or are developing guidelines for diagnosing
ADHD [attention-deficit/hyperactive disorder]; and even by CibaGeneva
Pharmaceuticals, the manufacturer of Ritalin, which issued similar guidelines
to doctors [recently].

Under the pressure of managed care, physicians are diagnosing ADHD in
patients and prescribing them Ritalin after interviews as short as 15 minutes.
And given Ritalin's quick action (it can "calm" children within days after
treatment starts), some doctors even rely on the drug as a diagnostic tool,
interpreting improvements in behavior or attention as proof of an underlying
ADHD—and justification for continued drug use.

Studies show that Ritalin prescribing fluctuates dramatically depending
on how parents and teachers perceive "misbehavior" and how tolerant they
are of it. I know of children who have been given Ritalin more to subdue
them than to meet their needs—a practice that recalls the opium syrups
used to soothe noisy infants in London a century ago. When a drug can
be prescribed because one person is bothering another—a disruptive child
upsetting a teacher, for example—there is clearly a danger that the drug will
be abused. That danger only increases when the problem being treated is so
vaguely defined.

ADHD exists as a disorder primarily because a committee of psychiatrists voted it so. In a valiant effort, they squeezed a laundry list of disparate symptoms into a neat package that can be handled and treated. But while attention is an essential aspect of our functioning, it's certainly not the only one. Why not bestow disorderhood on other problems common to people diagnosed with ADHD, such as Easily Frustrated Disorder (EFD) or Nothing Makes Me Happy Disorder (NMMHD)?

Once known as Minimal Brain Dysfunction and Hyperkinetic Syndrome, ADHD is considered a neurological disorder. Certainly, some people diagnosed with ADHD are neurologically impaired and need medication. But nervous system glitches account for the disruptive behavior of only a small minority of people who are vulnerable to distraction or impulsive behavior—perhaps 1 percent or 2 percent of the general population. Many more people have ADHD symptoms that have nothing to do with their nervous systems and result instead from emotional distress, depression, anxiety, obsessions or learning disabilities.

For these people, who exhibit the symptoms of ADHD but suffer from some other problem, Ritalin will likely be useless as a treatment. Taking it may postpone more effective treatment. And it may even be harmful.

No one knows how Ritalin works. Some miracle drugs, of course, have helped people for decades or even centuries before their mechanisms of action were understood. But we need to know more about the possible effects of a drug used mainly on children.

We're willing to overlook side effects when it comes to treating a life-threatening disease. But with a less weighty disorder like ADHD, therapeutic rewards must be weighed against possible adverse reactions. In a drug targeted at children, there is concern that harmful effects may crop up decades after treatment stops. Since Ritalin is a relatively new drug, in use for about 30 years, we still don't know whether long-term side effects await its young users. But we do know that more immediate problems can occur.

It's already clear that Ritalin can worsen underlying anxiety, depression, psychosis and seizures. More common but milder side effects include nervousness and sleeplessness. Some studies suggest that the drug may interfere with bone growth. And [recently] the United Nation's International Narcotics Control Board reported an increase in teenagers who were inhaling this stimulant drug, which is chemically similar to cocaine but not nearly as potent.

While Ritalin's mode of action isn't clear, the drug is known to affect the brain's most ancient and basic structures, which control arousal and attention. I question the wisdom of tampering with such crucially important parts of the brain, particularly with a drug whose possible long-term side effects remain to be discovered.

The surge in both ADHD diagnoses and Ritalin prescriptions is yet another sign of a society suffering from a colossal lack of personal responsibility. By telling patients that their failures, misbehavior and unhappiness are caused by a disorder, we risk colluding with their all-too-human belief that their actions are beyond their control, and we weaken their motivation to change on their own. And in the many cases where ADHD is misdiagnosed in children, we give parents the illusion that their child's problems have nothing to do with the home environment or with their performance as parents.

It must be true that bad biology accounts for some people's distracted and impulsive lifestyles. But random violence, drugs, alcohol, domestic trauma and (less horrifically) indulgent and chaotic homes are more obvious reasons for the ADHD-like restlessness that plagues America. We urgently need to address *these* problems. To do that, we need legislators who will provide support for good parenting, especially in the early years of childhood when the foundations for handling feelings, self-control and concentration are biologically and psychologically laid down.

Some people who can't concentrate probably do merit the diagnosis of ADHD and a prescription for Ritalin to treat it. But the brain, the neurological seat of the soul and the self must be treated with the utmost respect. With the demand for Ritalin growing, we must be increasingly wary about doling out a drug that can be beneficial but is more often useless or even harmful.

NO

Jerry Wiener

IS RITALIN OVERPRESCRIBED? NO

In defending the current use of Ritalin for treating ADHD [attention-deficit/hyperactive disorder], it's important first to emphasize that the disorder really exists.

Telling whether a child has ADHD is more complicated than a diagnosis of the mumps or chicken pox, but the diagnosis of ADHD can still be as valid as any in medicine. An analogous health problem would be multiple sclerosis: As with ADHD it's a distinct disease, yet we don't know what causes the illness and have no laboratory test for diagnosing it.

Since the 1950s what we now call ADHD has been a well-recognized syndrome involving, as all syndromes do, a group of signs and symptoms that occur together. Years of research have documented that some children differ from their peers in being inattentive and hyperactive as well as impulsive. Extensive field trials and numerous studies have established that hyperactivity and impulsivity are at the core of the diagnosis, with inattention a consequence of the other two, especially in school-age boys.

Adding to the evidence that ADHD is a legitimate clinical problem are recent results of magnetic resonance imaging (MRI) studies showing that children diagnosed with ADHD have subtle but significant anatomical differences in their brains compared with other children. Furthermore, studies of families suggest there is a genetic component for many cases of ADHD. More specifically, recent research has found a possible link between ADHD and three genes that code for receptors (proteins that jut from the surface of cells) that are activated by dopamine, a neurotransmitter (a chemical that conveys messages from one nerve cell to another). Defects in these genes could mean a reduced response to dopamine signals, perhaps accounting for the uninhibited behavior observed in ADHD.

A child suspected of having ADHD should be evaluated by a trained and experienced clinician who takes the time to assess the child's development, family history and behavior at school and at home. The clinician should require that the criteria set forth in the current *Diagnostic and Statistical Manual of Mental Disorders* (DSM-IV) are met before concluding that a child has ADHD.

From Jerry Wiener, "Is Ritalin Overprescribed? No," *Priorities*, vol. 8, no. 3 (1996), pp. 25, 27, 29. Copyright © 1996 by The American Council on Science and Health. Reprinted by permission of *Priorities*, a publication of The American Council on Science and Health, 1995 Broadway, 2d Floor, New York, NY 10023-5860.

To receive the diagnosis of ADHD, a child should display a significant number of symptoms and behaviors reflecting hyperactivity, impulsivity and inattention —and the symptoms and behaviors must be more persistent and severe than normally occur in children of that age. In addition and importantly, there must be impaired functioning in school, at home and/or in social relationships.

Are mistakes made in diagnosing ADHD? Of course. They usually occur when the clinician is rushed, inexperienced, untrained, pressured or predisposed either to "find" ADHD or to overlook it. As a result, there is both over- and underdiagnosis of ADHD. The reported fivefold increase in Ritalin prescriptions over the past five years is reason to reflect about possible overusage. However, repeated findings of a three-percent prevalence rate of ADHD among school-age children give as much cause for concern about underdiagnosis as for overusage: At these prevalence rates, up to 30 percent of children with ADHD may not be receiving sufficient treatment.

While there is no cure for ADHD, there is a very effective treatment to minimize its symptoms—through the use of stimulant medications such as Ritalin. Such drugs are by far the most effective treatment for moderating and controlling the disorder's major symptoms— hyperactivity, inattention and impulsivity—in 75 percent to 80 percent of children with this disorder.

The safety and effectiveness of Ritalin and other stimulant drugs, including Dexedrine (dextroamphetamine) and Cylert (pemoline), have been established more firmly than any other treatments in the field of child and adolescent psychiatry. Literally scores of carefully conducted blind and double-blind controlled studies have repeatedly documented the improvement—often dramatic—in symptoms of ADHD following the use of stimulant medication, with Ritalin the most common choice. By contrast, no other treatment, including behavior modification, compares with stimulant medication in efficacy; in fact, no treatment besides these medications has had much success at all in treating ADHD.

Stimulant medication is so effective that a parent with a child diagnosed with ADHD should receive an explanation if the clinician's judgment is *not* to prescribe medication. Appropriate considerations for not opting for Ritalin and similar drugs include a history of tic or Tourette's disorder, the presence of a thought disorder, significant resistance to such medications in the patient or family or insufficient severity of the symptoms or dysfunction. Other classes of drugs, such as antidepressants, can be effective and can be used when there is concern about the use of a stimulant medication or when side effects occur.

The issue should not be whether stimulants are overprescribed but the risk that they may be misprescribed. The most common example: children who are described as overactive or impulsive but who do not meet the criteria for the diagnosis of ADHD. Another example is the use of stimulants as a diagnostic "test" by a rushed or inexperienced clinician who may not realize that a favorable response was due to the placebo effect and therefore mistakenly assumes that the diagnosis of ADHD has been confirmed.

As effective as Ritalin can be for treating the symptoms of ADHD, it should rarely, if ever, be the only treatment for someone with the problem. The child or adolescent may also benefit from remedial work for any identified learning disability and from family therapy or psychotherapy for problems of self-image, self-esteem, anger and/or depression.

Is Ritalin overprescribed? Not when it's used for children who meet the criteria for the diagnosis of ADHD, including the requirement that the child's ability to function must be "significantly impaired." All too often, the mistakes in prescribing Ritalin are errors of omission, where children who could benefit from the drug never receive it. Instead, they go through school labeled as troublemakers, or as unmotivated or hostile. They'll have missed out on the opportunity for at least a trial on a medication that could have significantly improved their symptoms and allowed for improved academic performance, self-esteem and social interaction.

POSTSCRIPT

Are Too Many Children Receiving Ritalin?

To satisfy their own emotional needs, many parents push their physicians into diagnosing their children with ADHD. Parents believe that their children will benefit if they are labeled ADHD. The pressure for children to do well academically in order to get into the right college and graduate school is intense. Some parents feel that if their children are diagnosed with ADHD, then they may be provided special circumstances or allowances such as additional time when taking college entrance examinations. Some parents also realize that if their children are identified as having ADHD, then their children will be eligible for support services in school. In some instances, the only way to receive such extra help is to be labeled with a disorder. Some teachers favor the use of Ritalin to control students' behavior. During the last few years, there has been increasing emphasis on controlling school budgets. The result is larger class sizes and higher student-to-teacher ratios. Thus, it should not be surprising that many teachers welcome the calming effect of Ritalin on students whose hyperactivity is disruptive to the class.

Whether or not drug therapy should be applied to behaviors raises another concern. What is the message that children are receiving about the role of drugs in society? Perhaps children will generalize the benefits of using legal drugs like Ritalin to remedy life's problems to using illegal drugs to deal with other problems that they may be experiencing. Children may find that it is easier to ingest a pill rather than to put the time and effort into resolving personal problems. For many adults, drugs seem to represent a shortcut to correcting life's difficulties. Through its reliance on drugs, is American society creating a wrong impression for its children, an illusion of believing that there is a pill for *every* ill?

When to prescribe Ritalin for children also places physicians in a quandary. They may see the benefit of helping students function more effectively in school. However, are physicians who readily prescribe Ritalin unintentionally promoting an antihumanistic, competitive environment in which performance matters regardless of cost? On the other hand, is it the place of physicians to dictate to parents what is best for their children? In the final analysis, will the increase in prescriptions for Ritalin result in benefits for the child, for the parents, and for society?

The social consequences of and reasons for the explosion of Ritalin use in the last several years are discussed in Lawrence Diller's article "The Run on Ritalin: Attention Deficit Disorder and Stimulant Treatment in the 1990s," *Hastings Center Report* (March–April 1996). Several articles addressing whether or not Ritalin is overprescribed appear in the March 18, 1996, issue of *Newsweek*. Differences between the United States and Europe in the practice of prescribing Ritalin are described by Dorothy Bonn in "Methylphenidate: U.S. and European Views Converging?" *The Lancet* (July 27, 1996). And the effectiveness of Ritalin is studied by Thomas Spencer et al. in "A Double-Blind Crossover Comparison of Methylphenidate and Placebo in Adults With Childhood-Onset Attention Deficit Hyperactivity Disorder," *Archives of General Psychiatry* (June 1995).

ISSUE 13

Is Prozac Overprescribed?

YES: Mark Nichols, from "Questioning Prozac," *Maclean's* (May 23, 1994)

NO: Nancy Wartik, from "Prozac: The Verdict Is In," *American Health* (November 1996)

ISSUE SUMMARY

YES: Writer Mark Nichols states that many physicians prescribe Prozac too readily and that Prozac is used too often for ordinary problems of daily living such as discontent and irritability. He contends, moreover, that its long-term effects are not known and that some people experience negative psychological reactions while on Prozac.

NO: Health and psychology writer Nancy Wartik maintains that Prozac is helpful for treating chronic depression, especially among women, and that Prozac's purported dangers are overexaggerated. She asserts that if there were less adverse publicity surrounding Prozac, more people could benefit from its use.

One of the most common emotional problems in America is depression. It is estimated that approximately 10 percent of Americans experience some type of depression during their lives. The antidepressant drug most typically prescribed for treating depression is Prozac, whose generic name is fluoxetine. Although Prozac has been available only since 1987, the drug has already garnered several billion dollars in global sales. It is one of the most commonly prescribed drugs in the United States.

Although Prozac was originally developed for treating depression—for which it is believed to be 60–70 percent effective—the drug has been prescribed for an array of other conditions. These conditions include eating disorders such as bulimia and obesity, obsessive-compulsive disorders, and anxiety. It has even been prescribed for depressed pets. An important question about Prozac is currently under debate: Is Prozac being prescribed too casually? Some experts feel that physicians are giving Prozac to patients who do not need chemical treatment to overcome their afflictions. Sherwin Nuland, a professor at Yale University, believes that Prozac is relatively safe for its approved applications but that it is inappropriate for less severe problems.

As with most other drugs, Prozac can produce a number of adverse side effects, though they are reportedly fewer and less severe than those of other antidepressants. Short-term side effects from Prozac include headaches, sweating, fatigue, anxiety, reduced appetite, jitteriness, dizziness, stomach discomfort, nausea, sexual dysfunction, and insomnia. Because it is a relatively new drug, long-term side effects have yet to be determined.

Several lawsuits have been filed against Eli Lilly and Company, Prozac's manufacturer, as a result of one of the drug's alleged side effects: the drug has been linked to violent and suicidal behavior. Some individuals charged with violent crimes have even used the defense that Prozac made them act violently and that they should not be held accountable for their actions while on the drug. Prozac has also been implicated in a number of suicides, though it is unclear whether Prozac caused these individuals to commit suicide or whether they would have committed suicide anyway. Eli Lilly representatives emphasize that Prozac diminishes suicidal thoughts and may prevent violent behavior.

To date, hearings by the Food and Drug Administration (FDA) have concluded that Prozac is a safe and effective drug because the evidence linking it to violence and suicide is insufficient. One critic, author William Styron, asserts that the manufacturer has made a concerted effort to minimize the detrimental effects of Prozac. In 1990 the Prozac Survivors Support Group was formed to help people who have had adverse symptoms while on the drug.

Psychiatrist Peter R. Breggin, who feels that Prozac is being prescribed too frequently, argues that Prozac and other antidepressant drugs are being used to replace traditional psychotherapy. Breggin contends that psychiatry has given in to the pharmaceutical companies. Compared to psychiatry, Prozac is far less expensive and more convenient. But does Prozac get at the root of the problems that many people have? The U.S. Public Health Service recommends drug therapy for severe cases of depression but psychotherapy for mild or moderate cases of depression.

Psychiatrist Peter D. Kramer argues that Prozac brings about a positive transformation in the personalities of many individuals: people who are habitually timid seem more confident after taking the drug; sensitive people become more brash; and introverts improve their social skills. Kramer states that people become more real. Critics of this viewpoint ask, If one's personality changes as a result of a drug, what is that individual's real personality? Is the personality of a person on Prozac "real"? Also, does Prozac change one's personality or simply the way one perceives the world?

In the following selections, Mark Nichols maintains that Prozac is overprescribed and that it is being used simply to make people feel better. He contends that Prozac is employed as a quick fix and that people who are using the drug are not confronting the real sources of their problems. He discusses as well the social implications of the overprescription of Prozac. Nancy Wartik argues that Prozac is an invaluable drug in the treatment of mild depression and that more people could benefit from its use. She contends that Prozac has been unfairly criticized and that this criticism has prevented more people from using it.

YES

Mark Nichols

QUESTIONING PROZAC

With more than 11 million mostly satisfied customers around the globe, it is one of the most rapidly successful drugs in history. An antidote to clinical depression, the green-and-yellow capsule, introduced six years ago, has also been extolled by some enthusiasts as just the thing to help frazzled parents cope with their kids or to make chronic loners stop fearing rejection. Prozac—brand name for the chemical fluoxetine hydrochloride—has entered pop culture, as well, becoming the stuff of cartoons and stand-up comedy routines. And it has summoned the vision of an era of so-called cosmetic psychopharmacology, in which a society of pill-poppers, seeking relief from everything from shyness to fear or crowds, will have to look no further than the nearest medicine cabinet. That day may yet come. But it raises serious medical and philosophical questions—and the first wave of them is descending upon Prozac itself. Is Prozac—non-addictive and, according to some doctors, capable of transforming personalities for the better—a nearly perfect pill? Well, not quite.

There *are* some problems. Many medical experts worry that some doctors may be overprescribing Prozac and using it to treat relatively trivial personality disorders. As a result, far too many people—including some of the estimated 200,000 Canadians currently taking Prozac—may be using a drug whose long-term effects might not be known for decades. As well, there have been reports—contradicted by manufacturer Eli Lilly and Co. of Indianapolis and U.S. health officials—suggesting that a small number of Prozac patients may become violent or prone to suicidal thinking. Even more worrisome, Dr. Lorne Brandes, a Winnipeg cancer researcher, claims to have evidence that Prozac and some other widely used drugs may promote the growth of cancerous tumors. "I'm very concerned about Prozac," says Brandes, who reported in 1992 that rats and mice with artificially induced cancer showed an increased rate of tumor growth when they were given Prozac and another antidepressant. Brandes's findings alarmed some cancer researchers and prompted federal scientists to launch a similar study.

And although Prozac has fewer side-effects than earlier antidepressants, it does have some. Users may experience nausea, nervousness and insomnia and their sex life can suffer: a U.S. study, published in *The Journal of Clinical Psychiatry* in April [1994] found that among 160 patients taking Prozac, 54 reported that sexual desire or response diminished after they began using the drug. And even proponents wonder about the social implications of a medicine that promises to abolish angst—what would happen to the world's art and culture if future Vincent van Goghs and F. Scott Fitzgeralds were prescribed Prozac? Peter D. Kramer, a psychiatrist from Providence, R.I., who paints a largely favorable portrait of the pill in his best-selling book *Listening to Prozac*, allows: "We cannot escape entirely the fear that a drug that makes people optimistic and confident will rob them of the morally beneficial effects of melancholy and angst."

In defence of Prozac, which grossed $1.7 billion in worldwide sales last year, Eli Lilly officials say that it is one of the most thoroughly tested medications in history: more than 32,000 people took part in Prozac's clinical trials, and scientists have conducted at least 3,000 separate studies. "Nothing alarming has shown up," says Cameron Battley, corporate affairs manager for Eli Lilly Canada Inc. in Scarborough, Ont. Battley also insists that, despite reports of the drug being used to treat people who do not really need an antidepressant, "there is absolutely no indication of any inappropriate use of Prozac in Canada." Maybe, but there are signs that Eli Lilly suspects something amiss. In an advertisement that began appearing recently in North American medical publications, the company deplores the "unprecedented amount of media attention" given to Prozac and stresses that the drug is intended for use "only where a clear medical need exists."

While there are concerns about Prozac, there is also unstinting praise from doctors and patients for an antidepressant that has made it easier to treat a debilitating illness. The side-effects of older antidepressants—including a parched mouth, difficulty urinating and feelings of psychological detachment—made them hard to take. "There were serious problems involved in getting patients to tolerate those drugs in therapeutic doses," says Dr. James Brooks, a Toronto general practitioner. "With Prozac, you don't have this. I'm really pleased with Prozac."

Many patients are equally enthusiastic. Three years ago, William Pringle, Vancouver special events organizer, was flattened by a major depression. His doctor put him on Prozac. "I fell into this dark pit," says Pringle. "Prozac pulled me out and got me relaunched on my life." Pringle, 36, stopped using Prozac a year ago and says that he is still feeling fine. Maria Theresa Spagnuolo of Toronto began taking it in 1989, after three automobile accidents left her with chronic pain throughout her body—and serious depression. Married and the mother of a young son, Spagnuolo found that she "was crying about everything—spilled milk was a catastrophe." Prozac, adds the 38-year-old Spagnulo, "gave me energy and changed my outlook so that I can cope with life. I don't think I could function without it."

Interestingly, many doctors report that the majority of their Prozac patients are women. William Ashdown, a Prozac user who is executive director of the Winnipeg-based Society for Depression and Manic-Depression of Manitoba, says that "it is more acceptable for a woman to seek help for an emotional disorder. Most men are culturally pressured into other avenues of self-medication, alcohol being a common one."

Spurred by Prozac's success, competing drug companies have begun producing similar antidepressants, including Paxil (made by Britain's SmithKline Beecham PLC) and Zoloft (by New York City-based Pfizer Inc.). All the drugs tinker with the same delicate mechanism—the brain's chemical communication system. Over the past decade, scientists have made important strides in understanding how the brain works—and how to affect the intricate chemical activity that makes some people chipper and outgoing while leaving others habitually despondent. Among the key determinants are a group of chemicals known as neurotransmitters—they include serotonin, dopamine and norepinephrine—that help to flash signals among the brain's 50 billion cells. Discharged by one cell, the neurotransmitters lock onto the receptors of neighboring cells. In this chemical interplay, serotonin plays a powerful role in modifying mood and emotion—but some people apparently don't have enough of it.

To remedy that, Prozac and similar drugs—known collectively by scientists as selective serotonin re-uptake inhibitors (SSRIs)—prevent brain cells from reabsorbing used serotonin. That leaves a pool of serotonin available for further use, which can lighten the mood and thinking of depressed people. Rose Rancourt, a 42-year-old Vancouverite, began using Paxil last fall after battling severe depressions from the age of 16. A former computer information systems supervisor, Rancourt now devotes herself to working with other depressed people. Thanks to Paxil, she says, "I feel good. I feel fine. I have peace of mind."

Despite its success in blazing the way for other SSRIs, Prozac has been embroiled in controversy almost from the start. After taking about 15 years to develop the drug, Eli Lilly began marketing Prozac in the United States in 1988 and in Canada the following year. Then, in February, 1990, Dr. Martin Teicher, a psychiatrist at the highly regarded McLean Hospital in Belmont, Mass., and two of his colleagues reported that six depressed patients began to have suicidal thoughts after using Prozac. Writing in *The American Journal of Psychiatry,* Teicher said that when they began taking the drug, none of the patients were suicidal and all were "hopeful and optimistic" about their treatment. After that, a spate of anecdotal reports told of violence and suicide among Prozac users. And the drug acquired a tenacious enemy in the Los Angeles-based Citizens Commission on Human Rights, which has ties to the Church of Scientology, a movement that, among other things, opposes some aspects of psychiatry and drug therapy.

The Scientologists claim that by Sept. 16, 1993, no fewer than 1,089 suicides had been recorded among patients taking the capsule. If that figure is correct, it works out to about .01 per cent of the 11 million people who have used the drug. Eli Lilly's Battley denies that Prozac is to blame. "Sadly," he added, "it is impossible to eradicate the possibility of depressed people committing suicide, even if they are receiving medication." Hearings by the U.S. Food and Drug Administration exonerated Prozac, but the bad publicity cut into its sales and produced a flood of lawsuits against Eli Lilly. So far, U.S. courts have rejected 80 claims against the company, many alleging that Prozac caused violent or suicidal tendencies; another 170 lawsuits are pending. In Canada, five lawsuits

—at least one involving violence—are pending against the company.

Prozac weathered the bad notices and soon began getting good ones. Kramer's book, published last year, describes personalities transformed by Prozac and patients made "better than well." According to Kramer, the effect Prozac will have on a patient can never be accurately predicted. Sometimes, he writes, "you take Prozac to treat a symptom, and it transforms your sense of self." The pill seems "to give social confidence to the habitually timid, to make the sensitive brash, to lend the introvert the social skills of a salesman."

Boosted by Kramer's best-seller, Prozac took off in 1993, recording a 15-percent increase in North American sales over the previous year—and prompting concern that doctors now may be dispensing the drug too liberally. In Canada and the United States, Prozac has been approved for use in treating clinical depression, bulimia (habitual purging to lose weight) and obsessive-compulsive disorder (persistent irrational thoughts and actions). But many doctors have effectively expanded the definition of what constitutes clinical depression to include dysthmyia—chronic low-grade depression—and in some cases have prescribed Prozac to otherwise healthy patients suffering from low self-esteem or gnawing anxieties. Hubert Van Tol, an associate professor of psychiatry and pharmacology at the University of Toronto, says: "If it's a question of someone who isn't feeling so hot, or maybe a man who's nervous about addressing meetings—that's not what the drug was designed for."

As well, some psychiatrists argue that it is dangerous for Prozac or similar drugs to be used without accompanying psychotherapy sessions, which en-

able doctors to monitor the drug's effects. Some experts worry that general practitioners, who write the majority of Prozac prescriptions and see scores of patients a day, do not have time to do that. Others argue that far from being overprescribed, the drug has just begun to realize its potential. "In terms of sheer numbers," author Kramer told *Maclean's*, "you could probably double or triple the number of people using antidepressants, because depression is so underdiagnosed." Adds Kramer: "Prozac is not an enjoyable drug to use. It doesn't give you a high. With people who have problems but are less than clinically depressed, we would have no compunction about treating them with psychotherapy. So I don't see why we can't also treat them with a chemical that will ease their symptoms."

As compelling as that argument sounds, critics respond by insisting that any relatively new drug may have unforeseen consequences. Sidney Wolfe, director of the Public Citizen Health Research Group, a Washington-based consumer advocacy organization, compares Prozac to Valium, the popular tranquillizer that was on the market for more than 10 years before doctors discovered its highly addictive properties during the mid-1970s. "Prozac," declares Wolfe, "has become the Valium of the 1990s." Asks Dr. David Bakish, associate professor of psychiatry at the University of Ottawa: "Is there a chance that with Prozac some problem could show up in 15 or 20 years? Yes, it could happen."

Some doctors say they have seen disturbing reactions in Prozac patients. Dr. Shiva Sishta, a Fredericton psychiatrist who prescribes Prozac for people suffering form obsessive-compulsive disorders, says that one married woman who was on a fairly high dosage "became rather promiscuous—she recognized that she was not behaving properly." Shista took her off the drug, then resumed it later at a lower dosage with encouraging results. Dr. Randolph Catlin, a psychiatrist who is chief of the mental health service at Harvard University in Cambridge, Mass., says that "two or three" students he treated with Prozac reported "feeling split off from themselves. They feel as though they're not there any more." Adds Catlin: "One wonders if these reports that you hear about people acting aggressively with Prozac might be cases where patients who are out of touch with their feelings act on their impulses, without having any feeling of guilt or concern."

While controversy swirls around Prozac and the other SSRIs, a new generation of drugs—with an even greater potential for brightening moods and dispelling disruptive emotions—is fast coming of age.... New York City's Bristol-Myers Squibb Co.... introduce[d] Serzone, a more finely tuned serotonin-related drug designed to help people with depression and panic disorders while causing even fewer side-effects than the current SSRIs. Effexor, a new drug produced by Philadelphia-based Wyeth-Ayerst Laboratories Co. and already on the market in the United States, controls levels of serotonin and norepinephrine to help people suffering from depression; the company claims it has even fewer side-effects than Prozac.

Early in the 21st century, the next stage of drug development may give doctors more sophisticated tools for treating mental illnesses and correcting minor personality disorders—happy pills for every occasion. Because chemical imbalances in the brain are often the result of an inherited defect, says Rémi Quirion, director of the neuroscience division at the Douglas Hospital Research Centre in Montreal, "I think in 10 years' time we will be able to look at a patient's genetic background and choose the drug to use accordingly." Quirion thinks that eventually it will be possible for doctors to administer just the right mix of drugs "to fine-tune the behavior of a given person. We may be able to almost modulate personality." At that point, says the University of Toronto's Van Tol, society "will face an ethical question: do we think it's right to use drugs that change our behavior in a certain direction that we want it to go in? I don't know the answer." It is a question that society already has begun to grapple with as it struggles to come to terms with the unanswered questions about Prozac and the dawning of the age of cosmetic psychopharmacology.

NO   Nancy Wartik

PROZAC: THE VERDICT IS IN

Five years ago, a traumatic sexual encounter sent Cindy Thompson, [names have been changed] now 41, plummeting into depression. "It was agonizing," recalls Thompson, a public relations consultant in Baltimore. "I wanted to kill myself every day." Thompson's psychotherapist recommended Prozac. "But I resisted," she says. "I was concerned about using a chemical to alter my mind and emotions." Finally, poised between the knife drawer and the telephone, "I called my therapist." Thompson agreed to be briefly hospitalized—and to try Prozac. "I figured I'd hit bottom and had nothing to lose."

This year marks a decade since Prozac, the antidepressant that's achieved a celebrity normally associated with movie stars and rock groups, first hit the market. Since then, it's been glorified as a miracle cure and vilified in a backlash centering on claims that Prozac makes some users violent. It's also been attacked as a "happy pill," a quick fix that allows users to ignore the psychological issues at the root of their depression.

Yet even with its luster tarnished, Prozac prospers. With 1995 sales topping $2 billion, up 24% from 1994, it's the second biggest moneymaking drug in the U.S., after the ulcer medicine Zantac. According to the manufacturer, Eli Lilly, more than 14 million Americans have joined the Prozac generation.

The drug has touched the lives of women in particular, primarily because they're twice as likely as men to suffer from major depression—a partly genetic disorder marked by persistent symptoms including sadness, fatigue, sleep or appetite problems and suicidal thoughts. Women also tend to have higher rates of other disorders for which Prozac is now prescribed, such as dysthmyia (chronic mild depression), some forms of anxiety (panic attacks and obsessive-compulsive disorder), severe PMS and bulimia.

Has the advent of Prozac been a boon for women, or will it come to be seen as the 1990s equivalent of "Mother's Little Helper"? Has the drug transformed the treatment of mental illness, or will it cause as yet unknown health problems down the line? Such questions are all the more pressing in this era of managed care, when there's a growing tendency to treat psychological disorders with medication rather than prolonged (read: pricey) talk therapy.

And with a host of newer antidepressant clones such as Zoloft, Paxil and Serzone flooding the market, should Prozac still reign as the drug of choice? Ten years into the Prozac phenomenon, we're starting to get some answers.

A REVOLUTION IN TREATMENT

Antidepressants work by altering balances of mood-regulating chemicals, such as serotonin, in the brain. The most popular antidepressants used to be a class of drug known as tricyclics, which were developed in the 1950s and are still in use. But tricyclics affect not only the brain chemicals they're supposed to but also some they aren't. This can lead to side effects ranging from constipation, dizziness and weight gain to more dangerous problems such as heart rhythm abnormalities.

In contrast, Prozac, Paxil and Zoloft, which belong to a class of drugs known as selective serotonin reuptake inhibitors, or SSRI's, affect serotonin regulation much more directly, which means users tolerate them better. "It doesn't matter how well a drug works if, because of the side effects, people don't take it regularly," says Michael Norden, M.D., a psychiatrist at the University of Washington in Seattle and author of *Beyond Prozac*. "So Prozac was a tremendous step forward."

Women in particular seem to find Prozac and the other SSRI's easy to tolerate. In an ongoing multicenter study of people with chronic depression, women and men were randomly assigned to tricyclic or SSRI treatment. More than 25% of the women on tricyclics stopped taking them, largely because of the side effects, while less than 15% of women on SSRI's quit. They also reported better moods while using SSRI's. (Men, on the other hand, tended to do better on tricyclics.)

With findings such as these, it comes as no surprise that antidepressants are now prescribed more liberally than ever. Some 60% are given out by family doctors, rather than mental health specialists. They're also prescribed for a far greater range of ailments and for less serious disorders: Whereas tricyclics were once reserved only for those with severe depression, these days it's not uncommon for physicians to prescribe Prozac for a case of the blues.

HAPPY ALL THE TIME?

Prozac's easy accessibility has also raised fears that doctors are handing out the drug like M&M's and people are popping it for "personality face-lifts." The real story is more complicated. Plenty of experts agree that the drugs are too readily available. "Their popularity has led to some inappropriate use," says Sidney Zisook, M.D., a professor of psychiatry at the University of California at San Diego. "There are a lot of sloppy diagnosis, cases where they're given for the wrong reasons or for too long. There are also patients who just want to be perfect, to always enjoy themselves, and they think they can do it the easy way, with Prozac. But it's wrong to use these medicines to try to solve all of life's problems."

Others point to a tendency, encouraged by managed care, for doctors to prescribe a pill instead of steering patients toward psychotherapy. "There are maybe 20% to 30% of depressed patients who can just take a drug and get well," says New York University psychiatrist Eric Peselow, M.D. "But the majority need psychotherapy as part of treatment. Racing to Prozac isn't the only answer."

Unfortunately people who pop a pill without doing the hard work of self-examination may find themselves back where they started when they quit taking the medication.

Yet with only one in three depressed people today getting treatment, cries of "Prozac abuse!" can be misleading. "There are far more people who could benefit from these drugs and aren't taking them than there are people taking them inappropriately," says Dr. Zisook. Prozac's trendiness shouldn't obscure the fact that the drug and its progeny help many people dramatically.

Despite her initial skepticism, for instance, Thompson found the drug "life transforming. I felt like myself again." Prozac also pulled Isabel Leigh up from despair. Leigh, 41, a New York City editor who has struggled with depression on and off for years, was reluctant to try the drug. "I didn't want to be just one more trendy Prozac taker," she says. "I told myself it was a crutch I could do without." But about a year ago she found herself feeling lethargic, hopeless and unable to concentrate; she withdrew from friends and let work slide. Finally Leigh went to a doctor and got a Prozac prescription. "It took a few weeks, but the difference was incredible," she says. "I realized I'd been trying to overcome a biochemical problem with willpower alone."

PROZAC PITFALLS

Glowing testimonials aside, Prozac isn't perfect. Like any currently available antidepressant, it works in only 60% to 70% of cases. There's often a lag of up to eight weeks before the drug starts working. And Prozac isn't free of side effects either: Potential problems include agitation, insomnia, headache and weight gain or loss. What's more perhaps a third of those who stay on Prozac for nine months or more find that its uplifting effects fade away, a problem ingloriously known as "Prozac poopout." (Increasing the dose once or twice often helps.)

A growing number of studies also show that up to half of all Prozac users experience decreased libido and delayed or no orgasm. Sharon Keene, 39, a writer in Laguna Hills, CA, took Prozac for three months and "it seemed to help in just about every way," she says. "But I ended up stopping, because I couldn't achieve orgasm. If I wasn't married, maybe I wouldn't have cared so much, but it was affecting my relationship with my husband."

Though other SSRI's can impair sexual function too, Zoloft and Paxil leave the bloodstream faster than Prozac, so users may be able to circumvent trouble in bed by taking drug "holidays" a day or two before the act (so much for spontaneity). Serzone, on the market since 1995, is kinder to users' sex lives. So is Wellbutrin, a medication with a slightly different mechanism of action than Serzone and the SSRI's. It does add a very slight risk of seizures, though....

The bottom line: None of the new antidepressants is clearly superior. "They all have advantages and disadvantages," says Dr. Zisook. "We never know with certainty which drug will work best. There's always some trial and error involved."

THE PRICE OF FAME

As the leader of the pack, Prozac is often the drug of choice by benefit of name recognition alone. But its fame works against it too. Even today Prozac's reputation is clouded by rumors it can't quite shake. Within two years of its introduction in the U.S., headlines and lawsuits began claiming that Prozac drives some users to bizarre, violent behavior. One notorious 1989 incident, the subject of a new book called *The Power to Harm* by John Cornwell, involved a 47-year-old printing plant worker who shot 20 coworkers and then committed suicide after being on Prozac. Survivors and relatives of the victims sued Eli Lilly and lost, but the damage to Prozac's reputation was done.

Today you can surf the Net and still find horror stories from disgruntled folks in "Prozac survivor" support groups. Mary Beth Mrozek, a 33-year-old Buffalo, NY, mother of three who has bipolar illness, says that while on the drug she hallucinated, became convinced people were plotting against her and violently attacked loved ones. "I was a totally different person," she says.

Should the average Prozac user worry about having a Jekyll and Hyde reaction? Bipolar patients who take Prozac may be at slightly higher risk for an episode of mania. But that's a risk associated with any antidepressant (though possibly less so with Wellbutrin). Based on a substantial body of research, experts agree that Prozac users overall aren't at greater risk for violent or suicidal behavior. In fact, says Dr. Norden, "Depressed people who avoid Prozac are probably placing themselves in greater danger. Nothing increases suicide risk as much as depression itself."

A CANCER CONNECTION?

Perhaps a more realistic worry involves unknowns about the long-term effects of Prozac and the other SSRI's, especially since some users drugs are now staying on the drugs indefinitely. A slender body of evidence, based mostly on animal and very preliminary human studies, suggests that antidepressants, including Prozac, could accelerate tumor growth in some people who have a predisposition to cancer or preexisting tumors. Not surprisingly, Eli Lilly disputes these findings. "Lilly's long-term animal studies have bene extensively reviewed by the FDA," says Freda Lewis-Hall, M.D., a psychiatrist who heads the Lilly Center for Women's Health in Indianapolis. "There is absolutely no scientifically credible evidence that it either causes or promotes cancer."

Not everyone agrees. Oncologist Lorne Brandes, M.D., of the Manitoba Cancer Treatment and Research Foundation in Winnipeg, Canada, questions how carefully Lilly interpreted some of its data. But at the same time, he says that antidepressants are "absolutely warranted to treat depression. I'd just suggest trying to get off them as soon as you comfortably can."

Ultimately, however, we may remember Prozac not for its side effects, trendiness or even its effectiveness, but for the attention it has focused on depression —and that can only benefit women in the end. "Once, to be depressed was to be morally and spiritually weak," says Dr. Zisook. "Now people in line at the grocery story are talking about being on Prozac. The drug has brought depression out of the closet."

Leigh, for one, is grateful that it did. "It's not like I have a perfect life with Prozac," she says. "I still have ups and downs. But now I know that if I do get down, I'll come back up. Before Prozac, I was never sure."

POSTSCRIPT

Is Prozac Overprescribed?

Mental health practitioners generally agree that Prozac is effective for treating cases of moderate depression. It is also prescribed, however, for people who suffer from obsessive-compulsive disorders, eating disorders, and phobias. Most recently, Prozac has been shown to help women who suffer from premenstrual syndrome. Increasingly, Prozac is being employed just to improve people's moods. As a result, questions are being raised as to whether or not Prozac is being overprescribed. Opinion within the scientific community is divided over the drug's benefits.

The debate regarding Prozac has spurred other concerns: Should it be prescribed for common problems that people encounter on a daily basis, such as stress or feelings of irritation? Can one find happiness in a pill? Is Prozac a quick and easy fix? Is it ethical to chemically alter an individual's personality? Will psychopharmacology replace traditional psychotherapy? Is the rapid growth of Prozac a well-conceived promotion on the part of pharmaceutical companies? In a society that values solving problems quickly and easily, Prozac seems to effectively fulfill a need. However, do the advantages of Prozac outweigh its disadvantages?

A popular slogan years back referred to "better living through chemistry." If a drug is available that will make people feel happier, more confident, and more socially adept, shouldn't that drug be available for people who would derive some degree of benefit from it? One concern is that some individuals may rely on drugs to remedy many of their problems rather than work through the issues that caused the problems in the first place. Many people now use alcohol or illegal drugs to cope with life's problems. It is difficult to foresee what the effects would be if people could rely on legally prescribed drugs to remedy their problems.

In "Do Kids Need Prozac?" *Newsweek* (October 20, 1997), Mary Crowley raises some relevant issues regarding the prescribing of Prozac to children. Several articles in the August 19, 1994, issue of *CQ Researcher* deal with the controversy surrounding Prozac, how antidepressant drugs work, the early history of the drug, and the outlook for Prozac. In his book *Talking Back to Prozac* (St. Martin's Press, 1994), Peter Breggin, an outspoken psychiatrist who is very critical of Prozac, voices his skepticism of the efficacy of Prozac. Breggin argues that the research supporting the benefits of Prozac is highly questionable. Finally, Peter D. Kramer provides a brief outline of his experiences with Prozac in the revised edition of his best-seller *Listening to Prozac* (Viking Penguin, 1997).

On the Internet ...

http://www.dushkin.com

The Center for Substance Abuse Prevention (CSAP) Home Page
The Center for Substance Abuse Prevention promotes the development of comprehensive drug prevention systems related to community, state, national, and international needs. *http://www.covesoft.com/csap.html*

Join Together
Join Together is a resource center and meeting place for communities working to reduce the harms associated with the use of illicit drugs, excessive alcohol, and tobacco. Join Together helps communities to raise money to support prevention and treatment activities. *http://www.jointogether.org*

The Center for Substance Abuse Treatment (CSAT)
The Center for Substance Abuse Treatment works cooperatively with private and public treatment facilities to identify, develop, and support policies, approaches, and programs that enhance and expand substance abuse treatment. *http://www.samhsa.gov/csat/csat.htm*

The National Council on Alcoholism and Drug Dependence (NCADD)
The National Council on Alcoholism and Drug Dependence provides education, information, help, and hope in the fight against the chronic, often fatal, disease of alcoholism and other drug addictions. *http://www.ncadd.org*

The Higher Education Center for Alcohol and Other Drug Prevention
The Higher Education Center for Alcohol and Other Drug Prevention looks at drug-related issues as they apply to college campuses and their students, such as binge drinking on campus. The center addresses illegal drugs as well as legal drugs. *http://www.edc.org/hec/*

PART 3

Drug Prevention and Treatment

In spite of their legal consequences and the government's interdiction efforts, drugs are widely available and used. Two common ways of dealing with drug abuse is to incarcerate drug users and to intercept drugs before they enter the country. However, many drug experts believe that more energy should be put into preventing and treating drug abuse. An important step toward prevention and treatment is to find out what contributes to drug abuse and how to nullify these factors.

By educating young people about the potential hazards of drugs and by developing an awareness of social influences that contribute to drug use, many drug-related problems may be averted. The debates in this section focus on different prevention and treatment issues, the value of antidrug public service announcements, and the effectiveness of the most widely employed drug education program—Drug Abuse Resistance Education (DARE).

- Should the Food and Drug Administration Prohibit Tobacco Advertising?

- Is Total Abstinence the Only Choice for Alcoholics?

- Is Drug Abuse Resistance Education (DARE) an Effective Program?

- Should the Decision to Use Anabolic Steroids Be Left to Athletes?

- Does Drug Abuse Treatment Work?

- Are Antidrug Media Campaigns Effective?

ISSUE 14

Should the Food and Drug Administration Prohibit Tobacco Advertising?

YES: Richard W. Pollay, from "Hacks, Flacks, and Counter-Attacks: Cigarette Advertising, Sponsored Research, and Controversies," *Journal of Social Issues* (vol. 53, no. 1, 1997)

NO: Jacob Sullum, from "Cowboys, Camels, and Kids," *Reason* (April 1998)

ISSUE SUMMARY

YES: Richard W. Pollay, a professor of business, argues for greater regulation of the tobacco industry because it has a history of presenting misleading and inaccurate information. He also maintains that cigarette advertising influences the perceptions, attitudes, and smoking behavior of young people.

NO: Journalist Jacob Sullum disputes the contention that cigarette advertising influences young people to start smoking. He maintains that there is no proof that a ban on advertising would have any impact on smoking rates.

Scientific evidence clearly indicates that smoking causes numerous adverse health conditions. This debate, however, is not about whether or not tobacco is hazardous but whether or not the Food and Drug Administration (FDA) has the right to ban tobacco advertising. Several questions need to be considered: Do tobacco advertisements encourage smoking, especially among adolescents? Would a ban on tobacco advertisements reduce smoking behavior? Should tobacco companies have the right to promote their products as they wish, and do they have a constitutional right to freedom of speech? If tobacco advertisements are prohibited, should other potentially unhealthy products such as high-fat foods, tanning beds, and guns be prohibited also? Are tobacco companies being unfairly targeted? Would the prohibition of tobacco advertisements violate the rights of tobacco companies? How much responsibility does the consumer have for his or her own behavior?

In 1970 the Public Health Cigarette Smoking Act was passed, which banned cigarette advertisements from television and radio (advertisements for smokeless tobacco were unaffected). Since that time, cigarette advertisements have become much more prevalent in the print media and on roadside billboards. And although cigarettes are not directly advertised on television, their presence on television is unmistakable. Tobacco companies sponsor many televised sporting activities, especially automobile racing, and signs at various stadiums, which are frequently caught on camera, prominently display tobacco advertisements. Critics contend that many of these advertisements are geared toward target populations, notably adolescents and minorities. One of the most successful advertising campaigns is R. J. Reynolds Tobacco Company's Joe Camel. In one study, over 90 percent of 6-year-olds were able to match the Joe Camel cartoon character with the cigarette that it was promoting. Sales of Camel cigarettes escalated from $6 million to $476 million after the Joe Camel advertisements were introduced.

Many critics contend that stricter controls need to be put in place to eliminate the manipulative effects that tobacco advertising campaigns have on target audiences as well as on the general public. There is much concern that tobacco is a "gateway drug" that paves the way for other, illegal drugs, such as marijuana, cocaine, heroin, and LSD. Experts agree that the longer young people wait before they smoke cigarettes, if they even do choose to smoke, the less likely they will be to use other drugs. Young people often have difficulty internalizing the long-term consequences of their behavior because they are more concerned with meeting their immediate needs.

Supporters of the tobacco industry and advertising executives maintain that there is no compelling evidence that a causal link exists between advertising and smoking initiation and behavior. Moreover, advertisers contend that they do not market their tobacco products to young people. Advertising, they say, is used to enhance brand loyalty. They also argue that banning advertising violates their right to free speech.

How much of the responsibility for adolescent smoking lies with young people? Many people argue that smoking is done under one's own volition. What is the impact of parental smoking on children? Studies show that children of smokers are more likely to smoke than children whose parents do not smoke. Children with older siblings who smoke are also more likely to smoke than those whose immediate family members are all nonsmokers. Besides parents, children are exposed to other role models, such as teachers, civic leaders, athletes, health care workers, and clergy. What is the effect of their smoking (or not smoking) on the behavior of children around them? Curiosity and experimentation are very common among adolescents. If a young person experiments with cigarettes out of curiosity, can advertising be blamed?

In the following selections, Richard W. Pollay espouses the view that restricting tobacco advertising is an important first step in decreasing smoking rates, particularly among young people. Pollay maintains that tobacco companies misrepresent the research regarding the effects of tobacco advertising on smoking behavior. Jacob Sullum contends that banning or censoring cigarette advertisements is wrong because no one knows for sure what effect tobacco advertising has on smoking behavior. Additionally, a ban on cigarette advertising represents a serious threat to freedom of speech.

YES

Richard W. Pollay

HACKS, FLACKS, AND COUNTER-ATTACKS: CIGARETTE ADVERTISING, SPONSORED RESEARCH, AND CONTROVERSIES

The tobacco industry is acknowledged as outstanding for its ability to promote "friendly" research, to denigrate research inimical to its interests as prohibitionist propaganda (Jones, 1996), and "to produce and manage uncertainty" (Proctor, 1995, p. 105). At their extreme, critics are denigrated as a conspiracy of overzealous crusaders exhibiting totalitarianism (Boddewyn, 1986b). The industry's strategy doesn't require winning or resolution of the debates its principals manage to create or inflame. It is enough to foster and perpetuate the illusion of controversy in order to "muddy the waters" around potentially damaging studies and streams of research. This serves at least two important ends: offering reassurance and a basis for rationalization to the otherwise concerned, thereby calming public opinion; and encouraging friendly, ignorant, or naive legislators away from relying on scientific findings threatening to the industry. These tactics are now being used on many fronts of the tobacco battlefield.

The tobacco industry's first major success with this strategy was in combating the so-called "health scare" from the early lung cancer studies of the 1950s. Industry leaders gathered seeds of doubt from around the world, and reproduced and disseminated these through a massive public relations machinery (Pollay, 1990b). Encouraged by that success, they have continued to muddy the waters around the scientific findings relevant to almost every aspect of tobacco and its control, including: heart disease; passive or second-hand smoke; addiction; the medical and larger social costs consequential to smoking; the economic consequences of regulation, etc. Where necessary, as in the case of indoor air quality, they have even turned small local businessmen into apparent international authorities (Mintz, 1996). Of course, they prefer to employ those who seem to be independent from the industry, because trade organizations like the Tobacco Institute are admittedly biased. "We don't pretend to be objective, unbiased or fair. . . . We represent a

From Richard W. Pollay, "Hacks, Flacks, and Counter-Attacks: Cigarette Advertising, Sponsored Research, and Controversies," *Journal of Social Issues*, vol. 53, no. 1 (1997), pp. 53–74. Copyright © 1997 by Blackwell Publishers. Reprinted by permission. References omitted.

commercially vested interest" (Cosco, 1988, p. 8). It should be no surprise, then, that these tactics are also used to combat the issue of cigarette advertising and its effects, particularly its role in recruiting new smokers.

For example, when Fischer et al. (1991) measured product logo recognition of three-to-six-year-olds, they found over 90 percent of the six-year-olds could correctly match the cartoon Camel with cigarettes. So threatening was this result that industry-hired academic consultants attacked the study with or without the benefit of added research (Boddewyn, 1993; Martin, 1993; Mizerski, 1995). Their primary line of attack was to allege that this work was methodologically "inferior," in part because it had been authored, reviewed and published by and for medical experts, rather than marketing or advertising experts. The finding of high awareness among the very young has since been replicated by marketing academics (Henke, 1994), and even by the R. J. Reynolds–sponsored researcher (Mizerski, 1995), although this report is notable for downplaying this embarrassing fact and, instead, emphasizing allegations of methodological weaknesses of the original. More recently, Pollay's (1996) report that teens were three times as responsive to cigarette advertising as adults drew instant and inaccurate attacks from the Tobacco Institute as "a great deal of sound and fury signifying nothing" and "flatly contradicted" by a study sponsored by R. J. Reynolds (Stolberg, 1996).

The standard response of the industry to concerns about children and cigarette advertising has been to insist that "kids just don't pay attention to cigarette ads.... (Our advertising) purpose is to get smokers of competitive products to switch... virtually the only way a cigarette brand can meaningfully increase its business" (R. J. Reynolds, 1984), a thesis uncritically echoed by some others (e.g., Boddewyn. 1986b). The belief and assertion is that cigarette advertising is of little consequence, at least with respect to the young (e.g., Boddewyn, 1989; Reid, 1989; Ward, 1989). This assertion, so counter to common sense, is argued on theoretical grounds. Because cigarettes seem to be a so-called "mature" industry, i.e., one which has completed its dynamic growth and reached a stasis, it is claimed that its advertising and promotional activity can and does affect only brand-switching behavior among established adult smokers. By neither intent nor effect, tobacco industry magnates would have us believe, does cigarette advertising influence young people, reassure and retain existing smokers who might otherwise quit, or induce current smokers to smoke more—several of the ways in which advertising might conceivably influence primary demand....

No Known Industry Documents Employ the "Mature Market" Concept

To date, no corporate documents have been produced in litigation or research reports to verify that the "mature market" classification is relied upon by the industry in its internal strategic analyses, nor has any evidence of any kind been offered in support of the "mature market" opinions expressed by industry-advanced experts like Ward (1989). Reid (1989), when testifying for the industry, ignored the literature equivocal about the concept's validity, the literature specific to the cigarette industry, and the contradictory profit and advertising expenditure data. He ignored all the many corporate documents produced in the same litigation documenting the consumer research and advertising strategies focused on young starters (Pollay & Lavack, 1993). He even ignored his own observation, surely fitting cigarettes, that given "the existence of an undesirable image, advertising can play a major role" (Reid & Rotfeld, 1976, p. 26). Testimony like this that offers theoretical conjectures, while ignoring the relevant literature and the available case facts, is not merely speculative, but quite literally ignorant and prejudicial. . . .

Enormous Promotional Budgets Cannot Be Justified by "Adult Brand Switching" Alone

The cigarette market may seem, to the naive, to be stable and, therefore, to be a so-called "mature market" because total sales seem nearly constant. This appearance, however, hides the dynamics of substantial rates of quitting attempts, quitting successes, and dying—and the countervailing rates of recruitment of hundreds of thousands of new smokers. Maintaining constancy of market size involves recruiting over a million new smokers a year, and almost all smokers are recruited as minors, not as consenting adults.

Brand-switching alone cannot easily justify the enormous advertising and promotional expenditures, over $6 billion a year in 1993, larger than Hollywood's gross income from the United States and Canada combined (Kilday & Thompson, 1995). Brand switchers are an unattractive market segment, as they are typically older, health-concerned, or symptomatic smokers, thus relatively frail in constitution, in addition to being fickle by definition. They are also few in number. Siegel et al. (1996), after noting that less than 10 percent of smokers will switch in any

given year, estimate that the total profit from all "company switching" was $362 million, small compared to the costs of the battle of these brands. Accounting for sales in future years, the net present value of a new smoker to the cigarette companies has been estimated as US $1,085 (Tye, Warner, & Glantz, 1987).

If cigarette advertising had no effect on smoking recruitment, as the industry contends, a ban on advertising expenditures of this magnitude should and would be welcomed by savvy oligopolists like the tobacco industry. Indeed, a ban would benefit the larger firms the most, by saving them the enormous promotional expense and helping to freeze their large market shares. Thus, if advertising had no effect on primary demand, profit-maximizing firms and industries would curtail advertising competition, just as they would refrain from cut-throat price competition, and the largest firms would be expected to act as leaders in this self-restraint. Failing a tacit collusion to this end, the industry would eagerly seize the opportunity provided by regulatory proposals to ban advertising, with the larger firms the most motivated to do so. The fact that cigarette companies, led by the largest, are lobbying so hard against advertising bans or controls of any kind is illogical —unless the advertising and promotion has the effect of enticing new smokers. As Davis (1996, p. 3) stated: "The reason for the industry's failure to support a federal ban on tobacco advertising must be that . . . the companies must indeed perceive an industry-wide benefit to advertising and promotion." Failing that, they could save themselves all the spending on advertising that only attacked or defended market shares.

No Isolation or Immunity Protects Youth from Cigarette Ads

There is no way to isolate teens and pre-teens from popular culture and media, including cigarette advertising's inducements. The absence of a "magic curtain" around children obviates any "convincing defense of a view that would make young nonsmokers immune" (Cohen, 1990, p. 240–241). Those empowered with self-regulatory responsibilities in the National Association of Broadcasters (NAB) saw this vividly for the medium of television: "The difficulty in cigarette advertising is that commercials which have an impact upon an adult cannot be assumed to leave unaffected a young viewer, smoker or otherwise" (Bell, 1966, p. 30–31). Even a Marlboro ad man admitted after retiring, "I don't know any way of doing this that doesn't tempt young people to smoke" (Daniels, 1974, p. 245). Consistent with these views, newer research indicates that the likelihood of adolescent smoking is related to ad exposure rates (Botvin et al., 1993).

Advertising Gives the Cigarette "Friendly Familiarity"

Cigarette advertising is so pervasive and ubiquitous that cigarettes are a cultural commonplace, taken for granted by the public, and treated as less risky than appropriate. We are all aware of the reverse of this, when we feel suspicion of the unfamiliar. This positive effect is called "friendly familiarity" by advertising professionals (Burnett, 1961, p. 217).

"The ubiquitous display of messages promoting tobacco use clearly fosters an environment in which experimentation by youth is expected, if not explicitly encouraged" (Bonnie & Lynch, 1994, p. 34). "The kind of advertising that is al-most everywhere makes cigarets (sic) respectable and is therefore reassuring," according to Social Research Inc. (*Cigarets: who buys*, 1952, p. 23). Repetition, oft referred to as the soul of persuasion, likely biases both risk and social perceptions, such as assessments of smoking prevalence, and/or the social acceptance experienced by smokers, according to both consumer behavior and psychology experts (e.g., Cohen, 1990; Fishbein, 1977). This phenomenon is well known to psychologists as the "familiarity effect" (Zajonc, 1980).

The Perceptions and Judgments of Youth Are Known to Be Biased

The young do, in fact, overestimate the prevalence of cigarette smoking among both peers and adults, and the degree of this overestimation is among the strongest predictors of smoking initiation (e.g., Chassin et al., 1984). They also underestimate the negative attitudes of peers and the risks to which they personally are exposed should they smoke. Youths are also inclined to manifest an "invulnerability syndrome" (Greening & Dollinger, 1991). Youths tend to both "exaggerate the social benefit (by overestimating the prevalence and popularity of smoking among peers and adults) and to underestimate the risks (by underestimating the prevalence of negative attitudes toward smoking held by their peers)" (Bonnie & Lynch, 1994, p. 34). Another literature review concludes that "cigarette advertising appears to influence young people's perceptions of the pervasiveness, image, and function of smoking. Since misperceptions in these areas constitute psychosocial risk factors for the initiation of smoking, cigarette advertising appears to increase young people's risk of smoking" (USDHHS,

1994, p. 195). These facts seriously undermine the notion that the uptake of smoking is an informed choice or decision (Leventhal, Glynn, & Fleming, 1987). Irrespective of this naiveté, it is a misbehavior of minors, not consenting adults.

Cigarette Imagery Appeals to Adolescents

Cigarette ads often feature veritable pictures of health, depicting bold and lively behavior typically in pure and pristine outdoor environments (Pollay, 1991, 1993a; USDHHS 1994). The images of cigarette ads portray themes known to appeal to young people, such as independence, adventure seeking, social approval, and sophistication. The theme of independence, in particular, so well captured by the Marlboro Man, strikes a responsive chord with the dominant psychological need of adolescents for autonomy and freedom from authority. Adolescent girls feel the same needs for autonomy as do boys, accounting for the otherwise surprising popularity of the Marlboro brand among girls. Motivation research confirms the insights of previous advertisers and public relations professionals in seeing smoking as an expression of freedom and worldliness for women (Martineau, 1957). It seems no coincidence that marketers of female brands "try to tap the emerging independence and self-fulfillment of women, to make smoking a badge to express that" (Waldman, 1989, p. 81).

In addition, some of the models in cigarette advertisements appear particularly youthful (Mazis et al., 1992). This isn't all that common, however, as cigarette firms know that teens desire symbols of adulthood, not symbols of youth (e.g., hard rock vs. "bubble gum" music). Imagery-based ads are potentially insidious, in contrast to verbal assertions which require cognitive processing. Imagery is taken in at a glance, experienced more than thought about, tending to "bypass logical analysis." Because of this, imagery advertising is deemed "transformational" rather than informational (Cohen, 1990). The old adage says "seeing is believing," and cigarette ads use carefully tuned images to create positive experiences, while being careful to avoid precipitating cognitive counter-argumentation.

The Tobacco Industry Has Long Displayed a Strategic Interest in Youth

The industry has demonstrated an interest in the youth market in its planning documents, market research activities, and media plans for many decades (USDHHS, 1994, Pollay, 1995). Ads have been placed on billboards near schools and malls, and in after-school radio spots with effective reach into youth markets. The TV advertising schedules bought in the 1960s reflected a preference for those times with the higher proportions of delivered teenagers, not adults (Pollay, 1994a, 1994b). R. J. Reynolds' 1973 "Research Planning Document on Some Thoughts about New Brands for the Youth Market" described programs for appealing to "learning smokers" (Schwartz, 1995). Philip Morris found that almost half of the non-smoking girls "share many of the same values as the smokers and are highly exposed to the total smoking environment. We call them the 'Vulnerables' for, on the surface, they appear to be ready candidates for the next wave of new smokers" (Udow, 1976, H7664).

Copy concepts for many brands focus on independence, with the adolescent need for autonomy and self-reliance known by the industry to be a dominant one (USDHHS, 1994). The success of starter brands, according to trial evidence, is the result of carefully planned and executed strategies, guided throughout by extensive research (Pollay & Lavack, 1993). Corporate research documents discuss the behavior, knowledge, and attitudes of eleven-, twelve-, and thirteen-year-olds and media plans specify targets beginning at age fifteen, with willingness to pay as much for ad exposures to fifteen-year-old nonsmokers as to smokers. R. J. Reynolds' Canadian affiliate, for example, commissioned customization of "Youth Target Study '87" and got extensive data on subjects as young as fifteen.

The need to have a strategic interest in youth has long been recognized by the industry, and used to be freely admitted to. For example, just before the Surgeon General's Report of 1964, an advertising trade magazine, *Sponsor* ("What will happen," 1963), noted pro-health education with concern and asked: "If, however, impressionable youngsters are now approached mostly by the anti-smoking fraternity, how will cigarette sales fare 10 years hence?" Note, too, that this also demonstrates the long time spans appropriate in understanding cigarette advertising's effects, which are generational rather than instantaneous, inculcative rather than impulse-generating.

Adolescence Is a Time of Identity Formation and Advertising Attentiveness

"Cigarette advertising's cultural function is much more than the selling of cigarettes. Its collective images represent a corpus of deeply rooted cultural mythologies that are not simply pieces of advertising creativity, but icons that pose solutions to real, experienced problems of identity" (Chapman & Fitzgerald, 1982, p. 494). The National Association of Broadcasters knew this when trying to help the industry self-regulate TV ads. "The adult world depicted in cigarette advertising very often is a world to which the adolescent aspires.... To the young, smoking indeed may seem to be an important step towards, and a help in growth from adolescence to maturity" (Bell, 1966, p. 30–31).

Youths are alert to popular culture for cues and clues as to what's hot and what's not. They attend to advertising for symbols of adulthood, but pay only scant attention to warnings (Fletcher et al., 1995). "Teens are also more susceptible to the images of romance, success, sophistication, popularity, and adventure which advertising suggests they could achieve through the consumption of cigarettes" (Nichter & Cartwright, 1991, p. 242). Even brief cigarette ad exposures in lab settings can result in more favorable thoughts about smokers, enhance attitudes, increase awareness and change brand preferences of the young (Hoek, Gendall, & Stockdale, 1993; Pechmann & Ratneshwar, 1994).

This is consistent with consumer behavior knowledge as reflected in textbooks and journals. "Teenagers have become increasingly aware of new products and brands. They are natural 'triers'" (Loudon & Della Bitta, 1993, p. 151). They have "a lot of uncertainty about the self, and the need to belong and to find one's unique identity... (so) teens actively search for cues from their peers and from advertising for the right way to look and behave... (becoming) interested in many different products" that can express their needs for "experimentation, belonging, independence, responsibility, and approval from others" (Solomon, 1994, pp. 503–504). By high school, possessions and "badge products" like cigarettes are used as instruments for defining and controlling relations between people (Stacey, 1982).

As a 1974 RJR memo states: "To some extent young smokers 'wear' their cigarette and it becomes an important part of the 'I' they wish to be, along with their clothing and the way they style their hair" (Schwartz, 1996, p. A3). One starter brand in Canada, according to the R. J. Reynolds affiliate who marketed it, was popular with "very young starter smokers... because it provides them with an instant badge of masculinity, appeals to their rebellious nature and establishes their position amongst their peers" (Pollay & Lavack, 1993, pp. 268–269). Adults, in contrast, are not caught up in the processes of identity experimentation and formation. They are not as searching of their environment for consumption items symbolic of aspirational identities.

The image and badge aspects of brands are especially important to ethnic minorities. "While this is of utmost importance when marketing cigarettes in general, we feel it assumes even more importance when marketing cigarettes to blacks. Because blacks in general tend to be more insecure, for obvious reasons, it is critical that the public cigarette badge they adopt be one that supports what they are looking for in terms of psychological reassurance" (Reeves, 1979, p. 3). Thus, the Newport name has the virtue of connoting "quality and class," because of associations with status symbols such as Newport Beach and the Newport Jazz Festivals.

Youths Are Persuasion-Coping Novices
The young, as consumers, tend to be less experienced in counterarguing against advertising and selling tactics, as well as more brand-conscious than older consumers (Brucks, Armstrong, & Goldberg, 1988; McNeal, 1992). They are also less experienced as shoppers, with fewer experiences of salesmen and persuasion tactics. Friestad and Wright (1994, p. 7) note that "novices in coping with advertising or selling encounters may recognize only simple, superficial patterns in these events and have little proficiency with self-regulatory processes... (and) coping strategies." Adults, with their longer histories, particularly as smokers, have less interest in, and greater resistance to, the temptations and appeals of most new brands and/or ad campaigns.

Cigarette Addictiveness and Brand Loyalty Make Adults Proverbial "Old Dogs"
Cigarettes enjoy phenomenally high brand loyalty, the highest of all consumer products (e.g., Alsop, 1989). A relatively low rate of brand switching is the norm, usually 10 percent or less (Cohen, 1990, p. 239; FTC, 1985; Gardner, 1984; Siegel et al., 1996). Some of this nominal switching occurs only within brand families (e.g. from Brand X milds to Brand X lights), and is of little net consequence to the firm's sales or net profit. The high brand loyalty that naturally results from nicotine "satisfaction" of addictive physiological needs makes it very difficult and expensive to convert competitors' customers to your brands. Also, the bulk of the brand switching is the behavior of older, health-concerned or symptomatic smokers who are trading down, typically within a brand family, to products with lower tar and nicotine labeling, in the

mistaken belief that those products are safe(r), a belief fostered by years of advertising.

Youths Are Strategically More Attractive Than Adults
The trade of these older customers offers firms very little future and net present value, compared with the value inherent in attracting young starters, the bulk of whom will be brand-loyal (Tye, Warner, & Glantz, 1987). "This is a time when brand loyalties may be formed that could last well into adulthood" (Loudon & Della Bitta, 1993, p. 152, citing Moschis & Moore, 1981). The young are a "perpetually new market... thus a marketer must not neglect young consumers who come 'on stream' if the company's brand is to have continued success in the older-age market" (Loudon & Della Bitta, 1993, p. 155). Teens are a strategically important target audience, because brand loyalty is often developed during this time and this creates a "barrier-to-entry for other brands not chosen during these pivotal years" (Solomon, 1994, p. 504).

The death and quitting rates among aging smokers means that sales would drop rapidly were it not for a continuing influx of new starters. This strategic situation has been obvious to the industry for some time. R. J. Reynolds' research and development officers wrote in 1973: "Realistically, if our Company is to survive and prosper, over the long term, we must get our share of the youth market" (Schwartz, 1995). Contemporary corporate documents echo this idea, stating that "young smokers represent the major opportunity group for the cigarette industry," and "if the last ten years have taught us anything, it is that the industry is dominated by the

companies who respond most effectively to the needs of younger smokers" (Pollay & Lavack, 1993, p. 267).

Teens Are Three Times More Responsive Than Adults to Cigarette Ads
The latest research (Pollay et al., 1996) uses state-of-the-art techniques to analyze market share as a function of relative advertising, also known as *share of voice*. This measures the impact of cigarette brand advertising on realized market shares, allowing for both current and historical effects of advertising for nine major brands over twenty years. The results, which are robust under many alternative assumptions, show that brand choices among teenagers are significantly related to relative cigarette advertising. Moreover, the relationship between brand choices and brand advertising is significantly stronger among teenagers than among adults by a factor of about three. The greater advertising sensitivity among teenagers is in part due to *scale* (i.e., high fractions of teens concentrated on highly advertised brands), and in part due to *dynamics* (i.e., teen purchase patterns being more responsive to changes in advertising intensity). Further, the impact of advertising on brand choices among youth apparently cannot be dismissed as an inappropriate attribution (i.e., teenagers actually imitating adult brand choices rather than responding to advertising). Even when this aspect is factored into the analysis, the result remains consistent.

Greater advertising sensitivity among youth is consistent with earlier observations that brand choices of youth are highly concentrated on the most heavily advertised brands (CDC, 1992,

1994). California's Operation Storefront also found that "heavy advertising in stores exactly matches the brand preferences of children who smoke... but the ad prevalence does not match adult smoker preferences" (Hilts, 1995, p. B10). "Young people know advertising better, appreciate brand-stretching advertising more," and their ideal self-image matches the images offered by cigarette brands (Rombouts & Fauconnier, 1988; see also Aitken et al., 1987). A recent study (Pierce & Gilpin, 1995a, 1995b; Pierce, Lee, & Gilpin, 1994) reported data indicating that smoking rates among young women increased sharply in the late 1960s, coincidental with the launch of Virginia Slims and other nominally "female" brands.

Industry Apologists Typically Offer Weak Research, or None At All

The so-called "experts" that the industry gets to testify in courts and before legislative groups almost always offer opinions that are conspicuously ignorant of true corporate activity. Instead they opine based upon simplistic theorizing and conclusions. Martin told a court that cigarette ads can be of no appreciable import, no matter what their content or character, insulting the competencies of many advertising agencies, and judging their diverse efforts as all failing to alter public perceptions of the product, either individually or collectively. Perhaps the most simplistic and common position used to exculpate the industry is the "mature market" theory, discussed above, typically asserted with no corroborating evidence, perhaps because there is none to be had.

The industry has long relied on Boddewyn to argue that cigarette adver-

tising doesn't influence children, but the survey methodology and logic reported in Boddewyn (1987) is totally inadequate, biased, and superficial. This research was sponsored by the international tobacco industry lobbying organization, conducted by a British contract research firm, and published by an American advocacy organization, not by a peer-reviewed scholarly journal or scientific body. Its conclusion is based solely on a self-report question asking children to select, from a list of thirteen offered reasons, only the most important reason for smoking their first cigarette. This question is, to my knowledge, without precedent in either academic research or trade practice as the sole means of validly assessing advertising's role and effects. Not surprisingly, few choose "I had seen advertising" as the most compelling reason, since to do so requires that advertising's influence be consciously appreciated, willingly admitted to, and predominant among all of the prompted reasons, rather than just a contributing factor. One wonders how many might have agreed or disagreed with a statement like "advertising makes cigarettes seem attractive." While the apologists for the cigarette industry have ignored this grievous weakness, they dramatically raise their critical methodological standards when encountering results threatening their tobacco clients' economic or legal interests (e.g., Boddewyn, 1989). Martin (1993), for example, took the initiative to canvas researchers with a detailed questionnaire soliciting criticism of Pierce et al. (1991), who had found the cartoon Camel well known to the very young, while never commenting on the fallaciousness of Boddewyn's data and conclusions, and his client's political use of same....

Advertising Experts and Trade Journals Doubt the Industry's Stance

Many ad executives, when confronted with the pioneering Surgeon General's Report, admitted that cigarette advertising influenced minors. John Orr Young, whose agency, Young & Rubicam, had cigarette experience, said that: "Advertising agencies are retained by cigaret (*sic*) manufacturers to create demand for cigarets among both adults and eager youngsters. The earlier the teenage-boy or girl gets the habit, the bigger the national sales volume" ("Agency would refuse," 1964a). Another leading advertising executive, the president of Mc-Manus, Johns, & Adams felt that "There is no doubt that all forms of advertising played a part in popularizing the cigaret (*sic*)" ("Make cigarets," 1964b).

Emerson Foote, a founder of Foote, Cone, and Belding, and later CEO of McCann-Erikson, bluntly debunked the industry claims that its advertising affects only brand switching and has no effect whatsoever on recruitment. "I don't think anyone really believes this... I suspect that creating a positive climate of social acceptability for smoking, which encourages new smokers to join the market, is of greater importance to the industry.... In recent years the cigarette industry has been artfully maintaining that cigarette advertising has nothing to do with total sales. Take my word for it, this is complete and utter nonsense" (Foote, 1981).

More currently, one advertising CEO comments generally that cigarette advertising is "even sicker than war. If you were to choose the ultimate insanity of our society, I'd put cigarette advertising at the top" (Horovitz, 1996). Another wrote about the cartoon Camel: "Those of us in the marketing business know exactly what he's up to; we should be the first to denounce him" (DesRoches, 1994). A Philip Morris executive adds, "You don't have to be a brain surgeon to see what's going on. Just look at the ads. It's ludicrous for them to deny that a cartoon character like Joe Camel isn't attractive to kids" (Ecanbarger, 1993). This cartoon campaign has been described as "one of the most egregious examples in recent history of tobacco advertising targeted at children," encouraging even *Advertising Age* editors to urge that it be dropped (Cohen, 1994, p. 12).

The Industry's Latest Position Is Illogical and Ludicrous

The industry and its spokespersons would now have us believe that they have no influence at all on smoking onset, but that both their intent and the effect is exclusively on brand choice among existing smokers, now apparently admitted to include minors. When Pollay et al. (1996) reported on the impact of advertising on teens, a coalition of advertising groups, the Freedom to Advertise Coalition, said it "proves what we have been saying all along —that tobacco advertising is geared to influence market share among those people who already smoke" (Stolberg, 1996). This is saying that the firms' intentions and abilities are such that "we don't encourage children to smoke, only to switch brands." This has been satirized in editorial cartoons as a denial that cigarette advertisers entice kids to start smoking, because their marketing is aimed precisely at the second cigarette they smoke, not the first.

Research shows that the very young are aware of cigarette icons and associate these with both the product and brand. We also know that teens who have started smoking are substantially more affected by cigarette advertising than are adult smokers. Are the ones having their attitudes shaped at an early age all destined to make the perverse decision, from the advertisers' view, not to become smokers? Are the only ones who start smoking those who have had no awareness of, or attraction to, cigarette advertising they were exposed to while growing up (if, indeed, there can even be such a group of people)? Are those who start smoking, presumably despite their blindness and/or numbness to prior cigarette promotion, supposed to become instantly hypersensitive to it? Are we to believe that the children who have ignored advertising throughout their formative years suddenly are the only ones impacted by it?

As the perceptions, attitudes, and beliefs governing brand choice are influenced by cigarette advertising, it is totally implausible that those same brand perceptions, attitudes, and beliefs have no influence whatsoever on the temptation to start smoking. It is impossible to advertise a specific brand without also simultaneously advertising cigarettes as a product class. A Philip Morris marketing vice president, famous for managing Marlboro's success, once said, "A cigarette company's ads are not just competing with ads for other brands. You are competing with every other advertiser in America for a share of the consumer's mind" (Whiteside, 1974, p. 133). Advertising that makes a cigarette brand attractive inevitably also makes cigarette smoking attractive, at the very least the smoking of that brand. There is no known way to advertise so that only brand switching, but not product interest, is affected.

CONCLUSION

Creating the illusion of controversy is a worn-out tactic, and ought to be treated with incredulous cynicism by scholars and policymakers. In fact, there seems to be far less controversy about the role of advertising than a strong convergence of diverse streams of research and analysis. Strategic analysis indicates that new users are far more attractive to firms than the few, frail and fickle brand switchers. Historical analysis documents the industry's long-standing strategic interest in youth. Analysis of contemporary corporate documents shows this to be an intensifying interest, for it is among minors where virtually all starting of smoking occurs, and starting now occurs at younger ages than ever before. Content analyses of advertising show that cigarette advertising imagery is largely pictures of health and images of independence, known by the industry to resonate with adolescent needs for autonomy and freedom from authority. Behavioral analyses show that cigarette advertising constitutes a psychosocial risk factor. Not only is teen smoking behavior related to past and present advertising, but also this relationship is about three times stronger among teens than among adults. Meta-analysis has shown cigarette advertising elasticity to be positive.

This has important public policy implications. Whether intended or not, cigarette advertising is significantly related to youth smoking behavior. To the extent that advertising influences the use of cigarettes among a consumer group to whom their sale is illegal, the government has a legitimate interest in regulating cigarette advertising. Convergent analyses and results suggest that regulating cigarette advertising may be an effective policy intervention to influence smoking behavior among adolescents. This should at least address advertising whose character is likely to appeal to the young, and placement in media where exposure to the young is inevitable. The authors of the Institute of Medicine's literature review recommend that this be done at federal, state, and local levels, although this would require repealing current pre-emptive federal legislation (Bonnie & Lynch, 1994). For more on legislative options with respect to tobacco advertising, see Arbogast (1986), Blum and Myers (1993), Burns (1994), and Pytte (1990).

Given the many various analyses and diversity of evidence, it seems an inescapable conclusion that cigarette advertising plays a meaningful role in influencing the perceptions, attitudes, and smoking behavior of youth. It also seems appropriate for scholars to react to assertions that there are no such effects on youth with disbelief, and to suspect industry sponsorship as a likely basis for such assertions.

NO   Jacob Sullum

COWBOYS, CAMELS, AND KIDS

On January 1, 1971, the Marlboro Man rode across the television screen one last time. At midnight a congressional ban on broadcast advertising of cigarettes went into effect, and the smoking cowboy was banished to the frozen land of billboards and print ads. With the deadline looming, bleary-eyed, hung-over viewers across the country woke to a final burst of cigarette celebration. "Philip Morris went on a $1.25-million ad binge New Year's Day on the Dick Cavett, Johnny Carson and Merv Griffin shows," *The New York Times* reported. "There was a surfeit of cigarette ads during the screening of the bowl games." And then they were gone. American TV viewers would no longer be confronted by happy smokers frolicking on the beach or by hapless smokers losing the tips of their extra-long cigarettes between cymbals and elevator doors. They would no longer have to choose between good grammar and good taste.

This was widely considered an important victory for consumers. The *Times* wondered whether the ad ban was "a signal that the voice of the consumer, battling back, can now really make itself heard in Washington." A *New Yorker* article tracing the chain of events that led to the ban concluded, "To an increasing degree, citizens of the consumer state seem to be perceiving their ability to turn upon their manipulators, to place widespread abuses of commercial privilege under the prohibition of laws that genuinely do protect the public, and, in effect, to give back to the people a sense of controlling their own lives."

As these comments suggest, supporters of the ban viewed advertising not as a form of communication but as a mysterious force that seduces people into acting against their interests. This was a common view then and now, popularized by social critics such as Vance Packard and John Kenneth Galbraith. In *The Affluent Society* (1958), Galbraith argued that manufacturers produce goods and then apply "ruthless psychological pressures" through advertising to create demand for them. In *The Hidden Persuaders* (1957), Packard described advertising as an increasingly precise method of manipulation that can circumvent the conscious mind, influencing consumers without their awareness. He reinforced his portrait of Madison Avenue guile with the pseudoscientific concept of subliminal messages: seen but not seen, invisibly shaping attitudes and actions. The impact of such ideas can be seen in the controversy over tobacco advertising. The federal court that upheld the ban on broadcast ads for cigarettes quoted approvingly from another ruling that referred to "the subliminal impact of this pervasive propaganda."

Eliminating TV and radio commercials for cigarettes, of course, did not eliminate criticism of tobacco advertising. In 1985 the American Cancer Society, which decades earlier had called for an end to cigarette ads through "voluntary self-regulation," endorsed a government ban on all forms of tobacco advertising and promotion. The American Medical Association, the American Public Health Association, the American Heart Association, and the American Lung Association also began advocating a ban. Beginning in the mid-'80s, members of Congress introduced legislation that would have prohibited tobacco advertising, limited it to "tombstone" messages (black text on a white background), or reduced its tax deductibility. None of these bills got far.

In the '90s, since Congress did not seem inclined to impose further censorship on the tobacco companies, David Kessler, commissioner of the Food and Drug Administration, decided to do it by bureaucratic fiat. Reversing the FDA's longstanding position, he declared that the agency had jurisdiction over tobacco products. In August 1996 the FDA issued regulations aimed at imposing sweeping restrictions on the advertising and promotion of cigarettes and smokeless tobacco. Among other things, the regulations prohibited promotional items such as hats, T-shirts, and lighters; forbade brand-name sponsorship of sport-

ing events; banned outdoor advertising within 1,000 feet of a playground, elementary school, or high school; and imposed a tombstone format on all other outdoor signs, all indoor signs in locations accessible to minors, and all print ads except those in publications with a negligible audience under the age of 18.

The tobacco companies challenged the regulations in federal court, and in April 1997 U.S. District Judge William L. Osteen ruled that the FDA had no statutory authority to regulate the advertising and promotion of "restricted devices," the category in which the agency had placed cigarettes and smokeless tobacco. Under the nationwide liability settlement proposed last summer, however, the tobacco companies agreed not only to the FDA rules but to additional restrictions, including bans on outdoor ads, on the use of human or cartoon figures, on Internet advertising, and on product placement in movies, TV shows, or video games. Congress is considering that proposal now, and any legislation that emerges will dramatically change the way tobacco companies promote their products. Not content to wait, cities across the country, including New York, Chicago, and San Francisco, are imposing their own limits on cigarette signs and billboards. Elsewhere, the European Union plans to ban almost all forms of tobacco advertising by 2006.

These restrictions are based on the premise that fewer ads will mean fewer smokers—in particular, that teenagers will be less inclined to smoke if they are not exposed to so many images of rugged cowboys and pretty women with cigarettes. As a PTA official put it in 1967, "The constant seduction of cigarette advertising ... gives children the idea that cigarettes are associated with all they hold dear—beauty, popularity, sex, athletic success." For three decades the debate over tobacco advertising has been driven by such concerns. Yet there is remarkably little evidence that people smoke because of messages from tobacco companies. The ready acceptance of this claim reflects a widespread view of advertising as a kind of magic that casts a spell on consumers and leads them astray.

Today's critics of capitalism continue to elaborate on the theme that Vance Packard and John Kenneth Galbraith got so much mileage out of in the '50s and '60s. Alan Thein Durning of the anti-growth Worldwatch Institute describes the "salient characteristics" of advertising this way: "It preys on the weaknesses of its host. It creates an insatiable hunger. And it leads to debilitating over-consumption. In the biological realm, things of that nature are called parasites." When combined with appeals to protect children, this perception of advertising as insidious and overpowering tends to squelch any lingering concerns about free speech.

Busting Joe Camel's Hump

In 1988, R. J. Reynolds gave the anti-smoking movement an emblem for the corrupting influence of tobacco advertising. Introduced with the slogan "smooth character," Joe Camel was a cartoon version of the dromedary (known as Old Joe) that has appeared on packages of Camel cigarettes since 1913. Print ads and billboards depicted Joe Camel shooting pool in a tuxedo, hanging out at a nightclub, playing in a blues band, sitting on a motorcycle in a leather jacket and shades. He was portrayed as cool, hip, and popular —in short, he was like a lot of other models in a lot of other cigarette ads, except he was a cartoon animal instead of a flesh-and-blood human being. Even in that respect he was hardly revolutionary. More than a century before the debut of Joe Camel, historian Jordan Goodman notes, the manufacture of Bull Durham smoking tobacco ran newspaper ads throughout the country depicting the Durham Bull "in anthropomorphic situations, alternating between scenes in which the bull was jovial and boisterous and those where he was serious and determined."

But Joe Camel, it is safe to say, generated more outrage than any other cartoon character in history. Critics of the ad campaign said the use of a cartoon was clearly designed to appeal to children. *Washington Post* columnist Courtland Milloy said "packaging a cartoon camel as a 'smooth character' is as dangerous as putting rat poison in a candy wrapper." In response to such criticism, R. J. Reynolds noted that Snoopy sold life insurance and the Pink Panther pitched fiberglass insulation, yet no one assumed those ads were aimed at kids.

The controversy intensified in 1991, when *The Journal of the American Medical Association* published three articles purporting to show that Joe Camel was indeed a menace to the youth of America. The heavily promoted studies generated an enormous amount of press coverage, under headlines such as "Camels for Kids" (*Time*), "I'd Toddle a Mile for a Camel" (*Newsweek*), "Joe Camel Is Also Pied Piper, Research Finds" (*The Wall Street Journal*), and "Study: Camel Cartoon Sends Kids Smoke Signals" (*Boston Herald*). Dozens of editorialists and columnists condemned Joe Camel, and many said he should be banned from advertising.

In March 1992 the Coalition on Smoking or Health, a joint project of the American Cancer Society, the American Heart Association, and the American Lung Association, asked the Federal Trade Commission to prohibit further use of the smooth character. Surgeon General Antonia Novello and the American Medical Association also called for an end to the campaign. In August 1993 the FTC's staff backed the coalition's petition, and a month later 27 state attorneys general added their support. In June 1994, by a 3-to-2 vote, the FTC decided not to proceed against Joe, finding that the record did not show he had increased smoking among minors. (During the first five years of the campaign, in fact, teenage smoking actually declined, starting to rise only in 1993.) In March 1997, after several members of Congress asked the FTC to re-examine the issue, the commission's staff again urged a ban, citing new evidence that R. J. Reynolds had targeted underage smokers. This time the commission, with two new members appointed by the Clinton administration, decided to seek an order instructing RJR not only to keep Joe out of children's sight but to conduct a "public education campaign" aimed at deterring underage smoking.

The two dissenting commissioners were not impressed by the new evidence, which failed to show that Joe Camel had actually encouraged kids to smoke. One wrote, "As was true three years ago, intuition and concern for children's health are not the equivalent of—and should not be substituted for—evidence sufficient to find reason to believe that there is likely causal connection between the Joe Camel advertising campaign and smoking by children." But the FTC's action turned out to be doubly irrelevant. R. J. Reynolds, along with its competitors,

agreed to stop using cartoon characters as part of the proposed nationwide settlement, and last July it announced that it was discontinuing the "smooth character" campaign, replacing it with one that makes more subtle use of camels.

Although the *JAMA* articles were widely cited by Joe's enemies, including the FTC and President Clinton, they proved much less than the uproar would lead one to believe. In the first study, researchers led by Paul M. Fischer, a professor of family medicine at the Medical College of Georgia, asked preschoolers to match brand logos to pictures of products. Overall, about half the kids correctly matched Joe Camel with a cigarette. Among the 6-year-olds, the share was 91 percent, about the same as the percentage who correctly matched the Disney Channel logo to a picture of Mickey Mouse.

But recognizing Joe Camel is not tantamount to smoking, any more than recognizing the logos for Ford and Chevrolet (which most of the kids also did) is tantamount to driving. The researchers seemed to assume that familiarity breeds affection, but that is not necessarily the case. A subsequent study, funded by R. J. Reynolds and published in the Fall 1995 *Journal of Marketing*, confirmed that recognition of Joe Camel rises with age and that most 6-year-olds correctly associate him with cigarettes. Yet 85 percent of the kids in this study had a negative attitude toward cigarettes, and the dislike rose with both age and recognition ability. Among the 6-year-olds, less than 4 percent expressed a positive attitude toward cigarettes.

Animal Magnetism

In the second *JAMA* study, Joseph R. DiFranza, researcher at the University of

Massachusetts Medical School, led a team that showed Joe Camel ads to samples of high school students and adults. They found that the teenagers were more likely to recognize Joe Camel, to recall the ads, and to evaluate them positively than the adults, whose average age was about 40. Since R. J. Reynolds contended that the Joe Camel campaign was aimed at young adults, these results were hardly surprising. Based on such comparisons, it is impossible to distinguish between an ad aimed at 16-year-olds and an ad aimed at 18-year-olds (or 21-year-olds).

DiFranza et al.'s most striking claim was that the Joe Camel campaign had caused a huge shift in brand preferences. Using data from seven surveys conducted in three states between 1976 and 1988, they estimated that 0.5 percent of underage smokers preferred Camels before the campaign began. By comparison, 33 percent of the teenage smokers in their study, conducted during 1990 and 1991, said they smoked Camels—a *66-fold* increase. "Our data demonstrate than in just 3 years Camel's Old Joe cartoon character had an astounding influence on children's smoking behavior," the researchers wrote. But the pre-1989 surveys and the *JAMA* study were not comparable, and neither used random samples of the national population, so it's doubtful that the results are representative of American teenagers in general. Data from the Centers for Disease Control and Prevention's Teenage Attitudes and Practices Survey, which does use a nationwide sample, suggest a much less dramatic (though still sizable) shift toward Camels. In 1993, 13.3 percent of the TAPS respondents said they usually bought Camels, compared to 8.1 percent in 1989.

The third *JAMA* article presented data from a 1990 California telephone survey. The researchers, led by John P. Pierce, head of the University of California at San Diego's Cancer Prevention and Control Program, reported that teenagers were more likely than adults to identify Marlboro or Camel as the most advertised brand. The survey also found that Marlboro's market share increased with age until 24, when it started to decline gradually. Camel, on the other hand, was considerably more popular among teenagers than among young adults. Comparing the California data to the results of a national survey conducted in 1986, Pierce et al. concluded that the market shares for both Marlboro and Camel had increased among adults (the 1986 survey did not include minors). Camel's increase was bigger, particularly among adults under the age of 30 (i.e., the segment R. J. Reynolds claimed to be targeting).

Taken together, these studies suggested that 1) most children know Joe Camel has something to do with cigarettes and 2) the Joe Camel campaign helped increase the brand's market share, especially among young smokers. Since most smokers pick up the habit before they turn 18, it seems likely that the tobacco companies would take an interest in the brand choices of teenagers, and that inference is supported by internal documents. In 1974, for example, Philip Morris hired the Roper Organization to interview young smokers about their brand choices, and more than a third of the 1,879 respondents were described as 18 or younger. "To ensure increased and longer-term growth for Camel filter," said a 1975 RJR memo, "the brand must increase its share penetration among the 14–24 age groups, which have a new set of more liberal values and which represent tomorrow's cigarette business." Last year, as part of an agreement settling state lawsuits, the Liggett Group said tobacco companies have deliberately targeted underage smokers.

The other companies continued to deny that charge. R. J. Reynolds maintained that Joe Camel was aimed at 18-to-24-year-olds, although the company had no way of assuring that he would not also appeal to people younger than 18. In response, David Kessler told ABC's Peter Jennings, "Tell me how you design an advertising campaign that affects only 18-year-olds." Which is sort of the point. If cigarette companies have to avoid any ad that might catch the eye or tickle the fancy of a 16-year-old, they might as well not advertise at all (which would suit Kessler fine). In any case, the important question is whether advertising encourages teenagers to smoke, not whether it steers them toward Camels instead of Marlboros.

In each of the Joe Camel studies, the researchers' conclusions (and the subsequent press coverage) went beyond what the data indicated. Fischer et al., whose comparison between Joe Camel and Mickey Mouse got the most attention, were relatively cautious: "Given the serious health consequences of smoking, the exposure of children to environmental tobacco advertising may represent an important health risk and should be studied further." DiFranza et al. said, "A total ban of tobacco advertising and promotions, as part of an effort to protect children from the dangers of tobacco, can be based on sound scientific reasoning." Pierce et al. flatly concluded that "[c]igarette advertising encourages youth to smoke and should be banned." These are all statements of opinion that

have little to do with what the studies actually showed.

Information that came to light in a lawsuit challenging the Joe Camel campaign (a case that R. J. Reynolds settled for $10 million in September) suggests that at least some of the researchers may have prejudged the issue. In a letter he wrote to a coauthor before the research began, DiFranza complained that he had not been able to give reporters "proof that the tobacco companies are advertising to children. I can't point to any one piece of evidence as a smoking gun and say 'here, this proves it.' Well I have an idea for a project that will give us a couple of smoking guns to bring to the national media." He explained, "I am proposing a quick and easy project that should produce... evidence that RJR is going after kids with their Camel ads." Toward the end of the letter, he said, "There, the paper is all ready, now all we need is some data."

Switching Arguments
Neither DiFranza's "smoking gun" nor the other studies provided any evidence about the impact of advertising on a teenager's propensity to smoke, which is the crux of the issue. When critics complain that advertising encourages people to smoke, the tobacco companies reply that it encourages smokers to buy particular brands. Strictly speaking, these claims are not mutually exclusive. In principle, advertising can promote an industry's overall sales as well as drum up business for a specific company. An ad for a Compaq portable computer might encourage people to buy a Compaq (the company certainly hopes so), or it might get them thinking about laptops generally. But the tobacco companies argue that the U.S. market for cigarettes

is mature, meaning that the product is universally familiar, like toothpaste or deodorant, and attempts to boost overall consumption are no longer cost-effective. Indeed, with smoking rates declining, the tobacco companies are fighting for pieces of a shrinking pie. Tobacco's opponents say this trend makes cigarette manufacturers all the more desperate to maintain their profits; they need advertising like the Joe Camel campaign to attract replacements for smokers who quit or die.

Advocates of an advertising ban contend that brand competition does not adequately explain the industry's spending on advertising and promotion, which totals about $5 billion a year. In 1995, the most recent year for which the Federal Trade Commission has reported figures, coupons, customer premiums (lighters, key chains, clothing, etc.), and allowances to distributors accounted for about 80 percent of this money. Cigarette companies spent about $900 million on newspaper, magazine, outdoor, transit, direct-mail, and point-of-sale advertising.

According to a widely cited article published in the Winter 1987 *Journal of Public Health Policy,* "A simple calculation shows that brand-switching, alone, could never justify the enormous advertising and promotional expenditures of the tobacco companies." Anti-smoking activist Joe B. Tye and his co-authors started with an estimate, based on marketing research, that about 10 percent of smokers switch brands each year. Then they calculated that the industry's spending on advertising and promotion in 1983 amounted to nearly as much per switcher as a typical smoker would have spent on cigarettes that year. They also noted that, since each cigarette maker produces various brands,

smokers who switch are not necessarily taking their business to another company.

"Thus," the authors concluded, "advertising and promotion can be considered economically rational only if they perform a defensive function—retaining company brand loyalty that would otherwise be lost to competitors who promote their products—of if they attract new entrants to the smoking marketplace, or discourage smokers from quitting." If defending market share were the only aim, Tye et al. added, the tobacco companies should support a ban on advertising and promotion, which would eliminate the threat from competitors. On the other hand, "If advertising and promotion increase cigarette consumption, then less than two million new or retained smokers—5.5 percent of smokers who start each year or try to quit (most failing)—alone would justify the annual promotional expenditure."

There are several flaws in this argument. To begin with, the estimate for the number of brand switchers does not include people who usually smoke, say, Benson & Hedges but occasionally smoke Camels. Based on its own marketing surveys, R. J. Reynolds reports that about 70 percent of smokers have a second-choice brand that they smoke now and then. About 25 percent regularly buy more than one brand each month. Even smokers who don't have a second favorite sometimes try other brands because of coupons, premiums, and promotional offers.

Another problem is that, in estimating the value of brand switchers, Tye et al. did not take into account the continuing revenue from a new customer; they considered only the money he spends on cigarettes in one year. By contrast, when they estimated the gain from getting someone to start smoking or keeping a smoker who otherwise would have quit, they used the net present value of the additional profit over a 20-year period, which they calculated as $1,085, more than three times a year's revenue.

Most important, Tye el al. did not acknowledge that tobacco companies could be competing for new smokers without actually creating them. Although the companies deny that they target minors in any way, building brand loyalty among teenagers is still not the same thing as making them into smokers. Tye et al. considered the industry's opposition to an advertising ban prima facie evidence that tobacco advertising increases total consumption. But the tobacco companies might also have opposed a ban because it would help delegitimize the industry, opening the way to other kinds of regulation and defeats in product liability suits. Furthermore, a company's attitude toward restrictions on advertising (and brand competition in general) depends on its market position. Philip Morris and R. J. Reynolds, the market leaders, might well be less worried about an advertising ban than their competitors. Tellingly, these were the companies that spearheaded the settlement talks, and they included dramatic restrictions on advertising and promotion in their opening offer.

In any case, it is not clearly foolish for the tobacco companies to spend so much money on advertising and promotion, even without the hope of market expansion. More evidence is necessary to support the claim that tobacco advertising increases consumption. Broadly speaking, there are three ways of investigating this issue. You can look at the historical relationship between changes in advertising and changes in smoking. You can compare smoking trends in places with different levels of advertising. And you can ask people questions in the hope that their answers will suggest how advertising influences attitudes and behavior. None of these approaches has yielded consistent or definitive results. Each has limitations that leave plenty of room for interpretation. The state of the research was aptly, if unintentionally, summed up by the subtitle of a 1994 article in the *International Journal of Advertising* that made the case for a causal link: "The Evidence Is There for Those Who Wish to See It."

Does Life Imitate Ads?
Some analyses of historical data have found a small, statistically significant association between increases in advertising and increases in smoking; others have not. In a 1993 overview of the evidence, Michael Schudson, professor of communication and sociology at the University of California at San Diego, wrote, "In terms of a general relationship between cigarette advertising and cigarette smoking, the available econometric evidence is equivocal and the kind of materials available to produce the evidence leave much to be desired." This sort of research is open to challenge on technical grounds, such as the time period chosen and the methods for measuring advertising and consumption. There is also the possibility that advertising goes up in response to a rise in consumption, rather than the reverse. Industry critics often cite the increases in smoking by women that occurred in the 1920s and the late '60s to early '70s as evidence of advertising's power. "Yet in both cases," Schudson noted, "the advertising campaign followed rather than preceded the behavior it supposedly engendered." In other words, the tobacco companies

252 / 14. SHOULD THE FDA PROHIBIT TOBACCO ADVERTISING?

changed their marketing in response to a trend that was already under way.

International comparisons have also produced mixed results. There is no consistent relationship between restrictions on advertising and smoking rates among adults or minors. In some countries where advertising is severely restricted, such as Sweden, smoking rates are relatively low. In others, such as Norway, they are relatively high. Sometimes smoking drops after advertising is banned; sometimes it doesn't. It is hard to say what such findings mean. Countries where smoking is already declining may be more intolerant of the habit and therefore more likely to ban advertising. Alternatively, a rise in smoking might help build support for a ban. Furthermore, advertising bans are typically accompanied by other measures, such as tobacco tax increases and restrictions on smoking in public, that could be expected to reduce cigarette purchases. The one conclusion it seems safe to draw is that many factors other than advertising affect tobacco consumption.

The best way to resolve the issue of advertising's impact on smoking would be a controlled experiment: Take two groups of randomly selected babies; expose one to cigarette advertising but otherwise treat them identically. After 18 years or so, compare smoking rates. Since such a study would be impractical, social scientists have had to make do with less tidy methods, generally involving interviews, questionnaires, or survey data. This kind of research indicates that the most important factors influencing whether a teenager will smoke are the behavior of his peers, his perceptions of the risks and benefits of smoking, and the presence of smokers in his home. Exposure to advertising does not independently predict the decision to smoke, and smokers themselves rarely cite advertising as an important influence on their behavior.

Critics of the industry have been quick to seize upon studies indicating that teenage smokers disproportionately prefer the most advertised cigarette brands. But such research suggests only that advertising has an impact on brand preferences, which the tobacco companies have conceded all along. Several studies have found that teenagers who smoke (or who say they might) are more apt to recall cigarette advertising and to view it favorable. Such findings do not necessarily mean that advertising makes adolescents more likely to smoke. It is just as plausible to suppose that teenagers pay more attention to cigarette ads after they start smoking, or that teenagers who are inclined to smoke for other reasons are also more likely to have a positive view of cigarette ads.

In reporting on research in this area, the mainstream press tends to ignore such alternative interpretations. Consider the coverage of a 1995 study published in the *Journal of the National Cancer Institute*. The study, co-authored by John Pierce, found that teenagers who scored high on a "receptivity" index—which included "recognition of advertising messages, having a favorite advertisement, naming a brand [they] might buy, owning a tobacco-related promotional item, and willingness to use a tobacco-related promotional item"—were more likely to say they could not rule out smoking in the near future. Such "receptivity" was more strongly associated with an inclination to smoke than was smoking among parents and peers.

According to *The New York Times*, these results meant that "[t]obacco advertising is a stronger factor than peer pressure in encouraging children under 18 to smoke." Similarly, *The Boston Globe* reported that the study showed "cigarette advertising has more influence on whether adolescents later start smoking than does having friends or family members who smoke." The Associated Press went even further: "Of all the influences that can draw children into a lifelong habit of smoking, cigarette advertising is the most persuasive." In reality, the study showed only that teenagers who like smoking-related messages and merchandise are more receptive to the idea of smoking—not exactly a startling finding.

A study reported last December in *Archives of Pediatric and Adolescent Medicine* received similar treatment. The researchers surveyed about 1,200 students in grades six through 12 and found that kids who owned cigarette promotional items such as jackets and backpacks were four times as likely to smoke as those who did not. "Tobacco Gear a Big Draw for Kids," announced the headline in *The Boston Globe*. The story began, "If tobacco manufacturers hope to promote smoking by producing clothing or accessories emblazoned with cigarette logos, research by Dartmouth Medical School suggests that the tactic works well." Under the headline, "Study: Logos Foster Smoking," *Newsday* reported that "children who own cigarette promotional items . . . are far more likely to smoke."

Yet as the researchers themselves conceded, "The finding of an association between CPI [cigarette promotional item] ownership and being a smoker could easily be an expression of an adolescent who acquired these items after having made the decision to become a smoker." Later in the article, they wrote, "Our study and others published to date are subject to the usual limitations inherent in cross-sectional studies, in that we are unable to infer a direction between the exposure (ownership of a CPI) and smoking behavior, limiting our ability to invoke a causal relationship between CPI ownership and smoking." Translation: We would like to say that promotional items make kids smoke, but our study doesn't show that. This shortcoming did not stop the authors from concluding that "all CPI distribution should end immediately."

Marginal Effects

Overall, the evidence that advertising plays an important role in getting people to smoke is not very convincing. In 1991 the economist Thomas Schelling, former director of Harvard's Institute for the Study of Smoking Behavior and Policy, said: "I've never seen a genuine study of the subject. Most of the discussion that I hear—even the serious discussion—is about as profound as saying, 'If I were a teenage black girl, that ad would make me smoke.' I just find it altogether unpersuasive. I've been very skeptical that advertising is important in either getting people to smoke or keeping people smoking. It's primarily brand competition." The 1989 surgeon general's report conceded that "[t]here is no scientifically rigorous study available to the public that provides a definitive answer to the basic question of whether advertising and promotion increase the level of tobacco consumption. Given the complexity of the issue, none is likely to be forthcoming in the foreseeable future." The 1994 surgeon general's report, which focused on underage smoking, also acknowledged the "lack of definitive literature."

It's possible, of course, that tobacco advertising has an effect that simply cannot be measured. The 1989 surgeon general's report concluded that, while "the extent of the influence of advertising and promotion on the level of consumption is unknown and possibly unknowable," the weight of the evidence "makes it more likely than not that advertising and promotional activities do stimulate cigarette consumption." The 1994 report, based on suggestive evidence, said "cigarette advertising appears to increase young people's risk of smoking." Similarly, Michael Schudson—who says "[a]dvertising typically attempts little and achieves still less"—argues that cigarette advertising "normally has only slight effect in persuading people to change their attitudes or behaviors." But he adds, "It is reasonable to believe that some teens become smokers or become smokers earlier or become smokers with less guilt or become heavier smokers because of advertising."

Serious critics of tobacco advertising do not subscribe to a simple stimulus-and-response theory in which kids exposed to Joe Camel automatically become smokers. They believe the effects of advertising are subtle and indirect. They argue that the very existence of cigarette ads suggests "it really couldn't be all that bad, or they wouldn't be allowed to advertise," as Elizabeth Whelan of the American Council on Science and Health puts it. They say advertising imagery reinforces the notion, communicated by peers and other role models, that smoking is cool. They say dependence on advertising revenue from tobacco companies discourages magazines from running articles about the health

consequences of smoking. They do not claim such effects are sufficient, by themselves, to make people smoke. Rather, they argue that at the margin—say, for an ambivalent teenager whose friends smoke—the influence of advertising may be decisive.

Stated this way, the hypothesis that tobacco advertising increases consumption is impossible to falsify. "Fundamentally," writes Jean J. Boddewyn, a professor of marketing at Baruch College, "one cannot prove that advertising does *not* cause or influence smoking, because one cannot scientifically prove a negative." So despite the lack of evidence that advertising has a substantial impact on smoking rates, tobacco's opponents can argue that we should play it safe and ban the ads—just in case.

The problem with this line of reasoning is that banning tobacco advertising can be considered erring on the side of caution only if we attach little or no value to freedom of speech. If cigarette ads are a bad influence on kids, that is something for parents and other concerned adults to counter with information and exhortation. They might even consider a serious effort to enforce laws against cigarette sales to minors. But since we clearly are not helpless to resist the persuasive powers of Philip Morris et al.—all of us see the ads, but only some of us smoke—it is hard to square an advertising ban with a presumption against censorship. Surely a nation that proudly allows racist fulminations, communist propaganda, flag burning, nude dancing, pornography, and sacrilegious art can safely tolerate Marlboro caps and Joe Camel T-shirts.

POSTSCRIPT

Should the Food and Drug Administration Prohibit Tobacco Advertising?

A study in the *Journal of the American Medical Association* (vol. 266, 1991) reported that over half of children between ages 3 and 6 were able to identify Joe Camel, the mascot for Camel cigarettes. By age 6, as many children were able to recognize Joe Camel as readily as Mickey Mouse. Significantly, within four years after the Joe Camel campaign was initiated, Camel's share of the youth market escalated from 0.5 percent to 32.8 percent. Tobacco advertisers assert that they do not market to children but that advertising does affect what children know.

Smoking and tobacco advertising are highly charged political issues. U.S. senator Tom Harkin (D-Iowa) proposed an amendment to the Senate Tax and Urban Aid Bill to reduce the amount of money tobacco companies could deduct from their taxes for advertising expenses from 100 percent down to 80 percent. The additional revenue would go toward public education campaigns to dissuade people from smoking. In California an aggressive effort to discourage smoking and a 25-cent-per-pack tax increase resulted in a significant decline in smoking.

The tobacco industry feels that government does not have the authority to regulate their freedom of speech. The fear is that if government can regulate tobacco advertising, then it can regulate any activity that it deems unhealthy. Also, a portion of the revenue generated by the tobacco industry goes toward state and national treasuries, and thousands of people are employed by tobacco companies. The livelihood of many farmers comes from growing tobacco crops. Should these people be deprived of their livelihoods?

In "The Rights of Joe Camel and the Marlboro Man," *The Humanist* (January–February 1997), Barbara Dority argues that the government should put more emphasis on educating young people about the hazards of tobacco and less emphasis on restricting tobacco advertising. In "Evaluation of Antismoking Advertising Campaigns," *JAMA* (March 11, 1998), Lisa K. Goldman and Stanton A. Glantz write that the government should allocate more money for antismoking media campaigns. Two articles that take opposing views on banning tobacco advertisements are "Cowboys, Camels, and the First Amendment—The FDA's Restrictions on Tobacco Advertising," by George Annas, *The New England Journal of Medicine* (December 5, 1996) and "Controlling Tobacco Advertising: The FDA Regulations and the First Amendment," by Leonard Glantz, *American Journal of Public Health* (March 1997).

ISSUE 15

Is Total Abstinence the Only Choice for Alcoholics?

YES: Thomas Byrd, from *Lives Written in Sand: Addiction Awareness and Recovery Strategies* (Hallum Publishing, 1997)

NO: Stanton Peele, from "All Wet," *The Sciences* (March/April 1998)

ISSUE SUMMARY

YES: Professor of health Thomas Byrd maintains that Alcoholics Anonymous (AA) provides more effective treatment for alcoholics than psychiatrists, members of the clergy, or hospital treatment centers. Byrd contends that AA is the most powerful and scientific program, in contrast to all other therapies.

NO: Psychologist Stanton Peele questions the effectiveness of AA and supports instead alcohol treatment programs that are tailored to meet the different needs of alcoholics. Peele argues that for some alcoholics, the concept of a lifetime of abstinence may be counterproductive and that many alcoholics are capable of controlling their drinking behavior.

According to government figures, there are an estimated 10 to 20 million alcoholics in the United States. Cocaine addicts number between 250,000 and 1 million. Eating disorders, sexual addictions, compulsive gambling, excessive spending, and compulsive working affect millions more people. Knowing the best way to help people who engage in these compulsive or addictive behaviors is difficult. One way to control addictive behavior is to abstain from it. However, is abstention the best or only viable treatment goal?

The concept of helping people with addictions can be approached from opposing perspectives. Some critics take the view that addiction occurs when people lose control over their addictive behavior. Moreover, there is always some kind of reward or payoff that fuels one's addictive behavior. The benefit may be security, sensation, or power, but as long as one or more of these benefits are experienced, people will not stop their behavior. Not everybody needs to abstain from unhealthy behaviors; only those people whose behaviors have reached the addictive stage. With some potentially addictive behaviors, such as eating or working, it is impossible to abstain. However, with behaviors that are not necessary for survival, such as alcohol consumption, abstention is, according to some viewpoints, the only path to follow.

If addiction leaves people powerless, as some professionals maintain, then the only way to gain personal power and control is through abstention. If alcoholics are powerless against alcohol, then they cannot drink simply for the enjoyment of alcohol; they will invariably drink to excess. Furthermore, abstinence does not come naturally but must be learned. People need to learn to abstain each time they feel the urge to drink.

The abstinence model is currently the most popular approach for treating addiction. Abstinence is included in the 12-step model promoted by Alcoholics Anonymous (AA) and other self-help groups. Elements of this model include admitting to being powerless over one's addiction, accepting a higher power, and restructuring one's life. Opponents of the 12-step approach argue that it is not suitable for everyone and that it has not been proven effective. The idea of placing faith in a higher power, for example, is inconsistent with the values of many people, especially those who do not believe in the concept of a higher power. Another problem is that programs such as AA claim to be effective based on the testimonies of the program participants. However, because of the anonymity of people who attend or have attended AA meetings, follow-up studies are negligible.

A number of studies show that most people who stop addictive behavior do so on their own. Heroin addicts who quit using heroin generally do not go through any type of formal treatment. Likewise, the majority of individuals who quit smoking also stop without an organized program. It is unlikely that heroin addicts and tobacco users stop because they develop a belief in a higher spiritual power. Factors contributing to spontaneous remission are not well understood. It is believed that people stop self-destructive behaviors once they "hit bottom."

One criticism of the abstinence approach is that it stigmatizes people. The label "alcoholic" may deter people from receiving help because it connotes social deviance. Also, individuals who admit that they cannot control their own behavior are implying that they lack the strength to do so. That is, they are too weak to take care of their problems themselves. This stigma may prevent some people from seeking help.

In recent years alternative self-help groups to Alcoholics Anonymous have appeared. The Secular Organization for Sobriety (SOS) is one such group for alcoholics that does not have the same emphasis on a belief in a higher power. There is also Women for Sobriety/Men for Sobriety, which does not accept AA's disease model of addiction. Abstinence is a prominent aspect of this group, but overcoming alcoholism is based on self-acceptance and the role of love in relationships. Other programs are Rational Recovery (RR) and Moderation Management (MM). Unlike other models, RR and MM incorporate the belief that moderate alcohol use is possible.

In the selections that follow, Thomas Byrd makes the case that the abstinence-only, 12-step AA model is the only viable approach for overcoming alcoholism. Stanton Peele highlights the limitations of the approach taken by Alcoholics Anonymous, describes how AA may be counterproductive, and discusses alternative types of treatment.

YES

Thomas Byrd

LIVES WRITTEN IN SAND: ADDICTION AWARENESS AND RECOVERY STRATEGIES

ALCOHOLICS ANONYMOUS, WHAT WORKS BEST FOR MOST

Finding the words to describe an organization which has saved millions of lives and countless relationships is difficult. Fundamentally, Alcoholics Anonymous provides hope to those in despair. The contents of the "program" focus on feelings, and how to cope with them throughout life. It is not an intellectual program, rather focusing on problem resolution and the subsequent spiritual rewards. The fellowship teaches a philosophy whose rewards are immediate and practical. AA is not a religion where prime benefits may be promised in the afterlife. It is a group of people who share a common problem and experience. Members are committed to living in the solution, not in the problem. Only a distinct minority of alcoholics are able to put their disease in remission and enter recovery. Most alcoholics do not recover. AA is a simple program for complicated people. New members frequently ask "how" does the program work. If you dissect the word, the first letter stands for an honest appraisal of the problem; the second letter refers to being open-minded to new concepts from those in recovery; and the third letter stands for a willingness to devote the energy it takes to enter recovery. Members have committed two fundamental crimes. One is against the growth and development of another person. The second transgression is the indifference to the growth and development of self. Members are encouraged to make amends when possible and to carry the message to those still suffering. It is a program of attraction, not of promotion. The only requirement for membership is a desire to quit drinking.

Stopping drinking seems simple. You just don't drink. The problem is that there is a lot of failure. However, many of those who drink again will eventually stop drinking. Family members seem more likely to get their hopes up, only to suffer further discouragement if the alcoholic resumes drinking.

The problem drinker seems to be less upset with relapse, probably because drinking has played such a major role in his or her life.

The physician may help identify the problem but is best at tending to physical problems. The alcoholic is generally not a desirable patient in most medical offices. Rejection of prescribed treatment, dishonesty, evasiveness, and rationalization of drinking are typical. Alcoholism is best treated by the specialist, a fellow recovering alcoholic, where there is no barrier of misunderstanding. Fears, guilt and self-condemnation and other psychiatric problems are minimized in this relationship.

Most rehabilitation programs encourage their patients to participate in Alcoholics Anonymous as part of an aftercare program. This organization exists because alcoholics need help and AA is more successful than psychiatry, the clergy, hospitals or jails in providing that needed aid. The organization works one day at a time for anyone who thinks help is needed. Membership is anonymous unless the member desires to drop the anonymity.

Alcoholics Anonymous was founded by two prominent men whose lives had been seriously affected by excessive drinking. They set out simply to survive. What they did was to try anything and everything, keeping what works and rejecting the rest.

John D. Rockefeller made a $5,000 contribution to the co-founders Bill Wilson and Dr. Bob Smith to help the fledging organization. Bill Wilson had grandiose ideas of establishing a network of recovery centers throughout the United States. These plans were stilled by Rockefeller's son. At a dinner presided over by Nelson Rockefeller he declined to make any further family donations to the organization, stating "this is too good to be destroyed by money." This decision ultimately led to the establishment of a non-profit organization, which became self-supporting through their own membership's contributions. Wilson acquiesced to the condition of the one time gift, and the wealthy and visionary New York politician salvaged the organization by replacing profit with humanity.

AA is at the basis of all good treatment simply because it is the most powerful, and because it is the most scientific of all therapies. The first months of membership in Alcoholics Anonymous are most critical. Getting to the first meeting is difficult. Continuing to participate in your own recovery is also difficult. There are erroneously preconceived attitudes that can form barriers to recovery. The alcoholic needs to keep attending until he or she wants to attend. In other words, they need to give it a chance.

Help from another alcoholic is something that can be depended on. Service to others is one of the components of recovery. The drinker is accepted without question into the AA group. The 12 steps of Alcoholics Anonymous constitute a recovery program that begins with the admission that the member is powerless over alcohol and that strength is needed from another source to overcome the problem. A searching, fearless moral self-inventory is also part of the program. Restitution to those who have been harmed gives the alcoholic emotional strength. Knowing there is help if a person wants to stop drinking can be vital.

There are no rules, no dues, and participation is voluntary. It is a fellowship based upon a common problem. Sponsors in the organization are available to give support to the newcomer. Suggestions on how to stay sober are exchanged between members. "Tomorrow may never come, yesterday is a canceled check." The alcoholic can't be cured, but is only an arrested case. If the alcoholic takes a drink again, the problem will surface and the member will be right back in the depths of active alcoholism. The objective is to stay sober today. Alcoholics understand this, simple as it is. Personality reorientation can come later. *The Big Book of Alcoholics Anonymous* is an excellent source of information. The author also recommends another book, authored by Nan Robertson. It's titled, *Getting Better: Inside AA*, published by Fawcett Crest, New York, New York, 1988.

ACTIONS AMONG EQUALS

There are many approaches to the treatment of alcoholism, successful programs involve abstinence by whatever method it is achieved. Yet if one method of approaching a problem yields noticeably better and more striking results than others, then this method must contain some unique factor or factors that set it apart and form the basis of its supremacy.

"Alcoholics Anonymous is a fellowship of men and women who share their experience, strength and hope with each other that they may solve their common problem and help others to recover from alcoholism." The experiences of alcoholics are essentially the same, the theme is always the same: a progressive deterioration of the human personality. What then is the constant factor? What is AA's unique difference? I feel there are four distinctive characteristics that set apart this successful recovery program.

One of the answers lies in the manner in which this experience, strength and hope are shared and who is doing the sharing. Long before the average alcoholic walks through the doors of an AA meeting, help has been offered, in some instances even forced upon them. But these helpers are always superior beings. The moral responsibility of the alcoholic and the moral superiority of the helper, even though unstated, are always clearly understood. The overtone of parental disapproval and discipline in these authority figures is always present. Instead of the menacing, "This is what you should do," there is an instantly recognizable voice saying, "This is what I did." Therefore, one of the constant factors of a premium recovery program is where one alcoholic consciously and deliberately turned to another alcoholic, not to drink with, but to stay sober. I am personally convinced that the basic search of every human being is to find another human being, before whom one can stand completely without pretense or defense, and trust that person not to hurt them, because that person is exposed too. It is self-evident that the newcomer has been invited to share in the experience of recovery.

If the alcoholic responds to this invitation, the member then encounters a second unique factor: AA treats the symptoms first. The conviction that alcoholism is the symptom of deeper troubles. Even the cleverest diagnosis of these troubles is of little benefit if the patient dies. Autopsies do not benefit the persons upon whom they are performed. Total abstinence is the name of the game. Recovery can only begin with a decision to stay away from the first drink. No one can or will make that decision for the ill. In fact, one soon further learns that if he makes the decision, no one can or will force fulfillment of the goal. There are reports of action taken, rather than rules not to be broken. Action is the magic word. There are steps to be taken which are suggested as a program for recovery. Quoting from Chapter Five of the book, *Alcoholics Anonymous: Step One,* "We admitted we were powerless over alcohol, that our lives had become unmanageable." The newcomer finally sees that they must take these Steps before being entitled to report on them. It is important to "utilize, not to analyze."

The desire to make this decision often results from what appears to be a third unique quality: The intuitive understanding the alcoholic receives, while compassionate, is not indulgent. The new member is not asked what they are thinking, rather they are told what they are thinking. The companion "therapists" already have their doctorates in the four fields where the alcoholic reigns supreme: phoniness, self-deception, evasion, and self-pity. There's not much point in trying to fool people who may have invented the game that's being played. In the end, the member begins to achieve honesty by default.

There is a fourth factor which I feel is significant, and that is the recovering alcoholic's infinite willingness to talk about alcoholism. Without the newcomer's ever becoming fully aware of it, the fascination with alcohol is literally talked to death. There is a reversal of form which the educational process takes. The participant is asked, not so much to learn new values, as to unlearn those that brought the seeker to the doors of recovery; not so much to adopt new goals, as to abandon old ones. The real answer is that this unique therapy occurs wherever two alcoholics meet: at home, at lunch, in the street, at work or school, and on the telephone. Members may faithfully attend meetings waiting for "something" to rub off, namely the "miracle of AA." The sad part about it is that "something" is rubbing off on them. Death. The real miracle is simply the willingness to act.

The formless flexibility of AA's principles as interpreted by their different adherents finally pushes the alcoholic into a stance where he must use only himself as a frame of reference for personal actions, and this in turn means there must be a willingness to accept the consequences of those actions. In my viewpoint, that is the definition of emotional maturity. True freedom lies in the realization and calm acceptance of the fact that there may very well be no perfect answer. The search for perfection is the hallmark of the neurotic. In the final analysis, we are all striving to be a better human beings. The future is that time when you will wish that you had used the time that you have now. Live in the present.

Other programs such as Rational Recovery and S.T.A.R.T. emphasize self-management and recovery training. Both programs do not incorporate the "higher power" aspect of the AA program, neither use a 12 Step format, reject the recovering concept, sponsorship, nor a 'one at a time' philosophy.

GROWTH, A DAY AT A TIME

Recovering people can become overwhelmed by new responsibilities. Sometimes too, members wonder why we can't ever be finished and just stop for awhile.

Feeling this way can mean it is time to stop and rest. The process of recovery has plateaus and detours along the way, and it's okay at times to take a break. But the "it's too much trouble" feeling also can be a signal that we need to pay more, not less, attention to ourselves and our recovery program.

Just as the chemically dependent person chooses not to drink or use drugs on a daily basis, so must a codependent person choose to continue recovery one day at a time. It is easy to see progress or lack of it in the big choices—to abstain from chemicals, to dissolve destructive relationships, to change careers. Less visible, but at least as important, are the little choices we all make every day.

Recovery means choosing to confront small instances of abusive behavior instead of letting them go. It means choosing to set boundaries to protect your time for recreation and rejuvenation. It means saying "no" to demands you can't meet. It means deciding every day to take care of yourself by paying attention to your needs for sleep, exercise, and healthy diet.

We can let all these choices overwhelm us if we focus on the "every single day for the whole rest of my life" aspect of them. Or we can take them one day at a time, recognizing that some days are easier than others. And we can remember that, as choosing growth becomes a pattern, it gets easier. Each seemingly insignificant daily choice is a separate affirmation that recovery is worth the trouble.

NO

Stanton Peele

ALL WET

The week before Christmas 1996, as people dashed to the liquor store for reinforcements and clinked their glasses at holiday parties, the National Institute on Alcohol Abuse and Alcoholism (NIAAA) convened a press conference in Washington, D.C. The purpose was to herald the findings of Project MATCH, a government study devised to learn whether certain kinds of alcoholics respond best to specific forms of psychotherapeutic treatment. For example, twelve-step therapy and Alcoholics Anonymous (AA)—based in part on lifelong abstinence and personal surrender to a "higher power"—might work best for those seeking spiritual and religious meaning in their lives. Coping-skills therapy could help antisocial and emotionally disturbed alcoholics. And motivational therapy might best suit drinkers who show little desire for improvement, by spurring their desire to change.

Project MATCH had taken eight years to design and execute and had cost $27 million—the biggest and most expensive psychotherapy study ever mounted. It had encompassed thirty treatment sites and eighty therapists throughout the United States, along with dozens more of the country's most experienced investigators in alcoholism treatment, who had supervised and analyzed the study. The results of MATCH, much anticipated, promised to set firm guidelines for the therapy best suited to the particular needs of any given problem drinker.

Enoch Gordis, a physician and the director of NIAAA, stepped up to the microphone. "The good news is that treatment works," he announced. The therapies tested in Project MATCH all led to "excellent" overall results, he said.

But Project MATCH failed to find the links its organizers and most other alcoholism investigators had expected. The results showed virtually no differences in drinking reduction attributable to matching a patient's traits with a specific treatment. In fact, few clinical trials exist to show that the most popular American treatment for alcoholism, the twelve-step approach, is effective at all. Moreover, the results of both Project MATCH and a major 1996 NIAAA study showed that most people who had once struggled with alcohol abuse could later cut down on their drinking—a result that is anathema to the devotees of AA, to the U.S. medical establishment and to the American way of temperance.

Last December [1997] the MATCH collaborators published a further analysis of their study in the British journal *Addiction*, which basically repeated their earlier conclusions. Thus the group's official position remains the same as [before]: All is well with alcoholism treatment in America. In that view, whatever therapy people are pushed toward —which in the United States effectively means a twelve-step program with the aim of total abstinence—they will be fine. Such an outlook, Gordis's overoptimistic interpretation notwithstanding, represents a public-relations triumph for the alcohol-treatment industry in America. But the blanket assurance that "treatment works" does precious little for most people who drink too much.

* * *

I'll call her Alice (not her real name). She is a woman I interviewed who tasted liquor for the first time in college and promptly went on party alert. She dropped out of school and drank heavily throughout her early twenties. Three to five times a week she got drunk, both alone and with a shifting cast of friends. During one nine-month binge and for several shorter stretches she drank virtually every night, polishing off nearly a pint of Scotch before she went to bed. Several times during her decade of drinking she was homeless.

Nevertheless, when she went home to visit her parents, sometimes for a couple of weeks, there was a major change in Alice's behavior. All she drank was wine over dinner with her father (her mother was a teetotaler). She did not want her parents to know how badly she was messing up her life; she controlled herself so she would not lose their love and support.

Alice had attended a few AA meetings, but she found the confessional atmosphere stultifying and oppressive. The turning point for her came when, at age twenty-nine, she got a job as a receptionist in a dentist's office. The dentist reminded her of her father, a pharmacist; he was a new authority figure she wanted to please. She began spending her spare time with her coworkers—people who did not abuse alcohol. Alice realized she wanted to be like them: steady and productive. She took classes to become a dental hygienist, and she began drinking in moderation, wine with dinner only. In short, Alice's new job and new friends helped jump-start her desire for a stable life.

Alice is in her forties now, married with children, and still drinking moderately. Her case may sound unique: an alcoholic who recovered without treatment and who continues to drink. In fact, her story is typical of former alcoholics in the United States, according to NIAAA research. Indeed, Project MATCH, while finding no difference in results based on the kind of treatment received, did find that personal motivation and the drinking behavior of peers made a significant difference in a patient's success.

Alice and others like her demonstrate the need for a treatment focus besides AA and similar twelve-step programs. In the United States, unlike most other Western countries, alcoholism therapy clings to abstinence as the only acceptable goal. (In Britain and Australia, for instance, controlled drinking as a treatment goal is widely accepted.) According to a 1997 survey by the sociologists Paul M.

Roman of the University of Georgia in Athens and Terry C. Blum of the Georgia Institute of Technology in Atlanta, nearly 99 percent of the treatment programs in the United States advocate abstinence.

That black-and-white view of alcoholism stems not from scientific evidence but from attitudes forged in the early nineteenth century.... Drinking in colonial America was widespread, accepted and overwhelmingly benign. But as the American frontier expanded, between 1790 and 1830, healthy social customs began to warp. Taverns, once places for entire families to gather, became male preserves in which the only women likely to be present were prostitutes. In such an atmosphere of male independence, alcoholism rates rose dramatically. In response, the Anti-Saloon League and similar temperance organizations flourished, culminating in Prohibition in 1919.

Prohibition collapsed in 1933. But it did not die—it simply moved off the streets and into the hospitals. In the eighteenth century the Philadelphia physician Benjamin Rush had propounded the idea that the chronic drinking of hard liquor causes a specific disease, one that makes it impossible for the drinker to imbibe moderately. Rush's idea took hold. By the latter half of the twentieth century, both AA and the American medical establishment had elaborated it into the theory that some people have an inbred susceptibility to alcoholism. The disease theory of alcoholism and its attendant focus on abstinence became orthodoxy in the United States.

* * *

The medicalization of alcohol abuse has spawned much interest in fine-tuning treatments for the problem. Project MATCH (which stands for Matching Al-

coholism Treatments to Client Heterogeneity) was not the first effort to assess alcoholism therapies; a team led by the psychologist William R. Miller of the University of New Mexico in Albuquerque has been examining many smaller such studies for two decades. In 1995 Miller and his colleagues rated forty-three kinds of treatment by combining the results of 211 controlled trials that had compared the effectiveness of a treatment with either no treatment or with other alcoholism therapies. The treatment with by far the best overall score was "brief intervention"—followed by social-skills training and motivational enhancement.

Brief intervention shares elements with motivational enhancement, one of the treatments tested by Project MATCH, in that the patient and the therapist create a mutually agreed-upon goal. In brief intervention, the goal is usually reduced drinking; in motivational enhancement, it is either reduced drinking or total abstinence.

In a brief-intervention session, the health-care worker simply sums up the goal: "So we agree you will reduce your drinking from forty-two drinks a week to twenty, no more than four on a given night." Motivational enhancement is a bit more subtle: the therapist nudges, though does not direct, the patient's own values and desire for change. The dialogue in a motivational-enhancement session might go like this:

THERAPIST: What is most important to you?
PATIENT: Getting ahead in life. Getting a mate.
T: What kind of job would you like? What training would that take?
P: [Describes.]
T: Describe the kind of mate you want. How would you have to act, where

would you have to go, to meet and deal with a person like that?

P: [*Describes.*]

T: How are you doing at achieving this?

P: Not very well.

T: What leads to these problems?

P: When I drink, I can't concentrate on work. Drinking turns off the kind of person I want to go out with.

T: Can you think of any way to improve your chances of succeeding at work or with that kind of mate?

In both motivational enhancement and brief intervention, the discussion is non-judgmental and the patient helps make the decision to drink less or to quit. Both processes are far less confrontational than the one used by most treatment professionals in the United States. The Miller report described the standard treatment in the United States as "a milieu advocating a spiritual twelve-step (AA) philosophy, typically augmented with group psychotherapy, educational lectures and films, and . . . general alcoholism counseling, often of a confrontational nature."

Yet those same therapies ranked at the bottom of the Miller team's list, with far less proof of their effectiveness than other treatments. The conclusion, then, is startling: The most frequently used therapies in American alcoholism treatment are those for which there is the least evidence of success.

* * *

The 1996 NIAAA study mentioned earlier was also surprising. That study stemmed from the National Longitudinal Alcohol Epidemiologic Survey (NLAES), conducted in 1992 by the U.S. Census Bureau. Census field workers did face-to-face interviews with nearly 43,000 respondents across America, a general sample of U.S. adults eighteen years of age and older. Each interview probed the use of alcohol and drugs over a person's entire life, with a focus on the preceding year.

Deborah A. Dawson, an NIAAA epidemiologist, then analyzed interviews with 4,585 NLAES subjects who had at some time in their lives been alcohol dependent (the most severe diagnosis of an alcohol problem). Only a quarter of the group Dawson studied had ever been treated for alcoholism; those people had had somewhat worse drinking problems initially than the ones who had gone untreated. In the year before the interviews, about a quarter of all the subjects still had mild to severe alcohol problems; a similar proportion had not touched a drop; and the rest had drunk without abuse.

Those who had received some kind of treatment were slightly *more* likely than their untreated counterparts to have had a drinking problem in the previous year, Dawson reported in the June 1996 issue of the journal *Alcoholism: Clinical and Experimental Research*. For those whose alcohol dependence had first appeared in the preceding five years and who had been treated, 70 percent had had a drinking problem in the past year. For those whose drinking problems had emerged twenty years or more before, twice as many of the treated alcoholics as the untreated ones were still abusing booze (20 percent versus 10 percent). Among the long-term group, fully 60 percent of the untreated subjects had reduced their drinking to the point where they had no diagnosable problem.

On the basis of a study such as Dawson's, in which the treated and untreated groups differed in the initial severity of their problems, it would not be fair to claim that therapy leads to worse results than no therapy. But the finding that so many treated alcoholics still had a drinking problem, while so many untreated alcoholics could moderate their drinking over time, certainly contradicts the impression created by the MATCH report, as well as popular American ideas about alcoholism.

* * *

Why does Miller's and Dawson's research indicate that current treatments are ineffective, whereas MATCH purportedly showed that treatment works so well? It is worth taking a closer look at Project MATCH, to discover just what it did and what it found.

The MATCH results were published directly after the NIAAA press conference, in a detailed report in the January 1997 issue of *Journal of Studies on Alcohol*. The complicated design of MATCH included two groups of patients: an outpatient group and an aftercare group, made up of outpatients who had recently received hospital treatment. The patients were not deliberately matched to a treatment at the outset. Rather, each patient was assigned randomly to a treatment, and the success of the match was measured afterward on the basis of how well that person fulfilled predictions of success for that treatment, according to his or her personal traits.

Twelve-step and coping-skills treatment were each scheduled in twelve weekly sessions; motivational-enhancement therapy involved four sessions spaced over the twelve-week period. The year of follow-up showed comparably good results for all treatments. Before treatment, the subjects imbibed, on average, on twenty-five days out of thirty; that number fell to six days of drinking a month by the end of follow-up. The

amount consumed on drinking days also dropped markedly after treatment.

Going deeper into the MATCH methodology shows why its results could differ so dramatically from those of other research. Virtually all the subjects were alcohol dependent. But people simultaneously diagnosed with a drug problem were excluded from the study. The implications of that exclusion are substantial. According to a survey of treatment admissions published last year by the Substance Abuse and Mental Health Services Administration in Rockville, Maryland, the combined abuse of alcohol and drugs is the most frequent problem for patients at the time of admission to treatment for substance abuse. On that ground alone, the statistical validity of extrapolating from the Project MATCH sample to the alcohol-abuser population as a whole is seriously compromised.

But much more than that was going on in the selection of subjects for MATCH. Initially, 4,481 potential subjects were identified; fewer than 1,800 of them were actually included. The MATCH participants were volunteers. Yet in real life, patients are increasingly being referred for treatment by the courts, by their employers or by social agencies. They are threatened with prison, loss of a job or loss of benefits if they do not get help. Furthermore, Project MATCH dropped potential subjects for reasons such as lack of a permanent home address and for legal or probation problems. Others declined to participate because of the "inconvenience" of treatment. Compared with the volunteers excluded from the study, those who participated in MATCH were motivated, stable and free of criminal or severe drug problems—all of which predict a greater likelihood of success.

Not only were the patients in MATCH atypical, but they did not receive typical alcoholism treatment. Counselors were carefully selected and trained. Each treatment session was videotaped, and the tapes were monitored by supervisors. The quality of the treatments in MATCH seems to be a far cry from that of standard treatment programs in the United States. In such programs the counselors are generally former alcoholics themselves, whose subsequent training has exposed them only to more of the therapy they received—namely, the twelve-step philosophy.

In *The Truth About Addiction and Recovery*, a book I cowrote in 1991 with Archie Brodsky, a senior investigator in the psychiatry department at Harvard Medical School, we noted that twelve-step treatment is typically delivered in an authoritarian, directive fashion. Patients are told their behavior is wrong and their lives are not working, and they are lectured to quit drinking. Such behavior on the part of the therapist does not jibe with effective therapy, which helps patients to "own" their problems and participate in the solutions. For that reason patients in alcoholism treatment are regularly tagged as being "in denial." In our experience, when their values and perceptions are respected, patients are more willing to identify and address their problems rather than fight the process of treatment.

Yet twelve-step therapy could be delivered in many ways. One wonders whether the success of that treatment in MATCH arose in part from a style of twelve-step therapy different from the one in standard treatment programs. Unlike AA, the MATCH twelve-step treatment did not rely on group support; instead it concentrated on individual therapy sessions. The MATCH results, then, may point to the critical importance of the therapist's style of practice. Although MATCH did not find plug-in solutions, it did find that treatment success differed significantly depending on *where* the patients got help. That suggests that certain training programs, counselors and supervisors offer far better help than others, regardless of the kind of therapy they practice. Thus the research eye might do better to focus on how superior counselors deliver their therapy, whatever name that therapy goes by.

* * *

Other results of Project MATCH also challenge standard assumptions about alcoholism. The treatments that led to such excellent results required only about eight hours of outpatient therapy (the subjects, on average, attended only two-thirds of their scheduled twelve sessions). Yet the National Council on Alcoholism and Drug Dependence recommends hospital stays of several days for alcohol-dependent patients in the United States.

Although all the MATCH treatments led to equivalent results, not all were equal in effort and expense. The results of motivational enhancement were as good as those of the other therapies, but they required only a third as many sessions. And many studies show that even fewer sessions can be beneficial. Brief intervention is often restricted to a single session and follow-up. Although brief-intervention therapy has generally been reserved for nondependent alcohol abusers, several studies have looked at minimal treatments for people who are alcohol dependent. For example, in 1977 the psychiatrist Griffith Edwards and his colleagues at the Addiction Research Unit (now the National Addiction Center) of

London's Maudsley Hospital compared a full hospital treatment program with a single advice session for an alcoholic population. No differences in outcome were found. Comparable studies conducted throughout the 1980s in Missouri, New Zealand and Canada confirmed that conclusion.

But perhaps the biggest heresy that MATCH supports—inadvertently so—is the value of reduced drinking as a goal in alcoholism treatment. The MATCH organizers chose to present their success in terms of the number of drinking days and the amount imbibed on those days. They did not trumpet the news of their subjects' abstinence rates. That figure was not particularly impressive: about 20 percent of the outpatient group and 35 percent of the aftercare group abstained throughout the follow-up period. Yet in the outpatient group, a third drank without bingeing.

The data from Project MATCH and other mainstream research conflict in many ways, but they make this much clear: Since the majority of alcoholics do not stop drinking, whether treated or untreated, whether measured in the general population or following a gold-standard set of treatments, the ironclad insistence on abstinence as the only goal of therapy is perverse indeed.

Those who treat alcoholics—and American society as a whole—need to recognize that the aim of reduced drinking may be the best and only achievable goal for many alcoholics. Clinicians must also develop alternatives to traditional therapies—treatments that could well be briefer and less expensive than the ones now in use. Above all, everyone must acknowledge that alcoholics are *not* powerless. With the right resources, more often than not they hold the keys to their own recovery.

POSTSCRIPT

Is Total Abstinence the Only Choice for Alcoholics?

The fundamental question here is, Must alcoholics totally abstain from alcohol use, or can they benefit from other types of treatment? This issue was initially raised in the 1970s, when Linda and Mark Sobell presented research showing that alcoholics who were taught to drink socially were less likely to relapse than people who were told to abstain from alcohol. (This study was subsequently criticized for its methodology.) In another study supported by the RAND Corporation in the 1970s, it was found that the majority of alcoholics who went through formal treatment were drinking moderately or occasionally up to 18 months after treatment. Most did not resume their abusive use of alcohol. A criticism of this study was that it did not follow those in treatment long enough—a 4-year follow-up revealed that many had relapsed.

Many people who attempt to completely stop addictive behaviors fail. If a person tries several times to abstain from drinking alcohol (or other self-destructive behaviors) and cannot stop, perhaps other forms of treatment may be worth pursuing. However, moderation as a treatment goal may not prove to be productive because alcohol—the central element to the addiction—is still present in the alcoholic's life.

Rather than trying to identify the one best type of treatment, it may be better to match people with the type of treatment that is best for them. It may be shortsighted to think that one form of treatment is best for all addicts. One advantage of Alcoholics Anonymous (AA) over other forms of treatment is expense. In "Typical Patterns and Costs of Alcoholism Treatment Across a Variety of Populations and Providers," *Alcoholism: Clinical and Experimental Research* (April 1991), Harold Holder and James Blose report that the average stay for inpatient alcohol treatment lasts 22 days and costs $4,665. In contrast, there is no cost to be a member of AA.

Audrey Kishline, in her book *Moderate Drinking* (Harmony Books, 1996), discusses how principles of behavior modification can be applied in the treatment of alcoholism. In "Alcoholics Synonymous: Heavy Drinkers May Get Comparable Help from a Variety of Therapies," *Science* (January 25, 1997), Bruce Bower discusses an ongoing study in which clients are matched to appropriate therapies. An older, excellent essay that reviews the efficacy of alcohol treatment is William Miller and Reid Hester's "The Effectiveness of Alcoholism Treatment: What Research Reveals," in William Miller and Nick Heather, eds., *Treating Addictive Behaviors: Processes of Change* (Plenum Press, 1986).

ISSUE 16

Is Drug Abuse Resistance Education (DARE) an Effective Program?

YES: Michele Alicia Harmon, from "Reducing the Risk of Drug Involvement Among Early Adolescents: An Evaluation of Drug Abuse Resistance Education (DARE)," *Evaluation Review* (April 1993)

NO: Richard R. Clayton et al., from "DARE (Drug Abuse Resistance Education): Very Popular but Not Very Effective," in Clyde B. McCoy, Lisa R. Metsch, and James A. Inciardi, eds., *Intervening With Drug-Involved Youth* (Sage Publications, 1996)

ISSUE SUMMARY

YES: Researcher Michele Alicia Harmon reports that Drug Abuse Resistance Education (DARE) had a positive impact on fifth-grade students in terms of attitudes against substance abuse, assertiveness, positive peer association, association with drug-using peers, alcohol use within the previous year, and prosocial norms.

NO: Drug researchers Richard R. Clayton et al. maintain that despite DARE's popularity, it does not produce less drug use among its participants. They argue that the money that is spent by the federal government to fund DARE could be used for more effective drug prevention programs.

Drug education is arguably one of the most logical ways of dealing with the problems of drugs in American society. Drug-taking behavior has not been significantly affected by attempts to reduce the demand for drugs, and drug prohibition (as in the case of alcohol) has also failed. One remaining option to explore is drug education. Drug education is not an overnight panacea for eliminating drug problems. Rates of cigarette smoking have declined dramatically, but it took 25 years of public health efforts to achieve this. If drug education is to ultimately prove successful, it too will take years.

Many early drug education programs were misguided. One emphasis was on scare tactics. Experts erroneously believed that if young people saw the horrible consequences of drug use, then they would certainly abstain from drugs. Another faulty assumption was that drug use would be affected by knowledge about drugs, but it is obvious that knowledge is not enough. Over 400,000 people die each year from tobacco use, but 25 percent of adult Americans and increasing numbers of teenagers continue to smoke, even though most know the grim statistics about tobacco. Young people have a hard time relating to potential problems like lung cancer and cirrhosis of the liver (which is caused by long-term alcohol abuse), because these problems take years to develop. If drug education is going to be effective, it will need to deal with the immediate effects of drugs, not the long-term consequences. Another major problem with early drug education is that much of the information that teachers relayed concerning drugs was either incorrect or exaggerated. Teachers were therefore not seen as credible.

There is a lack of consensus as to what a drug education program should encompass. However, there is general agreement among drug prevention experts that drug awareness programs are counterproductive. Many schools conduct drug awareness programs in which, over the course of a week, former drug abusers talk to students about how their personal lives and families were ruined by drugs, pharmacologists demonstrate the physical effects of drugs, and films are shown that depict the horrors of drugs. These sensationalized programs stimulate curiosity, and it is not unusual for drug use to increase after one of these presentations.

Many drug prevention programs in the 1970s focused on self-esteem and values clarification. If low self-esteem is a factor in drug use, as many believed, then it would make sense to improve self-esteem to reduce drug use. However, self-esteem is not always a good indicator of drug use. Many young people who have good feelings about themselves use drugs. In addition, many believed that if students clarified their values, they would see the folly of using drugs. This approach overlooked the possibility that young people may turn to drugs because they want to be accepted by their peers, because drugs are forbidden, or simply because they enjoy the high that comes from drug use. The values clarification approach has been discarded by most drug educators.

The current emphasis in drug education is on primary prevention. It is easier to have young people not use drugs in the first place than to get them to stop after they have already started using drugs. The Drug Abuse Resistance Education (DARE) program—the subject of this debate—attempts to get upper-elementary students to pledge not to use drugs. The rationale is that putting energy into teaching elementary students about drugs rather than high school students will be more likely to reduce drug use because the latter are more likely to have already begun using drugs. The program focuses mainly on tobacco, alcohol, and marijuana. These are considered to be gateway drugs, which means that students who use other drugs are most likely to have used these first. The longer students delay using tobacco, alcohol, and marijuana, the less likely they will be to use other drugs.

In the following selections, Michele Alicia Harmon points out some of the benefits of Drug Abuse Resistance Education, especially on students' attitudes toward substance abuse, assertiveness, positive peer association, association with drug-using peers, alcohol use, and prosocial norms. Richard R. Clayton et al. seriously challenge the value of the DARE program.

YES

Michele Alicia Harmon

REDUCING THE RISK OF DRUG INVOLVEMENT AMONG EARLY ADOLESCENTS

The purpose of the current study is to evaluate the effectiveness of the Drug Abuse Resistance Education (DARE) program in Charleston County, South Carolina. Specific aims of the program include the stated DARE objectives—increasing self-esteem, assertiveness, coping skills, and decreasing positive attitudes toward drugs, actual drug use, and association with drug-using peers. The study also examines the program's effectiveness for reducing other known risk factors associated with adolescent drug use such as social integration, commitment and attachment to school, and rebellious behavior.

Much of what is known about adolescent drug use is a result of the annual High School Survey conducted by the Institute for Social Research at the University of Michigan (Johnston 1973). Data from a recent report examining drug use (Johnston, Bachman, and O'Malley 1991) show 90% of U.S. seniors reported drinking alcohol at some time in the lives, 64% said they had smoked cigarettes, 41% reported smoking marijuana, and 18% had taken stimulants.

High school survey data from Charleston show similar prevalence rates. For example, 77% of Charleston County seniors said they had drunk alcohol at some point in their lives, 47% had smoked cigarettes, and 31% reported smoking marijuana (South Carolina Department of Education and South Carolina Commission on Alcohol and Drug Abuse 1990).

Efforts to combat the drug problem have led to a variety of strategies over the past two decades. The three most widely used attempts to control drug use are supply reduction, treatment, and prevention.

Supply reduction efforts by law enforcement agencies to decrease production, importation, distribution, and retail sales of street drugs appears ineffective in reducing the drug problem. Increased arrests and imprisonment, given our crowded penal institutions, and the ready replacement of suppliers and dealers mitigates the actions of legal authorities.

From Michele Alicia Harmon, "Reducing the Risk of Drug Involvement Among Early Adolescents: An Evaluation of Drug Abuse Resistance Education (DARE)," *Evaluation Review*, vol. 17, no. 2 (April 1993), pp. 221–227. Copyright © 1993 by Sage Publications, Inc. Reprinted by permission. References omitted.

Similar to supply reduction, millions of dollars are spent every year on treatment as a means of curtailing drug use. Much like supply reduction strategies, treatment also shows little promise for eliminating drug use, particularly among adolescents (Polich et al. 1984; Stein and Davis 1982). Some feel adolescent drug problems stem from youth "life problems," not physiological dependence (Bennett 1983). This implies adolescent drug abusers are treated for the wrong problem. Subsequently, traditional drug treatment programs are often ineffective in treating adolescent clients (Sells and Simpson 1979).

Prevention holds more promise for controlling adolescent drug use than supply reduction or treatment. Reasons for promise include the timing of prevention programs and their focus on "gateway" substances—alcohol, tobacco, and marijuana. National data show youths initiating alcohol use as early as age 11 and marijuana and other illicit drugs at age 12 (Elliot and Huizinga 1984). Because drug use often begins at such an early age, prevention programs must target youths before they come in contact with drugs. Currently, many drug prevention programs (such as DARE) target youths while they are still in elementary school.

Targeting gateway substances is important because early use of such substances often follows a logical progression to experimentation with other drugs (Hamburg, Braemer, and Jahnke 1975; Kandel 1978; Richards 1980).

Prevention efforts have not always been as promising, however. Research clearly demonstrates the "first generation" of drug prevention programs such as information dissemination (stating facts about drugs), affective education (clarifying values and/or increasing self-esteem), and alternative activities to drug use have little or no impact on deterring adolescent drug use (Berberin et al. 1976; Hanson 1980; Kinder, Pape, and Walfish 1980; Schaps et al. 1981). In fact, some of these programs are associated with an increase in drug use (Gordon and McAlister 1982; Swisher and Hoffman 1975).

The "second generation" of drug prevention efforts has proven more effective in reducing adolescent drug use. This generation includes programs that focus on increasing general personal and social skills such as problem solving, decision making, coping, resisting peer pressure, and assertiveness through skill acquisition (Botvin and Dusenbury 1987; Schinke and Gilchrist 1985; Hansen et al. 1988; Telch et al. 1982).

DARE (DRUG ABUSE RESISTANCE EDUCATION)

DARE is a drug abuse prevention program that focuses on teaching students skills for recognizing and resisting social pressures to use drugs. DARE lessons also focus on the development of self-esteem, coping, assertiveness, communications skills, risk assessment and decision-making skills, and the identification of positive alternatives to drug use.

Taught by a uniformed police officer, the program consists of 17 lessons offered once a week for 45 to 50 minutes. The DARE curriculum can be taught only by police officers who attend an intensive two-week, 80-hour training. The DARE program calls for a wide range of teaching activities including question and answer sessions, group discussion, role play, and workbook exercises.

The DARE curriculum was created by Dr. Ruth Rich, a curriculum specialist with the Los Angeles Unified School District, from a second-generation curriculum known as Project SMART (Self-Management and Resistance Training) (Hansen et al. 1988).

DARE is one of, if not the most, widespread drug prevention programs in the United States. In 1989, over 3 million children in 80,000 classrooms were exposed to DARE ("Project DARE" 1990). Currently, there are DARE programs in every state in the United States and some counties have mandated DARE as part of the school health curriculum. It has also been implemented in several other countries including Canada, England, Australia, and New Zealand. In addition, it has been adopted by many reservation schools operated by the Bureau of Indian Affairs, and by the worldwide network of U.S. Defense Department schools for children of military personnel. There is a Spanish version and a Braille translation of the student workbook. Efforts are also under way to develop strategies for teaching DARE to hearing-impaired and other special-needs students.

Prior DARE Evaluations

Several DARE evaluations have been conducted over the past 9 years. Some show positive results, some show negative results, and most have serious methodological flaws. Recent DARE evaluations demonstrate an improvement in methodology over earlier studies. Initially, most of the DARE studies concluded that DARE was a "success." For these evaluations, success often meant students responded that they liked the DARE program. Still others claimed success if teachers and students rated DARE as "useful" or "valuable." For the most part success is based on the finding that students are more able to generate "ap-propriate" responses to a widely used 19-item questionnaire about drug facts and attitudes after the DARE program than before. In these last instances, almost all had no control group.

Many DARE studies contain such severe methodology problems that the results should be questioned. Methodological flaws contained in the evaluations include one or more of the following problems: (1) no control group, (2) small sample size, (3) posttest only, (4) poorly operationalized measures, (5) low alpha levels for scales ($< .50$), (6) no statistical tests performed, and (7) pretreatment differences not taken into account. Despite the lack of methodological rigor among most of these studies, three used rigorous methodology and should be mentioned because they have corrected many of the cited weaknesses.

The three studies are similar with respect to their evaluation designs but different in terms of their results. All three evaluations used adequate sample sizes and employed both pre- and posttest measures. They also randomly assigned schools to receive the DARE program or serve as controls.

Controlling on pretreatment differences, the dependent variable at Time 1 (pretest), and school type, Ringwalt, Ennett, and Holt (1991) in North Carolina reported significant differences in the expected direction for general attitudes toward drugs, attitudes toward specific drugs (beer, wine coolers, wine, cigarettes, and inhalants), perceptions of peers' attitudes toward drug use, assertiveness, recognizing media influences to use drugs, and the costs associated with drug use. However, no statistically significant effects were found for self-reported drug use, future intentions to use drugs, perceived benefits of drug use (alcohol and cigarettes), or self-esteem.

In Frankfort, Kentucky, Faine and Bohlander (1988) compared DARE to control students and found significant differences favoring the DARE students on all outcome measures, which include self-esteem, attitudes toward the police, knowledge of drugs, attitudes toward drugs, perceived external locus of control, and peer resistance scores.

The third DARE study worth mentioning took place in Lexington, Kentucky (Clayton, Cattarello, Day, and Walden 1991). The authors used analysis of variance to compare the treatment and control group outcomes. However, they only controlled on race despite other pretreatment differences. Statistically significant differences between the treatment and control group were found for general drug attitudes, negative attitudes toward specific drugs (cigarettes, alcohol, and marijuana), and peer relationships (interpreted as DARE students self-reporting more popularity among their peers). Differences were not observed for self-esteem, peer pressure resistance, or self-reported drug use.

A 2-year follow-up study (Clayton, Cattarello, and Walden 1991) examined the same cohort of sixth-grade students using two follow-up questionnaires (1 year apart) after the initial posttest. The only statistically significant difference occurred at the first follow-up for last-year marijuana use. Unfortunately, this finding occurred in the opposite direction than that expected. Significantly more marijuana use was reported by the *DARE students* than non-DARE students. Otherwise, no significant effects were found at any other time for any other drug type.

The only common outcome measures of the three studies mentioned are drug attitudes, self-esteem, and peer resistance (assertiveness). Inconsistent results were reported with respect to self-esteem and peer resistance (assertiveness) but the three evaluations agree that those in the DARE group had significantly less positive attitudes toward drug use compared to the control group.

Although some long-term studies have been attempted, the only one demonstrating adequate methodology is the Lexington, Kentucky study (Clayton, Cattarello, and Walden 1991) and the results do not warrant program success.

In short, studies of the DARE program have produced mixed results and DARE evaluations up to this point are inconclusive. Further replications are necessary in order to make more confident conclusions about the effects of the DARE program.

DARE Compared to Most Promising Prevention Approach

Several aspects of the DARE program make it a likely candidate for success. First, the program is offered to students just before the age when they are likely to experiment with drugs. Second, although there is little research on the effectiveness of law enforcement personnel as classroom instructors, uniformed police officers serve as teachers of the DARE curriculum in hopes of increasing favorable attitudes toward the law and law enforcement personnel. Third, the DARE program seeks to prevent the use of "gateway drugs" (i.e., alcohol, cigarettes, and marijuana), thereby decreasing the probability of subsequent heavier, more serious, drug use. Fourth, the DARE program draws on several aspects of effective drug prevention efforts from the second generation such as the development and practice of life skills (coping, assertiveness, and decision making).

Although DARE shows promise as a drug prevention strategy, more evaluation efforts need to take place before forming an overall conclusion about the program. This is especially important considering the fact that millions of government dollars are spent on this one particular drug prevention program every year and its dissemination continues to spread rapidly throughout the United States.

METHODS

Research Design

The current study used a nonequivalent control group quasi-experimental design (Campbell and Stanley 1963) to determine if participating in the DARE program had any effect on the measured outcome variables compared to a similar group that did not receive the program.

The 17-week DARE program took place during the fall and spring semesters of the 1989–1990 school year. A student self-report questionnaire was used to measure the outcome variables and all pre- and posttests were administered approximately 20 weeks apart.

The survey administration was conducted by the school alcohol and drug contact person. The administration was conducted in such a way as to preserve the confidentiality of the students. All students were assigned identification numbers prior to the time of the pretest. The identification number was used to link the pre- and posttest questionnaire responses. A questionnaire was distributed in an envelope with the student's name in the top right-hand corner.

Each name was printed on a removable label that the students tore off and threw away. The administrator read the cover page of the survey informing the students there was a number on the survey booklet that may be used to match their responses with questions asked later. The administrator also informed the students they had the right not to answer any or all the questions.

Response rates for the sample were high. The average pretest response rate was 93.5% for the DARE students and 93.7% for the comparison students. An average of 90% of the DARE students and 86.4% of the comparison students completed the posttest. The pre- and posttest (combined) response rates were similar for both groups; 86.5% (295) of the treatment and 83.7% (307) of the comparison students completed both surveys.

Analysis of variance procedures were employed to examine the differences between the DARE and non-DARE students at the time of the pretest. Controlling for any pretreatment differences between the two groups and the measured dependent variable on the pretest, analysis of covariance was used to detect significant differences at the time of the posttest.

Sample

From 11 elementary schools in Charleston County, South Carolina, 708 fifth-grade students participated in the present study. Students came from five schools receiving the DARE program and six that did not. Of the 708 students involved in the study, 341 received the treatment (DARE), and 367 served as comparison students. The students came from schools representing a cross section of those found in the Charleston County School

District. Three schools were urban, six suburban, and two rural.

Each of the DARE schools were paired with a comparison school based on the following characteristics: number of students, percentage of students receiving free or reduced lunch, percentage white, percentage male, percentage never retained, and percentage meeting BSAP (Basic Skills Assessment Program) reading and math standards....

In summary, the evidence shows DARE students had more beliefs in prosocial norms, more attitudes against substance use, more assertiveness, and more positive peer associations than the comparison group. The DARE students also reported less association with drug-using peers and less alcohol use in the last year. However, the DARE students were equivalent to the non-DARE students on social integration, commitment and attachment to school, rebellious behavior, coping strategies, attitudes about the police, self-esteem, and last-year and last-month drug use (with the exception of last-year alcohol use).

Current Findings and Comparisons

The current DARE evaluation demonstrates the program's effectiveness on some of the measured outcome variables but not on others. The current study shows DARE does have an impact on several of the program objectives. Among these are attitudes against substance use, assertiveness, positive peer association, association with drug-using peers, and alcohol use within the last year.

It should be noted that several of the variables showing no difference between the treatment and control groups are not specifically targeted by DARE (although they are shown to be correlated with adolescent drug use). Among these are social integration, attachment and commitment to school and rebellious behavior. It could also be argued that the DARE program does not specifically aim to change attitudes toward police officers, although this may be a tacit objective. Because the program does not target these outcomes specifically, it may not be surprising there were no differences found between the DARE and non-DARE groups. It was hypothesized that the DARE program may impact factors relating to later adolescent drug use, even if those factors were not specific aims of the program but this hypothesis did not hold true. In a sense this is evidence that helps to reject the selection argument. If the positive results were due to selection, they would not be found only for the outcomes targeted by DARE.

Much like the three previously reviewed DARE evaluations, the current study adds to the mixed results produced thus far with one exception. Across all studies using a pre-post comparison group design, DARE students' attitudes against drug use have consistently been shown to increase and differ significantly from the control students. Because favorable attitudes toward drug use have been shown to predict or correlate with later adolescent drug use (Kandel, Kessler, and Margulies 1978), this finding provides some of the most convincing evidence that DARE shows promise as a drug prevention strategy.

On the other hand, there are no other consistent findings for assertiveness (resisting peer pressure), self-esteem, or attitudes toward police. The current study found an increase in assertiveness among the DARE students as compared to the non-DARE students. Ringwalt et al. (1991) and Faine and Bohlander (1988) also found this to be true but Clayton, Cattarello, Day, and Walden (1991) did not. Effects on self-esteem were not demonstrated in the present DARE evaluation nor were they in Clayton's (Clayton, Cattarello, Day, and Walden 1991) or Ringwalt's (Ringwalt et al. 1991). However, significant differences in self-esteem were seen for the DARE participants over the controls in Faine and Bohlander's (1988) study. Thus the Charleston study helps to increase the consistency of the assertiveness and self-esteem results.

Faine and Bohlander's (1988) study also showed that positive attitudes toward police were significantly greater for the treatment group than the control group but the present study did not replicate such findings. However, the difference found between these two studies may be due to the measures used. The current DARE study uses only two single-item questions to assess students' attitudes about the police, whereas Faine and Bohlander (1988) used an 11-item scale that is likely to be more valid.

With reference to drug use, all of the stronger DARE evaluations found no effects with the exception of the current study, which found a significant difference on last-year alcohol use. Clayton's follow-up evaluation showed only one significant difference in the wrong direction on the first of two follow-up posttests (Clayton, Cattarello, and Walden 1991). As Clayton, Cattarello, and Walden (1991) point out, the lack of short-term drug use differences may be due to low base rates and thus should not be interpreted to mean DARE has no effect on adolescent drug involvement.

Recommendations
Replication studies of the evaluation of the DARE program should be continued because mixed evidence exists about the program's overall effectiveness. Conducting randomized experiments would certainly be best for drawing more confident conclusions about DARE program outcomes. Longitudinal studies would also aid in assessing the long-term program goal of deterring adolescent drug use.

There is one large problem with recommending a long-term study on a drug prevention program that is conducted in schools in the United States. The problem involves finding a true "no treatment" control group. Almost every school in the nation has some type of drug education component embodied in the school curriculum that is often mandated by the state. Therefore, it is likely the control group will receive some form of drug education. This problem has been documented as Clayton's (Clayton, Cattarello, and Walden 1991) study used a comparison group that received the school drug education unit and the ETI (Evaluation and Training Institute) had to discontinue their 5-year longitudinal study because the entire control group has essentially become a treatment group (Criminal Justice Statistics Association 1990).

In the future, it may be possible only to compare students' receiving some specified drug prevention program with the school system's drug education unit. However, this appears acceptable if the school system simply requires a unit session on factual drug information or a similar low-level intervention because prevention efforts such as these have consistently been shown to have no positive effects (Berberin et al. 1976; Kinder, Pape, and Walfish 1980; Schaps et al. 1981; Tobler 1986).

Should evaluations of the DARE program continue, it is suggested one national survey instrument be developed and used for all outcome evaluations. Currently, it is difficult to assess whether or not DARE is actually a success because different researchers use different survey instruments to examine a variety of outcome measures. Measuring DARE program objectives and other risk factors associated with later drug use with one survey would enable researchers to compare results across evaluations conducted in U.S. cities and other parts of the world.

Additional recommendations include employing peer leaders (i.e., high school students) as instructors instead of police officers. There are two reasons for this suggestion. First, it has not been consistently demonstrated that attitudes toward police become more positive upon receiving the DARE program, and second, there has been some evidence supporting the use of peer leaders as primary program providers (Botvin and Eng 1982; Botvin et al. 1984; Perry et al. 1980).

It would be not only interesting, but informative, to compare DARE program outcomes using peer leaders versus police officers as instructors. Should peer leaders provide equal or better outcomes, DARE programming costs would be considerably less and police officers would be more readily available to respond to citizen calls.

It is further recommended that DARE be restructured to incorporate components shown more consistently to be effective such as those found in second-generation approaches. Although DARE aims to increase resistance skills, coping, and decision making, the lessons specifically targeting these factors do so in the context of drug use only. Adolescents engaging in drug use behavior are often involved in other problem behaviors (Jessor and Jessor 1977). It would seem most practical and beneficial to target all of these behaviors using one program as Botvin (1982) and Swisher (1979) have suggested. The DARE program could serve as this one program, assuming several changes were implemented.

First, existing components would have to be expanded and additional components added in order to target more broad-based adolescent life problems such as family struggles, peer acceptance, sexual involvement, intimate relationships, and effective communication (expressing ideas, listening). Additional sessions should include components from second-generation programs such as setting goals, solving problems, and anticipating obstacles (Botvin, Renick, and Baker 1983; Schinke and Gilchrist 1985).

Second, skill acquisition is said to come about only through practice and reinforcement (Bandura 1977). It is proposed that any new skills taught, such as problem solving, be reinforced with "real life" homework where students practice these skills in the context of the "real world" rather than simply role playing them in the classroom.

The last recommendation is applicable not only to the DARE program but any drug prevention effort. It involves the addition of booster sessions following the prevention program. Because adolescence is a time of growth, individual attitudes and behaviors may continue to change and develop as the youth is maturing. Although short-term evidence of program effectiveness is encouraging, there is no guarantee a youth will continue to practice those same behaviors or hold those same beliefs years, or even months, after the program has ended. In fact, follow-up studies have documented the eroding effects of drug prevention programs (Botvin and Eng 1980, 1982) and the superior effects of booster sessions (Botvin, Renick, and Baker 1983; Botvin et al. 1984). For these reasons, DARE, or any other drug prevention program targeting adolescents, should include a series of follow-up sessions in order to increase the likelihood of sustaining any positive effects.

NO

Richard R. Clayton et al.

DARE: VERY POPULAR BUT NOT VERY EFFECTIVE

The purpose of this [selection] is to review and examine what is known about the most widely distributed school-based drug abuse prevention program in the world, DARE (Drug Abuse Resistance Education). It is likely that you know about DARE; you have seen the T-shirts, the bumper stickers, floats in Independence Day parades, DARE cars, and the hundreds of other ways that this program has been marketed. Perhaps you yourself were in a class or school that received the DARE curriculum in the fifth or sixth grade.

DARE is a social phenomenon (Wyson, 1993). In the 1983–84 school year, it was delivered to about 8,000 elementary school students in Los Angeles. Today, DARE is found in more than one half of all school districts in the United states and reaches at least 25 million students each year (Ennet, Tobler, Ringwalt, & Flewelling, 1994). Although the numbers are difficult to confirm, it is estimated that $750 million is spent on DARE each year in the United States. DARE can also be found in Australia, Canada, Mexico, New Zealand, Norway, and Sweden.

THE DARE PROGRAM

DARE began in Los Angeles in 1983–84 as a school-based drug prevention program. The curriculum is a result of the joint efforts of the Los Angeles Police Department and the Los Angeles Unified School District, one of the country's largest.

Unlike most other school-based prevention programs, which are taught by teachers, DARE is taught by uniformed police officers who must undergo 80 hours of rigorous training before they can teach the program (Falco, 1989).

The stated purpose of DARE is to "prevent substance abuse among school children." The principal way it seeks to achieve this goal is to teach students the skills for recognizing and resisting social pressures to experiment with tobacco, alcohol, and other drugs. The 17 DARE lessons also focus on enhancing students' self-esteem, decision making, coping, assertiveness, and communication skills and on teaching positive alternatives to substance use.

From Richard R. Clayton, Carl G. Leukefeld, Nancy Grant Harrington, and Anne Cattarello, "DARE (Drug Abuse Resistance Education): Very Popular but Not Very Effective," in Clyde B. McCoy, Lisa R. Metsch, and James A. Inciardi, eds., *Intervening With Drug-Involved Youth* (Sage Publications, 1996). Copyright © 1996 by Sage Publications, Inc. Reprinted by permission.

The curriculum and basic goals and structure of the DARE program have remained essentially the same since its beginnings. However, in 1992–94, additional lessons were added to place greater emphasis on the prevention of tobacco use and a new and enhanced focus was placed on violence prevention and conflict resolution. In addition, the actual classroom style became more "interactive" rather than one-directional from officer to student. The revisions were phased in during 1993–94, and beginning January 1, 1995, all DARE officers were required to use the "new" program.

The original DARE program was targeted at students in the fifth or sixth grade, preferably the grade immediately prior to entering junior high or middle school. Now there are DARE programs for kindergarten through third-grade students, middle-school students, and high school students (Kochis, 1995).

BEING AT THE RIGHT PLACE AT THE RIGHT TIME

National political interest in the drug problem was focused in 1986 with President Reagan's "War on Drugs" address to the nation. This led to broad support from both the Democratic and Republican parties and the passage of the Anti-Drug Abuse Act of 1986 (Falco, 1989). In both the Bush and the Clinton administrations, there was increasing recognition of the complexity of the problem and the requirements that law enforcement/supply reduction and prevention-treatment/demand reduction efforts be coordinated. The Office of National Drug Control Policy (ONDCP) is responsible for this coordination and has placed increasingly strong emphasis on prevention and drug education programs. In fact, federal spending for all "educational" prevention activities rose from $230 million in 1988 to $660 million in 1995.

DARE was at the right place at the right time, with just the right types of political support to become what the Justice Department called the "long term solution to the drug problem." In fact, the congressional testimony of Los Angeles Police Chief Daryl Gates and support from powerful members of Congress and President Bush led in 1990 to an amendment to the 1986 funding for DARE. The Drug Free Schools Act divided money given to the states into two parts: 70% of the money went to the departments of education in the states, and 30% went to the governor. The amendment required that 10% of the governor's portion be used to fund programs such as Project Drug Abuse Resistance Education (DARE). In fact, DARE was the only school-based prevention program singled out for mandated funding.

Congressional and other support for DARE continued into the mid-1990s, when it was again singled out for federal funding through a renewed commitment in Congress to what was now called the "Safe and Drug Free Schools and Communities Act."

DARE: MORE THAN JUST A DRUG PREVENTION PROGRAM

One of the reasons DARE has been so successful in spreading across the country is organizational. DARE America is a private, nonprofit corporation organized in 1987 with a goal of getting the program into all states and communities, developing and supporting a national DARE instructor training program, and getting funding nationally.

Training
The Bureau of Justice Assistance (BJA) within the Department of Justice started funding DARE in 1986 with a BJA grant of $140,000. In the late 1980s, BJA funded five regional DARE training centers. As part of the funding agreement, BJA appoints 5 of the 15 members of the DARE training center policy advisory board.

Additional Funding and Support
DARE America has been successful in attracting major corporate sponsors such as Bayliner, Herbalife, Kentucky Fried Chicken, Kimberly-Clark, McDonalds, Packard Bell, Security Pacific National Bank, and Warner Brothers. At the local and state level, there are thousands of large and small firms contributing to the program.

INCONSISTENCY: DARE'S POPULARITY AND ITS EFFECTIVENESS

The principal purpose of DARE is to reduce substance abuse among school children. About the only way to determine if DARE has achieved success (i.e., "works") is to conduct research on students who receive DARE and those who do not receive DARE. Both the experimental group (received DARE) and the control group should be examined prior to the start of the prevention effort and followed for 1 to 5 years to see if differences persist. DARE is the most widely research-evaluated school-based prevention program in the United States. There have been at least 15 evaluation studies conducted (Ennett et al., 1994), several of

which followed DARE and non-DARE students for up to 4 or 5 years (Clayton, Cattarello, & Johnstone, 1996). Although the results from various studies differ somewhat, all studies are consistent in finding that DARE does not have long-term effects on drug use (Kochis, 1995). It does seem to have some effects on knowledge and attitudes toward drugs, but even these effects diminish over time. In fact, two long-term follow-up studies show that after 3 or more years, students who received DARE do not even have more positive attitudes toward the police than students who did not receive DARE (Clayton et al., 1996; Wysong, Aniskiewicz, & Wright, 1994).

WHY IS DARE SO POPULAR IF IT IS NOT EFFECTIVE?

This is an important question because it reveals so much about the United States and its approach to social problems (Aniskiewicz & Wysong, 1990).

Police
DARE is popular among police for two reasons. First, it puts police officers into community institutions previously "off limits" to them. Before the advent of DARE, there was a widespread and deep-seated mistrust of police officers by school officials. In fact, police were seen by many community members and organizations as generally less educated and brutish. By entering school systems to teach DARE, police can change these stereotypes. Second, it allows police officers to do things that are seen as "positive." In most police departments prior to the mid-1980s, absolutely the worst assignment was what was then called "community relations." No police officer wanted that assignment. Now police of-

ficers are standing in line for an opportunity to be a DARE officer. Police officers perceive a different response to them from the public if they are involved with DARE. In fact, it could be said that DARE has had a major effect on the relationship between police departments and other community-based organizations. Police are now active players in a wide variety of positive community projects and initiatives.

Parents

DARE is popular among parents for at least two reasons. First, they are extremely concerned about drug abuse and violence, and most feel helpless in dealing with either. Therefore, if there is a police officer in the school teaching the DARE program, it might protect their child from being victimized by violent predators or by drug dealers. Second, most Americans have a naive and false sense of confidence in the power of "education." It is the panacea brought out to "solve" all our problems: If people just know the "facts," they will make rational choices. The DARE officer represents authority, and parents have faith that children will listen to and heed the advice of an authority. Besides, the prevailing orientation to drugs in this society is primarily concerned with legality/illegality—a law enforcement perspective. The DARE officer represents the prevailing perspective held by parents.

Teachers

DARE is also quite popular among teachers, and for two very good reasons. First, teachers, just like the parents, perceive the school to be a safer place when DARE officers are in the school. Second, the DARE officer teaches the drug prevention curriculum, which means that the teach-

ers do not have to teach the lessons. In fact, although the teachers are required to be "in the classroom" during the drug prevention lessons, they get a respite from their work, a break of sorts. This second reason is very important as an unintended consequence of how far and how quicly DARE has diffused across the country. At present, no colleges of education require preparation of teachers to deliver substance abuse prevention curricula. Even so, a significant proportion of fifth- and sixth-grade teachers in the United States could probably teach the DARE curriculum because they have seen and heard it taught one or more times. If the education establishment had been called on to provide 80 hours of training to teach a drug prevention curriculum such as DARE, it would have cost billions of dollars. Instead, such a curriculum has been provided at no cost to the education establishment in the course of the spread of DARE across America.

Administrators

School administrators, the principals and superintendents, seem to like DARE because it provides a sense of extra security at the school, it provides a respite for the teachers which makes them happy, it is generally very popular among parents and gets them more involved with the school than would otherwise be likely, and it links the school with another important institution of the community, the police department. A number of principals regularly request that the DARE officer be in the school on Mondays because attendance is noticeably higher when the DARE officer is in the school (Clayton, Cattarello, Day, & Walden, 1991).

THE "FEEL-GOOD" APPROACH TO DRUG PREVENTION

Someone might wonder: If everybody likes DARE and it makes students, teachers, administrators, parents, police, and politicians "feel good" because something is being done about drug abuse, why should we be worried by lack of evidence that it delays the onset or inhibits the continuance of drug use by adolescents? The answer to this question is quite simple and has three parts. First, publicly funded programs should be accountable for what they achieve. If they do not achieve their states goal (in this instance, a reduction in drug use), how can further expenditure of public funds be justified? Second, other similar programs consistently show some effects in the desired direction, although the effects are not huge (Botvin, Dusenbury, Botvin, & Diaz, 1995). Why should the American public pay for a program that has proven to be ineffective when programs that have proven to be successful exist? Third, a principal reason for evaluation research is to examine the effectiveness of public programming that may seem sound on the surface but is unsound in practice. The evidence for the lack of sustained effectiveness of DARE is strong, consistent, and impressive.

Why, then, the continued strong support of DARE? The answer to this question must be: Because it makes all the important groups (parents, teachers, administrators, police, politicians) "feel good." It is sad to say, but an overwhelming majority of people in the United States have a rather naive view of the world and how to solve social problems such as drug use and abuse by adolescents. DARE seems to reflect most of these naive notions and in some ways to exploit them.

Drug use is *not* a simple phenomenon. It will not be solved by simple slogans and bumper stickers and T-shirts and a bunch of people believing that DARE is "the" answer to drug abuse in America. If anyone really and truly believes this is true, we have some swamp land in Florida we would like for them to buy.

The "scientific" research on the effectiveness of DARE is clear. DARE does not produce sustained effects on drug use or on even attitudes toward police (Clayton et al., 1996). Furthermore, the most recent data suggest that drug use (marijuana, inhalants, LSD, stimulants, cigarettes) began to rise significantly among 8th, 10th, and 12th graders beginning in 1992 and continuing through 1994. The cohorts in which drug use began to rise for the first time since 1979 would have been 6th graders in 1990, 8th graders in 1992, and 10th graders in 1994. If we assumed that DARE had spread all across America by 1990, these would be the students who would have been most affected by the diffusion of DARE.

To be fair, DARE could not be expected to produce miracles and wipe out drug use among adolescents entirely. Many forces in society promote drug use or dilute efforts to fight drug use among adolescents. However, DARE could be expected to produce some reduction in drug use, or at the very least positive and sustained effects on attitudes toward drug use by adolescents. Instead, as has been shown, there are *no* sustained effects from the DARE program on attitudes or behavior. In fact, it is probably naive to think that any *universal* (one size fitting all students) type of school-based, curriculum-driven drug prevention program could exert enough influence to counter the forces driving youth toward experimentation with various drugs. These types of programs are simply not powerful enough, do not provide enough exposures to the intervention, and may not even directly address the primary causes of drug use by youth. For example, one entire lesson in the DARE curriculum is designed to heighten self-esteem. However, the extensive research literature on the relationship between self-exteem and drug use among adolescents indicates very little correlation between drug use and self-esteem. Therefore, even if the lesson helped to improve self-esteem for some of the students, that improvement would probably not be translated into a lower probability of drug use. So although DARE is very popular, it is not very effective. Therefore we as a nation should be ready to accept that fact and deal with its implications if we *really* want to have an effect on drug use among youth.

REFERENCES

Aniskiewicz, R., & Wysong, E. (1990). Evaluating DARE: Drug education and the miltiple meanings of success. *Policy Studies Review, 9,* 727–747.

Botvin, G. J., Dusenbury, L., Botvin, E. M., & Diaz, T. (1995). Long term follow-up results of a randomized drug abuse trial in a white middle class population. *Journal of the American Medical Association, 273,* 1106–1112.

Clayton, R. R., Cattarello, L., Day. E., & Walden, K. P. (1991). Persuasive communication and drug prevention: An evaluation of the DARE program. In H. Sypher, L. Donohew, & W. Bukoski (Eds.), *Persuasive communication and drug abuse prevention.* Hillsdale, NJ: Lawrence Erlbaum.

Clayton, R. R., Cattarello, A. M., & Johnstone, B. M. (in press). The effectiveness of Drug Abuse Resistance Education (Project DARE): Five year follow-up results. *Preventive Medicine.*

Ennett, S., Tobler, N., Ringwalt, C., & Flewelling, R. (1994). How effective is Drug Abuse Resistance Education? A meta-analysis of Project DARE outcome evaluations. *American Journal of Public Health, 84,* 1394–1401.

Falco, M. (1989). *Winning the drug war: A national strategy.* New York: Priority.

Kochis, D. S. (1995). The effectiveness of Project DARE: Does it work? *Journal of Alcohol and Drug Education, 40,* 40–47.

Wysong, E. (1993, October). *The frontier of drug education: D.A.R.E. as a social movement.* Paper presented at the annual meeting of the Indiana Academy of Social Sciences, Hanover College, Hanover, IN.

Wysong, E., Aniskiewicz, R., & Wright, D. (1994). Truth and DARE: Tracking drug education to graduation and as symbolic politics. *Social Problems, 41,* 448–473.

POSTSCRIPT

Is Drug Abuse Resistance Education (DARE) an Effective Program?

Before the effectiveness of drug education programs can be determined, it is necessary to define the goals of drug education. Are the goals of drug education to prevent drug use from starting? To prevent drug abuse? To prevent drug dependency? Perhaps the goal of drug education is to teach young people how to protect themselves and others from harm *if* they are going to use drugs. Without a clear understanding of the goals one wants to achieve in teaching about drugs, it is impossible to determine the effectiveness of drug education.

Before a drug education program can be designed, questions regarding what to include in the drug education curriculum need to be addressed. Should the primary focus be on teaching abstinence or responsible use? Is it feasible to teach abstinence from some drugs and responsible use of other drugs? Almost 90 percent of high school students have drunk alcohol; should they be taught they should not drink at all, or should they be taught how to use alcohol responsibly? Does the age of the children make a difference in what is taught? Do elementary students have the reasoning skills of high school students? Should the goal be for students to engage in a decision-making process or simply to adopt certain behaviors?

In the 1980s there was a significant reduction in drug use among high school seniors in the United States, although drug use has climbed since the early 1990s. How much of the reduction in the 1980s was due to drug education, and how much was due to other factors? Throughout American history drug use has been cyclical—perhaps the United States was in a down cycle in the 1980s and is currently in an up cycle in terms of drug use.

If drug prevention programs such as DARE are going to be effective in reducing drug use, schools and other institutions will need to work together. Many young people drop out of school or simply do not attend, so community agencies and religious institutions need to become involved. The media have a large impact on young people. What is the best way to incorporate the media in the effort to reduce drug use? Are antidrug commercial spots shown during programs aimed at teenage audiences effective?

Drug prevention efforts are reviewed in Mary Jansen's article "Prevention Research for Alcohol and Other Drugs: A Look Ahead to What Is Needed," *Substance Use and Misuse* (vol. 31, 1996). Another perspective on teaching about drugs is provided by Gail Milgram in "Responsible Decision Making Regarding Alcohol: A Re-Emerging Prevention/Education Strategy for the 1990s," *Journal of Drug Education* (vol. 26, 1996).

ISSUE 17

Should the Decision to Use Anabolic Steroids Be Left to Athletes?

YES: Ellis Cashmore, from "Run of the Pill," *New Statesman and Society* (November 11, 1994)

NO: Joannie M. Schrof, from "Pumped Up," *U.S. News and World Report* (June 1, 1992)

ISSUE SUMMARY

YES: Sociology professor Ellis Cashmore argues that anabolic steroids are no different from the aids and equipment that athletes commonly use to enhance their performance. He further contends that the notion that drug use violates the rules of fair play is illogical because competition has never been predicated on fair play.

NO: Joannie M. Schrof, an associate editor of *U.S. News and World Report,* asserts that athletes who take anabolic steroids are not fully aware of the potential adverse effects and that these athletes often use excessive quantities because they are under tremendous pressure to win.

Anabolic steroids are synthetic derivatives of the male hormone testosterone. Although they have legitimate medical uses, steroids are increasingly being used by individuals to quickly build up muscle and increase personal strength. Concerns over the potential negative effects of steroid use seem to be justified: an estimated 1 million Americans, half of whom are adolescents, have used illegally obtained steroids. Anabolic steroid users span all ethnic groups, nationalities, and socioeconomic groups. The emphasis on winning has led many athletes to take risks with steroids that are potentially destructive. Despite the widespread belief that anabolic steroids are primarily used by athletes, up to one-third of users are nonathletes who use these drugs to improve their physiques and self-images.

Society places much emphasis on winning, and to come out on top, many individuals are willing to make sacrifices—sacrifices that may entail compromising their health. Some people will do anything for the sake of winning. In an article in *Sports Illustrated* published prior to his death, football player Lyle Alzado spoke out not against the use of steroids but against the way *he* used steroids. His message was not necessarily that steroids were bad but that they can be used badly. For some, any use of steroids for athletic competition raises some ethical concerns. These people argue that steroid users gain an unfair advantage over competitors who do not take steroids. That is, of course, the precise reason athletes take steroids. Critics maintain that misinformation about the effects of steroids is fostered by the ban on their use.

The short-term consequences of anabolic steroids are well documented. Possible short-term effects among men include testicular atrophy, sperm count reduction, impotency, baldness, difficulty in urinating, and breast enlargement. Among women, some potential effects are deepening of the voice, breast reduction, menstrual irregularities, and clitoral enlargement. Both sexes may develop acne, swelling in the feet, reduced levels of high-density lipoproteins (which is the "good" cholesterol), hypertension, and liver damage. Also related to steroid use are psychological changes, including mood swings, paranoia, and violent behavior. The short-term effects of steroids have been thoroughly researched; their long-term effects, however, have not been substantiated.

The problem with identifying the long-term effects of anabolic steroids is that there are virtually no systematic, scientific long-term studies. Most of the information regarding long-term effects comes from personal reports, not well-conducted, controlled studies. Personal stories or anecdotal evidence is often accepted as fact. For example, anabolic steroids have been implicated in the development of liver tumors. Yet there are very few documented cases of liver tumors among steroid users. It is difficult to know if the effects from anabolic steroids are exaggerated.

The American Medical Association opposes stricter regulation of anabolic steroids on two grounds. First, anabolic steroids have been used medically to improve growth and development and for certain types of anemia, breast cancers, endometriosis, and osteoporosis. If stricter regulations were imposed, people who could benefit medically from these drugs will have more difficulty acquiring them. Second, it is highly unlikely that illicit use of these drugs will cease if they are banned. By maintaining legal access to these drugs, studies into their long-term consequences can be determined.

In the following selections, Ellis Cashmore argues that banning anabolic steroids from sports on the basis that they provide unfair advantages to athletes would be hypocritical because athletic competition is naturally unfair. He feels that better control of steroids can be accomplished if they are not prohibited. Joannie M. Schrof contends that people who use steroids are risking their lives and that stricter control of these substances is needed.

YES

Ellis Cashmore

RUN OF THE PILL

Amid the memories of [the 1994] World Cup finals, there is one that will remain. Not the record-breaking five goals of Russian striker Oleg Salenko against Cameroon, not the murder of Colombia's Andres Escobar, killed in a Medellín bar after conceding an own goal that hastened his country's exit from the competition, and certainly not the near-catatonic final. The abiding memory will be that of Diego Maradona, the third footballer in history to be ejected from a major tournament for taking banned substances—in his case a cocktail of five drugs, including ephedrine, found in over-the-counter decongestants. It transformed Maradona from the world's greatest player to the world's greatest cheat. The media all but changed his studs for cloven hooves.

Barely a week goes by, it seems, without a sports performer descending abruptly from the status of champion to cheat. Sports performers no longer prosecute the Corinthian ideal of competing for the sheer joy and gratification of competition. Athletes run for gold bars, boxers fight for millions, footballers play for monthly salaries big enough to buy an average family house. Hang incentives like this in front of performers and it's hardly surprising that they will do anything they can to augment the abilities they were blessed with. Taking drugs is an extension of the logic of competition.

Encouraged by television, which has successfully exploited sport and now almost depends on it, professional sport (which covers virtually all) offers incentives to its record-breakers and champions like never before. Performers can boost their performance by recruiting top coaches, nutritionists, acupuncturists; they can use state-of-the-art equipment and, if they can afford it, train in optimal climes. What they cannot do, of course, is take drugs. This sits oddly in a culture in which the preoccupation with health and fitness has all but commended a daily diet of chemicals. Even a relatively benign cold remedy, like Lemsip, will get an athlete banned for months, thanks to the presence of phenyephrine—and a set of rules that lacks both moral authority and common sense.

Sport's anti-drugs policies are so riven with hypocrisy, anomaly and contradiction that the only rational course of action is to abandon them and let competitors decide whether they want to take substances that purportedly enhance their performance. Sport hides behind two increasingly feeble justifications for maintaining an anti-drugs policy. The first has its origins in the policy's initial purpose: to protect competitors.

By the 1960s, it was known that, in cycling, competitors would often ingest amphetamine-based concoctions, some of them lethal, as the deaths of Knut Jensen and Tommy Simpson indicated. If the autobiography of ex-cyclist Paul Kimmage is to be accepted, the practice is still rife. A paternalistic impulse guided sport towards its early drug-testing, designed to prevent further tragedies.

Were this argument advanced today, it would seem a lot less credible than it did 30 years ago. A female runner using oral contraceptives to regulate her period and so maximise her training and performance, or a chess player who smokes to calm his nerves are allowed to compete, despite taking drugs with known harmful consequences. But there is woe for anyone who takes cough linctus without carefully checking the label.

There is also a paradox: evidence indicates that some sports activities themselves are more dangerous than many substances that are believed to enhance performance. Training at the intensity required to compete at the highest levels almost certainly takes its toll on the body's natural immunity system, exposing the competitor to infection.

Some sports clearly carry a risk. Ranked in terms of fatalities, boxing, a punishing pursuit in which brain damage is rife, is a relatively benign activity. Motor racing and air sports are killers. There are less visible casualties. In her teens, gymnast Olga Korbut charmed the world with her gentle play at the aesthetic borders of sport and art. By her late twenties, she was haggard and arthritic. There must be countless others who leave sport disabled by its physical demands. A genuinely paternalistic policy should examine that which it's meant to be safeguarding before banishing one of its lesser possible malefactors.

The argument most forcefully advanced nowadays is that using drugs violates the principle of fair play. But, has sport ever been fair? No: the conditions of actual competition may be equalised, but the advantages, whether natural or social, that some competitors enjoy can never be negated. Were you a runner, born in Bradford, following home Yobes Ondieki in a 5,000 metres race, you may wonder what difference it would have made if you, like your opponent, had been born and raised in Kenya, where the altitude encourages a naturally high haemoglobin count—a boon for middle-distance runners.

There is surely a degree of unfairness about a head-to-head meeting between Jennifer Capriati, born to a family well-off enough to provide top coaching facilities, and a ghetto child who picked up her tennis skills in the municipal parks of somewhere like Detroit.

Fair play and its antonym, cheating, are not preordained; they are products of how sports' governing organisations define them. If we need reminding of how arbitrary this can get, consider how devices, like starting blocks, or activities, including training, were once ruled out as unfair on the grounds that they gave competitors advantages.

Yet, there is still the question of sport's future to consider: we would be encouraging a generation of druggies, say querulous coaches and administrators. Sports stars today are potent symbols and their behaviour is often closely monitored and emulated by the young. The substances that supposedly enhance performance on the sports field are, of course, different from the ones that cause long-term distress at street-level. But the point is still a powerful one: drugs are drugs. So, why don't we drug-test Pavarotti after every concert, or expunge Suede's albums from the charts if they were recorded while the artists were under the influence? This is not *quite* as ridiculous as it sounds. The music of Charlie Parker, a heroin addict, the acting of Cary Grant, who used LSD, the writing of Dylan Thomas, an alcoholic: all these have not been obliterated, like Ben Johnson's 9.79 seconds.

Sports performers are different in the sense that they operate in and perhaps symbolise a sphere where all is meant to be wholesome and pure. But this puts competitors under sometimes intolerable pressure to keep their haloes straight. We know they are not saints; nor, given the business of sport, will they ever be.

The hearings of the Johnson case in 1989 and subsequent revelations all indicate that Johnson was not in a minority. This adds weight to the belief that the performers themselves are mere bit part players in a broader drama, the major roles being played by anonymous medics who prescribe competitors' training as well as their dope. "Scientist vs scientist" is how the future is sometimes envisaged: like dashing Svengalis, scientists might wield almost total control over their subjects were drugs allowed. The image is deliciously amusing rather than

sinister. Drugs are but one more of an ever-increasing portfolio of aids contemporary sports performers use to attain the levels of excellence demanded of them.

Nothing guarantees a product's arcaneness better than a ban. Intent as sport's governing bodies seem on stamping out drugs, their principal success has been in enlarging the mystique surrounding the likes of anabolic steroids and amphetamines. Making legal drugs available to performers means relegating them to the realms of the mundane.

Some research has shown that, when drugs are taken by performers, a placebo effect kicks in: the belief that they will enhance performance, rather than the substance itself, does the trick. One imagines how this type of disclosure would demystify drugs for young sports wannabes.

Sport harbours two naive beliefs, the first that competition is somehow pure. Yet, championships are prefixed with brand names, kits are plastered with logos, performers shamelessly endorse products. No one can disapprove of such commercialism, any more than the commercialism of SmithKline Beecham or Vaux breweries. But the marketplace brings with it imperatives, the central one of which is to win, not simply to compete.

The other is less explicit, but no less important, and concerns the assumption of a natural body state that shouldn't be corrupted by artificial means. Drugs are no more artificial than the entourage of aides and physical equipment commonplace in contemporary sport, and probably safer than tyrannical training regimes. The enhancing value of these is greater than any drug.

It is a foible of sport's governing organisations that they continue to search-and-destroy competitors who are, in a sense, merely following the dictates of commercial sport. The millions of dollars that are ploughed in the direction of Hewlett-Packard, which builds and equips testing centres, might more profitably be spent on research to discover the actual consequences of drugs currently favoured by competitors, rather than the imagined ones that continue to fascinate.

NO

Joannie M. Schrof

PUMPED UP

It's a dangerous combination of culture and chemistry. Inspired by cinematic images of the Terminator and Rambo and the pumped-up paychecks of athletic heroes with stunning physiques and awesome strength, teenagers across America are pursuing dreams of brawn through a pharmacopeia of pills, powders, oils and serums that are readily available—but often damaging. Despite the warnings of such fallen stars as Lyle Alzado, the former football player who died ... of a rare brain cancer he attributed to steroid use, a *U.S. News* investigation has found a vast teenage subculture driven by an obsession with size and bodybuilding drugs. Consider:

- An estimated 1 million Americans, half of them adolescents, use black-market steroids. Countless others are choosing from among more than 100 other substances, legal and illegal, touted as physique boosters and performance enhancers.

- Over half the teens who use steroids start before age 16, sometimes with the encouragement of their parents. In one study, 7 percent said they first took "juice" by age 10.

- Many of the 6 to 12 percent of boys who use steroids want to be sports champions, but over one third aren't even on a high-school team. The typical user is middle-class and white.

- Fifty-seven percent of teen users say they were influenced by the dozen or so muscle magazines that today reach a readership of at least 7 million; 42 percent said they were swayed by famous athletes who they were convinced took steroids.

- The black-market network for performance enhancers is enormous, topping $400 million in the sale of steroids alone, according to the U.S. Drug Enforcement Administration. Government officials estimate that there are some 10,000 outlets for the drugs—mostly contacts made at local gyms —and mail-order forms from Europe, Canada and Mexico can be found anywhere teenagers hang out.

- The nation's steroid experts signaled the state of alarm when they convened in April in Kansas City to plan the first nationwide education effort.

- Even Arnold Schwarzenegger, who has previously been reluctant to comment on his own early steroid use, has been prompted to speak out vigorously about the problem. The bodybuilder and movie star is the chairman of the President's Council on Physical Fitness and Sports.

Performance drugs have an ancient history. Greek Olympians used strychnine and hallucinogenic mushrooms to psych up for an event. In 1886, a French cyclist was the first athlete known to die from performance drugs—a mixture of cocaine and heroin called "speedballs." In the 1920s, physicians inserted slices of monkey testicles into male athletes to boost vitality, and in the '30s, Hitler allegedly administered the hormone testosterone to himself and his troops to increase aggressiveness.

The use of anabolic steroids by weight lifters in the Eastern bloc dates back at least to the 1950s, and the practice has been spreading ever since among the world's elite athletes. But recent sensations in the sports world—Ben Johnson's record-shattering sprints at the Seoul Olympics and the signing of Brian Bosworth to the largest National Football League rookie contract even *after* he tested positive for steroids—have attracted both young adults and kids to performance enhancers like never before, say leading steroid experts. These synthetic heroes are revered rather than disparaged in amateur gyms around the country, where wannabe Schwarzeneggers rationalize away health risks associated with performance-enhancing drugs.

Weighing in. The risks are considerable. Steroids are derivatives of the male hormone testosterone, and although they have legitimate medical uses—treatment of some cancers, for example—young bodybuilders who use them to promote tissue growth and endure arduous workouts routinely flood their bodies with 100 times the testosterone they produce naturally. The massive doses, medical experts say, affect not only the muscles but also the sex organs and nervous system, including the brain. "Even a brief period of abuse could have lasting effects on a child whose body and brain chemistry are still developing," warns Neil Carolan, who directs chemical dependency programs at BryLin Hospitals in Buffalo and has counseled over 200 steroid users.

Male users—by far the majority—can suffer severe acne, early balding, yellowing of the skin and eyes, development of female-type breasts and shrinking of the testicles. (In young boys, steroids can have the opposite effect of painfully enlarging the sex organs.) In females, the voice deepens permanently, breasts shrink, periods become irregular, the clitoris swells and hair is lost from the head but grows on the face and body. Teen users also risk stunting their growth, since steroids can cause bone growth plates to seal. One 13-year-old who had taken steroids for two years stopped growing at 5 feet. "I get side effects," says another teen who has used steroids for three years. "But I don't mind; it lets me know the stuff is working."

In addition to its physical dangers, steroid use can lead to a vicious cycle of dependency. Users commonly take the drugs in "cycles" that last from four to 18 weeks, followed by a lengthy break. But during "off" time, users typically shrink up, a phenomenon so abhorrent to those obsessed with size that many panic, turning back to the drugs in even larger doses. Most users "stack" the drugs, taking a combination of three to five pills and injectables at once; some report taking as many as 14 drugs simultaneously. Among the most commonly used are Dianabol ("D-Ball"), Anavar and Winstrol-V, the same type of steroid Ben Johnson tested positive for in 1988. "You wouldn't believe how much some guys go nuts on the stuff," says one teen bodybuilder from the Northeast. "They turn into walking, talking pharmacies."

Despite massive weight gains and sharply chiseled muscles, many steroid users are never quite happy with their physiques—a condition some researchers have labeled "reverse anorexia." "I've seen a kid gain 100 pounds in 14 months and still not be satisfied with himself," reports Carolan. If users try to stop, they can fall into deep depressions, and they commonly turn to recreational drugs to lift their spirits. Even during a steroid cycle, many users report frequent use of alcohol and marijuana to mellow out. "I tend to get really depressed when I go off a cycle," says one Maryland teen, just out of high school. "On a bad day, I think, 'Gee, if I were on the stuff this wouldn't be happening.' "

"Juicers" often enjoy a feeling of invincibility and euphoria. But along with the "pump" can come irritability and a sudden urge to fight. So common are these uncontrolled bursts of anger that they have a name in the steroid culture: "roid rages." The aggression can grow to pathological proportions; in a study by Harvard researchers, one eighth of steroid users suffered from "bodybuilder's psychosis," displaying such signs of mental illness as delusions and paranoia. So many steroid abusers are ending up behind bars for violent vandalism, assault and even murder that

defense attorneys in several states now call on steroid experts to testify about the drugs' effects.

What steroids do in the long run is still unknown, largely because not one federal dollar has been spent on long-term studies. Although Lyle Alzado was convinced that steroids caused his brain cancer, for example, there is no medical evidence to prove or disprove the link. But physicians are concerned about occasional reports of users falling ill with liver and kidney problems or dropping dead at a young age from heart attacks or strokes. Douglas McKeag, a sports physician at Michigan State University, is compiling a registry of steroid-related illnesses and deaths to fill the gaping hole in medical knowledge. McKeag sees preliminary evidence that steroid use might cause problems with blood-cell function that could lead to embolisms in the heart or lungs. "If that turns out to be true," he says, "then bingo—we'll have something deadly to warn kids about."

Dianabol desperadoes. Unfortunately, even that sort of documented health threat is unlikely to sway committed members of the steroid subculture. One widely shared value among users is a profound distrust of the medical community. Their suspicion is not totally unjustified. When steroid use was first becoming popular in the late 1950s, the medical community's response was to claim that they didn't enhance athletic ability—a claim that bulked-up users knew to be false. When that failed to deter users, physicians turned to scare tactics, branding steroids "killer drugs," again without hard evidence to back up the claim. As a result, self-styled "anabolic outlaws" and "Dianabol desperadoes" have sought guidance not from doctors but from the "Underground Steroid Handbook," a widely distributed paperback with detailed instructions for the use of more than 80 performance enhancers. "I know that proper steroid therapy can enhance your health; it has enhanced mine," writes author Daniel Duchaine. "Do you believe someone just because he has an M.D. or Ph.D. stuck onto the end of his name?" Or kids simply make up their own guidelines. "If you take more kinds at once, you get a bigger effect, and it's less dangerous because you're taking less of each kind," reasons one 18-year-old football player who has been taking steroids for two years.

Although even the steroid handbook mentions health risks particular to children and adolescents, in the end most young users seem unfazed by the hazards. In one poll, 82 percent said they didn't believe that steroids were harming them much, and, even more striking, 40 percent said they wouldn't stop in any case. Their motto: "Die young, die strong, Dianabol."

The main drawback to steroids, users complain, is that many brands must be administered with huge syringes. The deeper the needle penetrates the muscle, the less juice squandered just under the skin. Inserting the 1 1/2-inch needles into their buttocks or thighs leaves many teens squeamish, and they often rely on trusted friends to do the job. "The first time I tried to inject myself, I almost fainted, and one of my friends did faint," remembers a 19-year-old from Arizona. "Sometimes one of the guys will inject in one side of his butt one day and the other the next. Then, we all laugh at him because he can barely sit down for the next three days."

Local "hard core" gyms, patronized by serious weight lifters, are the social centers of the steroid culture. Teenagers caught up in the bodybuilding craze —typically white, middle-class suburbanites—commonly spend at least three hours a day almost every day of the week there, sometimes working out in the morning before school and again after school is out. Here they often meet 20-to-30-year-old men using steroids to bulk up for power lifting and bodybuilding shows or members of what steroid experts call the "fighting elite" —firefighters, bouncers, even policemen —synthetically boosting the physical strength they need to do their jobs. "Our role model is this older guy, the biggest guy at the gym," says one 17-year-old. "He's not a nice guy, but he weighs 290 pounds without an ounce of fat... that's our goal."

The older steroid veterans not only inspire kids to try the drugs but often act as the youngsters' main source for the chemicals. Sometimes, it's the gym owner who leads kids to a stash of steroids hidden in a back room; sometimes, it's a lifter who keeps the drugs in a dresser drawer at home and slips kids his phone number. Once in a while, it's a doctor or veterinarian who writes out endless prescriptions for the boys or for an unscrupulous coach. And too often, it's overzealous parents who push the drugs on their children. "My stepdad says he's going to start me up on steroids as soon as I'm done growing," says one freshman who wants to play pro football, "But I think he's just joking." Greg Gaa, director of a Peoria, Ill., sports-medicine clinic, says he has gotten calls from up to a dozen parents a year who want him to supply illegal performance enhancers to their children. A vast black market across America guarantees kids ready access to steroids in big cities and small towns alike. Typically, the drugs are shipped via private couriers from sources in other countries. Two order forms obtained by *U.S. News* require a minimum order of $75, offer 14 different steroids (ranging from $15 to $120 per bottle) and promise 48-hour delivery for an extra $20. Though the order forms, sent out six months apart, are identical and obviously the work of the same operation, the company name and address have been changed, apparently to outsmart investigators. In the earlier mailing, it's Mass Machine, located in Toronto. In the later form, it's Gym Tek Training, located in New Brunswick, Canada. Jack Hook, with the U.S. Drug Enforcement Administration in San Diego, describes a sting operation in which undercover agents from the DEA and the California Bureau of Narcotics posing as bodybuilders met up with a European gym owner and ordered $312,000 worth of steroids: the seller was nabbed in February when the shipment arrived via Federal Express.

Sometimes, kids themselves get into the act. Twenty-five percent say they sell the drugs to support their expensive habit. One Virginia 12th grader tells of fellow students who stole steroids from a drugstore where they worked and made "a killing" selling them around school. "Everybody knows you just go to this one guy's locker, and he'll fix you up," says the teen. A typical 100-tablet bottle of steroids—a month's supply—usually runs from $80 to $100 on the black market, but naive high schoolers often pay three times that amount.

"The challenge of getting ahold of the stuff is half the fun," admits one 17-year-old from Iowa, who tells of meeting dealers in parking lots and taste-testing drugs that look like fakes. Drug-enforcement agents estimate that 30 to 50 percent of the illegal muscle builders teens buy are phony. One Chicago-area youth spent $3,000 on what turned out to be a saline solution. Investigators have seized pills that turned out to be penicillin—deadly to some—and phony oils that were poorly packaged and rampant with bacteria. In April, two Los Angeles dealers were convicted of selling a counterfeit steroid that caused stomach pain, vomiting and a drop in blood pressure; the substance was a European veterinary drug used in show animals.

Subbing dangers. Since February 1991, when non-medical steroid distribution became a federal offense punishable by five years in prison, several drugs touted as steroid alternatives have also flourished underground. The top seller this year is a compound called clenbuterol, which is used by veterinarians in other countries but is not approved for any use in the United States. The drug recently led to problems in Spain, where 135 people who ingested it fell ill with headaches, chills, muscle tremors and nausea.

Human growth hormone, the steroid alternative Lyle Alzado used during his failed efforts at an NFL comeback, is medically used to treat dwarfism by stimulating growth. Its price, up to $1,500 for a two-week supply, is formidable, yet 5 percent of suburban Chicago 10th-grade boys surveyed in March by Vaughn Rickert of the University of Arkansas for Medical Sciences claim to have used the hormone. Although the body produces the substance naturally, too much can cause acromegaly, or "Frankenstein's syndrome," which leads to distortion of the face, hands and feet and eventually kills its victim.

Gamma-hydroxybutyrate (GHB) is a dangerous substance now popular among size seekers because it stimulates the release of human growth hormone. It also leads to comas. One Midwestern teen drank a GHB formula before going out to his high-school prom. He never made it. Within 20 minutes, he fell comatose and was rushed to the hospital to be revived. The Centers for Disease Control reports 80 recent hospitalizations from GHB use.

Many of the steroid alternatives that kids turn to come from an unlikely source: the local health-food store. For years, well-meaning coaches have persuaded kids to stay off steroids by opting for legal (and presumably safe) performance aids advertised ad nauseam in muscle magazines and sold in every shopping mall. Kids, happy to find a legal boost, empty their pockets on colorful packages that can cost up to $200 for a month's supply. But chemicals marketed as dietary supplements —essentially as food—undergo far less scrutiny than those marketed as drugs. "We have virtually no idea what's inside some of these products," warns Food and Drug Administration supplement specialist Don Leggett. "Just the other day someone asked about three new chemical compounds, and we couldn't even identify them. The substances aren't even on the books yet." Not long ago, he points out, clenbuterol and GHB were available in some health stores. Leggett is part of a task force now trying to assess the safety of a dozen common ingredients found in the bulking-up formulas, including chromium, boron and plant sterols.

Cracking the culture. Meanwhile, the ambience of gyms and health-food stores serves to cloak the use of performance-enhancing drugs in the veneer of a healthy lifestyle. Since all of the trappings of their world have to do with hard work, fitness and vitality, kids who use the substances see them as just another training aid, not much different from Gatorade or a big steak dinner. "We're not freaks or addicts," asserts one teen. "We're using modern science to help us reach our goals."

Educators agree that users tend to be mainstream kids. "These kids aren't your typical drug abuser," says Dick Stickle, director of Target, the high-school sports association that hosted a meeting in April [1992] of 65 experts who worked to plot a strategy for educating teens about the drugs' risks. "They have goals, they have pride; we've got to play on that pride." The group plans to send a book of guidelines for combatting the use of steroids and other performance enhancers to every secondary school, 37,000 in all.... But reaching secondary schools may not be enough: A Peoria, Ill., teacher was recently taken aback by a fourth grader who said he'd like to try the steroids his sixth-grade brother uses. Previous education efforts have at times backfired; in Oregon, students who learned about the dangers of steroids were more likely to use them than those who didn't. Testing all high-school football players alone would cost $100 million and be nearly useless, since most teens know how to beat the tests with the use of "masking" drugs available underground.

At the forefront of education efforts are Charles Yesalis, professor of health policy at Pennsylvania State University and the nation's premier steroid expert, and Steve Courson, a former NFL star who used steroids. Both say that curbing steroid use requires nothing less than a revamping of American values. "We don't allow our kids to play games for fun anymore," says Yesalis. "We preach that God really does care who wins on Friday night, when we should be teaching our children to be satisfied to finish 27th, if that's their personal best."

Courson, in his recent book, "False Glory," tells of being introduced to steroids at age 18 by a college trainer, using steroids throughout his college and pro career and developing an accelerated heartbeat during his heaviest cycle. He is currently awaiting a heart transplant. "In the NFL, I was nothing more than a highly paid, highly manipulated gladiator. I was spiritually bankrupt," says Courson, now a Pennsylvania high-school football coach. "I want kids to know they can be greater than gladiators, that they can use a sport to learn lessons about life and not let the sport use them."

Ultimately, to reach children, educators will have to crack the secretive steroid subculture. So inviting is the underground world that, according to one study, 1 in 10 users takes steroids primarily out of desire to belong to the tightknit group. Those who opt out are quickly ostracized. Bill, a 17-year-old junior from New England, says he was a wallflower with only a couple of friends before he got into steroids. Two and a half years and 16 cycles of steroid use made him part of the fellowship. But Bill vividly remembers one day last winter: It's the day his parents found a needle he forgot to discard. Since then, he hasn't seen much of his friends. "I had to switch gyms because they were all teasing me about shrinking up and pressuring me to use the stuff," he says. "I never see them now—we don't have anything to talk about anymore—but they're all betting I'll go back on it. Right now, the only way I know I'll stay off steroids is if I can find a guarantee that I'll reach 220 pounds without them. No, make that 230."

POSTSCRIPT

Should the Decision to Use Anabolic Steroids Be Left to Athletes?

There are several reasons why long-term research on steroids is lacking. First, it is unethical to give drugs to people that may prove harmful, even lethal. Also, the amount of steroids given to subjects in a laboratory setting may not replicate what illegal steroid users actually take. Some users take more than 100 times the amount of steroids that are being clinically used.

Second, to determine the true effects of drugs, double-blind studies need to be done. This means that neither the researcher nor the people receiving the drugs know which subjects are receiving the real drug and which are receiving a placebo (an inert substance). This is not practical with steroids, because subjects can always tell if they received the steroids or the placebos. The effects of steroids could be determined by following up with people who are known steroid users. However, this method lacks proper controls. If physical or psychological problems appear in a subject, for example, it cannot be determined whether the problems are due to the steroids or to other drugs the person may have been using. Also, the type of person who uses steroids may be the type of person who has emotional problems in the first place.

Even though the Drug Enforcement Administration estimates the black-market trade in anabolic steroids to be over $400 million a year, one could argue that they are a symptom of a much larger problem. Society emphasizes appearance and performance. From the time we are children, we are bombarded with constant reminders that we must do better than the next person. We are also reminded of the importance of appearance; to either starve ourselves or pump ourselves up (or both) in order to satisfy the cultural ideal of beauty. If we cannot achieve these standards through exercising, dieting, or drug use, then we can try surgery. Steroid use fits into the larger social problem of people not accepting themselves and their limitations.

Problems related to the use of anabolic steroids are described in "Anabolic Steroid Use and Associated Health Risk Behaviors," by Amy Middleman and Robert DuRant, *Sports Medicine* (April 1996) and in "Psychological and Behavioral Effects of Endogenous Testosterone and Anabolic-Androgenic Steroids: An Update," by Michael Bahrke et al., *Sports Medicine* (December 1996). An article that explains why it is difficult, if not impossible, to eliminate the use of anabolic steroids is "A Little Steroid Goes a Long Way," by Ian Anderson, *New Scientist* (October 1, 1994). In "Athletes on Anabolic-Androgenic Steroids," *Physician and Sportsmedicine* (June 1992), Mark Frankle and David Leffers detail a program that they instituted to prevent and reduce health problems related to steroids.

ISSUE 18

Does Drug Abuse Treatment Work?

YES: John B. Murray, from "Effectiveness of Methadone Maintenance for Heroin Addiction," *Psychological Reports* (vol. 83, 1998)

NO: Robert Apsler, from "Is Drug Abuse Treatment Effective?" *The American Enterprise* (March/April 1994)

ISSUE SUMMARY

YES: Psychology professor John B. Murray contends that drug abuse treatment, especially methadone maintenance, has been shown to reduce illegal opiate use, curtail criminal activity, and lower rates of HIV infection.

NO: Assistant professor of psychology Robert Apsler questions the effectiveness of drug abuse treatment and whether or not drug addicts would go for treatment if services were expanded.

Numerous drug experts feel that more funding should go toward preventing drug use from starting or escalating and toward treating individuals who are dependent on drugs. Today, when budget battles loom and taxpayers dispute how their tax monies are spent, the question of whether or not government funds should be used to treat people who abuse drugs is especially relevant. Questions surrounding this debate include: Does drug abuse treatment reduce criminal activity associated with drugs? Will drug addicts stop their abusive behavior if they enter treatment? Will more drug addicts receive treatment than currently do if services are expanded? and, Will the availability and demand for illegal drugs decline?

The research on the effectiveness of drug treatment is mixed. In *The Effectiveness of Treatment for Drug Abusers Under Criminal Justice Supervision* (National Institute of Justice, 1995), Douglas S. Lipton states that drug abuse treatment not only reduces the rate of arrests but also reduces crime and lowers the cost to taxpayers over the long run. Also, it has been shown that illicit drug use is curtailed by drug abuse treatment and that treated drug addicts are better able to function in society and to maintain employment. Perhaps most important, drug treatment may prove beneficial in curbing the escalation of HIV (human immunodeficiency virus), the virus that causes AIDS. The logic here is that when drug users (a high-risk population for HIV) enter treatment, they can be advised about the behaviors that lead to HIV transmission. Drug treatment is less costly than hospitalization and incarceration.

Some experts contend that reports regarding the effectiveness of drug treatment are not always accurate and that research on drug abuse has not been subjected to rigorous standards. Some question how effectiveness should be determined. If a person relapses after one year, should the treatment be considered ineffective? Would a reduction in an individual's illegal drug use indicate that the treatment was effective, or would an addict have to maintain complete abstinence? Also, if illegal drug use and criminal activity decline after treatment, it is possible that these results would have occurred anyway, regardless of whether or not the individual had been treated.

There are a variety of drug treatment programs. One type of treatment program developed in the 1960s is *therapeutic communities*. Therapeutic communities are usually residential facilities staffed by former drug addicts. Although there is no standard definition of what constitutes a therapeutic community, the program generally involves task assignments for residents (the addicts undergoing treatment), group intervention techniques, vocational and educational counseling, and personal skill development. Inpatient treatment facilities, such as the Betty Ford Center, are the most expensive type of treatment and are often based on a hospital model. These programs are very structured and include highly regimented schedules, demanding rules of conduct, and individual and group counseling.

Outpatient treatment, the most common type of drug treatment, is less expensive, less stigmatizing, and less disruptive to the abuser's family than other forms of treatment. Vocational, educational, and social counseling is provided. Outpatient treatment is often used after an addict leaves an inpatient program. One type of treatment that has proliferated in recent years is the self-help group. Members of self-help groups are bound by a common denominator, whether it is alcohol, cocaine, or narcotics. Due to the anonymous and confidential nature of self-help groups, however, it is difficult to conduct follow-up research to determine their effectiveness.

Individuals who are addicted to narcotics are often referred to methadone maintenance programs. Methadone is a synthetic narcotic that prevents narcotic addicts from getting high and eliminates withdrawal symptoms. Since methadone's effects last about 24 hours, addicts need to receive treatment daily. Unfortunately, the relapse rate is high once addicts stop treatment. Because there is much demand for methadone maintenance in some areas, there are lengthy waiting lists.

In the following selections, John B. Murray examines methadone maintenance programs and finds that such drug treatment programs effectively curtail illegal drug use and reduce criminality and the spread of AIDS. Robert Apsler contends that the benefits of drug treatment are not as significant as proponents of drug treatment profess.

YES

John B. Murray

EFFECTIVENESS OF METHADONE MAINTENANCE FOR HEROIN ADDICTION

Summary.—Methadone maintenance programs have effectively reduced heroin dependency and are available in most countries affected by heroin addiction. Methadone, developed in Germany during World War II as a pain killer, does not have the euphoric effects of heroin and the goal of treatment is to substitute methadone for heroin use. Recidivism is probably a life-long risk. Methadone maintenance programs began in the 1960s in the United States in New York City. Once tolerance is developed, it may be used continually without harmful side effects. Dosage is important for effectiveness as are counseling, rehabilitation services, and employment support. Reduction in criminality and AIDS has been associated with methadone maintenance programs.

Many reports in the past few decades have documented the effectiveness of methadone maintenance treatment for heroin addicts (Newman, 1995). This treatment is most often used for opiate addiction and has been the first outpatient treatment that heroin patients would attend reliably (Sorenson, 1996). It began after World War II in community-based programs and now exists in most countries where there is heroin addiction (Ball, Lange, Myers, & Friedman, 1988; Digiusto, Seres, Bibby, & Batey, 1996). Worldwide 250,000 heroin addicts are being treated in such programs (Farrell, Ward, Mattick, Hall, Stimson, Des Jarlais, Gossop, & Strang, 1994). Reviewed here are research on the effectiveness of methadone maintenance for heroin addiction as well as studies indicating contribution to employment, reduction in criminal activity, and improved life style.

Methadone hydrochloride, which has a pharmacological profile similar to morphine, is an opioid developed during World War II in Germany as a substitute pain-killer (Blaine & Renault, 1976). It does not produce euphoria in those who develop tolerance and metabolizes to inactive substances more slowly than morphine thereby extending its action to 24 hours and permitting

From John B. Murray, "Effectiveness of Methadone Maintenance for Heroin Addiction," *Psychological Reports*, no. 83 (1998), pp. 295-300. Copyright © 1998 by *Psychological Reports*. Reprinted by permission of the author and publisher. References omitted.

a dosage per day. The effectiveness of methadone maintenance in reducing use of opiates was first reported in the United States by Dole and Nyswander (1965) and Dole, Nyswander, and Warner (1968) in research at Rockefeller University and Beth Israel Medical Center in New York City. Methadone maintenance can be continued indefinitely on a single dose administered daily without harmful effects (Cushman, 1977; Dole & Nyswander, 1965). Fatal overdose of methadone has occurred more often in those who did not have a prescription and obtained methadone from others (Bell, Digiusto, & Byth, 1992; Cairns, Roberts, & Benbow, 1996).

Methadone maintenance has been extensively evaluated (Dole, 1988; Farrell, et al., 1994; Kirn, 1988; Public Policy, 1991). Many well controlled studies, conducted mostly in the United States, have compared groups on methadone maintenance with control groups over a year or more of treatment and have shown the programs' superiority in reducing, although not always eliminating, use of opiates (Sorenson, 1996). However, evaluations of these programs go beyond reduction of heroin dependency (Ball, et al., 1988; Newman, 1987). Observational studies have indicated that they have an influence in reducing criminal activity of participants (Bell, Hall, & Byth, 1992; Cushman, Trussel, Gollance, Newman, & Bihari, 1976; Dole, et al., 1968; Sechrest, 1979). Those with good psychosocial adjustment more often benefit but also many who come from populations lacking strong social support and from lower social economic status (Sorenson, 1996; Vaillant, 1988). Research has indicated a high incidence of coexisting mental disorders in the patients treated, particularly depression, alcoholism, and antisocial personality disorder (Kosten & Rounsaville, 1986; Milby, Sims, Kauder, Schumacher, Huggins, McLellan, Woody, & Haas, 1996).

Because methadone treatment is effective in reducing needle use, the program has contributed to reducing the risk of HIV infection (Ball, et al., 1988; Brown, Burkett, & Primm, 1988; Cooper, 1989; Katz, Galanter, Lifshutz, & Maslansky, 1995; Public Policy, 1991; Stimmel, 1993). Methadone maintenance does not significantly impair the immune system and it is safe for those with HIV (Wodak, Capelhorn, & Crofts, 1995). It does not complicate pregnancy for the mothers who are in the programs (Blinick, Wallach, Jerez, & Ackerman, 1976; Nadelmann & McNeely, 1996). Effective counseling, rehabilitation services, and employment support are components of effective methadone programs (Farrell, et al., 1994; Sechrest, 1979).

Programs in the United States have focused on long-term use of methadone. The programs aim at voluntary rehabilitation of hard-core addicts who are motivated to escape heroin and its debilitating effect on their health and lifestyle (Alexander & Hadaway, 1982; Belding, Iguchi, Lamb, Lakin, & Terry, 1995, 1996; Bellis, 1993). As they progress in treatment, clients are encouraged to undertake more difficult rehabilitation steps to move away from street drug subcultures in favor of a more stable life style (Cushman, 1977).

These programs are not panaceas and always have been controversial (Dole, 1995; Kirn, 1988; Sorenson, 1996). Patients are often disadvantaged, and rehabilitation may be long with relapses (Sechrest, 1979). The criteria for eligibility vary and often are controlled by government agencies at different levels (Bell, et al., 1992). Some long-term drug abusers do well when methadone is terminated but the majority experience a return of symptoms so recidivism is a lifelong risk (Dole, 1988; Newman, 1987). Approximately 70% of the patients may relapse within one year after they are discharged and with relapse, criminal activities and sharing needle injections may reoccur (Zanis, McLellan, Alterman, & Cnaan, 1996). The programs are designed for maintenance of heroin addicts in a manner similar to that of chemotherapy for other chronic illnesses (Des Jarlais, Joseph, Dole, & Nyswander, 1985).

Since patients often are polydrug users, one particular problem is that others for whom methadone was not prescribed may obtain it from patients (Grapendaal, 1992). Where the programs are well supervised, diversion of methadone to others is less likely (Sorenson, 1996), but the hazards of diversion appear to have been overestimated since methadone is readily available on the black market (Dole, 1995). The demand for illicit methadone results in part from its limited legal availability.

STRUCTURE AND REGULATION OF METHADONE MAINTENANCE PROGRAMS

Methadone maintenance programs may vary in the structure of their treatment (Ball, et al., 1988; Bell, Hall, & Byth, 1992; Bellis, 1993). Length of time in the program varies although it has been significantly related to improvement. Longer stays in treatment have been associated with better outcomes (Farrell, et al., 1994; Stimmel, 1993). French, Zarkin, Hubbard, and Rachal (1993) who interviewed 11,000 addicts in a long-term follow-up of drug abusers in North Carolina reported that time in treatment

was negatively and significantly related to outcome variables and appeared to have a stabilizing effect. The programs were concerned with reducing the use of heroin but patients' polydrug abuse may confound estimates of effectiveness (Belding, et al., 1995). For example, use of cocaine correlated highly with incident of criminality in a study wherein 65% to 70% of 150 drug users were clients in methadone clinics (Grapendaal, 1992).

Dosage is an important factor in effectiveness of the programs (Caplehorn, Bell, Kleinbaum, & Gebski, 1993; Cooper, 1992). Because these treatment programs vary in organization and practices, dosage may vary in different studies (Ball, et al., 1988; Dole, Nyswander, Des Jarlais, & Herman, 1982; Farrell, et al., 1994; Fisher & Anglin, 1987). Dosage in many programs was stabilized at 40 mg despite research data over 15 years indicating that this should be individualized, and that the most effective daily dosage is between 50 and 100 mg (D'Aunno & Vaughn, 1992; Nadelmann & McNeely, 1996). In early research heroin addicts accepted into the programs began as inpatients, and the methadone dosage administered every day began with 10 mg a day and was gradually increased to a tolerance level (Dole & Nyswander, 1965; Dole, et al., 1968). Once the methadone tolerance level was reached. patients could be shifted to outpatient status and maintained on a daily dose of methadone between 50 mg and 100 mg. If taken by someone who has not developed tolerance, a dosage of 70 mg to 75 mg can be fatal. Flexible dosage according to need has been associated with longer stays in treatment.

When supervised by a nurse or medical doctor, administration of methadone is less subject to abuse (Des Jarlais, *et* al., 1985). In most research methadone has been taken in pill or liquid form. Injections may be preferred by patients but it is more likely to be abused if patients are also using cocaine. In a national mail survey of 25% randomly sampled community pharmacies in England and Wales almost 80% of patients used the oral liquid form and 11% used pills (Strang, Sheridan, & Barber, 1996). In one program patients received a daily cup of orange juice in which a methadone diskette was dissolved (Kirn, 1988). The use of injections also may encourage needle sharing and reduce any benefits of methadone maintenance of HIV. Daily visits to the clinic for medication and frequent checks by urinalysis reduce diversion of methadone to others. When patients have proven themselves, take-home medication may be allowed one day or more weekly (Ball, et al., 1988).

Urinalysis is a regular part of the programs as well as a way of monitoring the patients' progress in treatment. In a study of 341 heroin addicts who were applying for acceptance into four clinics in Sydney, Australia, concordance between self-reported use of drugs and the results of urinalysis was acceptably close (Digiusto, et al., 1996). Agreement between self-report and urinalysis was better for heroin than for psychostimulants. Magura, Goldsmith, Casriel, Goldstein, and Lipton (1987) checked the validity of self-reports of drug use against the urinalysis readings in 248 methadone maintenance patients. The two methods complemented each other in that self-reports indicated drug users' problems which were not detected in patients through urinalysis. Self-reports tended to be more accurate for older patients.

Counseling, psychosocial services, and rehabilitation facilities are components of many effective programs (Public Policy, 1991). Employment and employment counseling contribute to the effectiveness of treatment because patients who are without jobs are more likely to slip back into the lifestyle of the drug culture (Platt & Metzger, 1985; Vaillant, 1988). However, psychosocial components may not be the important factors in the effectiveness of programs, and controlled provision of methadone alone may be effective. Because waiting lists were so long, 301 addicts in 22 units sponsored by New York City, who were unable to get into the regular program, were assigned randomly to either an experimental or a control group (Yancovitz, Des Jarlais, Peyser, Drew, Friedmann, Trigg, & Robinson, 1991). Waiting time for an opening in a regular clinic was three months. Both groups received initial medical evaluation. The experimental group received education on the dangers of AIDS and methadone treatment beginning at 20 to 30 mg a day increasing gradually to 80 mg daily but received no counseling or vocational rehabilitation. Urinalysis was used once a month to check on possible use of opiates and indicated there was significant reduction in heroin use for the experimental group versus the control group. The two groups were equivalent in their initial drug use. A higher percentage of the experimental group entered the regular program when an opening occurred.

McClellan, Arndt, Metzger, Woody, and O'Brien (1993) studied the cost-effectiveness of psychosocial services in methadone maintenance programs. In a veterans hospital 92 opiate addicts were randomly assigned to one of three groups who differed in the available psychosocial services. One group received only methadone; in the second group counseling was added to methadone; and the third group received methadone, counseling, family therapy, as well as medical and psychiatric assistance on site. The second and third groups showed significantly more improvement than the first group. The two groups receiving psychosocial assistance showed significant reduction in opiate use and illegal activity, and more of them stayed longer in the program. Minimum treatment with methadone alone appeared effective only for a minority of eligible addicts.

Kraft, Rothbard, Hadley, McLellan, and Asch (1997) also addressed the question of the cost-effectiveness of psychosocial support services in programs. They compared three groups of patients receiving methadone for treatment of opiate addiction, with 100 patients randomly assigned to each of three groups during a 24-wk. clinical trial. One group received only methadone, the second group received methadone along with counseling, and the third group received methadone along with extensive counseling that included family therapy and employment services. Analysis of data at 6 months follow-up showed that the group with extensive counseling had the highest rates of abstinence but their treatment was not as cost-effective as that for a second group, a combination of methadone and moderate amounts of counseling. Methadone alone also was less cost effective as measured by fewer abstinent patients. Cost-effectiveness appeared to be best with the moderate counseling and methadone treatment group but the authors pointed out that there is a level of support below which supplemental services should not fall.

DISCUSSION

Methadone maintenance has demonstrated effectiveness in reducing opiate use in many controlled studies. In addition, reduced criminal activity has been reported and psychosocial adjustment improved in those who remain in the programs. Recently the programs have been credited with reducing HIV on the basis of reduction of patients' opiate use and less frequent sharing of needles.

Methadone maintenance is expensive. Estimates of annual cost per patient vary with the amount of supplemental support offered. This outlay can be considered to be offset somewhat by lower costs in reduced criminal activity, increased employment, and reduction in public assistance. These trade-offs, along with reduction in hospitalization for comorbidity, have not been computed but are involved in estimates of the real cost of methadone maintenance.

The consensus that methadone maintenance is helpful in preventing HIV transmission is encouraging. It is discouraging that many, even most patients, in these programs do not overcome their addiction and must continue in treatment indefinitely, perhaps because methadone reinforces associated physiological and behavioral habits. Better counseling methods may improve the chances of complete recovery and decrease likelihood of relapse. However, details of psychotherapeutic interventions have not been included in reports on these programs so it would be difficult to know how counseling might be introduced or improved. Figures or percentages of vocational rehabilitation have rarely been reported.

To be effective methadone maintenance programs should be oriented towards encouraging participants to remain in treatment. This is not only useful for their health but retention in maintenance programs may be a key to reduced criminal involvement of addicts. Methadone maintenance has provided an alternative to life-long heroin addiction. Success in these programs has grown to include not only reduced opiate use but also less crime in the community, social and vocational rehabilitation, and improved general health. In sum, many realize a more productive and socially acceptable life style. Social stability, especially stable employment, is an effective predictor of long-term outcome.

A major concern for research will be identifying the possible specific defi-ciency in heroin dependency and what to do. Discovery of the process by which methadone blocks the euphoric effects of heroin might be translated into a means of reversing dependency on heroin as well as on cocaine and alcohol. Differences in dosage of methadone might be resolved into minimum and maximum doses with range in between being important for effective treatment. Finally, one more issue addressed in research on the program's effectiveness would be the necessity for total abstinence from all opiates. Those structuring treatment for alcoholism have wrestled with this issue of partial versus total abstinence but it has not been given attention in current research.

NO   Robert Apsler

IS DRUG ABUSE TREATMENT EFFECTIVE?

In early February [1994], the Clinton administration spelled out its national antidrug strategy. Much of the debate over the new program will turn on how much federal support should be made available for treating drug addicts. The administration plans to spend $355 million in new grants for the states to use to treat hard-core drug users, while cutting funds for interdiction. Many years of massive federal investment in interdiction—including involvement of the U.S. military—have failed to reduce the availability of low-cost street drugs. And the policy momentum is now toward shifting federal funds from supply reduction to demand reduction, a move that would benefit treatment and prevention programs. Also, news stories about the administration's deliberations often report on drug treatment programs with long waits for new admissions. What is implied if not stated is that the size of the country's drug abusing population, estimated by the Institute of Medicine to be 5.5 million people, would be significantly reduced if more money were spent for drug abuse treatment.

But missing from the news stories and analyses of proposed antidrug strategies is any frank discussion of the underlying assumption that drug abuse treatment is effective. This assumption is based largely on reports from clinicians and recovered drug addicts. It is encouraged by a growing drug treatment industry and accepted by a public that wishes for a solution to the drug problem. The premise may be accurate, but it is not yet supported by hard evidence. We do not know that drug abuse treatment is effective. Clinicians' reports in other areas have not always been reliable. For example, many medical procedures developed through clinical experience alone have been abandoned when researchers showed, through carefully controlled comparisons, that placebos or other alternatives matched their effectiveness.

With a few exceptions, drug abuse treatment has not been subjected to rigorous tests for effectiveness. Good research doesn't exist for a number of reasons. Researchers are hampered by fundamental conceptual issues. Even

From Robert Apsler, "Is Drug Abuse Treatment Effective?" *The American Enterprise* (March/April 1994). Copyright © 1994 by The American Enterprise Institute, Washington, DC. Reprinted by permission.

defining basic ideas is difficult. There are significant practical obstacles that make conducting research difficult as well, and little federal support for drug treatment research has been available for over a decade.

WHAT IS "DRUG ABUSE TREATMENT"?

One of the conceptual and practical problems of research is the simple fact that no one process or combination of procedures comprises "drug abuse treatment." Nor do the various types of drug programs have much in common beyond the shared objective of reducing drug abuse.

There are four major types of drug treatment. *Residential therapeutic communities* are highly structured residential settings for drug addicts and typically employ a mixture of psychological and behavioral therapies. Duration of treatment varies widely among these programs. *Inpatient/outpatient chemical dependency treatment* begins with a three- to six-week residential stay in a clinic or hospital that uses the Alcoholics Anonymous philosophy. These clients are then encouraged to attend self-help groups for the rest of their lives. A third type, *outpatient methadone maintenance programs,* involves supervised addiction to methadone hydrochloride as a substitute for addiction to other narcotics, such as heroin. Programs may include counseling and other social services for clients. The fourth category, *outpatient nonmethadone treatment,* joins many different types of programs whose main similarity is that they tend not to treat individuals who are dependent on opiates such as heroin, morphine, and codeine.

This four-group classification is crude because the programs within each category differ markedly from each other. For example, methadone maintenance programs differ in the size of the methadone dose, the number and type of additional services provided, the frequency of urine testing, the strictness of program regulation enforcement, and whether clients are permitted to take their methadone dose home. Some programs focus on illicit drug use and criminal activity, while others target the overall functioning of clients. Some demand abstinence from all illicit drugs; others help clients gain control over their drug use. They differ in whether they concentrate on a particular drug and, if they do, on which drug. Some programs rely heavily on professional practitioners; others employ nonprofessionals, often ex-addicts, as counselors. Programs also differ in the clients they serve: those in the private sector cater mainly to employed drug abusers, whose care is covered by health insurance. The public sector programs serve large numbers of indigent clients.

The differences within each of the four major categories of drug programs are so great that information about the effectiveness of one program in a particular category tells us little about the effectiveness of other programs in the same category. In fact, some differences among programs within a classification group may prove to be more important than the differences among the four groups of programs. For example, new evidence shows that the sheer quantity of treatment provided to clients is crucial to a program's effectiveness. Thus, the amount of counseling and auxiliary services provided by a program may be a more important defining characteristic with respect to efficacy than the types of drug abuse it treats, its treatment philosophy, or whether it operates through a residential or outpatient setting.

WHAT IS "EFFECTIVE" TREATMENT?

Just as there is no simple answer to what comprises drug abuse treatment, neither is there an agreed-upon definition of what constitutes *effective* drug abuse treatment. Definitions clash in two important ways. First, strongly held views divide the treatment community on whether abstinence from illicit drug use is necessary. One position holds that successful treatment is synonymous with total abstinence from illicit drugs. The other position holds that treatment is successful if it ends clients' *dependence* on drugs. Continued, moderate drug use is accepted for those clients able to gain control over their drug use and prevent it from interfering with their daily functioning.

Definitions of effectiveness also differ in the number of behaviors they measure. The most common view of effectiveness judges treatment by its ability to reduce the two behaviors most responsible for society's strong reaction against drug abuse: illicit drug use and criminal activity. Others argue that a broader definition of effectiveness is necessary to describe treatment accurately. Advocates of the broader definition believe that treatment should not be considered effective if it can only demonstrate reductions in drug use and illegal activity, since these changes are likely to dissipate rapidly unless clients undergo additional changes. Returning clients who have completed treatment to their previous drug using environment, it is argued, subjects them to the same social and economic forces that contributed to their drug use. According to this view, sustained changes occur only when clients are willing and able to survive and prosper in new environments. To do so, clients must first develop the necessary employment, social, and other skills. Broad definitions of effectiveness usually include: (1) drug abuse, (2) illegal activities, (3) employment, (4) length of stay in treatment, (5) social functioning, (6) intrapersonal functioning, and (7) physical health and longevity.

MOTIVATION AND CRISIS

Without having resolved even basic definitions about drug abuse treatment, the administration is nevertheless proceeding on the assumption that more money for treatment will mean more help. Doing so ignores the fact that we don't know very much in this area and also ignores the little we do know. We don't know much about client differences, for instance. But we do know that a drug addict's motivation for seeking treatment is crucial. Most clinicians believe that successful treatment is impossible if a client does not want help. Addicts must admit the existence of a serious problem and sincerely want to do something about it. Only then will they accept the assistance of clinicians. However, most experts in the drug abuse field reluctantly acknowledge that almost no drug abusers actually *want* treatment. The news reports implying that thousands of needy addicts would enter treatment and soon be on their way to recovery if the country were willing to spend more money and increase the number of drug programs are inaccurate. While waiting lists exist for some programs, others have trouble attracting addicts.

Furthermore, most drug abusers enter treatment when faced with a crisis, such as threats by a judge, employer, or spouse, or a combination of the three. As a result, the drug abuser's objective may be limited to overcoming the current problem. When the crisis has abated, patients often admit they do not intend all drug use to stop. A national survey of admissions to public drug programs from 1979 to 1981 found that pressure from the criminal justice system was the strongest motivation for seeking treatment. Thus, the existence of long waiting lists may tell us more about judges' efforts to find alternatives to incarceration in overcrowded jails than about the actual intentions of drug abusers or the effectiveness of treatment programs.

The assumption that drug addicts enter treatment at a crisis point has another important ramification for interpreting research on the effectiveness of treatment programs. Studies of treatment effectiveness typically measure clients at least twice: when they enter a program and when they complete treatment. If the first measurement occurs during a time of crisis, it will reflect clients' negative circumstances by showing high levels of drug use, criminal behavior, unemployment, and so on. The second measure of clients, taken at the conclusion of treatment, will likely occur after the precipitating crisis has passed or at least lessened. Consequently, a comparison of the measurements taken at the beginning and end of treatment will show significant improvement for many clients. Is this improvement evidence of effective treatment? Or does it merely reflect the natural cycle of a passing crisis? The main problem is that

the research designs used in nearly all drug treatment research cannot separate the effects of treatment from other factors such as these.

RESEARCH PROBLEMS

Questions about drug treatment effectiveness must be answered the same way as similar questions about treatments for the common cold, AIDS, or other ailments, that is, by obtaining evidence that compares the outcomes of treated and untreated individuals. While this may seem obvious, most drug treatment research has neither compared the necessary groups of drug users nor employed the types of research designs capable of producing strong conclusions. In addition, serious measurement and attrition problems weaken the conclusions of most studies of drug treatment effectiveness.

Research design.   Comparisons between drug users who receive treatment and others who do not are almost nonexistent. Researchers study only treated drug users. Yet the observed behavior of drug users who do not enter drug programs reinforces the need for researchers to include untreated addicts in their studies. We have known for years, for instance, that some drug abusers, including heroin addicts, end drug use largely on their own. Researchers have also observed large reductions in drug use among drug abusers waiting for, but not yet receiving, treatment for cocaine abuse.

The phenomenon of people ending their use of highly addictive *legal* substances on their own is well documented. For example, there is mounting evidence that smokers quit on their own at about the same rate as those attending smoking treatment programs. Estimates of remission from alcoholism and alcohol problems without formal treatment range from 45 to 70 percent. No comparable estimate is available for the number of drug users who quit on their own. Until we know the recovery rates for untreated drug abusers, it is impossible to claim that treatment is more effective than the absence of treatment.

Furthermore, the research designs and methods employed in most drug treatment research are so seriously flawed that the results can be considered no more than suggestive. Many investigations study a single group of treated clients and attempt to draw conclusions without a comparison group. Other investigations compare different groups of clients receiving different treatments. In nearly all such cases, the types of clients differ from group to group. Consequently, it is impossible to distinguish between effects caused by treatment differences and effects caused by client differences.

Measuring the outcomes of treatment. One major need in drug treatment research is for an objective, reliable, and inexpensive method for measuring treatment outcomes. Presently most treatment researchers rely entirely on clients' own reports of past and current behavior. Much of the behavior that clients are asked about is illegal, occurred while they were intoxicated, and may have taken place months, and even years, earlier. As one would expect, clients underreport their drug use and other illegal activities. Yet the drug treatment field continues to rely heavily on these dubious reports because there are no suitable alternatives. Chemical tests, such as urine and hair testing, are important adjuncts for validating clients' reports. But at best these tests confirm use or abstinence; they do not indicate anything about quantity or intervals of use. So they are crude measures that cannot easily track patterns of drug use over long periods after a client leaves a treatment program.

Many treatment studies measure clients at the beginning and end of treatment because it is so difficult and expensive to keep track of them after they have completed a program. Some studies do attempt to assess the impact of treatment six months, a year, or even longer after completion. But investigators can seldom locate more than 70 percent of clients, if that. Clients who cannot be contacted are often deceased, in prison, unemployed, and/or homeless. Leaving them out of the studies may skew the findings, making the conclusions appear more positive than is warranted.

Length of treatment. The length of drug abuse treatment is a complex and confusing element in the overall picture of treatment effectiveness. To begin with, simply keeping clients in treatment is a major challenge for many drug programs. Most clients are forced into treatment. And many leave shortly thereafter. Therefore, merely remaining in treatment has become a widely accepted measure of treatment effectiveness. While it makes sense that clients can only benefit from treatment if they remain in a program, there is the risk of confusing happenstance for cause and effect.

Addicts who truly want to change their lifestyles are likely to make many changes. Such changes include entering and remaining in a treatment program, reducing drug use, holding a steady job, eschewing illegal activities, and so on. Other individuals not willing to change their lifestyles are more likely to drop out of treatment after being forced into a drug program. They continue using drugs, do not hold steady jobs, engage in illegal activities, and so on. Thus, to prove that drug programs are effective, researchers must show that (1) drug programs help addicts commit to changing their lifestyles, and/or that (2) the resulting improvement among treated clients is greater than the improvement expected anyway from individuals who have already chosen to change their lifestyles.

Another challenge is determining the length of an optimum stay in a drug treatment program. Most private chemical dependency residential programs used to run for 28 days, though cost-reduction pressures have shortened this time. Outpatient nonmethadone treatment averages roughly six months of once-or-twice-a-week counseling sessions. Some therapeutic communities provide treatment for a year or more, while methadone maintenance programs may involve lifetime participation for clients. How much treatment is enough? Some research shows that methadone clients remain in treatment for an unnecessarily long time. This may mean that programs with waiting lists should consider ending treatment for long-term clients to make room for new ones. The impact of treatment may be much greater on someone receiving treatment for the first time than on an individual who has been on methadone for years.

The complex treatment histories of many drug addicts increase the difficulty of judging treatment effectiveness. Over the course of their addiction careers, typical drug addicts enter several different treatment programs. They may enter the same programs on different occasions for different lengths of time. At

any point during this involved treatment history, addicts may find themselves participating in a study of treatment effectiveness. However, that study is likely to examine only the most recent treatment episode without taking into account previous treatment stays. Perhaps even small amounts of treatment accumulate over time until they influence an individual. Some drug addicts may try different forms of treatment until they find a type of treatment or a particular counselor that helps them. However, existing treatment research cannot disentangle the effects of multiple treatment episodes in different types of drug programs that last for varying amounts of time.

WHAT WE KNOW ABOUT TREATMENT PROGRAMS

Because of research problems, very little is known about the effectiveness of three out of the four categories of drug abuse treatment identified earlier in this article —*residential therapeutic communities, inpatient/outpatient chemical dependency treatment,* and *outpatient nonmethadone maintenance programs.* Surveys of *residential therapeutic communities* have produced promising results, but important questions remain unanswered. Two longitudinal studies of many drug treatment programs reported reductions in drug use and criminal activity among therapeutic community clients who remained in treatment for at least several months. But therapeutic communities are highly selective in at least two ways. First, they appeal only to clients willing to enter a long-term residential setting. Second, most addicts who enter therapeutic communities quickly drop out. Thus, therapeutic communities may influence the drug addiction of only a small and select group of individuals. Furthermore, there is almost no research about the factors that affect success and failure in therapeutic communities.

As for the other two, almost nothing reliable has been produced on *inpatient/outpatient chemical dependency treatment*, though it has become the dominant approach of privately financed inpatient programs. Nor are there reliable findings on *outpatient/nonmethadone treatment*.

The strongest evidence that drug abuse treatment can be effective comes from randomized clinical trials of the remaining category of treatment programs, *methadone maintenance treatment* programs. Randomized clinical trials are powerful studies that randomly assign a pool of subjects to different conditions, such as different types of treatment; researchers are able to conclude that if some groups of subjects improve more than others, the improvement is probably due to the treatment condition, not to preexisting differences among the individuals. The first of three rigorous trials of methadone treatment, a U.S. study conducted in the late 1960s, randomly assigned highly motivated criminal addicts to either a methadone program or a waiting-list group that received no treatment. All 16 addicts on the waiting list quickly became readdicted to heroin, as did 4 addicts in the treatment group who refused treatment. Eighteen of the 20 untreated individuals who became readdicted returned to prison within 1 to 10 months. Only 3 of the 12 addicts who received treatment returned to prison during this period, and their heroin use decreased.

A test in 1984 of a methadone maintenance program in Sweden provides further evidence of treatment effectiveness, though the stringent client selection criteria make it difficult to generalize the findings. Heroin addicts became eligible for this study only after (1) a history of long-term compulsive abuse, and (2) repeated failures to stop, despite documented serious attempts to do so. Thirty-four addicts meeting these eligibility requirements were randomly assigned to either treatment or no-treatment. Two years later, 12 of the 17 drug addicts assigned to treatment had abandoned drug use and started work or studies. The remaining 5 still had drug problems, and 2 had been expelled from the program. Conversely, only 1 of the 17 addicts in the no-treatment group became drug free; 2 were in prison, 2 were dead, and the rest were still abusing heroin.

A very recent randomized clinical trial in the United States compared three levels of methadone treatment: (1) methadone alone without other services, (2) methadone plus counseling, and (3) methadone plus counseling and on-site medical/psychiatric, employment, and family therapy. The results showed that methadone alone was, at most, helpful to only a few clients. The results for clients who received methadone plus counseling were better, and clients who received additional professional services improved most of all. In sum, these three studies demonstrate that methadone treatment has the potential to reduce illicit narcotics use and criminal behavior among narcotics addicts.

To what extent do these findings apply to methadone maintenance programs in general? We do not know, and we must remain skeptical about the level of effectiveness of most methadone programs; their results could be quite different. For example, two of the three studies described above restricted their research to clients who were highly motivated to end their addiction. But methadone programs in this country typically treat individuals who are forced into treatment, many of whom exhibit little desire to change their addict lifestyles. The third study did not restrict the research to highly motivated clients. However, the study took place in a well-funded, stable, hospital-based, university-affiliated setting. Most methadone programs operate on small budgets that severely restrict their ability to provide services and hire qualified staff. Therefore they differ in important ways from the study program.

To learn about the impact of less extraordinary methadone programs, a U.S. General Accounting Office study examined the efficacy of 15 methadone programs in a five-state survey. The survey found that (1) the current use of heroin and other opiates ranged from 2 to 47 percent of clients enrolled in the clinics, (2) many clients had serious alcohol problems, (3) clients received few comprehensive services despite high rates of unemployment, and (4) clinics did not know if clients used the services to which they were referred. Other research has shown that many methadone programs administer doses of methadone smaller than those known to be effective. In sum, typical methadone programs differ significantly from the methadone programs evaluated in the randomized clinical trials discussed above, and they may be less effective.

CONCLUSIONS

Drug abuse treatment features prominently in discussions of how the Clinton administration should respond to the country's concern about drug abuse. Yet little hard evidence documents the effectiveness of treatment. Almost nothing is known about (1) the effectiveness of three of the four major treatment modalities, (2) the relative effectiveness of different versions of each major treatment modality, and (3) the prognosis for different types of drug abusers. Instead of answering questions, drug treatment research raises troublesome issues for policymakers. How can treatment work when clinicians claim that success depends on clients wanting help, and we know that most clients are forced into treatment? What happens to drug abusers who never seek treatment?

What can be said with some certainty is that (1) methadone maintenance programs can help clients who are highly motivated to end their drug abuse, and (2) a model program that provides counseling along with methadone has been able to help less well-motivated clients. But there is little good news here since most drug addicts do not want to end their drug use, and typical methadone maintenance programs may not possess the resources to duplicate the impact of the model program.

The absence of convincing evidence about the effectiveness of drug abuse treatment results from the lack of rigorous evaluations. Only a handful of randomized clinical trials have been conducted to date. More need to be done, and valid and comprehensive measures of treatment effectiveness need to be employed in these studies in order to end the reliance of treatment researchers on clients' self-reports of sensitive behaviors. Treatment research also needs more post-treatment follow-ups to show that treatment effects persist once clients leave their programs.

Finally, researchers must learn what happens to untreated drug abusers. Past and current research focuses almost exclusively on drug abusers who enter treatment. This research does not make comparisons between treated and untreated drug abusers and cannot answer the most fundamental question of all: is treatment more cost-effective than no treatment?

POSTSCRIPT

Does Drug Abuse Treatment Work?

Much of the research on drug treatment effectiveness is inconclusive; furthermore, researchers do not agree on what the best way is to measure effectiveness. Determining the effectiveness of drug treatment is extremely important because the federal government and a number of state governments are now contemplating increasing the amount of funding allocated to drug treatment. Many experts in the drug field agree that much of the money that has been used to deal with problems related to drugs has not been wisely spent. To prevent further waste of taxpayer funds, it is essential to find out if drug treatment works before funding for it is increased.

Another concern related to this issue is that addicts who wish to receive treatment often face many barriers. One of the most serious barriers is that there is a lack of available treatment facilities. In *Improving Drug Abuse Treatment*, NIDA Research Monograph No. 106 (1991), C. L. Veatch states that there are an estimated 291,000 drug abusers in California but fewer than 15,000 licensed treatment slots for methadone patients. Compounding the problem is the fact that many communities resist the idea of having a drug treatment center in the neighborhood, even though there is little research on the effects of treatment facilities on property values and neighborhood crime rates. Another barrier to treatment is cost, which, with the exception of self-help groups, is high. Furthermore, some addicts avoid organized treatment altogether for fear that if they go for treatment, they will be identified as drug abusers by law enforcement agencies.

Many addicts in treatment are there because they are given a choice of entering either prison or treatment. Are people who are required to enter treatment more or less likely to succeed than people who enter treatment voluntarily? Early studies showed that treatment was more effective for voluntary clients. However, a study conducted by the federal government of 12,000 clients enrolled in 41 publicly funded treatment centers found that clients referred by the criminal justice system fared as well as if not better than voluntary clients in terms of reduced criminal activity and drug use.

In "Experts Fear Get-Tough View of Drug Treatment May Backfire," *American Medical News* (September 16, 1996), Christina Kent reports that the medical community supports expanding addiction treatment services because it believes that such expansion would still be cost-effective over the long term. Marsha Rosenbaum et al., in "Treatment as Harm Reduction, Defunding as Harm Maximization: The Case of Methadone Maintenance," *Journal of Psychoactive Drugs* (September 1996), argue that methadone maintenance reduces drug use, crime, and the risk of HIV.

ISSUE 19

Are Antidrug Media Campaigns Effective?

YES: Barry McCaffrey, from *Testing the Anti-Drug Message in Twelve American Cities: National Youth Anti-Drug Media Campaign, Phase I (Report No. 1)* (September 1998)

NO: David R. Buchanan and Lawrence Wallack, from "This Is the Partnership for a Drug-Free America: Any Questions?" *Journal of Drug Issues* (Spring 1998)

ISSUE SUMMARY

YES: Barry McCaffrey, director of the Office of National Drug Control Policy (ONDCP), argues that the attitudes and behaviors of young people regarding drug use are affected by antidrug media campaigns. He therefore supports the federal government's spending millions of dollars for antidrug public service announcements.

NO: David R. Buchanan, an assistant professor of community health studies, and professor of health education Lawrence Wallack argue that antidrug media campaigns are not only ineffective but may result in a backlash. They maintain that many drug-prevention messages are inaccurate, and they question the value of the scare tactics that are part of most antidrug announcements.

There has been a significant proliferation in drug use by young people since the beginning of the 1990s. Because drug use can have a negative effect on one's health, interpersonal relationships, emotional and social development, family relations, and academic success, most people would agree that reducing drug use is a desirable, if not necessary, goal. However, what is the best strategy for achieving this goal? Experts disagree on the best course of action to take to decrease drug taking. Some experts feel that more effort should be put into enforcing laws against drug use. Others believe that the federal government should make a greater commitment to stopping drugs from entering the country. Still others maintain that more money should be used for drug education.

Among the different approaches being explored for curtailing drug use by young people is the use of antidrug public service announcements. The question being debated in this issue is whether or not antidrug public service announcements affect drug-taking behavior. Do young people who watch announcements that denounce and ridicule drug use alter their drug-taking behavior? Moreover, should the federal government spend millions of tax-payer dollars on antidrug public service announcements, especially if it is unclear that they have any effect?

Assessing the effectiveness of antidrug public service announcements is problematic. Many young people seem to scoff at antidrug advertisements. Yet could these advertisements have a subtle effect on their attitudes? Teen-agers may laugh at the advertisements, but the idea that drug use is harmful might be planted in the heads of these young people. Also, although antidrug announcements appear to be aimed at teenagers, preteens could also be affected by these messages.

According to the researchers for the annual Monitoring the Future Survey of drug use by 8th-, 10th-, and 12th-grade students, one of the several factors behind the increase in drug use by young people in the 1990s was the lack of attention in the media to the detrimental effects of drugs. News accounts and stories detailing the physical, emotional, and social problems caused by drugs were shown less frequently. Consequently, say the researchers, many young people became less concerned and aware of the potential problems of using drugs. Public service messages highlighting what may occur because of drug use is an attempt to combat this previous neglect by the media.

Supporters of the antidrug media campaign acknowledge that this is just one element of a much larger effort to halt drug use by young people. They affirm that community-based prevention activities and school-based drug education programs need to be continued. Supporters of reducing drug use through media campaigns also feel that the media *promote* drugs in various ways. For example, a number of musical groups appear to advocate drug use through their songs. Also, although movies such as *Trainspotting* and *The Basketball Diaries* illustrate the personal problems that can result from drug use, others show drug use in a matter-of-fact way. Hence, some young people may discount the potential hazards of drug use.

Critics of antidrug public service announcements feel that these messages are not effective because many young people do not view them seriously. It is also argued that these announcements sometimes lack credibility because the effects of drugs are exaggerated. Thus, they are disregarded by young people who have used drugs without experiencing the problems that are depicted.

In the following selections, Barry R. McCaffrey argues in favor of the federal government's spending millions of dollars on antidrug media messages because he feels that they may have a positive effect on the attitudes and behaviors of young people toward drug use. David R. Buchanan and Lawrence Wallack maintain that the antidrug media campaign is not only ineffective but may result in increased drug use because the messages are based on scare tactics and inaccuracies.

YES

Barry McCaffrey

TESTING THE ANTI-DRUG MESSAGE IN TWELVE AMERICAN CITIES

THE MEDIA CAMPAIGN DESIGN

Existing research provides the foundation for the initial design of the [National Youth Anti-Drug] Media Campaign. Data from the *Monitoring the Future* study reveal an apparent link between the erosion of anti-drug attitudes among youth since the early 1990s and increases in drug use among this group (Johnston, 1996). Early research suggested that mass media may have a role in decreasing drug use, and that long-term exposure to anti-drug images, ideas, and attitudes is needed to foster anti-drug behavior among youth (Becker, 1978; Schramm, 1954). However, research conducted in the 1980s and 1990s found that few media campaigns successfully met their objectives because, among other things, they were poorly disseminated and were not targeted to the interests of their intended audience (Flay and Sobel, 1983; Shilling and McAlister, 1990).

ONDCP [Office of National Drug Control Policy] has drawn from this body of research to structure its Media Campaign. The Media Campaign was proposed by the President and approved by Congress. Under the Appropriations Act of 1998, the House and Senate approved funding (H.R.2378 and S.1023) for "a national media campaign, to reduce and prevent drug abuse among young Americans." The legislation also states that in order to comply with the Government Performance and Results Act of 1993, "the Director shall report to Congress within two years on the effectiveness of the national media campaign based upon the measurable outcomes provided to Congress previously."

ONDCP began implementing its Media Campaign in January 1998, in 12 target sites, by using purchased slots on radio and television, as well as space on billboards and in the print media, for a series of anti-drug use advertisements. The radio and TV advertisements were designed to air during prime

From Barry McCaffrey, Office of National Drug Control Policy, *Testing the Anti-Drug Message in Twelve American Cities: National Youth Anti-Drug Media Campaign, Phase I (Report No. 1)* (September 1998). Washington, DC: Government Printing Office, 1998.

time and other times when youth and parents would be listening or watching, as opposed to very late evening and other time slots typically reserved for public service announcements (PSAs). The timeframe for launching the first phase of the Media Campaign did not allow for the development of new advertisements; thus, the messages are the same as earlier PSAs developed by the Partnership for a Drug-Free America (PDFA). ONDCP and the PDFA are now collaborating on new advertisements, which are being developed especially for the Phase II and Phase III Media Campaigns. The new advertisements will be based on recommendations included in the National Youth Anti-Drug Media Campaign Communication Strategy Statement (Porter Novelli, 1998).

It is important to note that this Media Campaign, like other public information or health promotion campaigns, employs an array of ongoing efforts that include supplemental public education and information initiatives to encourage community-based prevention activities. Furthermore, while this Media Campaign is under way other media interventions will occur (e.g., locally sponsored media campaigns); thus, in evaluating the Media Campaign, one must recognize that youth and their parents are being exposed to advertisements other than those paid for by ONDCP. For example, during Phase I, 12 target sites are being exposed to the official intervention (i.e., the Media Campaign), as well as to other advertisements and information campaigns ongoing in the communities. Twelve comparison sites, though not targeted by the Media Campaign, are exposed to other advertisements as well. The primary focus of the Phase I Media Campaign evaluation is to determine if there are changes

in awareness and attitude toward drugs resulting from exposure to paid anti-drug messages compared with changes resulting from exposure to free public service messages on local radio and TV stations. The evaluation will make every effort to distinguish between effects resulting from the Media Campaign and those resulting from other ongoing public information and education campaigns in the communities studied.

The Media Campaign is designed to reach five target groups: youth, ages 9–10 (13% of the Media Campaign effort); youth, ages 11–13 (25%); youth, ages 14–18 years (12%); partners (40%); and other influential adults (10%). The following are the goals of the Media Campaign:

- To educate and enable America's youth to reject illegal drugs;
- To prevent youth from initiating use of drugs, especially marijuana and inhalants; and
- To convince occasional users of these and other drugs to stop using drugs.

Through realistic portrayals, the Media Campaign is designed to show the harmful effects of drugs and the benefits of a drug-free lifestyle, make drug use appear to be abnormal by reminding people that most youth do not use drugs, and empower parents with information and strategies to prevent their children from using drugs.

The Media Campaign has three Phases: Phase I was a 25-week pilot test airing from January through May 1998 in 12 target sites. The Phase I evaluation also included 12 matched comparison sites where the Media Campaign was not launched but where other advertisements or PSAs were being aired. Phase I, described as the "learning lab" phase, targeted youth between the ages of 9 and

18 and the adults who influence them, such as parents, teachers, and mentors. As mentioned above, Phase I included airing paid advertisements developed by the PDFA on radio and TV, as well as in print media, and a matched donation of advertising time. In some sites, billboards and book covers also were used, if extra funding was available. These advertisements emphasized prevention of entry-level drug use (marijuana and inhalants) in all target sites and focused on local epidemics of heroin, cocaine, and methamphetamine use, where appropriate.

Phase II is a national anti-drug use media campaign that began in July 1998.... As in Phase I, radio and TV slots, billboards, and print-media spots constitute advertising. As Phase II matures, other media such as magazines and the Internet will be included. New media ads will be developed and implemented as the Media Campaign continues through Phases II and III. The effort is nationwide, rather than being limited to the 12 target sites of Phase I. Some new advertisements specially developed for the Media Campaign are being introduced during the first few months of Phase II.

Lessons learned from Phase I and Phase II will be used to inform important decisions about the focus, messages, and audiences to be targeted, and the most effective delivery vehicles to be used as the nationwide Phase III Media Campaign is developed, launched, and updated during the next 4 years....

Media Influences on Youth

This section presents findings on the types of media and the drug-related media information that youth indicate as being influential.

General information and mixed messages The majority of youth in target and comparison sites mentioned television shows and movies as general sources of information (both anti- and pro-) about drugs. They regarded the media as conveying mixed messages, citing TV shows with anti-drug or anti-alcohol messages being aired back-to-back with beer commercials as an example. Youth noted many TV shows that included profanity, violence, drinking, smoking, drug use, and poor values. They thought that, in general, TV glamorized violence and drug use; TV characters would use drugs, but there would always by a happy ending.

Pro-drug media messages Youth mentioned being aware of relatively few pro-drug messages in the media compared with anti-drug messages. But they were aware of ads for beer on TV, billboards and magazines advertising cigarettes, and cigarette use in movies. Young people understand very clearly that these ads are trying to sell them something, and high school youth in particular are aware that the ads are promoting an image. In a non-urban high school focus group, one participant said "some things you listen to or watch, you kinda say, 'ooh', you know, 'they're kinda cool, I kinda wanna be like that, and if I wanna be like that I have to do that'... "

Most young people were critical of cigarette use in films: members of a non-urban 7th–9th grade focus group questioned why smoking in films was necessary and saw it as "adding on to the problem if they're, you know, glamorizing smoking." Participants in a non-urban 4th–6th grade group thought that beer ads should be removed from TV and that cigarette ads should be removed from magazines.

Radio, music tapes and compact discs, and videos were seen as focusing heavily on drugs and sex, and youth described them as almost totally pro-drug. "Heavy metal" groups like Acid Rock are named after drugs and music groups like "Kiss" reportedly have members who are known to use drugs. A non-urban focus group in Denver mentioned the Internet as a source of drug information. In particular, youth reported that some Internet personal home pages had directions for making a "bong" (a device used to smoke marijuana). An urban high school student in one focus group said that even if young people did not want to drink or smoke, some of the neighborhood billboards had advertisements that tempted them to start.

One non-urban focus group in Portland summarized media influence by saying "You learn a lot about drugs on TV. TV teaches you how to use drugs, drink booze, and smoke cigarettes." Elementary school children in some focus groups mentioned having seen, for example, *Menace* movies on how to "cook crack"; intravenous drug use; using rubber to "wrap the arm" on "The Promised Land" [television show]; marijuana use on "Murphy Brown" [television show]; and the movie *Kingpin* that showed how to manufacture homemade water pipes (used for smoking marijuana) from ordinary objects. They also mentioned the promotion of majors sports events by alcohol and tobacco companies.

Anti-drug media messages Although they acknowledged that there was some good anti-drug programming on radio and television, most youth reported that the pro-drug messages simply overwhelmed the anti-drug messages. However, they felt that anti-drug programming could be effective if it was of high quality and was shown often enough. They mentioned movies like *The Class of 1999* and *The Goat* and television documentaries featuring real drug addicts as examples of effective anti-drug programming.

Age group differences Older teens understood that movies such as the *Menace* series and TV shows such as "Full-House" and "Jerry Springer" have a graphic anti-drug message and depict lives ruined by drugs. Younger children, however, often interpreted these graphic movies and shows simply as "pro-drug." Irony and symbolism were lost on these younger viewers, who are very literal. For them, the image is the message. For example, elementary students generally reported how they acted out what they saw in movies and ads. For example, they would pretend to be "cutting" cocaine by using chalk dust to simulate cocaine, cut up dried glue as pretend "rock," and even act out the *Frying Pan* ad in the play kitchen at school.

Middle school and high school students of all backgrounds understood how literal younger children were; older youth indicated their wish to protect younger children and strongly objected to any movie with a graphic drug theme, even an anti-drug theme, being shown during prime time. For example, many high school students had seen the film *Pulp Fiction*. Although they thought it was "fun," they also understood that it portrayed drugs positively to an extreme degree, and were outraged that it was shown on prime time TV where young children could see it. Even drug-experienced youth from neighborhoods where drugs are the norm felt this way.

Youth critique of anti-drug advertising Youth of all ages were aware of anti-drug ads in the media. Young people in both target sites and comparison sites reported seeing anti-drug messages. Overwhelmingly, youth mentioned TV and the movies, with some mentions of radio and a few of posters or billboards. For the most part, older students (7th–12th graders) were highly critical of these ads: "you don't really listen" [to the message] and "those who say 'don't use drugs' are using drugs" (Atlanta urban high school student). Some participants pointed out that some people perceived the anti-drug ad as "just a commercial" and would change the channel because they do not like commercials.

In the 4th–6th grade groups, it was difficult to elicit reactions to ads. Some participants remembered images from a few ads but typically did not offer reactions to them. When probed, some of the youth said they thought such ads might be effective. In 7th–9th grade groups, participants were attracted by ad images (for example, Joe Camel) but were ambivalent about the effects of the ads. It was this age group that most often said anti-drug information should come from parents—not from ads; this age group also reported worrying that ads may induce youth to try drugs. Youth in 7th–9th grades frequently reported that they thought the anti-drug ads were intended for significantly younger children. By 10th–12th grade, participants watched and clearly remembered ads but typically found them laughable. They were articulate about feeling disconnected from the people depicted in the ads. In general, the high school focus groups reported that

the ads did not influence them but might be effective with much younger children.

A number of participants said, in effect, that anti-drug messages in the media seemed remote to them. An urban high school student in Sioux City stated "It's like a nickel a day to save the starving families in Rwanda. I have nickel a day; I don't pay 'em because you're not connected with what's going on. It's no way involved in your life. You just let it go in one ear and out the other." Two other participants in the same group said, "It has to be more real than just on TV because everyone knows TV's not real," and "TV is not teaching them. If something happens to their friend or interview someone like it's personal, then [they] will listen."

A number of youth emphatically said that ads would have no effect—except, perhaps, to make people use drugs more —because, as one student said, "people do what they want to anyway." Middle and high school students joked among themselves about anti-drug ads; they laughed about them in the focus groups and mimicked the ads while giggling at their effects. The words "funny" and "stupid" were frequently used by middle school and high school students to describe ads they had seen.

These responses were distributed almost equally across urban and non-urban groups, although urban groups seemed to be more cynical about the ads. Participants in one urban focus group were especially negative about the use of celebrities in ads. One person commented, "I wouldn't even listen, 'cause I don't see them [celebrities] at home everyday. You know what I mean?" This sentiment was widely shared by other youth. The findings across target site focus groups were surprisingly similar to findings across comparison site focus groups.

Intermediate Findings for Youth
The following sections report the intermediate site visit findings from focus groups with elementary, middle, and high school students in each of the 12 target sites. Youth were asked to describe how and when they were exposed to anti-drug messages in the media, including television, radio, printed material, and the Internet. They also were asked about their levels of awareness of anti-drug messages, what impacts these messages had, how effective and culturally relevant these ads were perceived to be, and how ads might be improved. Although youth in comparison sites also were asked to comment on anti-drug ads they had seen in their communities (e.g., PSAs or ads run through local campaigns), this discussion focuses on the reactions of youth in the 12 ONDCP Media Campaign target sites.

Youth Awareness of Anti-Drug Ads
Target site youth were keenly aware of increases in the number of times anti-drug ads were being shown in their cities and were cognizant of increases in the number of different anti-drug ads they had seen on television and on billboards. Radio, print media, and the Internet were rarely mentioned. Youth in each target site could name, on average, approximately 13 TV ads they had seen, while youth in comparison sites could name, on average, only 5. Memory of sponsorship was not a good indicator of awareness because of variation in the way sponsorship was "tagged." In some sites, for example, sponsorship was displayed in large letters, and in others, all that was shown was a small, difficult-to-read symbol at the bottom of the screen. Sometimes multiple sponsorships were displayed or telephone numbers were included for those interested in obtaining additional information. While youth's specific descriptions of advertisements were indicative of their seeing ads that were part of the ONDCP Media Campaign, many youth did not mention being aware of the "Partnership for a Drug-Free America/Office of National Drug Control Policy" tag.

Older youth could name more ads than younger youth, and they had a better understanding of the intended message. For example, San Diego 4th–6th graders could remember parts of (but could not name) only one cartoon ad. Urban 7th–9th graders mentioned a few ads—both anti-smoking and anti-drug; while both non-urban and inner city 10th–12th grade groups recalled six different TV anti-drugs ads. The non-urban high school students correctly recalled PDFA and ONDCP sponsorship; their inner-city counterparts did not recall the sponsors but remembered the ads in detail. As was the case at baseline, younger youth were at times confused by the ads and were as likely to discuss anti-smoking ads as they were to talk about the ONDCP ads. For example, while most Baltimore non-urban 4th–6th graders remembered the messages in the ads, they were sometimes confused about which drug the ads referred to. Portland urban 4th–6th graders had only limited recall of anti-drug ads, and several focus group members focused on the negative effects on cigarette smoking. In contrast, Portland's middle and high school focus groups recalled more ads, understood the messages, and were not confused about which ads referred to illicit drugs and which referred to cigarettes.

Youth who perceived that anti-drug television ads were "dumb" or "stupid" often were the same youth who had watched these ads most intently and had the strongest reaction to them. Research has shown that a strong negative reaction to these kinds of ads may be indicative of youth's awareness of the ads and the fact that they are paying attention to them (Eagly and Chaiken, 1993; Reeves, Newhagen, Maibach, Basil, and Kurtz, 1991).

Youth Perceptions of Impact and Effectiveness of Ads

At the time of the intermediate site visits, youth participating in focus groups were asked to assess the impact of ONDCP Media Campaign ads, in terms of the influence these ads had on their own thinking and on their intent to act as well as on their view of how effective these ads were in influencing youth. Across all age groups, youth expressed mixed views and qualified their responses, noting that the ads could be useful in certain ways for themselves or for specific groups of people, but not necessarily useful for everyone.

Some youth in all age groups cited positive impacts of the television ads. (Even though they were asked about other media outlets such as radio, print, and the Internet, their responses almost always pertained to what they saw on television.) For some youth, the ads made drugs seem scary, made them think about potential adverse health effects, gave them a mental image about drugs that stayed with them, or showed them how to resist peer pressure. However, there were equal numbers of youth who stated that they did not pay attention to the ads, the ads would not influence them because they had already made up their minds, or

peer pressure was more influential than ads at middle or high school age.

Some 4th–6th grade children expressed uneasiness about the ads, believing that they might introduce youth to drugs and encourage them to experiment. Additionally, youth of all ages said they did not believe the ads would influence those who already were users, but they felt the ads might impact children between 8 and 12 years of age or those deciding whether or not to use. Very few of the youth in any age group had discussed the ads with their parents or among themselves, and only youth from a few sites had discussed the ads with their teachers.

While a number of focus group youth did perceive that anti-drug ads could be effective, they also spoke about the competing influences in their environment that encourage drug use. Youth of all ages reported that they receive messages encouraging drug use from four major sources including peers, the media, family, and the neighborhood. Youth in all sites mentioned peers and schoolmates as the most likely source of pro-drug information. Peers promoted the message that although drugs may be dangerous, they are "cool." As they had done at baseline, the youth who participated in focus groups during intermediate visits discussed exposure to pro-drug messages from TV and popular music. They talked about the cleverness of beer commercials and the promotion of major sports events on TV by alcohol and tobacco companies.

Messages encouraging drug use also came from the family and neighborhood. Youth in nine target sites mentioned having personal experience with close family members and adult relatives who use drugs. Participants in one-quarter of the youth focus groups specifically mentioned parents who use drugs, and the same proportion of youth mentioned older siblings and friends who use drugs. Although this pressure was more intense for inner-city youth, it also was prevalent in non-urban communities. Inner-city youth have the additional pressure of strong pro-drug messages from their neighborhood. Inner-city youth reported strong economic and social pressure to sell drugs, even if they do not use.

NO

David R. Buchanan and
Lawrence Wallack

THIS IS THE PARTNERSHIP FOR A
DRUG-FREE AMERICA: ANY QUESTIONS?

The paper examines the impact and possible unintended side effects of the privately sponsored Partnership for a Drug-Free America (PDFA) media campaign to reduce illicit drug abuse. The paper describes the history, goals, organization, production processes, and process and outcome evaluations of the PDFA advertising campaign. It also reviews major criticisms that have been leveled at the PDFA campaign, including its dissemination of false information, the narrow scope of its message, a number of unintended iatrogenic side-effects, potential conflicts of interest arising from the sources of its funding, and the agenda-setting function of the PDFA campaign in defining which drugs are dangerous and how the attendant problems should be addressed.

INTRODUCTION

There is a prevailing belief in American society—perhaps more a desperate wish—that information is the "magic bullet" to solve our drug problems. If we could just get the right information to the right people in the right way for the right number of times, then seemingly dangerous or unhealthy behaviors could be eliminated. There is no clearer manifestation of this belief than the Partnership for a Drug-Free America (PDFA). For more than a decade, the PDFA has sought to generate a $1-million-a-day media campaign, creatively packaged by seasoned advertisers, to deliver the right message to the American public.

Politically, the PDFA media campaign is the perfect strategy in many respects. It capitalizes on our belief in education (although 30-second, fear-oriented media spots might not reasonably be considered serious education). It reinforces the notion that America's drug problems can be resolved through changing individual attitudes, without addressing fundamental social conditions such as poverty and discrimination. And it takes the heat off of legal —and widely advertised—drugs such as alcohol and tobacco, which are far more dangerous and costly to society. To wit, according to the most authoritative estimates, cigarette smoking causes 320,000 premature deaths annually, alcohol another 200,000 premature deaths every year, yet according to the federal Office of National Drug Control Policy (ONDCP), the total number of deaths for all illegal drugs combined *rose* to a total of 14,000 in 1994 (ONDCP 1997; Surgeon General 1991; Ravenholt 1984; Trebach 1987).

This paper examines the work of the PDFA. It raises practical questions about its effectiveness and ethical questions about its strategy and implications. It challenges the work of the PDFA by bringing to light the implicit assumptions of their mass mediated messages. Fundamental to the analysis is the question of whose interests are being served by PDFA's approach. "Unselling drugs," as the PDFA attempts to do, is a laudable enterprise and on the surface a seemingly significant public service. But the relationship of the PDFA to alcohol, tobacco, pharmaceutical, advertising, and mass-media industries confounds their intents and provokes unavoidable questions about the differences between public versus private interests and public health versus public relations.

The article begins with a brief description of the PDFA, its history, goals, organization, production process, output, and evaluations of its effectiveness. We then review the major concerns raised by critics of the PDFA. Supporters of the PDFA see it as the quintessential example of the American spirit of voluntarism and service to the country, successfully harnessed to the discipline of free market principles. Critics see the PDFA as a self-serving front for the advertising industry and other private corporations, deflect-

ing both attention and material resources from more serious responses to America's alcohol and other drug problems. This paper reviews and discusses these competing claims.

DESCRIPTION OF THE PARTNERSHIP FOR A DRUG-FREE AMERICA

History

People may be surprised to learn that the PDFA is an entirely privately funded mass-media campaign created by professional marketing personnel, with no other organizational base or purpose. It is financed entirely through donations from large corporations, advertising agencies, and private foundations.

Started in 1986, the PDFA is the brainchild of Phil Joanou, then chairman of the Los Angeles advertising agency, Daley & Associates. Joanou introduced the idea of creating the PDFA at the 1986 annual meeting of the American Association of Advertising Agencies (AAAA).

To put this occasion in context, 1986 was the year that college basketball star Len Bias (University of Maryland) and pro football star Don Rogers (Cleveland Browns) died within 8 days of each other from cocaine overdoses, the use of crack cocaine had become much more widespread, and President and Mrs. Reagan launched a new War on Drugs. Media coverage of America's drug problems leaped from obscurity to front-page headlines (Merriam 1989). The Washington *Post* had seven stories on drugs in 1985, but over 400 stories on drugs in 1986 (Boldt 1992). *Newsweek* ran an unprecedented six front-page cover stories on drugs in 1986. On television, we saw such widely viewed news programs as CBS's "48 Hours on Crack Street" (one of the most widely watched news documentaries in television history, with more than 15 million viewers), ABC's "A Plague Upon the Land," and NBC's "One Nation, Under Siege." The nation was aroused. President Reagan signed the Omnibus Anti-Drug Abuse Act in 1986, which has since become the vehicle for more than a 10-fold increase in federal funding for anti-drug efforts.

Against this backdrop, Joanou asked the AAAA for a $300,000 grant of seed money to launch what was originally called the Media-Advertising Partnership for a Drug-Free America. Based on discussions with leading advertising agencies and campaign consultants, the PDFA was originally conceived as a temporary 3-year effort that would require $1.5 billion worth of advertising to achieve success in "unselling drugs" (Alter 1987; Colford 1988a). With money from the AAAA, the PDFA shortly thereafter set up its offices in New York City and hired its first Chief Executive Officer, Dick Reilly, and president, Tom Hedrick. After a series of minor delays (Alter 1987), the first PDFA ads were aired on April 13, 1987 (Associated Press 1992).

During the first 3 years, the PDFA generated about $150 million worth of donated advertising placements each year, for a total of $434 million over the 3-year period (PDFA 1992). Although this amount was far short of their original, ambitious $1.5 billion goal, it is nonetheless impressive. Since then, the directors of the PDFA have set their expectations on the current goal of attaining $1 million worth of advertising every day, or $365 million over the course of 1 year (see figure 1). In response to recent increases in drug use among youth, Disney's ABC-TV gave the PDFA

$100 million worth of airtime in 1 month alone—one ad per hour during the entire month of March 1997—as part of a concerted 'march against drugs' media effort (Goldman 1997).

Goals

The goals for the PDFA have been variously stated. In their campaign literature the PDFA has identified three major objectives: (1) to reduce demand for drugs by changing attitudes through media communications, (2) to track changes in attitudes toward illegal drugs, and (3) to evaluate the impact of PDFA messages on attitude changes (PDFA 1992). In a personal interview with PDFA President Tom Hedrick,... he stated that the most clearly defined objective for the PDFA is in management terms: to attain $1 million worth of advertising every day. They project that this level of advertising will ensure that every single American receives at least one anti-drug message every single day (Colford 1989b).

One million dollars a day is a staggering sum. In relative terms, the PDFA is now the second largest advertiser in America, second only to McDonald's, which spends approximately $450 million per year (Levine 1991). The PDFA's corner on media space is about five times that spent selling Coca-Cola™ (Levine 1991).

Beyond monetary goals, the PDFA proclaims that its mission is to unsell drugs. This theme has been variously stated as:

- "to produce a fundamental reshaping of social attitudes toward the use of illegal drugs;
- to make drug use socially unacceptable;

Figure 1
Partnership for a Drug-Free America Annual and Cumulative Media Values

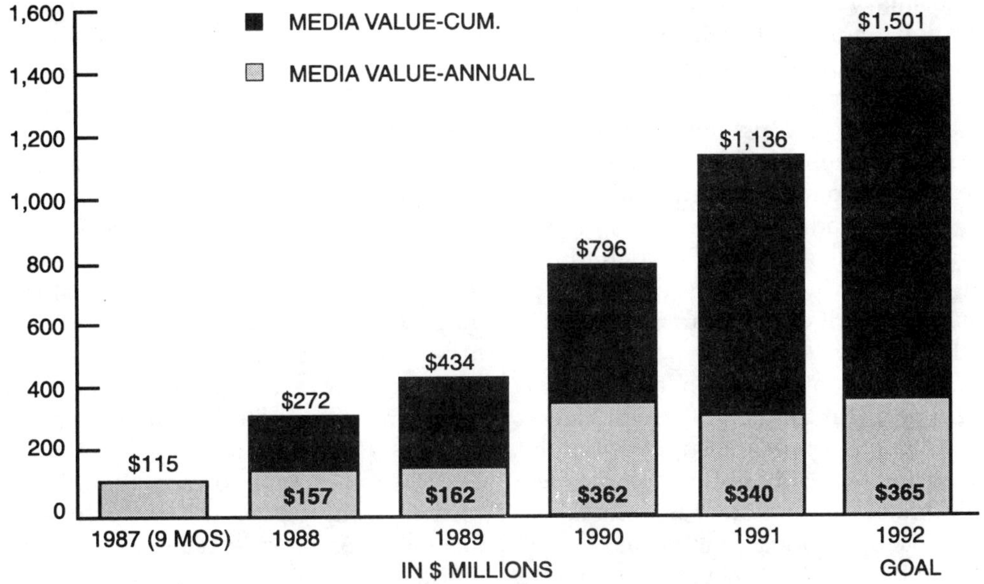

- to accelerate trends in decreasing drug use;

- to push the public's leanings further and faster;

- focused primarily on reducing the number of people trying drugs for the first time, with messages aimed at those who might influence those decisions;" and, more typical of their genre,

- "to compete with drug pushers for the market share of non-users."

In an oft-repeated phrase of their own making, their goal is to "denormalize" drug use. The current CEO, Jim Burke, states that the purpose of the PDFA is to bring America "closer to the day when not one more child tries an illegal drug" (PDFA n.d.).

Organizational Operations

The PDFA is headed by Jim Burke. A man well connected among America's corporate executives and prominent politicians, Burke retired from his position as Chairman of the Johnson & Johnson Corporation to come to the PDFA. When asked about whether the marketing efforts of the $8 billion Johnson & Johnson Corporation—manufacturer of products including Valium™, Librium™, Tylenol-3™ with codeine, and numerous over-the-counter painkillers—might inure the public to the idea that drugs are a solution to life's problems, Burke replied,

"I worry about that. I agree we are a society . . . that believes if you have a pain, take a pill. That can contribute to the problem" (Colford 1989b).

Upon leaving Johnson & Johnson, Burke obtained a $3 million grant for the PDFA from the Robert Wood Johnson

(RWJ) Foundation, a large private foundation whose endowment derives from the profits of the Johnson & Johnson Corporation. In 1994, PDFA was awarded another $7.5 million from RWJ (Health Care Financing Review 1994). As another indication of his—and by extension the PDFA's—influence, Burke chaired the President's Council on Drug Abuse during the Bush administration. During the 1992 electoral debates, President Bush singled out Mr. Burke by name to applaud his spirit of voluntarism in service to the country.

The PDFA operates on about a $3-million annual budget, of which almost two-thirds is spent on support for the approximately 30 full-time employees. This amount is consistent with its labor-intensive operations, as indicated below. The PDFA is staffed by career corporate marketers and sales personnel. Their primary job function is to sell the PDFA, constantly, year in and year out. They must sell the PDFA to: (a) corporate sponsors, (b) advertising agencies, and (c) media executives.

Because the PDFA is funded entirely through private donations, the first sales task for the staff is to persuade the top 100 corporate advertisers to make financial contributions to underwrite the campaign. Each year the PDFA staff ask those corporations with the largest advertising accounts to donate a percentage of their marketing budget to support the PDFA. Based on tax records uncovered by Cynthia Cotts (1992), a reporter for the *Nation*, the major contributors to the PDFA at that time were the leading pharmaceutical, alcohol, and tobacco companies (see table 1). We will return to this point [later].

After soliciting corporate donations, the next major sales assignment targets the advertising agencies. The PDFA staff must convince America's leading advertising agencies—from Ogilvy and Mather to Daley & Associates—to donate *pro bono* staff time and resources to develop the ads themselves. Except for minority ad agencies, all "copy" for the PDFA campaign is developed through *pro bono* contributions.

Finally, the staff must sell the idea of airing or running the ads to the networks, local television stations, newspapers, and magazines. Many of the charts in this paper are drawn from the materials used in presentations to corporate clients. In reviewing these materials, the sales pitch appears to cover the major points typical of any marketing presentation (e.g., themes from formative research with focus groups representative of different market segments).

Given the labor-intensive nature of its operations, more than two-thirds of the PDFA's operating budget is thus spent supporting staff making these sales presentations to potential corporate sponsors, advertising agencies, and media outlets. Only a small portion (< 25%) is spent on the actual production or distribution of materials. This amount is disbursed mainly to smaller, minority advertising agencies who can not afford major *pro bono* work....

Inaccuracies

There are now several ads known to contain inaccuracies or falsehoods for which the PDFA has been reproached. The first such ad to receive national notoriety was the "If you're using marijuana, you are not using your brain" ad. As mentioned earlier, this ad created the impression that the electroencephalogram shown was that of someone who was high on marijuana,

Table 1

Corporate Contributors, 1991

Contributor	Amount
Robert Wood Johnson (RWJ) Foundation	$3 million
J. Seward Johnson, Sr., Charitable Trust	$1.1million
Dupont	$150,000
Proctor & Gamble	$120,000
Bristol-Meyers Squibb	$110,000
SmithKline-Beecham	$100,000
Merck Foundation	$75,000
Hoffman-LaRoche	$50,000
Phillip Morris	$150,000
Anheuser-Busch	$150,000
R.J. Reynolds	$150,000
American Brands	$100,000
Total (less the RWJ grant)	$2.25 million

Note: adapted from Cotts 1992.

when in fact it was the ECG of someone in a coma. The discrepancy was first called to the nation's attention by Dr. Donald Blum of the UCLA medical school and later reported in the *Journal of the American Medical Association* (JAMA) (Dubay 1992).

The next major error concerned figures about the consequences of cocaine use in ads appearing in medical journals, which claimed one-third of users, 5 million people, require medical help. These figures are mistaken—the true figure is closer to 1 in 10, similar to rates of alcohol abuse—and were first challenged in an article in *Scientific American* (Horgan 1990). Other similar sorts of misinformation include: reports on the symptoms of marijuana use that are extremely rare (Dubay 1992), reports on the effects of cocaine extrapolated studies of monkeys in cages reinforced under an operant conditioning paradigm (Waldorf et al. 1991), and ads suggesting marijuana use lowers one's sperm count.

Narrow Message

The PDFA has also been criticized for offering an exceedingly narrow range of messages regarding America's drug problems, relying primarily on fear arousal as the basis for motivating change. PDFA messages have been characterized by journalists in the advertising industry as "the hard sell, equating drugs and death," which "invoke hard-hitting images of death, dependency, mental and physical destruction and wasted lives," guaranteed to "make the mind reel with [their] depiction of horror and waste" (Alter 1987; Reed 1988). For example, one ad equates marijuana use with Russian roulette. In another, "A Sleep Over Date Run Amok" aimed at 6 to 8 years olds, a little boy, after agreeing to spend the night at a friend's house, is greeted by an ambulance conveying the friend's older brother who has just died of an overdose. In a more recent effort, a gunman approaches a drug dealer in his car with his girlfriend and their baby; while watching the unfolding scene through the pistol's sight, the viewer then sees the trigger being pulled just as the baby comes into sight.

The resort to fear tactics is further compounded by the gatekeeping function of local media outlets, who have shown an unwavering preference for the more sensationalistic ads over milder alternatives. Critics raise three points here. There is a long history of communication studies on fear appeals and it is well known that fear-oriented messages work only under very limited conditions. Unless recipients are provided with a clear, viable means for reducing their fears, this type of message has consistently been shown to be ineffective in producing behavior change (McGuire 1985; Severin and Tankard 1988; Soames 1988). Other than "just say no," PDFA ads rarely depict viable outlets to reduce one's fears.

Second, despite the promotional hyperbole about the potent fear quotient in PDFA ads, they are on the whole relatively tame, especially in comparison with the current genre of horror and action films to which adolescents flock. It is unlikely that anyone is really shocked or frightened by their content. Third, PDFA ads have never presented the dangers of alcohol, tobacco, or prescription drugs, which constitute a far greater risk to society (U.S. Surgeon General 1991).

In a comprehensive review of substance-abuse prevention messages, DeJong and Winsten (1990) conclude that more effective messages include positive portrayals that model how one might handle an offer to try drugs and ones that depict pro-social alternatives, such as active, healthy lifestyles. With few exceptions, the PDFA has failed to deploy such alternative approaches.

Side Effects

The errors in presentation and resort to scare tactics create the potential for backlash against drug-prevention messages. Just as teens in the 1960s discovered marijuana was not the "killer weed" their parents and teachers said, so the PDFA's current efforts threaten to destroy the credibility of any anti-drug campaign. What happens when the young people find out that smoking marijuana is really not like playing Russian roulette? How will they then react to messages about other more dangerous drugs?

Other potential side-effects from the campaign include the reinforcement of negative stereotypical images. In a relatively new campaign against heroin use, one PDFA ad features a young addict describing how, after losing his job, he had to "have sex with men for money to support his habit." As the Gay and Lesbian Alliance against Defamation noted, the commercials suggest that homosexuality "is merely an extreme reaction made by young people in life-threatening situations" and that "if there is one thing worse than being an addict, it's being a homosexual" (Elliott 1996). Like the ECG ad, the PDFA pulled this ad only in response to the ensuing public outcry (Levere 1996).

Similarly, the PDFA ads may serve to harden public sympathies toward drug treatment, and more specifically, toward the location and expansion of drug-treatment centers. The PDFA campaign sets out explicitly to portray drug users as "aggressive, depressed losers." (These terms are taken from items used to measure changes in attitudes in the mall intercept tracking surveys, i.e., a measure of success of the campaign is the extent to which it makes an increasing number of people think drug users are aggressive, depressed losers.) When drug users are perceived to be highly aggressive types, people become (more) concerned about locating treatment facilities in their neighborhood. Vilifying drug abusers as pariahs makes it harder for people to see that they are not all that different from the rest of us, perhaps just people in need of a better set of coping skills. By the same token, these ads serve to legitimate the criminal justice response to America's drug problems, in lieu of alternatives such as treatment and education.

Another side effect is that air time for PDFA ads has come at the cost of displacing other worthy causes. There has not been an increase in time allocated to PSAs since 1986 (on the contrary, the deregulatory mood has eased pressure on broadcasters), so other public service concerns have been sacrificed. Finally, there is evidence that the PDFA is crowding out other approaches to drug prevention, too. For example, in 1989 and 1990, the 10 largest foundation grants for alcohol and substance abuse prevention totaled $12.4 million. Of that sum, the PDFA took $4.7 million, or 38% of the total.

Other people worry that the hypocrisy of advertisers and the media can only reinforce public cynicism. ABC-TV offers the PDFA $100 million worth of airtime, while at the same time accepting $626 million in ads to push beer sales, which has consistently been demonstrated to be the "gateway" to further involvement with drugs (Scheer 1997). The ads aired during the march against drugs campaign in March 1997 were developed by the Omnicom Group advertising agency, the same agency that handles a $156 million Anheuser-Busch account (Scheer 1997). The lack of integrity adds to public distrust and jaded withdrawal, fueling feelings of suspicion that undermine the message of the ads.

Conflicts of Interest

As indicated in table 1, the PDFA receives major contributions from the pharmaceutical, alcohol, and tobacco industries. In a written response to Cotts's article (1992) in the *Nation*, PDFA President Hedrick stated that contributions from these industries amount to less than 3% of their total revenues. But if one totals the contributions from these three industries, they come to $2.25 million, which is 75% of the PDFA's stated annual operating budget. When asked during an interview for this [selection], Hedrick refused to be drawn into trying to reconcile the discrepancy.

Further, when questioned about whether they would consider foregoing these funds, Hedrick has responded with increasing irritation to questions about their acceptance. He contends:

"We've been called a front for the alcohol industry. We take contributions from cigarette and alcohol companies. I have no apologies whatsoever. Anheuser-Busch, R. J. Reynolds are top 100 advertisers. Now am I going to turn down $100,000 or $50,000 from them? Absolutely not! Are they impacting what I'm doing, do I run a different creative? Absolutely not! What is it W. C. Fields said, 'No good deed goes unpunished' " (Associated Press 1992).

... Hedrick indicated that the only problem he saw with their funding might be if large numbers of people learned about it, which could then undermine the PDFA's credibility. Barring this, the omission of alcohol, tobacco, and other legal drugs was justifiable on the eminently plausible grounds that the PDFA could not take on everything. However, after receiving a large $7.5 million grant from the RWJ Foundation in 1994, the PDFA ceased soliciting donations from the alcohol and tobacco industries, albeit they steadfastly defend their on-going acceptance of funding from the pharmaceutical industry.

The absence of alcohol, tobacco, and other legal drugs in PDFA materials constitutes one of its major agenda-setting functions. Whenever anyone things about America's drug problems, the polished, professionally crafted images conceived by the PDFA invoke images of marijuana and cocaine, not Budweiser™, Marlboro™, or Valium™. By setting the national tone, the ability of public health professionals to call attention to the health consequences of alcohol and tobacco use is constantly compromised.

Another agenda item for the PDFA is to keep advertising *per se* out of public discussions about the causes of America's social problems. As the war on drugs began to unfold back in 1986, there was tremendous public concern and debate about the effects of the mass media in promoting an irresponsible, hedonistic way of life in America. When the Reagans started criticizing the Hollywood film industry, advertisers were aware of the potential for broadening the debate to include the role of advertising. Thus, the PDFA was conceived at a time when it was important for the advertising industry to appear as much as possible as good, positive, benevolent, responsible corporate citizens. But a couple of examples will serve to illustrate the less than altruistic motives behind this part of the PDFA's agenda.

In a first example, paired editorials ran in the industry's leading trade journal, *Advertising Age,* on November 13, 1989. The lead editorial, titled "Thank you Mr. President," applauds President Bush for his prominent public support on behalf of the PDFA. The editorial immediately below the lead is titled "New Risks in the Courts." It cautions the readership to be vigilant about new efforts to hold advertisers—not just manufacturers —legally accountable in product liability suits. The political agenda is clear.

In another example, the legislature in Florida was considering a new tax on advertising in 1991. Recognizing both the threat and an opportunity, the PDFA introduced a stepped up effort to assist local communities in designing drug-prevention media materials. The result? From an article appearing in *Advertising Age:*

"I suspect there is another benefit as well. State and local governments share the public's concerns over drug abuse and the terrible financial burden it creates. These are the same governments that are often ignorant and critical of advertising. A positive industry response to a critical public concern could help create a more favorable climate and attitude for advertising that it deserves but rarely achieves. In Florida, where the threat of an ad tax has resurfaced, the governor recently held a special reception to personally thank everyone involved in the Florida Partnership" (Bell 1992).

Finally, although the voluntary *pro bono* nature of the enterprise is intended to demonstrate good corporate citizenship, the work may be undertaken for less altruistic motives. Many agencies are more interested in winning prestigious advertising awards than solving social problems. Cliff Freeman, for example, submitted one of their ads, "Lenny," developed for the PDFA, to the Andy Awards (where it won a silver award). For many, the work was an entirely self-serving act. "It's completely scandalous what they did," says copywriter Richard Yelland of Kirshenbaum Bond. "They just did it for the award—it was all about publicity for Tony Kaye and Cliff Freeman" (Cooper 1996).

Ideological Implications
The final criticism raised about the PDFA concerns its larger ideological implications. Beyond an agenda-setting function that defines which drugs are— and are not—considered social problems and which industries are—and are not —legitimate targets of reform, there are other, even more disturbing repercussions from the PDFA campaign. In the final analysis, the PDFA has a deeply political message.

The PDFA's model regarding the causes of substance abuse is not objective, neutral, nor reflective of research on its etiology. The PDFA propagates a particular point of view regarding the causes of America's drug problems, which, by the power of its reach, thereby marginalizes

and delegitimates other perspectives. The model promoted by the PDFA is that problems like drug abuse are best understood to be the result of individual choices.

In the PDFA perspective, drug abuse is like any other consumer behavior. Individuals enter the marketplace and make free and unfettered choices in pursuit of their own self-interests. Following this premise, the PDFA campaign is designed wholly around the idea of making abstinence the more attractive, preferred consumer choice. The solution to America's drug problem lies in stimulating each and every individual to reappraise his/her self-interests in light of the PDFA message.

But when decisions about drugs are equated with consumer preferences, then the causes of substance abuse must be located within the individual's mental calculus, presumably ill-informed in those who choose to try drugs. As the PDFA pushes this individual consumer behavior model, the effects of social, political, and environmental factors are not afforded the same level of visibility and consideration. Questions about the role and responsibility of private corporations, for instance, in generating and/or resolving social problems are never raised, let alone made part of everyday public discourse. Questions about the justice and consequences of the current distribution of wealth and power in America are relegated to marginal, quirky interjections outside the mainstream. When a model that locates responsibility for resolving America's drug problems within the individual is zealously promoted, the feasibility and truth value of other perspectives are diminished in the public eye. By framing the issue in these terms, the PDFA makes serious consideration of the need for other approaches, such as changes in socioeconomic conditions, more distant and removed. As such, the PDFA message is promoting a particular point of view, and a particularly conservative point of view: The problem is solely the property of individuals, and has nothing to do with society, the social structure, poverty, unemployment, discrimination in opportunities for advancement, etc.

The conservative slant of the PDFA's message is further compounded by the limitations of the medium. When solutions to social problems are packaged in 30-second sound bites, they have to convey a very simple message. The medium does not allow for more complex discussions. The impact of this constraint became apparent in discussions with the PDFA leadership.

When discussing the relative consequences of alcohol versus marijuana use, Hedrick and colleagues repeatedly referred to people who wanted to include alcohol among America's drug problems as "prohibitionists" and those who questioned the dangerousness of marijuana as "legalizers." The PDFA did not want to take on alcohol problems because, among other things, the message would be too complicated. Similarly, to suggest that some illegal drugs might not be as bad as others would muddy the waters in ways that cannot be accommodated in 30-second solutions.

Given this mindset, the PDFA is not equipped to help the public grapple with the idea that our drug problems may be more complex than the labels, legalizer and prohibitionist. The public is not becoming better educated nor more perceptive in its deliberations about our drug problems as a result of their campaign. In this sense, the PDFA may be contributing more to the problem than to the solution.

Finally, one of the more intriguing questions concerning the ideological interests of the PDFA goes back to their resistance to public funding. Wouldn't it be easier for the PDFA to accept a stable, guaranteed level of funding from government coffers, rather than having to hustle donations year after year? There are many reasons for their aversion.

As mentioned earlier, the heads of the PDFA prefer private control over message content. Absent public interference, they are free to pursue their creative muse, accountable only to themselves and their corporate sponsors. In addition, the advertising industry itself has self-interested concerns in protecting alcohol, tobacco and pharmaceutical industries from counter-ads that might run if a publicly financed, publicly controlled media campaign was initiated. The tobacco industry withdrew their ads from television in 1971 after the initiation of a publicly mandated counter-ad campaign, at great loss to the myriad of advertising agencies on contract. But perhaps even more intriguing is the role the PDFA would like to play in demonstrating the effectiveness of private market solutions to social problems.

In meeting with the staff of the PDFA, there is no question that they are sincere in their desire to see the PDFA campaign be successful, to see lives saved, and needless suffering stopped. Many of them have been touched personally by the tragedy of substance abuse. But it became clear that they also want to be able to show that the recourse for government programs may be unnecessary and unwarranted. The private market can provide everything a society needs, and better.

In one of the more eye-opening exchanges in the interview, one of the authors described current public health knowledge about risk factors that make substance abuse problems more likely in populations.... When asked if the PDFA tried to address these known risk factors, Hedrick responded that he thought that this approach was what was wrong with the field of public health, and why the PDFA had a better program. In his mind, there is nothing one could do about changing "any of the classic, stereotypical environmental factors." Notions of improving schools, strengthening families, and providing programs to enhance students' social and academic skills are infeasible and misguided.

As he continued, his "fear ... of taking the broader public health point of view" is that public health looks to "institutional solutions for individual problems." But, for Hedrick and the PDFA, one cannot change the way things are. All anyone can do is get people to "buy into" the idea of "why they shouldn't be into the drug business." It is the free market mentality—people are self-interest maximizers freely choosing in a marketplace devoid of other considerations. According to Hedrick, attitudes toward drug use are "much more important" than the effects of poverty or broken families. The "two most important things" are telling every kid "stay in school and stay off drugs." If successful, the PDFA can show the world that all these other issues really are irrelevant.

CONCLUSION

There is a general agreement that public information campaigns can be an important adjunct in promoting public health. But they are not synonymous with effective prevention. Public health agencies learned a long time ago that you cannot "unsell" unhealthy behaviors through advertising alone (Wallack 1989; Wallack et al. 1983). This has been the lesson of the Stanford Heart Disease Prevention Program and many other comprehensive efforts to change behavior and improve public health. We have long known that, without local interpersonal involvement and participation, behavior change interventions are destined for failure.

Advertisers, too, know that advertising by itself does not produce change. That is why private corporations use advertising as only one part of a comprehensive marketing approach, distilled in its most basic terms in the 'four Ps': product, price, place, and promotion. Successful marketing campaigns incorporate all four elements, at a minimum, delivering local tie-ins, widespread product availability, attractive pricing, and products that promise personal and immediate gratification. As an advertising campaign, the PDFA fails on most counts applied in their own circles.

But more importantly, not only has the PDFA been ineffective, it has neglected America's more serious drug problems —alcohol and tobacco. Alcohol and tobacco, in terms of years of potential life lost and total number of deaths, do far more to destroy individual opportunity and family well-being than the illicit drugs targeted by the PDFA (Ravenholt 1984). By defining America's drug problem as marijuana, cocaine and heroin, the PDFA is not providing a public service. It deflects attention away from corporate behavior that affects millions—to focus on individual behavior. It deflects attention away from social issues that must be addressed—to point to individual failures that ultimately lead to blaming the victim.

Public health concerns have a clear message: social and environmental changes are necessary to improve health. Education may be necessary and good, but it is not sufficient to change health behavior. History has shown that significant improvements in the health of the public come about only when the underlying socioeconomic conditions correlated with poor health are ameliorated (Mckinlay and McKinlay 1977). By conveying the false sense that something adequate and successful is being done, the PDFA may well be "enabling" our drug problems, rather than contributing to their solution.

In the end, we need to ask whose interests are served by the PDFA. Even with the best of intentions, they may also serve to divert us from more important goals and more effective strategies. It may well be that we continue to turn to—and be impressed by—media strategies because we feel the need to do something, even when it is something merely comfortable and easy. The PDFA does not ask anything of us collectively, what we might do as a society to address our social problems. It lets each of us off the hook. Drug abuse is their problem, the ones who make those foolish decisions. But at some point, we will reap the results of our actions and inactions. At some point, America must come to terms with questions about the kind of society we want to create. The problems are not going away. At some point, we need to do what is right, not what is expedient.

POSTSCRIPT

Are Antidrug Media Campaigns Effective?

In the United States, companies spend large sums of money on advertising because it is an effective way to promote use of their products. Thus, one could argue that it is logical to try to curtail drug use by young people by advertising through the media. That is, if advertisements can promote desirable behaviors, then they should be able to discourage undesirable behaviors.

One concern about antidrug announcements is that they may bring the issue of drugs to the attention of youngsters who had previously never considered using drugs. McCaffrey contends that if the media focus a great deal on the effects of drugs, then young people who have had little interest in trying drugs may become more curious and experiment with them. At what point do warnings against drugs become invitations to use drugs?

One organization that is devoted to antidrug advertisements is the Partnership for a Drug-Free America (PDFA). Although the Office of National Drug Control Policy provides funding to the PDFA, it is a private organization that receives money from charitable organizations as well as from pharmaceutical companies, beer manufacturers, and tobacco companies. One criticism of PDFA advertisements is that they do not address cigarette and alcohol use by young people because the organization is afraid of losing income from the beer and tobacco companies.

Buchanan and Wallack note that PDFA advertisements contain inaccuracies about the effects of drugs and statistics on drug addicts. They also indicate that PDFA advertisements have been criticized for utilizing primary fear arousal techniques. At best, Buchanan and Wallack argue, fear arousal has short-term benefits. Buchanan and Wallack maintain that depicting prosocial alternatives, such as a healthy lifestyle, is a more effective strategy. Furthermore, they are concerned that the misleading advertisements from the PDFA may create a backlash against antidrug messages.

Two articles that examine the effects of drug messages are "Evaluation of Antismoking Advertising Campaigns," by Lisa Goldman and Stanton Glantz, *Journal of the American Medical Association* (March 11, 1998) and "Male Adolescents' Reactions to TV Beer Advertisements: The Effects of Sports Content and Programming Context" by Michael Slater et al., *Journal of Studies on Alcohol* (vol 57, 1996). An interesting article that looks at how music videos depict tobacco and alcohol is "Tobacco and Alcohol Use Behaviors Portrayed in Music Videos: A Content Analysis," by Robert DuRant et al., *American Journal of Public Health* (July 1997).

CONTRIBUTORS
TO THIS VOLUME

EDITOR

RAYMOND GOLDBERG is a professor of health education at the State University of New York College at Cortland. Since 1977, he has served as coordinator for graduate programs in the School of Professional Studies. He received a B.S. in health and physical education from the University of North Carolina at Pembroke in 1969, an M.Ed. in health education from the University of South Carolina in 1971, and a Ph.D. in health education from the University of Toledo in 1981. He is the author of *Drugs Across the Spectrum*, 3rd ed. (Morton Publishing, 2000) and the author or coauthor of many articles on health-related issues, and he has made many presentations on the topic of drug education. He has received over $750,000 in grants for his research in health and drug education.

STAFF

Theodore Knight List Manager
David Brackley Senior Developmental Editor
Juliana Poggio Developmental Editor
Rose Gleich Administrative Assistant
Brenda S. Filley Production Manager
Juliana Arbo Typesetting Supervisor
Diane Barker Proofreader
Lara Johnson Design/Advertising Coordinator
Richard Tietjen Publishing Systems Manager
Larry Killian Copier Coordinator

AUTHORS

ROBERT APSLER is an assistant professor of psychology in the Department of Psychiatry at Harvard Medical School in Boston, Massachusetts, and president of Social Science Research and Evaluation, Inc.

JAMES B. BAKALAR is a lecturer in law in the Department of Psychiatry at the Harvard Medical School. He has coauthored a number of books with Lester Grinspoon, including *Psychedelic Drugs Reconsidered*, 3rd ed. (Open Society Institute, 1997).

JANET BRIGHAM is a research psychologist at SRI International, a nonprofit research center in Menlo Park, California, where she focuses on tobacco use and nicotine dependence. Her work on addiction has been published in such journals as *Biological Psychiatry, The American Journal of Public Health,* and *Psychiatry Research.*

RICHARD BROMFIELD is a clinical instructor in psychology in the Department of Psychiatry at Harvard Medical School in Boston, Massachusetts. He is the author of *Doing Child and Adolescent Psychotherapy: The Ways and Whys* (Jason Aronson Publishers, 1999).

DAVID R. BUCHANAN is an assistant professor of community health studies in the School of Public Health at the University of Massachusetts–Amherst.

THOMAS BYRD is a professor of health at De Anza College in Cupertino, California.

ELLIS CASHMORE is a professor of sociology at Stafford University in England.

RICHARD R. CLAYTON is a professor of psychology at the University of Kentucky in Lexington, Kentucky, and chair of the Tobacco Etiology Research Network. He was a coprincipal investigator for the 1985 National Household Survey on Drug Abuse, and he has been director of the Center for Prevention Research at the University of Kentucky since 1987.

RICHARD J. DeGRANDPRE is a visiting assistant professor of psychology at Saint Michael's College in Winooski, Vermont. He is coeditor, with Warren Bickel, of *Drug Policy and Human Nature* (Plenum, 1996).

ROBERT L. DuPONT, former director of the National Institute on Drug Abuse (NIDA), has been a leader in the field of substance abuse prevention and treatment for more than 25 years. Currently, he is president of the Institute for Behavior and Health, a nonprofit research and policy organization, and a clinical professor of psychiatry at the Georgetown University School of Medicine. He has published more than 150 professional articles and 10 books and monographs, including his edited book *Stopping Alcohol and Other Drug Use Before It Starts: The Future of Prevention* (DIANE Publishing, 1996).

MATHEA FALCO is president of Drug Strategies, a nonprofit policy institute in Washington, D.C. He was also assistant secretary of state for international narcotics matters from 1977 to 1981. He is the author of *Making a Drug-Free America* (Times Books, 1994).

LESTER GRINSPOON is chair of the board of directors for the National Organization for the Reform of Marijuana Laws. He is also executive director of the Massachusetts Mental Health Research

Corporation and an associate professor of psychiatry at the Harvard Medical School in Boston, Massachusetts. He has been involved in marijuana research for over 20 years, and he received the Norman E. Zinberg Award for marijuana research in 1990.

WAYNE HALL is director of the National Drug and Alcohol Research Centre at the University of New South Wales in Australia.

MICHELE ALICIA HARMON is a former faculty research associate in the Department of Criminology and Criminal Justice at the University of Maryland in College Park. She also did research at the Urban Institute, a nonprofit policy research organization in Washington, D.C.

JOHN HOOD is a contributing editor for *Policy Review.*

JAMES A. INCIARDI is director of the Center for Drug and Alcohol Studies at the University of Delaware, a professor in the Department of Sociology and Criminal Justice at Delaware, an adjunct professor in the Comprehensive Drug Research Center at the University of Miami School of Medicine, and a member of the South Florida AIDS Research Consortium. He has done extensive consulting work nationally and internationally and has published approximately three dozen books and more than 180 articles and chapters in the areas of substance abuse, criminology, criminal justice, history, folklore, social policy, AIDS, medicine, and law.

BENJAMIN JUNGE is senior research coordinator with the Department of Epidemiology at the Johns Hopkins School of Hygiene and Public Health. He is also evaluation director for the Baltimore Needle Exchange Program.

EDWARD L. KOVEN is the author of *Smoking: The Story Behind the Haze* (Nova Science Publishers, 1996).

PAUL A. LOGLI is state's attorney for Winnebago County, Illinois, and a lecturer at the National College of District Attorneys. A member of the Illinois State Bar since 1974, he is a nationally recognized advocate for prosecutorial involvement in the issue of substance-abused infants. He received a J.D. from the University of Illinois.

TRENT LOTT is the Republican U.S. senator from Mississippi and the current senate majority leader. He served as administrative assistant to Representative William Colmer (D-Mississippi) from 1968 to 1972, and he represented the Fifth District of Mississippi in the U.S. House of Representatives from 1972 to 1988.

ALBERT B. LOWENFELS is a professor of surgery at New York Medical College.

ROBERT J. MACCOUN is a professor of public policy at the University of California, Berkeley, and a consultant to the RAND Corporation in Santa Monica, California. He is also a member of the editorial advisory board of *Law and Society Review* and a member of the National Consortium on Violence Research. He is coauthor, with Peter Reuter and Mathea Falco, of *Comparing Western European and North American Drug Policies: An International Conference Report* (RAND Corporation, 1993).

SUE MAHAN is an associate professor in the Department of Criminal Justice and Legal Studies at the University of Central Florida in Orlando.

BARRY McCAFFREY is director of the Office of National Drug Control Policy at the White House. He serves as the senior drug policy official in the executive branch and as the president's chief drug policy spokesman, and he is also a member of the National Security Council. Upon his retirement from the U.S. Army, he was the most highly decorated officer and the youngest four-star general.

JOHN B. MURRAY is a distinguished professor in the Department of Psychology at St. John's University in Jamaica, New York.

ETHAN A. NADELMANN is director of the Lindesmith Center, a New York–based drug-policy research institute, and an assistant professor of politics and public affairs in the Woodrow Wilson School of Public and International Affairs at Princeton University in Princeton, New Jersey. He was the founding coordinator of the Harvard Study Group on Organized Crime, and he has been a consultant to the Department of State's Bureau of International Narcotics Matters. He is also an assistant editor of the *Journal of Drug Issues* and a contributing editor of the *International Journal on Drug Policy.*

MARK NICHOLS is the health and science editor of *Maclean's.*

OFFICE OF NATIONAL DRUG CONTROL POLICY (ONDCP) was created by the Anti-Drug Abuse Act of 1988 to advise the president on a national drug control strategy, a consolidated drug control budget, and other management and organizational issues. The principal purpose of the ONDCP is to establish policies, priorities, and objectives for the nation's drug control program, with the overall goal of significantly reducing the production, availability, and use of illegal drugs both in the United States and abroad.

STANTON PEELE is a social and clinical psychologist who has taught at Harvard University, Columbia University, and the University of California. He has authored or coauthored several highly influential books on the nature of addiction and on treatment efficacy and social policy with respect to substance abuse, including *Love and Addiction* (Taplinger, 1975), *The Meaning of Addiction* (Lexington Books, 1985), and *Diseasing of America* (Lexington Books, 1989). The author of numerous journal articles that have challenged and helped redirect mainstream thinking about addiction, he was awarded the Mark Keller Award by the *Journal of Studies on Alcohol.*

RICHARD W. POLLAY is on the faculty of commerce and business administration at the University of British Columbia in Vancouver, Canada.

MARSHA ROSENBAUM is a sociologist and director of the San Francisco, California, office of the Lindesmith Center, a policy research institute that focuses on broadening the debate on drug policy and related issues. She also serves on the boards of the Harm Reduction Coalition and the Humanistic Alternatives to Addiction Research and Treatment. She is coauthor, with Sheigla Murphy, of *Pregnant Women on Drugs: Combating Stereotypes and Stigma* (Rutgers University Press, 1999) and, with Jerome Beck, of *Pursuit of Ecstasy: The MDMA Experience* (State University of New York Press, 1994).

CHRISTINE A. SAUM is a research associate at the Center for Drug and Alcohol Studies at the University of Delaware. She is coauthor, with James A. Inciardi and Hilary L. Surratt, of *Cocaine-*

Exposed Infants: Social, Legal, and Public Health Issues (Sage Publications, 1997).

JOANNIE M. SCHROF is a senior editor of *U.S. News and World Report.*

NADIA SOLOWIJ is a research psychologist at the National Drug and Alcohol Research Centre with interests in the field of cognitive psychophysiology and the addictions, particularly in the long-term effects of substance abuse upon cognitive functioning. Her current research is prospective, assessing cannabis users before and after quitting, and she is a coinvestigator on a multisite treatment trial for cannabis dependence in the United States. She is the author of *Cannabis and Cognitive Functioning* (Cambridge University Press, 1998).

JACOB SULLUM is a senior editor for *Reason* magazine. He writes on several public policy issues, including freedom of speech, criminal justice, and education. His work has appeared in the *Wall Street Journal*, the *New York Times*, and the *Los Angeles Times*. In 1988 he won the Keystone Award for investigative reporting. He has been a fellow of the Knight Center for Specialized Journalism.

DAVID VLAHOV is a professor of epidemiology and medicine at the Johns Hopkins School of Hygiene and Public Health. He is also principal investigator of the evaluation of the Baltimore Needle Exchange Program.

ERIC A. VOTH is chairman of the International DrugStrategy Institute and a clinical assistant professor with the Department of Medicine at the University of Kansas School of Medicine. He is also medical director of Chemical Dependency Services at St. Francis Hospital in Topeka, Kansas. He has testified for the Drug Enforcement Administration in opposition to legalizing marijuana, and he is recognized as an international authority on drug abuse.

LAWRENCE WALLACK is a professor of public health at the University of California, Berkeley, and codirector of the Berkeley Media Studies Group, an organization that conducts research and training in the use of the media to advance public health policies. He has published extensively and lectures frequently on policy issues related to health promotion. He is the recipient of several awards, including the Beryl Roberts Prize in Health Education (1980). He is the principal author of *Media Advocacy and Public Health* (Sage Publications, 1993) and coeditor, with Charles K. Atkin, of *Mass Media and Public Health: Complexities and Conflicts* (Sage Publications, 1990).

NANCY WARTIK is a contributing editor of *American Health.* She specializes in the areas of health and psychology.

PAUL D. WELLSTONE is the Democratic U.S. senator from Minnesota. Before being elected to the Senate in 1990, he was a professor at Carleton College in Northfield, Minnesota, for 20 years.

JERRY WIENER is on the faculty of George Washington University Medical School in Washington, D.C.

INDEX

Please remember that this is a library book,
and that it belongs only temporarily to each
person who uses it. Be considerate. Do
not write in this, or any, library book.

Date Due

AUG 3 1 2000			
MR 08 03			

BRODART, CO.   Cat. No. 23-233-003   Printed in U.S.A.